Grand Canyon

A Century of Change

Grand Canyon
A Century of Change

Rephotography of the 1889-1890
Stanton Expedition

Robert H. Webb

The University of Arizona Press
Tucson

First printing 1996
The University of Arizona Press
Copyright © 1996
The Arizona Board of Regents
All Rights Reserved

Library of Congress Cataloging-in-Publication Data
Webb, Robert H.
Grand Canyon : a century of change : rephotography of the
1889–1890 Stanton Expedition / Robert H. Webb.
   p.   cm.
Includes bibliographical references and index.
ISBN 0-8165-1554-9 (cloth). — ISBN 0-8165-1578-6 (paper)
1. Grand Canyon (Ariz.)—Description and travel.   2. Grand
Canyon (Ariz.)—Surveys.   3. Repeat photography—Arizona—
Grand Canyon.   4. Landscape changes—Arizona—Grand
Canyon.   5. Colorado River (Colo.-Mexico)—Description and
travel.   6. Colorado River (Colo.-Mexico)—Surveys.   7. Repeat
photography—Colorado River (Colo.-Mexico)   8. Landscape
changes—Colorado River (Colo.-Mexico)   9. Stanton, Robert
Brewster, 1846–1922.   I. Title.
F788.W437   1996
979.1'32—dc20   95-32536
                                                        CIP

British Cataloguing-in-Publication Data
A catalogue record for this book is available from the British
Library.

Frontispiece: Mile 113.3, view replicated by Liz Hymans,
February 21, 1992.

To Toni, who helped me see it through,

to Ray, who inspired this,

and to the crews of 1990–1995,

who worked hard to make it possible.

Contents

Sidebars

Figures

Acknowledgments

Many colleagues aided and abetted this research. I am indebted to Glenn Rink for his contribution to the idea of replicating Stanton views and his extremely hard work in making the initial river trip of 1990 a success. I particularly thank Jan Bowers for her enthusiasm for interpreting plants in the Stanton views; Jan always served as a reality check for my wild ideas concerning desert plants and ecology. Jack Schmidt encouraged our interpretation of changes in sand bars and helped train my crews. Ted Melis contributed many ideas concerning debris flows and their effect on the Colorado River. Larry Stevens shared information on riparian vegetation of the river corridor. Countless others have contributed directly or indirectly to this effort; I particularly acknowledge the contributions of Mimi Murov and Tom Wise.

Many friends have helped with the effort required to reoccupy and photograph so many views in such an exacting manner. We were fortunate to have had highly skilled and professional river guides on the four trips; I especially thank head guides Gary Bolton, Kenton Grua, and Glenn Rink. I admire the pride and professionalism of the guides I worked with: Jane Bernard, Gary Bolton, Tom Brownold, Michael Collier, Dave Edwards, Kenton Grua, Liz Hymans, Jano Kempster, Archie McPhee, Glenn

Rink, Dennis Silva, Drifter Smith, and Tom Wise. Also, Tom Workman guided us into Glen Canyon in December 1989. Gary Bolton, Liz Hymans, Glenn Rink, Dennis Silva, and I identified the location of most camera positions from our memories of Grand Canyon geography; I remain particularly impressed with Bolton's "photographic memory." Mimi Murov, my "photo wrangler," deserves special thanks for her tireless efforts on all of the repeat photography trips. Tom Wise helped plan the trips in 1991–1993, and his efforts were largely responsible for our success in replicating all the Stanton views.

In our three-person crews, all positions were of equal importance. Jane Bernard, Tom Brownold, Dave Edwards, Ralph Hopkins, Jim Hasbargen, Liz Hymans, Ted Melis, Glenn Rink, Steve Tharnstrom, Ray Turner, Tom Wise, and I were photographers during one or more of the trips. Of the numerous note takers, Diane Grua, Mimi Murov, and Toni Yocum excelled. I thank Gary Bolton, Jan Bowers, Jeff Clark, Michael Collier, Steve Cox, Lenore Grover, Ginger Harmon, Jim Hasbargen, Mimi Murov, Clive Pinnock, Karen Reichhardt, Glenn Rink, Renee Rondeau, Jack Schmidt, Dennis Silva, Drifter Smith, Doug Stephens, Ray Turner, Rosalee Winn, Tom Wise, and Toni Yocum for their tireless work in trying to decipher changes from ancient photographs. I particularly thank Mia Hanson for her help with logistical support; Mia was always ready to help out in tight situations.

Two long-time river runners and Grand Canyon aficionados helped this work immeasurably. I especially thank P. T. Reilly, who contributed in one way or another to most of the interesting aspects of this work. I also thank Bob Euler, who shared his experiences tracking down Stanton camera stations and gave other valuable information. Both Reilly and Euler graciously loaned photographs they had taken that replicated Stanton views or showed other aspects of change in Grand Canyon.

I especially thank Raymond M. Turner and Janice E. Bowers of the U.S. Geological Survey for their encouragement and help during the repeat photography trips. Ray taught me the value of repeat photography during numerous excursions around the western United States, and he introduced me to Grand Canyon in 1984. Ray has been an inspiration for my research and career, and I am greatly indebted to him. Jan was an essential part of most of the river trips and made repeated efforts to teach me how to write. This book was improved immensely through her efforts.

Parts of the manuscript were read by many trip participants and scientists, but reviews by several individuals notably increased the quality of the text. I am indebted to Jan Bowers, Bryan Brown, Mia Hanson, Waite Osterkamp, Duncan Patten, John Weisheit, and Dave Wegner for their critical reviews of the entire manuscript. Paul Martin, Mimi Murov, Glenn Rink, Jack Schmidt, Larry Stevens, Ray Turner, Steve Tharnstrom, and Tom Wise critically reviewed various chapters. Critiques by Rose Houk and Sally Bennett greatly improved the manuscript. I particularly thank Bryan Brown, Steve Carothers, Bob Euler, Paul Martin, Connie McCabe, and P. T. Reilly for contributing accounts of their experiences or research in Grand Canyon.

This research was funded partially by the U.S. Bureau of Reclamation, Glen Canyon Environmental Studies Program; a grant from the Grand Canyon Natural History Association to Glenn R. Rink; and the National Research Program of the U.S. Geological Survey. The Defense Nuclear Agency, Department of Defense, generously contributed Steve Tharnstrom's expertise to this project. For work upstream of Lees Ferry, the National Park Service, Glen Canyon National Recreation Area, provided a boat and guide in December 1989, and Steve Carothers graciously loaned us a boat in October 1992. For the 1990 trip in Grand Canyon, Rob Elliott of Arizona Raft Adventures generously donated the use of four boats and equipment and Dick McCallum of Expeditions, Inc., helped with the logistics of putting in and taking out. Subsequent trips in 1991, 1992, and 1993 were outfitted by O.A.R.S, Inc., and the U.S. Geological Survey.

Paul Martin thanks Robert Webb and Roy M. Johnson for tolerating his revisionisms and Jennifer Shopland for clarifying them. Peter Bennett, Ken Cole, Bob Euler, Jim King, Vera Markgraf, Jim Mead, Peter Mehringer, Mary Ellen Morbeck, Mary Kay O'Rourke, Art Phillips, Barbara Phillips, Eleanore Robbins, Geoff Spaulding, and Tom Van Devender helped with Martin's ideas and research.

The staff of the Still Picture Branch of the National Archives was of invaluable help to this research. All the Stanton photographs in this book were obtained from the Still Picture Branch of the National Archives. I especially thank Betty Hill and Ed McCarter for preserving the negatives of the Stanton expedition and for their help with my unreasonable requests to obtain duplicates. I owe Connie McCabe and her assistants a debt of thanks for restoration of the original negatives, which made many of the detailed scientific interpretations possible. Six of the more than four hundred Stanton photographs used in this rephotography project were obtained from the Stanton papers at the New York Public Library. I obtained additional, non-Stanton views from the Huntington Library in San Marino, California; the University of Utah Special Collections; Special Collections at Northern Arizona University; and the U.S. Geological Survey Photographic Library in Lakewood, Colorado.

We printed photographs for interpretation and presentation in this book, and the two jobs were significantly different. Making the prints for the fieldwork in the canyon was an arduous task. Ted Melis printed most of the images we used in 1990; Ted Melis, Ray Turner, and Sara Light-Waller printed those used on the second trip in 1991. For subsequent trips, several people including Sara Light-Waller, Ted Melis, and Dave Ring made prints. Chuck Sternberg graciously provided the line art.

The black-and-white images reproduced in this book were printed by Steve Tharnstrom, Sara Light-Waller, Dave Ring, and myself. The original and replicate views are printed as close to full frame as possible; we cropped the edges of some views to hide tears and imperfections in the original negatives.

Several of the Stanton photographs were retouched to eliminate or subdue glaring imperfections caused either by the nature of the film Stanton and Nims used, by poor development after the negatives were exposed, or by cracking or tearing related to a century of storage. Nims and Stanton masked most of the sky in their photographs because the film they used would often yield fantastic and unrealistic patterns. Bill Boyer retouched objectionable cosmetic defects in the sky of six photographs presented in this book. Photographs at the bottom of 209 Mile Rapid, at mile 119, and at Forster Rapid were retouched to eliminate chemical stains or subdue light-dark bands across the landscape. The photographs were evaluated for change before retouching occurred.

Introduction

My inspiration to work with historical photographs of Grand Canyon came during an unlikely moment. In early October 1987, Jack Schmidt, Glenn Rink, and I were browsing through books at Marble Canyon Lodge near Lees Ferry. We were about to launch a research trip down the Colorado River in Grand Canyon.

There was a new book on the shelf, an account of the second successful river trip through Grand Canyon. Edited by Dwight L. Smith and C. Gregory Crampton, *The Colorado River Survey*[1] is Robert Brewster Stanton's diary of an abortive expedition in the summer of 1889 and a successful one in the winter of 1889–1890 undertaken to document the proposed route of a water-level railroad through the canyons of the Colorado River. Like most river runners, I had read with great interest John Wesley Powell's account of his pioneering 1869 river expedition. What struck me about *The Colorado River Survey*, however, were the many photographs that illustrated the book. I later learned that these photographs were only a sampling of the 2,200 negatives taken during the Stanton expeditions.

My research in Grand Canyon involved debris flows from the side canyons into the Colorado River.[2] These flows, a type of flash flood that has the consistency of wet concrete, occur in steep terrain around the world where torrential rainfall occurs. They occur infrequently in Grand Canyon: the average time between flows seems to be twenty to fifty years. I was having difficulty determining when flows had occurred in the past; how do you determine when a pile of boulders was deposited? Written accounts of historic debris flows are sparse, and there is seldom enough organic material among the boulders for standard techniques like radiocarbon dating.

I needed a new approach, and the photographs of the proposed railroad route suggested what that approach might be. I was already familiar with repeat photography from earlier work in tributaries of the Colorado River in Grand Canyon.[3] Looking through Stanton's diary, I realized that I could use his photographs, which consisted of 445 views between Glen Canyon Dam and the upper end of Lake Mead, to make a canyon-long survey of debris-flow frequency. In addition, we could commemorate the centennial of Stanton's successful expedition if we launched a river trip in the winter of 1990. The combination of scientific gain and historical reenactment was irresistible, and we began planning to replicate the Stanton photography.

In theory, replicating old photographs seems easy. Holding a print of the view, you find the location where the original photographer stood, aim, and press the shutter. In reality, the process is much more difficult. Besides assembling the prints and associated information, the would-be repeat photographer must have some idea as to the most appropriate photographic equipment. Time of year, and even time of day, may be essential. It helps to know approximately where the original camera stations were; even then, the repeat photographer expends considerable effort in placing a camera as close to the original camera position as possible.

The first problem was to obtain prints of the Stanton photography. Footnotes in *The Colorado River Survey* indicated the existence of several albums containing prints. Ray Turner had purchased prints from the New York Public Library, which has an archive of Stanton papers and an album of prints. A few phone calls established the existence of an album of prints in the National Archives in Washington, D.C. Betty Hill, head of the Still Picture Branch, told me that the negatives also were stored in the National Archives but had become tightly rolled and were too brittle to make prints. Restoration would be expensive, so I purchased poorer-quality copy negatives of the deteriorated album prints. Greg Crampton graciously loaned us the copy negatives used to prepare some of the photographs in *The Colorado River Survey*. We used the copy negatives to prepare approximately 110 sets of prints, primarily of views that could be readily identified.

Our first trip was into what is left of Glen Canyon, a fifteen-mile reach between Glen Canyon Dam and Lees Ferry. On December 19, 1989, Ray Turner, Ted Melis, and I began the work reported in this book. Ray had been replicating views in Grand Canyon for nearly two decades and in the Southwest for thirty years, but he had never concentrated on a group of photographs such as was available from the Stanton expeditions. In two days, Ray replicated nine Stanton views and began to realize the amount of geological and ecological information they contained. Together, Ray and I determined the most appropriate types of lenses for our medium- and large-format cameras. We agreed that the views should be replicated in winter, because most had deep shadows and the vegetation was dormant.

Our trip commemorating the centennial of Stanton's 1890 trip launched from Lees Ferry on January 17, 1990, a cold and overcast day. Photo crews consisted of a photographer, a note taker, and others performing the essential task of determining what had changed or not changed in the view. The river guides helped with the repeat photography, and the scientists helped with work normally performed by guides. We used a combination of memory, guessing, and luck to find the old photo positions. We replicated as many of the historic views as we could relocate, but inevitably we passed some camera positions accidentally and guessed wrong on the locations of others.

During the thirty-four-day trip, we replicated 101 views from the Stanton expeditions and discovered a number of significant changes a century after the originals were made. Rocks in the foreground that had not changed often allowed quick, close occupation of the original camera station. Although my primary objective was to interpret the occurrence of debris flows in the past century, the Stanton views yielded abundant information on a wide variety of environmental changes in Grand Canyon.

I received a pleasant surprise in June 1991 when I revisited the National Archives. Connie McCabe of the Still Picture Branch had begun the process of restoring the original negatives and making duplicates. The duplicate negatives generally yielded clearer prints that allowed a more detailed interpretation of foreground plants and distant objects, such as sand bars and debris fans, that previously had been fuzzy. With considerable help from Ed McCarter of the Still Picture Branch, I obtained a nearly complete set of duplicate negatives.

In the winters of 1991–1993, we devoted most of four river trips to replicating Stanton views. We timed these trips to overlap as much as possible with Stanton's 1889–1890 itinerary to attain similar shadows, lighting, and vegetation conditions in certain parts of the canyon. In 1991, we were primarily interested in views of western Grand Canyon, and we launched on a thirty-day trip January 29. We were able to replicate 168 Stanton views between Lees Ferry and Diamond Creek. The 1991 trip also produced many new hypotheses concerning long-term change in Grand Canyon. In the winter of 1992, we devoted two trips to repeat photography. In eleven

days in late December and early January, we replicated 51 views between Lees Ferry and Phantom Ranch. In February and March 1992, we replicated another 75 views.

Replicating all of the Stanton negatives appeared to be a futile goal because "new" ones kept turning up at the National Archives and the New York Public Library. The value of this group of photographs is so great, however, that I doggedly pursued the acquisition of prints and the replication of Stanton views on trips that were devoted to other research goals. Additional views in Grand Canyon were replicated in November 1990; November 1991; October 1992; and February and March 1993, 1994, and 1995. Replications of views in Cataract Canyon, Utah, which are discussed only briefly, were completed during research trips in July 1991 and 1992, May 1993, and March 1994.

On the 1889 and 1890 expeditions, Stanton and his crew had spent eighty-two days to make the original views, but most of their time was spent getting boats and equipment around rapids. In about a hundred days over six winters, we found and replicated 445 views of the Stanton expedition. We spent most of our effort in finding the exact location of the original view and interpreting changes. We exposed perhaps 2,000 negatives on these trips, and despite the rare double exposure or problems with commercial photographic labs, we secured emulsion for every Stanton view taken between Glen Canyon Dam and Lake Mead for which we could find an original print or negative.

It would have been easy just to make this an album of repeat photographs or a paean to Robert Brewster Stanton. Instead, I chose to write the rudiments of an environmental history of Grand Canyon. Although it might seem limiting to attempt such a history from one set of old photographs, the Stanton photographs are exceptional for recording evidence of environmental conditions in 1890 and thus allowing us to determine the most significant changes in the river corridor over the last century. In almost every key place, we found a Stanton view to test a hypothesis about what has or has not changed in Grand Canyon.

The scope of this book is limited to the river corridor, specifically to those areas recorded in Stanton views. Many other interesting environmental changes in Grand Canyon are not covered—for example, decreases in the populations of native fishes in the Colorado River.[4] The choice of issues treated in this book reflects my desire to report as completely as possible an environmental history of Grand Canyon reconstructed using one extraordinary set of old photographs.

Grand Canyon

A Century of Change

CHAPTER 1

The Denver, Colorado Canyon and Pacific Railroad

On the afternoon of March 1, 1890, Robert Brewster Stanton anxiously scanned the left side of the Colorado River near the western end of Grand Canyon. His expedition, reduced to two boats and ten men, was approaching Diamond Creek, and Stanton did not want to pass the creek accidentally. The expedition members knew that a wagon road entered Grand Canyon at the creek[1] and that the town of Peach Springs, Arizona (and a railroad depot), was a day's hike to the south. The alternative was grim; Stanton knew that he and his men would have to run sixty-two river miles and the dreaded Separation Rapid before the next possible contact with civilization.

Stanton's expedition was low on supplies, but he was not desperate. On December 10, 1889, the original group of twelve men had left Crescent Creek (now called North Wash) near Hite, Utah, intending to spend most of the winter traveling through the canyons of the Colorado River.[2] After a sumptuous Christmas dinner at Lees Ferry, the expedition had entered Marble Canyon on December 28. Four months' supplies had been packed into three boats, and although Stanton had lost one boat upstream, he still had plenty of provisions left as he looked for Diamond Creek. The men longed for tobacco and sugar, which they had run out of two weeks before, but conditions could not have been too bad; Stanton claimed he had gained fourteen pounds since the trip began.[3]

Using the only map available, Stanton landed late in the afternoon at the mouth of what is now called 224 Mile Canyon and hiked up the channel. Finding no footprints or other signs of visitation, he returned to the boats in disappointment and launched again. At 5:05 P.M., the crew landed at the mouth of a side canyon with a large creek. Scouting quickly, they were delighted to find signs of recent visitation. They had reached Diamond Creek, and a celebration ensued at the boats.

The next day, Stanton and Elmer Kane, one of his most trusted crew members, hiked nearly twenty-five miles to Peach Springs in less than six hours. He sent telegraphs to his wife and some friends, sent mail and supplies back to his men at the mouth of Diamond Creek, and then found a room at the local boardinghouse. Nearly a week later, he received the news he had awaited for so long: a telegram arrived March 7 from the W. H. Jackson Company of Denver, saying "negatives all right."[4] Before the trip began, Stanton had never taken a photograph in his life, but at that moment he learned that the 1,600 negatives he had exposed would probably yield clear prints.

Stanton boated through Grand Canyon to demonstrate the feasibility of building a water-level railroad along the Colorado River. His expedition in many ways was the last of the great surveys to develop transportation systems in the West. The region had been systematically explored and mapped twenty years before by federal government agents and surveyors,[5] and several transcontinental railroads were in use. Stanton's was a can-do era, and his proposed railroad would have been on the same scale of engineering achievement as the construction, forty years later, of Hoover Dam on the Colorado River.

Had Stanton's railroad been built, it would have irrevocably changed the Colorado River and would have had incalculable consequences on what is now

Grand Canyon National Park. But because he systematically photographed the entire river corridor, Stanton unintentionally established the basis for an excellent long-term monitoring program for a national park.

The Prospector's Idea

The Colorado River in Grand Canyon had been visited only rarely before 1890, the year of Stanton's successful expedition. John Wesley Powell had received great acclaim for his widely publicized pioneering expeditions down the river in 1869 and 1871–1872 and for subsequent geological surveys. Powell opened the river corridor to further exploration with the publication of his book *The Exploration of the Colorado River of the West and Its Tributaries* (1875).[6]

A few prospectors impressed by the possibilities of mineral deposits explored the region after Powell.[7] One such prospector was S. S. Harper, who searched for minerals in northern Arizona in 1870. After traversing the line of the Santa Fe Railroad through the Rocky Mountains, Harper conceived the idea of building a water-level railroad through the canyons of the Colorado River to avoid the "saw-tooth effect" of numerous mountain crossings.[8] Such a railroad could deliver coal from the Rocky Mountains to San Diego, and supplies could be brought to the isolated miners and ranchers in the intermountain West.[9]

Completely naive about the canyons,[10] Harper persisted in trying to interest friends and potential investors in the project for nearly twenty years. In January 1889, he finally found a willing partner in Frank M. Brown, a successful real estate investor in Denver. Brown saw great commercial potential in this railroad project and organized the Denver, Colorado Canyon and Pacific Railroad (DCC&PRR) Company on March 25, 1889. Despite his lack of experience with railroads, Brown became president of the company.

The proposed route for the railroad was down the

Colorado River (then called the Grand River) from Grand Junction, Colorado, to the confluence of the Green and Colorado Rivers. Downstream from the confluence, the railroad was to be built about a hundred feet above water level along the Colorado River through Cataract, Narrow, Glen, Marble, and Grand Canyons. The railroad would end in San Diego. Enthusiastic about the project, Brown initiated the survey of the proposed railroad route by launching a river trip downstream from Grand Junction on March 28, 1889. This expedition, headed by assistant engineer Frank C. Kendrick, surveyed the route to the confluence of the Green and Colorado Rivers by May 4. The main expedition that would finish the survey through the canyons would be launched later in May, and Brown began purchasing the necessary equipment.

Brown was convinced that a railroad could be built through the canyons of the Colorado River and that such a line would be profitable. He traveled to the East to enlist investors, who were hesitant about the project. He even discussed the railroad project with Powell, who was decidedly negative about the prospect of construction in the sheer walls of Grand Canyon.[11] Eventually, Brown managed to secure enough funding for an exploratory trip. But before construction could begin, he needed to find a competent engineer and get a favorable report on the route. The engineer he found was Robert Brewster Stanton.

Brown, Stanton, and Nims

In 1889 Stanton was, at age forty-three, a successful civil and mining engineer. He had attended college at Miami University, a small college in Oxford, Ohio, of which his father was president. Although his education was not in engineering, Stanton learned surveying and began his career in 1871 as a rod man with the Atlantic and Pacific Railroad. Advancing rapidly to the stature of project engineer, Stanton worked on various railroad construction projects until he engineered the Georgetown Loop for the Union Pacific spur line between Georgetown and Silver Plume, Colorado, between 1880 and 1884.[12] In 1889, Stanton became a consulting engineer based out of Denver and occasionally worked as a mining engineer.

To Brown, Stanton must have seemed the ideal choice for chief engineer. Besides his reputation for engineering railroads, Stanton was an experienced outdoorsman in the still-frontier West. He had worked for two years as general manager of a mine in Idaho and had explored railroad routes from horseback in Oklahoma and Texas. He was a religious man; he did not work on Sundays and abhorred heavy drinkers. Married to Jean Oliver Moore, Stanton was also raising a family. Like Powell before him, Stanton had a handicap: he had been dropped in early childhood, and his left arm had not grown normally. Nonetheless, Stanton did not shrink from danger or hard labor in the wilderness, although he "could not swim a stroke."[13]

Stanton became chief engineer for the DCC&PRR on May 13, 1889. Immediately, he had disagreements with his employer, Brown, who was then planning the second river expedition to demonstrate the feasibility of the railroad route, this time from Green River, Utah, to Needles, California. Stanton had only ten days after his appointment as chief engineer to hire men and obtain surveying equipment for the expedition. Of the men Stanton requested, four were to be experienced boatmen; Brown replaced these men with two inexperienced friends. Stanton realistically estimated six to eight months for completion of the survey; Brown asked that it be completed in two to three months.

Brown was in a hurry to explore the railroad route because he needed a favorable report of the

Figure 1.1 (pages 6–8). The Colorado and Green Rivers in Utah and Arizona

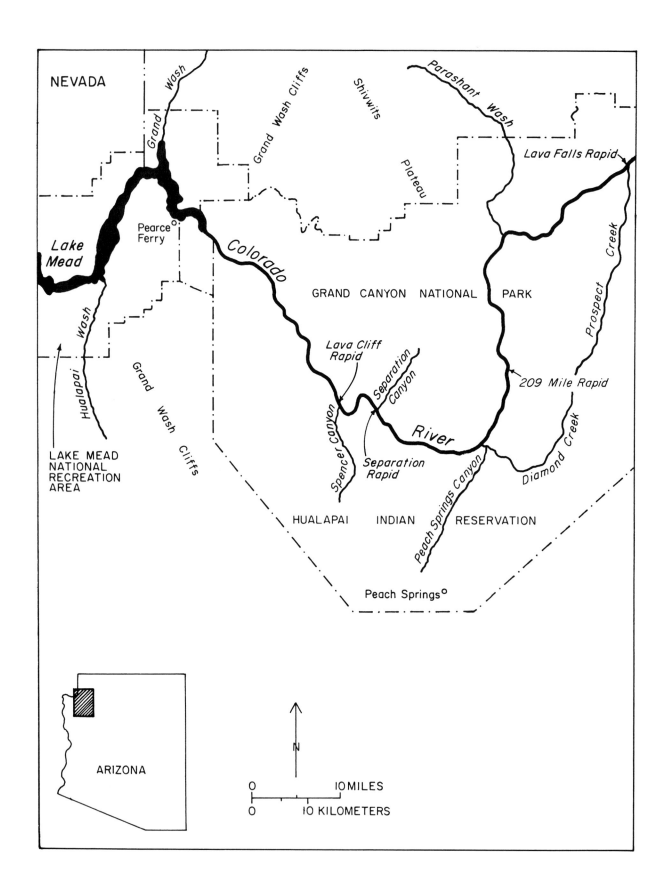

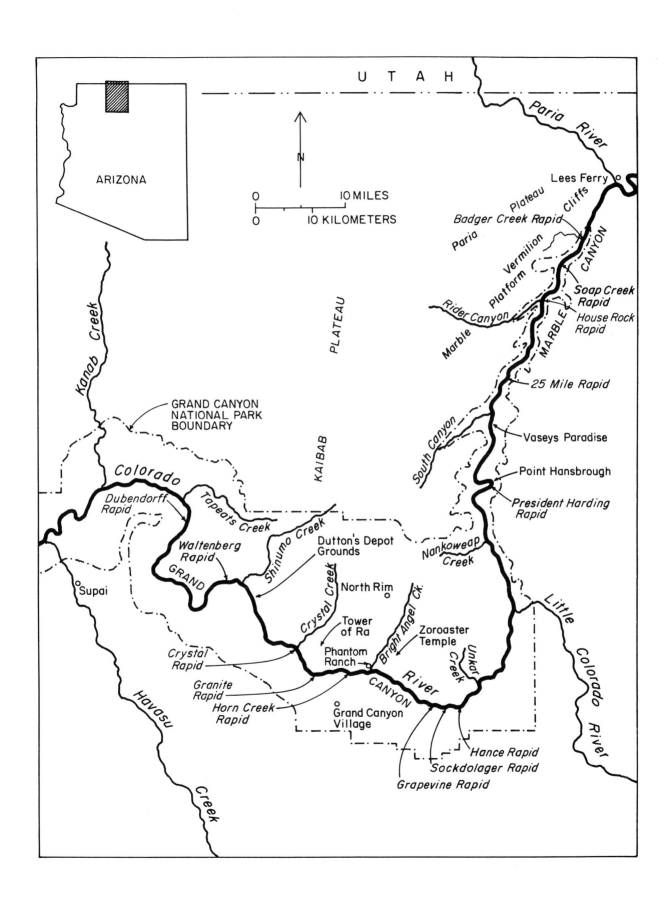

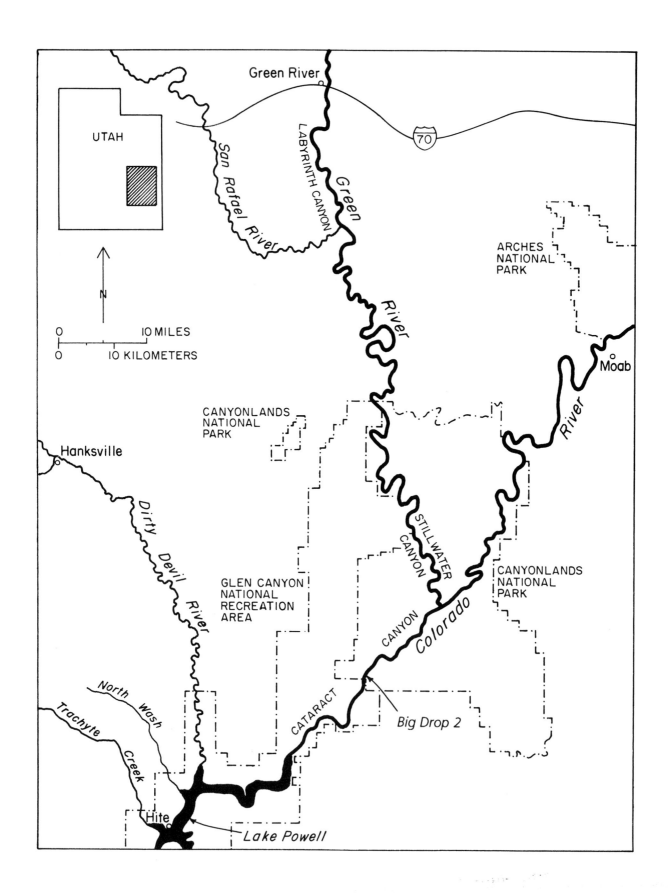

engineering feasibility by August 15 to secure fifty million dollars in backing. At one point, he offered Stanton a bonus of ten thousand dollars if the survey could be completed in thirty days. Perhaps because of his haste, or perhaps because he was unwilling to purchase appropriate and expensive gear, Brown outfitted the expedition with cheap boats and poor equipment. More important, he failed to procure life jackets despite Stanton's protest. Because he wanted no advantage over his men, Stanton refused to take a life jacket for himself.

Stanton was disappointed on viewing the boats at Green River; two were made of thin red cedar and already had split bottoms from handling in transport. Brown had purchased light boats to make portaging easier, but Stanton was justifiably concerned about what would happen when they struck rocks. Brown had bought watertight zinc boxes for provisions, but the crew could not fit all the boxes and gear inside the small, open boats. Instead, the watertight boxes were lashed together into a raft to be towed behind the cook's boat.

Stanton was convinced that Brown did not understand the dangers of a trip down the Colorado River. Stanton had reread Powell's report, which suggested that extreme caution was required for safe passage through the canyons. Powell had described a typical run through a Colorado River rapid in this fashion:

> About eleven o'clock we hear a great roar ahead, and approach it very cautiously. The sound grows louder and louder as we run, and at last we find ourselves above a long, broken fall [Sockdolager Rapid], with ledges and pinnacles of rock obstructing the river. There is a descent of perhaps 75 or 80 feet in a third of a mile, and the rushing waters break into great waves on the rocks, and lash themselves into a mad, white foam. We can land just above, but there is no foothold on either side by which we can make a portage . . . we must run the rapid or abandon the river. There is no hesitation. We step into our boats, push off, and away we go, first on smooth but swift water,

then we strike a glassy wave and ride to its top, down again into the trough, up again on a higher wave, and down and up on waves higher and still higher until we strike one just as it curls back, and a breaker rolls over our little boat. Still on we speed, shooting past projecting rocks, till the little boat is caught in a whirlpool and spun round several times. . . . Hurled back from a rock, now on this side, now on that, we are carried into an eddy, in which we struggle for a few minutes, and are then out again, the breakers still rolling over us. Our boat is unmanageable, but she cannot sink, and we drift down another hundred yards through breakers—how, we scarcely know.[14]

In hindsight, we know that Powell's report greatly exaggerated the hazards of the river, but Stanton was right to be deeply concerned for the crew's safety. However, he wanted the job and did not protest strongly to Brown. This attitude, which Stanton later attributed to his engineering background,[15] probably explains why he did not abandon the first expedition earlier than he did.

The relationship between Brown and Stanton was complex, and the two men's different personalities may explain actions that appear at variance on the ill-fated trip. At age forty-four, Brown was athletic, healthy, and daring, and he chose not to believe Powell's account of the dangers of the Colorado River. He took the job of demonstrating the feasibility of the railroad route lightly and considered the expedition little more than an outing with his friends. Stanton, in the typical fashion of engineers, was realistic and methodical. He tried to anticipate the dangers and expected much hardship and work. Yet the two appear not to have been at odds on the first trip; Stanton's diary suggests that their disagreements were mostly professional and that Stanton deferred to Brown. While traveling through Glen Canyon, Brown and Stanton learned that they were members of the same college fraternity and became close friends. Of more importance, both shared the strong opinion that a railroad could be built through the canyons of the Colorado River.

Brown, knowing the value of publicity, also hired a photographer to accompany the expedition and document the proposed railroad. Franklin Asa Nims was born in Manlius, New York, and studied at the National Academy of Design in New York City.[16] He moved to Colorado in 1879 and worked as a professional photographer in Colorado Springs. When Brown hired him for the job, Nims was about thirty years old and had experience in the gallery of Denver photographer W. H. Lawrence. He also worked briefly as Brown's secretary.[17] Nims's first assignment was to obtain quickly the necessary photographic equipment and film for the expedition.

Disaster in the Summer of 1889

The sixteen men of the Brown-Stanton expedition assembled at Green River, Utah, on May 23, 1889, at the Denver and Rio Grande Railroad bridge crossing. On May 25, they stopped repairing boats and started rowing downstream. They rowed only forty minutes before they had to stop and caulk one of the six boats. Three hours after launching, another boat struck rocks in their first rapid and needed repair. This poor start was a preview of the disasters awaiting them downstream.

Nims began photographing as soon as the expedition launched from the Green River. He used his camera only sporadically on the Green River because Brown was in a hurry to reach the confluence with the Colorado River. However, Stanton kept notes on this 120-mile reach should a spur line be proposed between the Denver and Rio Grande Railroad at Green River and the DCC&PRR at the confluence. Most of the Green River is flat water, and the trip was quick and uneventful.

The expedition reached the confluence of the Green and Colorado Rivers on May 29. The following morning, Stanton and his crew took up the surveying line where the team led by Kendrick had left off in early May. They began surveying into Cataract Canyon along the left side of the Colorado River, which is where the route would have been constructed through Cataract, Narrow, Glen, and the upper part of Marble Canyons. Nims started photographing the railroad route at the confluence; Brown's intention was to document as much of the proposed railroad line as possible.

In the first rapid of Cataract Canyon, the expedition had its first disaster. The combination of the cook's boat, named the *Brown Betty*, and the raft of watertight boxes it was towing was unwieldy. To avoid being swept into the whitewater, the crew cut the raft loose at the top of the rapid. They lost, at least temporarily, one-third of their provisions in what is now called Brown Betty Rapid.[18]

The Colorado River was near the crest of its annual flood when the expedition entered Cataract Canyon.[19] As a result, many rapids that are distinct at low water were continuous whitewater for Brown and his crew. The waves concealed enormous boulders, and the eddy fences, which separate swiftly downstream-moving water from upstream-moving eddies, were treacherous zones of whirlpools and turbulence. Brown tried running rapids, but the light boats flipped or were damaged on rocks. When the crew tried lining boats down the side of rapids, the ropes broke, with disastrous consequences. Instead of the pleasure trip Brown appeared to have expected, the expedition became a continuous cycle of portaging and repairing boats. By June 10, the men had lost two boats, the provisions raft, and more than half of their food supply. Luckily, the crew found a few of the zinc boxes intact and were able to salvage some food. Accidents and near escapes were frequent, although cuts and bruises were the only physical injuries. Open dissention began in the group.

Stanton urged Brown to split the expedition on June 5. The alarming rate of loss of provisions frightened the men, and Stanton wanted Brown and his friends, who were not helping with the survey, to go downstream to Hite and secure additional provisions. Brown refused, and the crew continued to lose provisions faster than they could recover their own flotsam. Somehow, the instrumental survey and systematic photography continued between the portaging and lining of boats. On June 13, Stanton again proposed splitting the trip. Upon learning of Stanton's determination, and recognizing that only six days' provisions were left, Brown agreed.

On June 17, Brown, with three boats and eleven men (including Nims), set off for Hite to acquire provisions. They passed quickly through the lower part of Cataract Canyon and Narrow Canyon, reaching Hite on June 19. The fast transit prevented Nims from photographing this reach, which is now under Lake Powell. Brown sent back provisions to Stanton's small group, which had tenaciously continued to survey downstream, content with the work despite low rations. Provisions reached Stanton on June 20, and the surveyors completed their work to Hite on June 24. The expedition had completed only 54 miles of the 1,037-mile railroad survey in one month.

The expedition regrouped at Hite and split into two teams. Three men quit the expedition, including two that Stanton had found worthless. Sensing the need for someone with experience, Brown hired Harry McDonald, who was working at the placer mines near Hite. Brown and Stanton, with three boats and eight men including Nims and McDonald, proceeded downstream into Glen Canyon. Stanton was to make an "eye survey" during the fast-paced run to Needles. Members of the second group—five men under assistant engineer William Bush—were to move more slowly downstream in one boat with the goal of completing the instrumental survey to Lees Ferry.

Brown and Stanton's group passed through Glen Canyon without incident and reached Lees Ferry on July 2. It is unlikely that Nims made many views in Glen Canyon on this trip, because the men covered 160 miles in only four days. On July 9, the resup-

plied trip launched from Lees Ferry and rowed into Marble Canyon. Because Brown wanted to reach Needles quickly, Nims had only a few opportunities to photograph in Marble Canyon. After portaging the first two rapids, the crew camped on a sand bar just below Soap Creek Rapid.

That evening, Brown was troubled and talked at length with Stanton. They stayed up late, smoking their pipes and talking of home. During a restless night, Brown dreamed of rapids. The next morning, Brown and McDonald launched first, and at Salt Water Riffle (mile 11.8),[20] their boat flipped on an eddy fence. With no life jackets, Brown and McDonald were trapped in the turbulence. Both were sucked under the surface, but only McDonald emerged safely downstream. An inscription marks the spot at Salt Water Wash where the president of the DCC&PRR drowned, and Nims photographed the eddy for documentation. The boat was recovered a mile downstream; Brown's body was seen several days later but was not recovered.

Stanton's diary entry for July 10, largely consisting of information on the railroad route and emotionless accounts of the accident, might seem callous. But in his later narrative account, he says he grieved greatly after Brown's death. The diary entries may have reflected the matter-of-fact treatment of death on the frontier, because even Nims's diary gives little indication of grief. Though it may seem inexplicable that Stanton chose to continue rather than take the easy hike up Salt Water Wash and back to Lees Ferry, he had already risked starvation to survey the lower part of Cataract Canyon, and his strong sense of duty prevailed. The expedition, demoralized and poorly equipped though it was, continued downstream.

Stanton and his men cautiously entered what is now called the Roaring Twenties, a group of closely spaced rapids that begins about twenty miles downstream of Lees Ferry. This fast-water reach is similar to the terrifying whitewater the men had traversed in Cataract Canyon. The crew lined and portaged their

Figure 1.2. Big Drop 2, Cataract Canyon, Utah

A. Franklin Nims made this upstream view from the middle of Big Drop 2, also known as Rapid 22, in early June 1889 (number 73). At high water levels, this rapid is the most severe in Cataract Canyon. The expedition paused in its portage of the left side of this rapid for a group photograph. Discharge in the Colorado River is about 40,000 cfs.

boats around most of the rapids in the summer heat. On July 13, they stopped for lunch under the shade of a juniper tree at what Stanton named Lone Cedar Rapid, now called 23½ Mile Rapid. McDonald carved his initials "H.McD." into the trunk of this tree, and those initials are still visible on the living tree.

Disaster struck again on July 15 at 25 Mile Rapid. The crew lined their boats around the head of the rapid on the left, then launched below. The current below 25 Mile Rapid impinges on a vertical bedrock wall on the left as the river makes a right bend. At the water level of July 15, 1889, an overhanging ledge was exposed about three feet above the water. The boat containing Peter Hansbrough and Henry Richards flipped under this ledge, and both men drowned. Their bodies drifted downstream.

Stanton no longer had a choice. The men were shattered, and even had they not been mutinous, there were no longer enough of them to portage the boats. He began searching for a place to hike out of the canyon. On July 17, the expedition reached South Canyon (mile 31.6), where the men found Anasazi ruins and a trail out of Marble Canyon to the north. Stanton thought the creek was Nankoweap, which

B. The repeat view was made by Ted Melis at 3:00 P.M. on July 24, 1991. The water level, about 7,000 cfs, is much lower than in 1889, exposing the big rock in the center of the rapid. Careful examination of the skyline at right reveals a large debris-flow deposit that was not present in 1889; this debris flow may have been the source for the new rocks on the left side of the rapid. The fractured rocks throughout the foreground indicate that a rockfall occurred sometime during the intervening 102 years. The tamarisk at right center is testament to the invasion of this exotic species throughout the Southwest during the twentieth century.

actually was another twenty miles downstream. The crew stashed the remaining gear in what is now called Stantons Cave,[21] and they all hiked out. They reached a cattle camp in House Rock Valley on July 19 and made their way back to Denver by July 27.

Another Try

Despite the tragedy of the first trip, Stanton's evaluation of the upper part of the proposed route led him to believe that the railroad could be built. He became the biggest booster of the DCC&PRR project; he bought the stock of a major shareholder and was elected to the board of directors. When Powell attacked the absurdity of the project, Stanton defended it in the engineering press.[22] With only $13,500 in donations and some promises of more, Stanton decided to proceed with a second trip scheduled for the winter of 1889–1890.[23]

Stanton had learned the hard and tragic lessons

of the first expedition. His crew had completed an instrumental survey to a point only thirty-four miles upstream of Lees Ferry under conditions of extreme heat and low supplies. Upon viewing Nims's photographs of upper Cataract Canyon and the few that survived the aborted trip into Marble Canyon, Stanton realized that he could convince investors of the railroad's feasibility by systematically photographing the proposed route. He would finish the instrumental survey to Lees Ferry, but photography would save valuable time in Grand Canyon, where only very bad sections for a railroad line would be surveyed. Because the canyons were tortuous and Stanton wanted as much of the line as possible recorded on film, camera stations would be in bends, which had the longest possible view of the river corridor and cliffs.

Stanton carefully planned the boats and equipment for the upcoming trip. He retained frontiersman McDonald to supervise the construction of three new twenty-two-foot boats in Waukegan, Illinois.[24] Each boat was made of oak and had ten airtight compartments. The best cork life jackets were purchased, and the men were required to wear them constantly while on the river. Clothing and bedding were stored in specially made rubber bags. Remembering that the earlier expedition had recovered floating boxes of food, Stanton stored provisions in five-gallon kegs that he believed could float free of wrecked boats and be retrieved downstream. He also bought kegs of brandy and whiskey, which were used as medicine and "restorative" after dunkings.

For the second trip, Stanton carefully selected men for their compatibility and willingness to see the project through. McDonald became his head boatman. John Hislop, a veteran of the first trip, became Stanton's assistant engineer. Stanton also retained Nims's services as photographer, perhaps partly because of his loyalty in Cataract Canyon. Eight other men were selected for the trip, none with previous whitewater experience. One of these men, William H.

Edwards, kept the only other complete diary of the second expedition.[25]

Ever pragmatic, Stanton avoided Cataract Canyon because the instrumental survey had already been completed there. The expedition moved overland 110 miles from Green River to the mouth of Crescent Wash (now North Canyon) at the head of Glen Canyon. Here, it launched in midmorning on December 10 and began the routine of halting at appropriate spots for photographs. The crew also panned for gold and discussed placer mining with people they met in Glen Canyon. One of the people they met was Jack Sumner, a boatman on Powell's 1869 expedition, who had encouraging words about their chances for successfully running the canyon.

On December 21, the expedition took up the instrumental survey where Bush had left off the previous July. During that day, the expedition passed the site where Glen Canyon Dam would be built seventy years later. While Stanton surveyed down to Lees Ferry, Nims photographed the railroad route, delaying arrival at Lees Ferry and forcing an unwanted camp. After a Sunday rest, Stanton carefully surveyed and had Nims photograph a tight bend two to four miles above Lees Ferry. Even high winds could not prevent their arrival at Lees Ferry that evening. The next day, Christmas Eve, the men rowed back upstream and continued the instrumental survey.

Stanton took December 25 as an opportunity to reprovision his trip and rest his men at Lees Ferry. Warren Johnson, the ferryman, was a gracious host for a Christmas dinner that Stanton arranged as a surprise for his men. The crew launched into Marble Canyon on December 28, portaged supplies and lined boats around the right side of Badger Creek Rapid, and camped. The day had been brilliantly sunny, but the next morning the crew found ice on the boats. In contrast to the previous summer, the water level was much lower, and the rapids appeared much different.[26]

After a day of rest, the crew arrived at Soap Creek

Rapid and began a portage on the right. Soaked after working in the freezing water, they drank some restorative whiskey, built a fire, and camped. Snow surrounded their beds the next morning. The weather affected the quality of the expedition's photographs of Marble Canyon, which typically are stark without strong shadows.

The weather became the least of Stanton's concerns on New Year's Day. Nims fell twenty-two feet off a cliff and landed on his back and head. He was bleeding from his nose and right ear and had broken bones in his right ankle and foot. Eventually, it became clear that the semiconscious Nims would survive, but he could not continue downstream. Stanton had two large problems to confront: how to evacuate Nims and how to complete the photographic survey. Because photographs would sell the project to potential investors, the photographer was the most important person on the trip.

While others attended to Nims, Stanton decided to assume photographic duties himself. He had never taken a photograph, but he had watched Nims. Stanton relates the story this way:

> I had never adjusted a camera, had never seen the inside of a roll-holder. How did the thing work anyway? The photographer's book of record was at hand. It was full of columns, headed with all sorts of abbreviated notes and signs. They were so much Choctaw to me. All that was known, and all that could be found out from anyone in the party, was that the film should not be exposed so long in a bright sun as in a dark night. With that stock of knowledge and information the work began. The camera . . . was focused, adjusted, turned and twisted. Every moment I became more excited and worried. At last the roll-holder was put in place; the instrument carefully covered up with the focusing cloth, and the slide drawn; but, as I attempted to take off the [lens] cap, I hesitated, dashed my hat upon the ground, and tore my hair in desperation at the complicated state of affairs. While [I was] thus engaged the cook picked up our little

camera, took a snapshot at me, and preserved for my future contemplation the absurd picture I was making of myself.[27]

Unfortunately, the cook's snapshot does not appear to have survived.

Evacuation of Nims began on January 3 at House Rock Canyon, a mile and a half downstream of the accident site. Stanton, Hislop, and McDonald scouted up the canyon and managed to climb above a waterfall. Convinced that the crew could evacuate Nims in this canyon, Stanton sent the other two back while he continued up and out to summon Johnson and bring a wagon from Lees Ferry. He reached Lees Ferry at midnight after a thirty-five-mile walk that took twenty hours. After McDonald and Hislop returned to the boats, the crew rigged up a litter and began the arduous task of carrying Nims to the top of the cliff the next day. Four men carried Nims, who lapsed in and out of consciousness, while four others scouted the trail and carried blankets and food. They used ropes to haul the litter up and over waterfalls and cliffs. Finally, they climbed up through a crack and reached the rim in late afternoon.

Three members were sent back to the boats for more food and water while the remainder endured a cold night on the rim huddled in rain and snow around a sagebrush fire. The three returned early on the morning of January 5, and Stanton appeared several hours later with news that a wagon was on the way for Nims. After a two-week convalescence at Lees Ferry, Nims returned to Denver, where he recovered in about six months. He was bitter that his pay was cut off on January 1, but he was prepared for his accident in one way: he had purchased life and accident insurance before the trip.[28]

On January 6, the crew packed in a light snowstorm and resumed their journey. Progress through the seemingly endless rapids of the Roaring Twenties was slow. The men lined the boats through each rapid, the only choice being whether to carry some

Figure 1.3. Where Hansbrough and Richards died

A. Nims documented the sites where Frank M. Brown, Peter Hansbrough, and Henry Richards died in July 1889. Just below 25 Mile Rapid, where Hansbrough and Richards died, Nims made this upstream view (number 310) on July 15 around midday. The boat carrying Hansbrough and Richards upset under the low bedrock wall at the center of the view.

of the gear around or to lower the boats fully loaded. Stanton took photographs of the railroad route while his men worked in the freezing water. His diary entries for Marble Canyon refer almost exclusively to trip logistics and engineering considerations for the railroad route.

The weather remained cold through Marble Canyon.[29] Below one rapid, after waves broke over his boat, Stanton noted, "Rather severe to take such a bath during a snowstorm." At another place, Stanton watched ice form on his wet shoes. In this narrow part of the canyon, the sun rarely shines at water level during winter. When the crew saw a patch of sunlight, they rejoiced; Stanton consistently describes the occasional "beautiful sunshine" in Marble Canyon.

At 24½ Mile Rapid, near a pedestal of Redwall Limestone that Stanton named Marble Pier, the men

B. P. T. Reilly replicated Nims's view on April 29, 1964 (not shown), and Jim Hasbargen made our repeat view on January 2, 1992, at 1:31 P.M. Snow mantles the cliffs in the background of Hasbargen's photograph. The foreground boulders are unchanged, but small cobbles have shifted at bottom center. A small debris flow has deposited small boulders on the debris fan at right center, and the sand bar at extreme right has changed little in size.

halted to repair boats. The crew stayed in camp three nights and weathered another snowstorm. Stanton learned to change the film and was gaining confidence in his recently acquired duties. Evacuating Nims and repairing boats had cost valuable time, and Stanton was eager to move downstream. Problems continued the next day at 25 Mile Rapid, where Hansbrough and Richards had drowned the previous summer; this time, a boat was stuck on a rock and much of the kitchen equipment sank. Stanton

lost another day to boat repair.

The expedition began moving downstream in earnest on January 13. The crew retrieved supplies from Stantons Cave, thereby offsetting their losses in 25 Mile Rapid. After a day of repair and photographs at South Canyon, they quickly rowed through lower Marble Canyon. Stanton decided that a crossing was required just below Vaseys Paradise, and the attention of the survey crew switched to river right. The sun broke through the clouds, and Stanton began to note spring flowers and mesquite trees, a welcome sign of warmer temperatures.

On January 16, the crew found Hansbrough's remains near what Stanton called Boulder Rapid, later renamed President Harding Rapid (mile 43.8) by members of the 1923 U.S. Geological Survey expedition. The crew buried Hansbrough the following morning under a cliff and carved an inscription in the rock. On January 20, the men reached the mouth of the Little Colorado River (mile 61.4), stopped briefly for photographs, and rowed into Grand Canyon.

The expedition then entered the relatively calm waters of Furnace Flats, an open reach of about seven miles. Gaining confidence, the boatmen began to run most of the riffles and rapids, although they lined boats and portaged supplies around Lava Canyon Rapid (mile 65.5). Potential for economic mineral deposits appeared high here, and Stanton's men, particularly McDonald, spent time prospecting. In so doing, they met Felix Lantier, a prospector, at Tanner Rapid (mile 68.3) on January 22.[30] Stanton took the opportunity of this chance encounter to send out his field notebooks and rolls of exposed film to Flagstaff. He was uncertain whether his negatives were good; not until five weeks later at Peach Springs did he learn the welcome news.

Stanton had criticized Nims for climbing to precarious vantage points for more aesthetic photography; he wanted only "pleasing" photographs that showed the nature of the canyon and railroad route. Up to this point, he had mostly followed his own advice. But as photographs of the granaries at Nankoweap (mile 52.4) and Cardenas Hilltop Ruin (mile 72) indicate, Stanton (like Nims) was succumbing to the lure of the canyon's scenery. He began including more descriptions of the scenery in his diary in addition to the engineering details.

After they lined Unkar Rapid (mile 72.6) on January 24, the going got rougher. The portage and lining of Nevills Rapid (mile 75.5) took a morning. Hance Rapid (mile 76.8) had no distinct channel. They had to lift the boats over some rocks along the left bank and portage all supplies. Including passage of Lower Hance, the men labored a day and a half here and promptly entered Upper Granite Gorge on the evening of January 27. The next day, the men lined Sockdolager Rapid (mile 78.6) on the left, an option Powell did not have because of higher water in 1869 and 1872. Although Stanton was looking for Sockdolager, which Powell had described as a seventy-five-foot drop, he did not recognize the famous rapid. Concerned with finding the obstacle to navigation that Powell had described, Stanton and his men continued cautiously downstream.

Stanton's impression of the canyons was changing. The expedition stopped for photographs at what is now a heavily used camping beach at mile 81.3. After making an image of the mouth of Vishnu Creek, Stanton, Hislop, and McDonald climbed up the steep schist on the south side. They found a particularly well vegetated place that they thought would make a "wonderful place for sheep and goats." Stanton noted in his diary the differences among the canyons he had traversed:

> One thing I note today on all these granite walls: being broken up into crags and little valleys between, the valleys are full of grass, greasewood, cacti, and mesquite bushes. So that, while the rocks are black and sombre, the whole picture is enlivened by the green colors. And where one can get a glimpse of the red, grey, and bright-colored sandstones above, the contrast is most beautiful. Of course, the bright colors of the canyons above—Cataract, Glen, and Marble—are wanting in the Granite, but the vegetation gives an appearance of usefulness, as in contrast to the utter barrenness of some portions of the sandstone country.[31]

His notice of the desert plants, and his recording of them on film, became a very significant aspect of his expedition to us a hundred years later.

Search for the Site of the Hansbrough-Richards Tragedy

P. T. REILLY

My first trip through Grand Canyon was in 1949 as a boatman for Norman D. Nevills. For my own records, I usually took a picture looking both upstream and downstream from each camp and from our noon stops. At the conclusion of the trip I began to wonder what our predecessors had done at various places, if their solutions to obvious problems in river running had been different from ours. Otis R. "Dock" Marston had been working on the same problems, and it was not long before Marston and I pooled our efforts. We spent years trying to find some answers, and others remain unknown to this day, but we uncovered some from time to time. One of the most interesting follows.

Among the difficult problems was locating the place where Hansbrough and Richards of the Stanton party had drowned on July 15, 1889. Nims took a photograph of the site to document the drownings. Richards's body was never found, but Stanton's crew discovered Hansbrough's skeleton during the second expedition on January 16, 1890, at mile 43.7. The crew buried the skeleton at the base of a great limestone cliff. Since the location of the grave was discovered in the 1950s, it has been visited by thousands of river travelers.

My photographic coverage of the Colorado River through Marble and Grand Canyons was extensive, but sometimes I was too busy at the oars to take the pictures I wanted. One such occasion occurred in the early 1950s. I had run 25 Mile Rapid and was resting at the oars when the strong current swiftly carried the boat toward an overhanging cliff on the left. I became alert in time to prevent my boat from crashing head-on into the downsloping cliff. I noticed the strong current as it hit the cliff and plunged downward, and I realized that this probably was the place where Hansbrough and Richards had overturned and lost their lives in 1889.

Convinced that I had located the site of the double drowning, I intended to prove it on another trip. I was all set to do so when, with one passenger, I piled into 24½ Mile Rapid on June 23, 1959. My attention was riveted on the overhanging cliff below the next rapid when a heavy lateral smashed into us on the port, capsizing the boat. After we came up I yelled to my passenger to swim to the eddy and come down with the other boat. I grabbed the safety line of my capsized boat and hung on as the boat and I floated down the center of 25 Mile Rapid. At one point I thought my boat might be flipped right-side-up, but that stroke of fortune was not to be. As the boat and I cleared the rapid, a very strong current caught my legs and straightened them out toward the left wall. I was sure then that I knew how Hansbrough and Richards had drowned. I finally landed my capsized boat at mile 26.7. After a while, the other boat with my passenger aboard came down, and we continued downstream.

In the 1950s, water higher than that which the Stanton crew had experienced in 1889 prevented my positive identification of the site, but on April 29, 1964, our party landed on a small fan at mile 25.3. I walked directly to the location from which Nims had taken the picture documenting where Hansbrough and Richards had drowned. Though Nims had used a camera with a wide-angle lens, I was able to duplicate the photo. However, I could not afford to wait for the exact lighting shown in the 1889 view, and we continued the trip. Comparison of Nims's and my photographs reveals that despite several years of very high runoff in the Colorado River, the same rocks are present in the same position after seventy-five years.

Figure 1.4. Rebuilding the *Marie* in Grapevine Rapid

A. Mistakes made while lining rapids had severe consequences on early river expeditions. During a lining in Grapevine Rapid, the *Marie* broke loose and became lodged among boulders, which tore a large hole in the boat's side. More than three feet of damaged wood had to be removed from the center of the boat during reconstruction. Stanton photographed the repair of the *Marie* on February 1, 1890, in this upstream view (number 429).

The first major problem with boats occurred January 29 while the men tried to line the right side of Grapevine Rapid (mile 81.5). Stanton thought this was Sockdolager, because Grapevine was the only rapid in this reach that remotely resembled Powell's description. The *Marie* became pinned on a rock and filled with water. Unable to move the boat, the crew unloaded it and camped on a gravel beach in the middle of the rapid. During the night, rising water floated the damaged boat off the rock, and the next morning the crew recovered it. The men spent five

days cutting the *Marie* in half, removing the damaged center, and reassembling the boat at a length of eighteen feet. At night, the crew slept on rocks in the middle of the rapid. They hurried with the repair, because the river rose three feet during their forced stay.

Horn Creek Rapid (mile 90.2) finished what Grapevine had started. Stanton saw the rapid at its worst in the low water of February 6. A large boulder blocks the center of the channel, and the left side is shallow and rocky. On the lower right, the

B. Modern river runners will find reoccupation of the makeshift boat workshop nearly impossible. Typical dam releases now make landing above Grapevine Rapid on the right very difficult, so we chose to run the rapid, pull in below, and scramble back up to the site. Steve Tharnstrom replicated Stanton's view on January 7, 1992, at 3:18 P.M.

current impinges on a large piece of black schist. The crew decided the right side was the best place to line but could not hold the first boat in the swift water. Amazingly, the boat ran the rapid and was retrieved undamaged, so Stanton decided to turn the next boat loose at the top. The *Marie* crashed into the black boulder and disintegrated. Stanton's men then carried the remaining boat around the rapid, the first time a boat had had to be portaged since the previous July.

By this time, McDonald had become disgusted with the expedition. He watched as the boat he had spent five days rebuilding turned to splinters.

Eleven men were crammed into two boats, and the hard work of portaging and lining continued relentlessly. The most experienced outdoorsman on the trip, McDonald felt abused because several members of the crew were not working as hard as he was. Also, he had seen the potential for prospecting upstream and was eager to go back. When the expedition reached Crystal Creek (mile 98.3), he decided to hike out after consulting with Stanton. On February 10, he began his successful climb to the North Rim and civilization.[32] For "a little recreation," Stanton, Hislop, and Kane climbed the Tower of Ra, an isolated butte on the north side of the river.[33]

Figure 1.5. The Tower of Ra

A. On February 10, 1890, after Harry McDonald left the expedition, Stanton and two crew members began their climb of the Tower of Ra. They took a camera and film. After a "pretty good rest" on the top, Stanton was impressed with the sunrise over Grand Canyon. The number of negatives still in existence indicate that he exposed more film on this view than any other in the canyon, and his railroad route is nowhere to be seen (number 487). He did not record the time; but the length of shadows suggests that he probably took the photograph before 7:30 A.M.

After returning to the boats, the crew portaged goods and lined boats around Crystal Rapid, as they did at Tuna Creek Rapid (mile 99.2), the next one downstream. Launching below, Stanton had a wild ride in Lower Tuna Rapid, which resulted in a boat full of water and wet cameras. The expedition had entered what is now called the Jewels, a rough reach in which most of the rapids are named for semi-precious gems. The crew worked three and a half days to move eight river miles. They portaged the

B. Robert C. Euler became aware of the Stanton view from the Tower of Ra in the mid-1960s. He landed in a helicopter on the Tower of Ra to replicate Stanton's view on September 20, 1979. Several of the shrubs and plants in the foreground, notably bear grass, appear to have survived the past century.

boats over the head of 104 Mile Rapid, and other rapids required combinations of lining and portaging. On February 17, the expedition landed at the top of Bass Rapid (mile 107.9), and Stanton immediately recognized the potential of the right side as a switching yard and depot. Had the railroad been built, Stanton would have named this site "Dutton's Depot Ground" after Clarence Dutton, a geologist of the Powell Survey. Both Dutton and Powell had expressed doubts to Stanton that a place could be found for a switching yard among the sheer cliffs of Grand Canyon.

Below Shinumo Creek (mile 108.7), the crew found the rapids less threatening and the scenery more beautiful. Stanton wrote less about engineering and devoted long passages of his journal to the plant life and the colors of the cliffs. The weather, however, turned worse. Rain fell most of the time, and while eating lunch in Fossil Canyon (mile 125), the crew had to run from a flash flood. In camp the night of February 21, they discovered that their tobacco supply had been exhausted. They continued to make good time; they traveled six miles despite lining 128 Mile, Specter, and Dubendorff Rapids and running Bedrock Rapid. They camped upstream of Tapeats Creek (mile 133.7) and rested the following Sunday.

On February 24, sunshine and rising water greeted the men after a week of rain. After lining Tapeats and 135 Mile Rapids, the crew ran all the whitewater down to just above Havasu Creek (mile 156.9) on the rising flood.[34] Their confidence in their whitewater abilities increasing, they continued to run all but the largest rapids. As the river continued to rise, however, they became worried as rapids seemingly appeared and disappeared in what should have been calm stretches.[35] Some waves were so frightening that Stanton camped instead of attempting to run them. Their "worrying day" was allayed somewhat by the discovery of a pouch of tobacco in one of the rubber bags.

The expedition rode the high but slowly dropping water for a quick trip to Lava Falls Rapid (mile 179.3). The crew spent a cold night camped above its roar.[36] The next morning, February 27, Hislop set fire to the dense vegetation surrounding the warm springs below the rapid so the crew could warm up during the portage. The blaze filled the canyon with smoke.[37] The crew portaged boats and supplies along the left side of Lava Falls while Stanton waited for the smoke to clear from his view of the rapid. While waiting, Stanton or one of his crew built a cairn on the spot where he made three views of the canyon; the cairn still stands. The combination of the portage, the cold weather, and smoke delayed the trip half a day.

Lava Falls Rapid proved to be the last serious navigational obstacle of the trip. After running every

The Climb to the Tower of Ra

ROBERT C. EULER

Stanton and his crew were camped at the mouth of Crystal Creek on February 10, 1890. Stanton decided to lay over and attempt a climb to the North Rim, where he hoped to attain a broader perspective and photographs of what lay ahead. Stanton's brief journal entries[1] give us a "bare bones" account of the hike, while his later writings[2] provide more detail.

Stanton, Hislop, and Kane left the riverside camp early in the morning. Kane had the tripod and camera strapped to his back. The three men took biscuits, coffee, and bacon but carried no water; they assumed they would obtain water from snow on the rim by evening.

It was an extremely difficult climb; as far as I know, only two men in recent times have been able to accomplish it.[3] By evening, Stanton and his companions found themselves on one of the buttresses at the north side of the Tower of Ra, far out from and below the North Rim. There they made a dry camp with "a crackling fire, some dry biscuits and toasted bacon" for supper.[4] In the morning, Stanton was ecstatic about the view and took several pictures. Stanton claimed that he climbed from that point to Osiris Temple, although two veteran Grand Canyon hikers, Harvey Butchart and Donald Davis, who followed the Stanton route believe that Stanton started down the same day by another, easier route before reaching Osiris. (Davis and Butchart, who made their climb in 1966, also were attempting to replicate a few of Stanton's photographs.)[5]

Given the difficulty of the climb, one might assume that no one had been at the Tower of Ra before Stanton in 1890. However, while Davis was exploring the saddle between Ra and Osiris, he spotted a small cave in the Redwall Limestone. Inside, he found a prehistoric Anasazi ceramic jar and several corncobs. Two months later, while on an archaeological survey by helicopter, I visited Davis's cave and recorded two complete vessels of a type known to archaeologists as Moenkopi Corrugated. The vessels had been deposited in the cave by Anasazi some eight hundred years before and are clear evidence that the Indians had cached them with corn on a route out of the canyon.[6]

In ensuing years, I was preoccupied with archaeological research in Grand Canyon, and although I knew of Stanton's climb, I was not aware of the photographs he had taken. However, in 1979, the late Otis R. "Dock" Marston sent me a poor-quality copy print of Stanton's view from the Tower of Ra and asked me to try to locate the original camera station and replicate the view.

As luck would have it, such an opportunity presented itself not long after. On September 20, 1979, together with two colleagues, Frank Tikalsky and Trinkle Jones, I helicoptered to the north buttress of the Tower of Ra. Within two hours I had located rock features that were in the foreground of Stanton's view. He had used a wider angle lens than I had, and I was not able to encompass in my picture all of the features in Stanton's view.

As I set up my tripod as closely as I could ascertain to where Stanton had stood, I looked down at my feet and there was the broken ground glass from a camera. It could have belonged only to Stanton, since no one else to my knowledge had ever photographed with a view camera from that precise spot.[7]

Neither in Stanton's journal nor in his later writings did he mention that he had broken his ground glass on the Tower of Ra. In the type of camera he was using, the ground-glass focusing screen had to be removed after the scene had been composed and focused.[8] Apparently during this operation Stanton dropped the glass, and it broke. Why, I wondered, had Stanton failed to note this accident in his journal, and how had he made other photographs without the focusing screen? Not until I read the list of photographic equipment carried on the Stanton expedition did I realize that he had been equipped with six ground-glass focusing screens,[9] so the loss of one would have been insignificant.

I noted while I was replicating Stanton's view that not only were most of the rocks in the same places, but so was a dead juniper branch, attesting to the degree of preservation in this dry climate. Furthermore, I observed some plants (notably, bear grass) growing in what appeared to be the same place in both photographs, suggesting the minimum longevity of some types of Upper Sonoran Desert flora. Thus, the replication of this Stanton view adds a bit to our knowledge of history, botany, and environmental change in Grand Canyon.

rapid except 205 Mile, which required a short portage, the expedition reached Diamond Creek (mile 225.5) on March 1. After the resupply, the crew launched again on March 12 and ran all the rapids down to Separation Rapid (mile 239.5). By this time they were easily running rapids of the same magnitude that they had chosen to line in Marble Canyon. Seeing no other choice, Stanton quickly decided to run Separation Rapid. When the boat struck a rock at the bottom, Stanton was washed overboard and had to swim to safety downstream; his life jacket saved him from Brown's fate. Stanton later remembered that he had failed to photograph Separation Rapid, a serious mistake considering his later interest in what had happened there during the Powell expedition.[38]

The following day, March 14, the expedition reached Lava Cliff Rapid. Unable to portage, the crew carefully lined the top of the rapid on the left and ran the remainder. Stanton thought Lava Cliff was the worst rapid he had seen. Before the closure of Hoover Dam in 1935, Lava Cliff, Lava Falls, and Separation Rapids were considered the worst whitewater on the river, although inclusion of Separation Rapid with the other two has been questioned.[39] Lava Cliff and Separation Rapids are now covered by the waters of Lake Mead.

Lava Cliff was the last difficult rapid. With only photography to slow progress, the expedition reached the end of Grand Canyon on March 17. It passed scattered settlements and mining operations and reached Fort Mojave near Needles, California, on March 22. Stanton halted the expedition temporarily and took a train to Denver for business. The expedition resumed April 19 for a ten-day run down to Yuma, the conclusion of the journey.

Aftermath

As Robert Brewster Stanton floated out of Grand Canyon in March 1890, he certainly did not share the opinion of Lieutenant Joseph C. Ives, who in 1857

had declared, "The region is, of course, altogether valueless. It can be approached only from the South, and after entering it there is nothing to do but leave. Ours has been the first, and will doubtless be the last, party of whites to visit this profitless locality. It seems intended by nature that the Colorado River along the greater portion of its lonely and majestic way, shall be forever unvisited and undisturbed."[40] In Stanton's opinion, the Grand Canyon was ripe for development, and he expected that his railroad would open the region to mining and even tourism. Neither Stanton nor Ives had a correct vision of things to come.

Of course, the railroad was never built. Stanton attempted to convince investors that the project was feasible, but the financial panic of 1890 ended any possibility of financing. Stanton wrote several popular accounts of the expedition; one was the impetus for the next successful run of Grand Canyon in 1896. Harry McDonald returned to Grand Canyon in 1891 and staked claims in Chuar Creek (mile 65.5). His finds encouraged a speculator, James Best, to organize a river expedition down the Green and Colorado Rivers in 1891, with McDonald as head boatman and William Edwards as another boatman. John Hislop, Stanton's assistant engineer and loyal friend, continued his engineering career by building a railroad in Alaska. After surviving Arctic winters and the Grand Canyon expedition, Hislop was killed by a train in Chicago while on his honeymoon in February 1901.[41]

Franklin Nims evidently remained bitter about his treatment by Stanton. Not only had his pay been cut after his fall, he did not even receive copies of his own photographs. Instead, by chance, he was able to purchase eighty-five of them for five dollars from a bookstore in Denver.[42] Nims published several accounts of the expedition, neglecting to mention his accident and filling in the details of the expedition from Stanton's accounts.[43] Nims's career as a photographer apparently ended with the Stanton expedition. In the 1890s, he worked as a bookkeeper, a stenographer, a photo engraver, a journalist, and even an insurance agent. He moved to Greeley, Colorado, in 1900 and died January 2, 1935, in Indiana.

Stanton turned his attention to other projects and his family, but his expedition through Grand Canyon had changed his life. He became a historian of the Colorado River, perhaps spurred on by criticism of his expedition by Frederick Dellenbaugh, an admirer of Powell and a member of Powell's 1871–1872 expedition.[44] Stanton wrote a history of river running titled *The River and the Canyon* that was more than a thousand manuscript pages long; however, he died in 1922 before the unwieldy manuscript could be published. It became a part of his papers, which were donated to the New York Public Library after his death.

Julius Stone, a wealthy industrialist from Ohio who ran the Colorado River in 1909, took an interest in parts of Stanton's manuscript. One section dealt with James White's purported first run of the canyon on a log raft in 1867; Stanton had interviewed White and doubted that the published accounts were accurate.[45] Stone was also keenly interested in the events that caused three men to leave the Powell expedition at Separation Rapid in 1869, because the names of these men, whom Dellenbaugh labeled "deserters," had been left off a monument to the Powell expedition at the South Rim of the canyon. Stanton had interviewed several members of Powell's expedition, who gave accounts that contrasted with Powell's version, and he believed that Powell had forced the men to leave.[46]

Stone hired James M. Chalfant to edit these sections, and *Colorado River Controversies* was published in 1932. The issue of the monument's alleged inaccuracy remained. Dr. Russell G. Frazier, a river-running physician from northern Utah, financed a Grand Canyon trip in 1934 to place a plaque at Separation Rapid commemorating the three men.[47] The plaque was placed too low on the cliff, however, and the rising waters of Lake Mead submerged it. In 1939, Frazier financed a trip up Lake Mead with the eighty-year-old Stone to replace the plaque; a new plaque had to be placed higher on the cliff in 1943.[48] The new plaque refers to *Colorado River Controversies* and Stanton's version of the events at Separation Rapid.

Interest in Stanton's manuscript was revived in the 1960s. Dwight Smith, a professor of history at Miami University of Ohio, became interested in Stanton's narrative of his two expeditions. Smith extracted Stanton's narrative account from *The River and the Canyon* and published it as *Down the Colorado* in 1965. Smith and C. Gregory Crampton, a renowned western historian from the University of Utah, published Stanton's diary as *The Colorado River Survey* in 1987. With the publication of these three books, most of the material included in *The River and the Canyon* became widely available.

The fate of the photographs taken by Nims and Stanton was less publicized. Stanton had published many of them in an attempt to gain financial backing for his railroad, and he made several albums of prints. However, the negatives became useless in his eyes soon after the expedition ended. Stanton realized the historical importance of his account of the 1889 and 1890 expeditions, and his diary and narrative are fundamental to the human history of Grand Canyon. In viewing the useless negatives, Stanton likely did not suspect that they would become a resource for evaluating environmental change in Grand Canyon.

CHAPTER 2

The Science and Art of Repeat Photography

Repeat photography of landscapes is the science of locating and reoccupying as exactly as possible the camera position of a previous photographer. It is also an art, because replicating photographs requires astute choice of the appropriate camera system and film, careful timing to achieve the correct shadows and time of day, and appropriate use of filters to highlight or subdue important subjects. Generally, the object is not merely to make the replicate but to identify and interpret changes in the view as well. Interpretation of landscape changes is broadly inter-disciplinary and is based on natural sciences such as geology and biology.

Franklin Nims's and Robert Brewster Stanton's views of Grand Canyon are ideal for repeat photog-raphy. In attempting to document a railroad route, Nims and Stanton systematically photographed the river corridor through Grand Canyon. These photo-graphs represent an unbiased and, for all intents and purposes, random sampling of the environment of the canyon, which makes them an ideal scientific tool. Still, the amount and quality of scientific data that can be obtained from a pair of photographs of the same view depends largely on precise relocation of the original camera station. Fortunately, most of Stanton's camera positions are on stable slopes or bedrock with detailed foregrounds. The combination of unchanged foreground rocks and background cliffs allows precise reoccupation of camera positions.

Repeat Photography in Grand Canyon

Repeat photography has been long accepted as a technique for quantitatively assessing landscape changes. The first scientist to use repeat photography apparently was Sebastian Finsterwalder, who in 1888–1889 mapped changes of glaciers in the Alps using pairs of photographs.[1] Finsterwalder's technique is still employed in analyses of glacier mass balance. Since this pioneering effort, use of repeat photography has expanded into the natural and social sciences, architecture, and engineering.

In the southwestern United States, researchers have extensively used repeat photography to document biological and geomorphic changes associated with land use and climatic fluctuations.[2] The classic work in this area is *The Changing Mile*, written in 1965 by Rodney Hastings and Raymond Turner. In their work, Hastings and Turner documented vegetation changes caused by climatic change and livestock grazing in the Sonoran Desert. Repeat photography has served similar purposes in eastern Colorado, the Great Basin, and other areas in the western United States,[3] as well as in Grand Canyon for historical documentation and analysis of change in geology and vegetation.[4]

Who purposefully replicated the first photograph in Grand Canyon is difficult to determine.[5] P. T. Reilly, a river runner and avid photographer intrigued by Grand Canyon history, collected old photographs so he could locate and document several sites of historical interest. In July 1953 and again in 1964, he replicated the view of the abandoned boats from Powell's expedition at the mouth of Kanab Canyon. Also in 1964, Reilly replicated Nims's photographs of the sites where Frank Brown and Peter

Hansbrough and Henry Richards had drowned.

Repeat photography for scientific documentation began with the U.S. Geological Survey expedition of 1968, which traced the route of the 1869 Powell expedition while replicating photographs from the 1871–1872 expedition.[6] The purpose of the 1968 trip was twofold: to commemorate Powell's expeditions and to determine changes, primarily geologic, over the intervening years. Hal Stephens, a geologist who was the trip photographer, replicated twenty-eight views.

Systematic repeat photography of the canyon began in the early 1970s. Raymond Turner and Martin Karpiscak of the U.S. Geological Survey were interested in recent changes in riparian vegetation related to regulation by Glen Canyon Dam. They replicated views by numerous photographers, including Jack Hillers (of the Powell expedition) and Stanton. In particular, Turner and Karpiscak worked with the views of Eugene C. LaRue, who systematically photographed Grand Canyon during the U.S. Geological Survey expedition of 1923.[7] Turner continued his work with old photographs and had replicated about a hundred views of Grand Canyon, including seven by Nims or Stanton, by 1989. The remainder of the photographs from 1889 and 1890 had not been replicated or interpreted for change.

Photographs to Document a Railroad Route

Franklin Nims had worked for William Henry Jackson, preeminent photographer of western landscapes, and was fully aware of state-of-the-art camera equipment and films. Nims's Albion cameras, made by the Scovill and Adams Company of New York, had a format of 6½ by 8½ inches. Neither Nims nor Stanton wrote about the type and characteristics of lenses used in these cameras. However, Stanton refers flippantly to a "blister on his heel about the size and shape of a No. 4 Dallmeyer lens" in one account, indicating his familiarity with this lens.[8] His diary lists an "8 × 10 WA lens" among supplies taken on the second trip.[9] The lenses were not equipped with shutters; photographers removed the lens cap to expose the negative, then replaced the lens cap.

In replicating their views, we found that Nims and Stanton must have used at least two lenses with different fields of view: one had a normal field of view of about 48°, and the other was a wide-angle lens with a field of view of approximately 86°. The normal lens may have been a No. 4 Dallmeyer wide-angle landscape lens with a focal length of 12 inches, and the wide-angle lens may have been a No. 1A Dallmeyer wide-angle rectilinear lens with a focal length of 5.25 inches.[10] These lenses have rotating diaphragm plates to allow for variable apertures. Most of the photographs have a large depth of field, which indicates that Nims and Stanton mostly preferred smaller apertures, as would be suitable for photographing outdoors. They likely used other lenses, but I could not distinguish others when I inspected the existing negatives.

Although the Albion cameras could accept glass-plate holders, Nims chose to use roll film and equipped the cameras with Walker roll holders, which had only recently been invented.[11] Roll film could be developed after the trip, took up less cargo space, and weighed considerably less than glass plates. The films available to Nims were less sophisticated than today's films. All were blue-sensitive emulsions (orthochromatic) that, when properly exposed for typical landscapes, severely overexposed the sky. The result was minimal sky detail on the printed image. The most advanced medium available before Stanton's first expedition in May 1889 was George Eastman's American Film, also known as paper-stripping film.

In addition to the Albion cameras, Nims included a "detective" camera that produced a 4 by 5–inch image. This camera, used for informal views, possibly was a Kodak Junior 4, which used a roll of forty-eight exposures.[12] The 6-inch lens had a shutter and a fixed aperture of f8; the slightly telephoto field of view was about 44°. The film was paper backed, and after exposure the film had to be immersed in castor oil to make it translucent for printing. Seventy negatives made with this type of camera are housed in the National Archives. Various members of the expedition used the detective camera to take snapshots.

Nims left Green River with three Albion cameras, the detective camera, and an unknown amount of film. The wind blew one of the Albion cameras over a cliff on June 3, but Nims was able to repair it. His diary indicates he wrapped film and equipment in a blanket and rubber coat for protection from water damage. This was insufficient protection, because Nims had to overhaul the equipment on June 6, and on June 17 he "ruined all photograph stock, wet all instruments."[13] He had only three hundred unexposed negatives when the expedition left Lees Ferry on July 3, because he could not obtain photographic supplies in Kanab.[14] The detective camera was lost in 25 Mile Rapid when Hansbrough and Richards overturned, and the remaining cameras were stashed in Stantons Cave.

For the second expedition, Nims used the first flexible, transparent roll film. Stanton and Nims used extreme care to ensure that the film was protected from the perils of river travel. Some 2,200 negatives were exposed on the second trip; Nims exposed 600 before his accident, and Stanton exposed the remaining 1,600. Approximately half of these negatives were made on American Film; the remainder were made on transparent film. Apparently, Nims and Stanton did not trust the new transparent film enough to use it exclusively: they made at least one view using each type of film. To ensure that the film stayed dry, Stanton put the unexposed film into tin boxes sealed with adhesive plaster and packed the boxes into rubber bags. After the film was exposed, he put it into the tin boxes, soldered them shut, and stored duplicate rolls on different boats.[15]

Photography on the Stanton expeditions must have been tedious. Stanton would first choose a location with the longest view of the river corridor and cliffs and would order the boats to land. The photographer (either Nims or Stanton), with assistants, would carry the equipment to the camera station, which generally was some distance upslope from the boats. The photographer would aim and focus the Albion camera by viewing the image on a ground glass at the back of the camera; he would place a dark cloth over the camera and his head so he could see the image clearly. He would then remove the ground glass and install a Walker roll holder. Next he would judge the exposure, set the aperture, and remove the lens cap for the required time. After replacing the lens cap, he would have to remember to advance the film. When completely exposed, the rolls had to be changed in a dark tent.

The numerous steps required to capture an image provided many possibilities for poor-quality negatives. Some of the views are slightly out of focus. Moreover, Stanton occasionally aimed the camera into the sun, with predictable consequences. Nims's views, which generally have good exposures, reflect his expertise with photography; many of Stanton's views, especially those taken on cloudy days, were underexposed.[16] Stanton and Nims may have forgotten to advance the film only once, because only one of the negatives is a double exposure.[17] Although Stanton admits fumbling with loading the roll holders on occasion, he had no major disasters with unloading the exposed film.

After the negatives were developed, they were numbered in what Nims or Stanton thought was downstream order. Some negatives were numbered three times; the large and very conspicuous set of numbers is used to reference the images. Nims conscientiously labeled his negatives made in the summer of 1889 with the name of the railroad company, the date, and the location where he thought the exposure was made. Unfortunately, his memory of canyon geography was faulty; for example, photograph number 50, taken at mile 21.4 in Marble Canyon, has a number and caption that suggests it was taken in Cataract Canyon. Stanton made extensive notes about his views; as a result, few of his numbered views are out of order. Stanton was not completely successful in his attempt to collate Nims's views with his own, and he mislabeled some views of upper Marble Canyon made by Nims in July 1889.[18]

The Fate of the Prints and Negatives

Stanton attempted to use the images from the 1889 and 1890 expeditions to prove that a railroad could be built through the canyons.[19] He published some images of Cataract Canyon on September 21, 1889,[20] and loaned some to E. A. Reynolds for use in a popularized account of the first trip.[21] Eventually, Stanton made at least four albums of photographs from both expeditions. Stanton gave albums to the Engineering Societies Library in New York City and the Institution of Civil Engineers in London; both libraries still have the albums. One album was entered as evidence in a mineral-rights trial in 1932,[22] after which Stanton's wife regained possession of the album and the negatives. This album was donated with his papers to the New York Public Library in 1941.

Colonel Claude Birdseye led a U.S. Geological Survey expedition through Grand Canyon in 1923 with the intent of locating potential dam sites.[23] He wanted to obtain as much information as possible from other river trips to supplement the data he collected. Birdseye contacted Stanton's daughter, Anne Stanton Burchard, to obtain photographs and notes made by the Stanton expedition. Burchard complied, and Birdseye acknowledged receipt of the album, the remaining negatives, and numerous other items on July 10, 1924.[24]

However, Birdseye was very disappointed with the negatives he received. Expecting glass plates,[25] he was instead confronted with a mess. The transparent film had rolled up tightly and was brittle, and the paper on the unstripped paper negatives had turned brown, making the negatives nearly opaque. He wrote Burchard to say that transfer of the negatives to the more stable glass plates would cost about five hundred dollars. Given this large expenditure, Birdseye shelved the negatives. After Birdseye retired, the U.S. Geological Survey transferred the negatives and the remaining album of photographs to the Still Picture Branch of the National Archives, the repository for historic materials from federal agencies. After initial inquiries, the transfer—which consisted of the album containing 835 prints, 1,335 negatives, and some miscellaneous glass plates Stanton had used for illustrations of publications—was made June 6, 1949, and was accepted June 29 of that year.[26]

The Stanton Views and Repeat Photography

Stanton's photographs are invaluable for the interpretation of environmental change because of the systematic way in which they were made. The average distance between camera stations was 1.1 river miles, although the actual distance depended on the width and curvature of the river corridor. Because Stanton wanted to document a railroad route, he placed his camera where he could record the widest and longest view of canyon walls. He often made views at bends in the river where the line of sight upstream and downstream was greatest. Typically, he climbed above the high-water level of the Colorado River and thus produced downward-looking views that captured many details of the river and canyon. He needed to document bridge crossings, so many of the views depict tributary canyons. The large format (6½ by 8½ inches) produced remarkably clear images.

Many important riverine features can be easily interpreted from Stanton's views. Because canyon walls just above high-water level were frequent subjects, any change in riparian vegetation is readily apparent. Sand bars, which are now used for camping and serve as the soil in which riparian vegetation grows, are commonly depicted in the views. The rapids of the Colorado River and the debris fans at the mouths of tributary canyons were also typical subjects. When Stanton climbed above the high-water level, he often captured desert vegetation in the foreground of his views.

Some of Stanton's and Nims's sites have been covered by Lake Powell or Lake Mead, rendering them inaccessible for repeat photography. Of the 443 accessible views in the National Archives, 4 were unusable because they were out of focus, were too dark, or had deteriorated excessively. We used the remaining 439 views and 6 from the New York Public Library, referred to here as the Stanton photographs, for repeat photography.

Equipment and Methods

To replicate Stanton's views, we used cameras of 2¼ by 3¼–inch and 4 by 5–inch formats equipped with normal- and wide-angle lenses. These formats are preferable to 35-mm camera systems because of larger image size and improved ability to carefully compose the view. For the most part, we used panchromatic and extremely fine grained black-and-white film. Our procedure for replicating views began long before we reached the approximate site of a Stanton camera station. River trips are costly affairs involving many people; our primary objective in the fieldwork was to replicate as many views each day as possible. Long-term river guides who accompanied us determined (based on their memory of Grand Canyon) approximately where Stanton's views had been taken. Their efforts were in large part the reason we managed to replicate 445 Stanton views in a relatively short time.

Preservation of the Stanton Negatives

CONSTANCE McCABE

The Stanton expedition represents an important milestone in the history of photography. Nims was perhaps the first of his profession to choose not to carry a single glass dry plate to document a survey expedition. Rather, he took two flexible films in continuous rolls: Eastman's paper-based American Film and rollable transparent plastic film. These films had the distinct advantages over glass plates of convenience, light weight, less bulk, and freedom from breakage.

American Film was readily available commercially in 1886.[1] The film's soluble gelatin sublayer required that the gelatin emulsion be stripped from its paper support and be transferred to a flexible, transparent gelatin film support. At the time of Stanton's expedition, American Film was considered a dependable substitute for glass-plate negatives. However, the handling of exposed film was awkward and the stripping process cumbersome. Once a roll of paper negatives was exposed, exposures were cut into individual frames before development. This procedure was occasionally inaccurate; sometimes images were cut through the middle.[2]

After chemical processing, the paper negatives were squeegeed onto a collodion-coated glass plate, emulsion down.[3] Hot water was poured over the negative to dissolve the soluble gelatin subbing. This allowed the paper support to be peeled away, leaving the thin emulsion attached to the glass. Another thin sheet of gelatin was then soaked in a cool solution of water and glycerine before being squeegeed over the glass-supported emulsion.

A protective solution of dilute collodion was then applied to the gelatin pellicle and allowed to dry thoroughly. The gelatin-based film was stripped from the glass, and prints were made from the finished negative.

The rollable transparent film, which had a flexible plastic base rather than a paper support, was made available to the public in 1889.[4] The new film was processed like American Film, except that the troublesome steps involving stripping were eliminated.

At the time of the Stanton expedition, few practitioners of photography had experience with the new products. However, the promise of ease of use persuaded Nims to use both film types on the trip. Nearly all the exposures made during the Stanton expedition, on both paper- and plastic-based film, were successful. Many of these original negatives are in the holdings of the Still Pictures Branch of the National Archives in Washington, D.C. Most exist as single plastic or unstripped paper negatives, although some examples of the gelatin-based American Film are present as well.

To preserve the extant images and to make the views available for research, a preservation project was developed. The project was carried out by staff members and interns from the conservation and photographic laboratories of the National Archives. The primary goals of the preservation project were to create a high-quality duplicate negative of each of the Stanton views and to withdraw the original historically valuable negatives from use. The production of permanent duplicates from which prints are made not only protects the original negatives from the hazards of handling but also provides facsimiles that make the visual information accessible should the originals undergo natural deterioration. The original negatives can then be retired from darkroom use and reserved as artifacts.

The paper- and gelatin-based negatives, which were in reasonably good condition, posed no serious duplication problems. Flat and fairly flexible, they could be handled safely during the reproduction process. In contrast, the transparent plastic negatives, which were tightly curled and slightly brittle, could not be unrolled without risk of cracking or tearing. This inconvenience was described by photographers as early as 1890: "The emulsion that is placed on celluloid strips, on drying, naturally tends to curl up. The fact that they are rolled on the spool sensitive side inward increases this permanent set, so that if the washed films are simply suspended like paper from one corner, on drying they will curl up into thin spills like pencil cases. . . . [A]fter a short time, if not left under pressure, they will begin to curl again."[5]

The archive's negatives had to be flattened before being duplicated. Each negative first had to be relaxed by being gently humidified within small chambers, initially with warm water vapor and several hours later with cool water vapor and gentle restraint. Once it was relaxed and sufficiently flat, the film was removed from the chamber to dry. While the negative was still under restraint, two sheets of purest-quality archival paperboard with nonstick porous interleaving sheets were placed above and below the film; these were held in place as the restraints were carefully removed. This "negative sandwich" was placed under weight. After drying, the "negative sandwiches" were inserted into transparent polyester sleeves, and the paperboard and interleaving were carefully slipped out. Because the film still has a strong tendency to curl, the negatives were duplicated while in their sleeves.

From each original negative, an "interpositive," or print, was made on a permanent transparent film support. The interpositive, which reproduces the tonal range and detail of the original negative, is the archival preservation master from which new duplicate negatives can be made for routine printing. The last step in the preservation project was to rehouse all plastic negatives in high-quality paper enclosures to provide chemical and physical protection, thus maximizing the life of the negatives.

For the repeat photography project in Grand Canyon, high-quality prints were made from the duplicate negatives, resulting in much clearer views than those produced using copy negatives of century-old prints. The original negatives, which are unusual examples of early flexible film, are now protected in the National Archives from possible damage that might be incurred through use and handling. The Stanton negatives remain available for future scholarly research.

Figure 2.1. 164 Mile Rapid

A. Stanton was "almost frozen" by the time he stopped at the head of 164 Mile Rapid to make this downstream view (number 609). Stanton exposed the negative at 9:00 A.M. on February 26, 1890, the day after the expedition was forced to camp because of rising floodwaters. The camera station is on the left bank at mile 164.5, across from Tuckup Canyon.

We scheduled the river trips during the same months as Stanton's expedition to attempt to duplicate lighting, shadows, and condition of perennial vegetation. Despite attempts to follow Stanton's itinerary, we replicated fewer than ten views on the same date that Stanton made his original ones. Because Stanton noted the time at which he made his views, we also attempted to duplicate shadows as closely as possible. We managed to replicate many views successfully in this manner, although we had less cloud cover than Stanton had during the 1890 expedition. Also, the length of shadows changed considerably

with the number of days between the date Stanton made his view and the date we replicated it; therefore, we often found that despite being at a camera station at the same hour that Stanton was, we observed considerably different shadows.

Once our boats landed near a camera station, all three members of the photo crew helped locate the general camera position. While the photographer worked to place the camera in the exact position as Nims's or Stanton's camera, the interpreter and note taker compared the local geology and vegetation with that shown in the historic photograph. One

B. The repeat view was made by Ralph Hopkins on February 20, 1990, at 10:51 A.M. The two views illustrate the desired precision of repeat photography; the camera position for the repeat view is in exactly the same spot as the original camera. Inspection of the sides of either photograph shows the same rocks and projections at the same places. The lighting is different between the two views because Stanton had diffuse light when he made his view whereas Hopkins had bright sunlight and deep shadows. The foreground shows desert vegetation typical of the Muav Gorge, including catclaw, Mormon tea, and hedgehog cactus; some of the catclaw trees in the middle distance persist. The resolution of the original photograph is good enough to permit identification of mistletoe in the catclaw tree to the right of the figure standing at lower center. Despite the lower water level in 1990, the rapid does not appear to have changed significantly. A photo-to-photo comparison of boulders on the debris fan indicates that no significant aggradation or degradation has occurred. The sand bars downstream of the debris fan are now smaller.

or both of these members of the photo crew would take a print (measuring 8 by 10 inches) of the 1889 or 1890 view, punch a small hole in revealing features of the view, and identify or describe the features. The note taker would record the location and orientation of the camera and camera station and information on camera settings, such as exposure time and aper-

ture, as the photographer secured the images. The whole process typically required one to two hours for completion.

How close did the photographers get to the exact camera positions? Repeat photography is a game of getting as close as possible, with perfection being approached only rarely. We placed the cameras by

Figure 2.2. Hance Rapid

A. At Hance Rapid (mile 76.8), the Stanton expedition found "an immense and long rapid full of huge boulders both above and under water. . . . It is so broad there is no distinct channel." Stanton made this view (number 411) of the mouth of Red Canyon and across the top of Hance Rapid on January 27, 1890, at 11:30 A.M.

lining up foreground and background objects on either side of the view; this is an elementary use of a photogrammetric tool called parallax. Our photographers worked hard to replicate views exactly, but usually they were off by a few inches in one or more directions. We could get seriously distracted by lining up an object or objects that did not appear to have changed over the intervening century but which in fact had. In one case, I was about six feet too far into one view, but another photographer who later revisited the site corrected my error.

We learned many small details of Nims's and Stanton's techniques as we replicated their views. Nims tended to be artistic with his views; his composition involved unusual camera positions chosen, it seemed, to get large depth of field, much as Hillers of the Powell expedition had done in 1872. After Stanton replaced Nims as photographer, we noticed a change in selection of views and camera positions. At first, Stanton seemed uncertain about where to place his tripod; he would ignore obvious flat or prominent places, such as Nims used, and instead

B. Tom Brownold replicated Stanton's view on January 27, 1990, at 11:40 A.M. He waited patiently until the shadow exactly replicated the shadow in Stanton's view, 100 years later to the day. One Mormon tea (left center) and several mesquite trees are still alive.

would choose the side of a slope or cliff, which often left us cursing his poor judgment. However, Stanton gained experience as his expedition moved through the canyon, and we found that his camera stations became more predictable and easier to reoccupy as we followed him through the canyon.

Stanton's limited knowledge of photography made him cautious with lenses. He mostly used the wide-angle lens upstream of Phantom Ranch, with a very rare normal view included, usually as a duplicate of a wide-angle shot. Either something happened to that wide-angle lens between about miles 130 and 150 or Stanton was learning photographic composition, because he switched to using mostly his normal lens

with a rare wide-angle shot. We had to be on our toes between miles 90 and 130, where Stanton appeared to use the two types of lenses almost interchangeably.

Fortunately, we easily replicated most of the Stanton views. Complications occurred when the camera station was in a spot that was dangerous to reoccupy or where major changes had occurred. Only one camera station could not be reoccupied; it was buried beneath many tons of rock that had fallen from a cliff below House Rock Rapid (mile 17.0). Others were difficult because of changes in the intervening century. We typically had to approximate camera positions on eroded sand bars by placing our tripod on five-gallon buckets to raise the camera height. At one camera position on an island near Vaseys Paradise (mile 31.8), the photo crew had to abandon their work prematurely when water began to rise around their feet. At another site, the crew built a platform of oars and tables over the river to replicate a pair of views near mile 85.5. The people who worked on this project were unanimous in their admiration for the clarity and information content of Stanton's views, especially in comparison with photographs by other historic photographers of Grand Canyon.

Appropriate Technology:
The Rate of Change and Photographic Interval

Rate of environmental change is extremely pertinent to what one might expect to learn from repeat photography. Something that fluctuates considerably from year to year—for example, the number of annual wildflowers—may not be an appropriate subject of study in views made a century apart, whereas slow-growing trees and shrubs with long life spans make excellent subjects. In Grand Canyon, the rate of change of trees and shrubs is difficult to determine using standard techniques, such as permanent plots, because establishment of individuals occurs too infrequently. Repeat photography of century-old views rectifies the problem. Many shrubs (particularly Mormon tea) visible in Stanton's views were still alive a century later, which suggests that their rate of establishment and mortality is very slow. The interval between Stanton's photographs and our replicates is thus appropriate for examining the life spans of the longest-lived Grand Canyon plants.

Evaluation of change in riparian species was both difficult and easy. Riparian species typically grow in dense clusters, making the evaluation of change in individuals very difficult. For example, Apache plume, a common shrub in upper Marble Canyon, reproduces from root suckers in addition to seeds, making determination of individuals difficult. However, we were able to evaluate change in the riparian zone as a whole.

Documentation of debris flows is one of the most appropriate applications of repeat photography. Debris flows deposit large boulders and levees of coarse sediments that are easily identified and interpreted using repeat photography. These flash floods occur on average every twenty to fifty years in tributaries of the Colorado River in Grand Canyon, and the hundred-year interval between Stanton views and our replicates was generally ideal. Problems of interpretation were common at tributaries with a high frequency of debris flows, because successive debris flows cover evidence of previous ones. In the case of Lava Falls Rapid, we examined about 209 historic views other than the one made by Stanton to determine when debris flows had occurred in the past century and how the Colorado River had responded.

Change in sand bars was the most difficult interpretation made in the Stanton views. Sand bars change over minutes and hours, and certainly over weeks and months, yet we attempted to evaluate changes in sand bars over a century. As with riparian vegetation, flow releases from Glen Canyon Dam changed sand bars in a systematic fashion, which alleviated much of the difficulty in interpretation. We were unwilling to draw conclusions about specific sand bars, particularly important camping beaches; instead, we determined change in sand bars more generally, by lumping together large numbers of sand bars within long reaches of the canyon to determine if gross patterns of change were present.

What we did not interpret is equally important: for example, someone asked if we could determine whether air quality in Grand Canyon had deteriorated over the past century. Obviously views made a century apart, on days with different meteorological conditions, would preclude such a comparison. (As a point of interest the winter of 1890 was much stormier than the winters of 1990 to 1993. The amount of cloud cover revealed in the Stanton views suggests that the expedition had few sunny days.) Other attributes not evaluated include any features in the river that would be covered with water at a discharge of about 5,000 cubic feet per second, change in the distribution of insects or animals, and change in the distribution of rare or uncommon plants.

The varied and abundant interpretations of change made here reveal the value of repeat photography for assessing environmental change. Stanton's railroad would have caused considerable scarring of the natural landscape in Grand Canyon, but his careful photographic documentation of the proposed route provides invaluable data on environmental conditions in 1890 and changes in those conditions during the past century.

CHAPTER 3

The Century Club

Beyond the inviting green ribbon of riparian plants that lines the Colorado River is another important ecosystem in Grand Canyon—the desert. Drab, gnarled shrubs and cacti above the influence of the river cling unassumingly to the sun-baked rocky slopes away from the river and on the sheer cliffs that rise to the South and North Rims. The desert plants impart an enduring impression of extreme age, as if they had always been present and the canyon had never changed. This sense is more than an illusion, for in the absence of disturbances, desert plants may indeed change little over many human lifetimes.

Robert Brewster Stanton's systematic photography provided a means of evaluating longevity and change in desert plants at the bottom of Grand Canyon. Perhaps the most startling aspect revealed by repeat photography is the number of desert species that have survived for at least a hundred years—earning membership in what I call the Century Club.

Desert Plants in Grand Canyon:
The Product of 12,000 Years

For perspective on the longevity of desert plants, one must appreciate the rather brief period in which those plants have inhabited Grand Canyon. The best source of information on prehistoric vegetative change is the refuse piles left by one of the largest herbivores below the rims: the packrat. Also known as wood rats, these rodents are widespread in the southwestern United States.[1] Packrats construct middens of woody debris; in steep terrain, these houses are often built in crevices or caves that offer protection from the weather. Little nearby plant material or other lightweight debris escapes use by the packrats as building material. Untidy housekeepers, packrats drop pieces of their food and defecate and urinate in their houses. After the packrats die or leave, the mixture of debris and animal waste dries and solidifies.

Analysis of packrat middens has proved an ingenious tool for studying ancient plant distributions. In arid climates, the middens, solidified by urine, remain plastered to the sides or ceilings of crevices and dry caves for tens of thousands of years. By analyzing the stems, seeds, needles, and other plant parts in thousands of packrat middens, paleoecologists have obtained enough information to precisely determine the distribution of vegetation during the last 40,000 years in the southwestern United States. Much of the paleoecological research based on packrat middens has been conducted in Grand Canyon, thoroughly documenting changes in plant distributions from the end of the Pleistocene to the Holocene, or the last 11,000 years.[2]

Plant Distributions in the Pleistocene

On July 13, 1889, Stanton and his crew measured an oppressive 132°F in the sun in the upper part of the Roaring Twenties. When they reached 23½ Mile Rapid, they faced yet another portage. The men were desperate for shade until they spotted a solitary juniper tree on the downstream side of the debris fan. Underneath this large tree, they ate lunch and slept to avoid working in the heat. After a heavy thunder-storm arrested their sleep, they resumed their portage of the rapid, which Stanton called "Lone Cedar Rapid."

Juniper is now rare along the river corridor, but it was not scarce during the Pleistocene. In fact, the plant community that was adjacent to the Colorado River in the Pleistocene is termed "juniper-desertscrub."[3] Before about 11,000 years ago, the climate in the region undoubtedly was cooler, and possibly wetter, than that of today;[4] consequently, juniper grew at much lower elevations in Grand Canyon. In addition, most of the precipitation probably occurred in winter. The summer thunderstorm Stanton and his crew experienced under the lone juniper would probably have been unusual 13,000 years ago.

The cooler climate created significantly different plant distributions in the Pleistocene. The presence of woodlands where desert now occurs is typical of Pleistocene vegetation in most of the southwestern United States.[5] Like the zone dominated by juniper, other plant zones in the region were 2,000 to 3,300 feet lower in elevation, and the distribution of some species was considerably different.[6] For example, 13,000 years ago shadscale was the most common shrub among the juniper trees; Mormon tea also was common.[7] Blackbrush was relatively rare in eastern Grand Canyon but commonly occurred near the level of the river in western Grand Canyon. Prickly pear, particularly Mojave prickly pear, grew in eastern Grand Canyon, whereas barrel cactus was present in western Grand Canyon.[8] In some sections of Grand Canyon, desert plant communities may have looked much like those in upper Marble Canyon today.[9]

The Holocene Invasion

The climate of the southwestern United States warmed very quickly after about 12,000 years ago,[10] and desert plants responded slowly to the opening of more favorable habitats along the river corridor in Grand Canyon. For a variety of ecological reasons, the slowness, termed "vegetational inertia,"[11] is expected when plants respond to climatic change. One of the reasons for vegetational inertia in the canyon is the tenacity of junipers, which remained at low elevations until about 8,500 years ago.[12] Another is the distance the seeds of some species traveled to get to Grand Canyon, which delays the entrance of new species into the favorable habitat.

Creosote bush, perhaps more than most desert species, typifies the concept of vegetational inertia in Grand Canyon. Around 13,000 years ago, this shrub was confined to the lower Colorado River valley about three hundred miles south of its current northerly limit.[13] Shortly after 8,200 years ago, creosote bush was established at least in southern Nevada but probably was not present in western Grand Canyon.[14] Creosote bush arrived at its most northerly position in California about 4,000 years ago; likely, it is still adjusting its range there.[15]

Other species arrived in Grand Canyon at different times. White bursage, a common associate of creosote bush, was present 10,000 years ago in Death Valley, and its presence is well documented west of the mouth of Grand Canyon by 8,200 years ago.[16] Catclaw and mesquite probably arrived at different times; catclaw (closely related to mesquite) was present 9,000 years ago, whereas mesquite was first recorded only 1,300 years ago in eastern Grand Canyon.[17]

During the Holocene, plant species altered their distributions at different rates, responding as an assemblage of individuals, not collectively as a community.[18] Analysis of fossil packrat middens has dispelled the notion that plant communities merely moved upward in elevation or northward in response to the warmer temperatures of the Holocene. However, paleoecologists do not know when the modern plant distribution of Grand Canyon stabilized, or even if the current distribution is stable. I have surmised from regional studies that the desert in Grand

Canyon has existed in its present state for many thousands of years.

Modern Distribution of Desert Plants

The desert vegetation in Grand Canyon consists of vegetation with affinities to the four North American deserts: the Great Basin, Mojave, Sonoran, and Chihuahuan Deserts.[19] For example, in the first thirty miles of river corridor downstream of Glen Canyon Dam, plants are representative of lower-elevation assemblages of the Great Basin Desert: in what remains of Glen Canyon downstream of the dam, the assemblages most commonly found include Mormon tea and four-wing saltbush, whereas between Lees Ferry and mile 15, shadscale, Mormon tea, and beavertail cactus are the most conspicuous species. Between miles 14 and 94, a combination of Mormon tea, snakeweed, and wolfberry dominates; this type of assemblage is characteristic of upper-elevation sites in the Mojave Desert.

Beginning at mile 39, plant assemblages are more similar to those of the Sonoran and Chihuahuan Deserts than to the more northerly deserts. Mesquite and catclaw are common along the old high-water zone and are also established in the desert above. Brittlebush begins to appear at about mile 43 along south-facing slopes, typically in association with Mormon tea and catclaw.[20] Mormon tea and catclaw, together with perennial grasses and herbaceous perennials, are the most common desert species between miles 93.5 and 175.

Downstream of mile 175, the mixture of species is characteristic of lower-elevation parts of the Mojave and Sonoran Deserts. Creosote bush occurs between mile 167 and Lake Mead.[21] Between mile 183 and 193, a combination of creosote bush, white bursage, and Mormon tea dominates (the definitive vegetation type of the Mojave Desert); ocotillo also is common. Where ocotillo and barrel cactus are abundant, this mixture of species is more representative

Figure 3.1. Above Lees Ferry

A. The Stanton expedition reached Lees Ferry (mile 0.0) for the second time on December 23, 1889, after a hard row against an upstream wind. The following day, crew members rowed back into Glen Canyon to complete their instrumental survey of the railroad route. Nims did not take notes as thoroughly as Stanton; he probably made this downstream view (number 250) at mile +1.2 in Glen Canyon on the afternoon of December 24. Although Stanton states that the day was "clear and beautiful," the photograph shows partly cloudy skies.

of the northern Sonoran Desert than of the Mojave Desert.

The Longevity of Desert Plants in Grand Canyon

Several hundred plant species grow in the desert zone along the Colorado River. The few species of desert plants visible in the Stanton views are only a fraction of the total number of species in Grand Canyon. This minimal representation is not surprising, given the limited distribution of some species and the brief flowering season of others. Altogether, some 136 different trees, shrubs, perennial grasses, and cacti and other succulents might reasonably be visible at the sites where the old photographs were taken.[22] These plants include all cacti, succulents, and perennial grasses that are not obligate riparian

B. Tom Wise replicated Nims's view on a cloudy October 28, 1992, at 2:25 P.M. The most obvious changes in the view are the erosion of the sand bar at lower right and the invasion of tamarisk at left center. Few changes have occurred in the blackbrush-dominated vegetation in the foreground. All eight individuals of blackbrush survived the century despite livestock grazing; only one became established in the past century. Prickly pear has increased in density. The line at left center is Stanton's road, built in 1899 as assessment work to validate upstream mining claims; rocks displaced from the road appear at bottom left.

species (that is, confined to riparian areas). In the 259 Stanton views that showed desert vegetation, we were able to identify 59 species; in other words, the photographs yielded information on fewer than half of the perennial desert plants one could reasonably expect to see at the bottom of Grand Canyon.

By comparing our replicate photographs with the Stanton views, we observed individuals of 41 species that have survived for at least a century. Of these species (see table 1 in the appendix), 22 are shrubs, 5 are grasses, 7 are cacti, 1 is a different type of succulent, and 6 are trees. Moreover, 28 species had persistent individuals in more than one replicated view, and 31 had more than one individual that was still alive after a century. Two hybrid species of cactus also have survived for at least a century. We observed

Figure 3.2. Cardenas Hilltop Ruin

A. The Cardenas Hilltop Ruin at mile 72 was once called Stanton's Fort. Built and abandoned approximately eight hundred years ago by the Anasazi, the walls had mostly fallen by the time Stanton photographed it on January 23, 1890, at 4:15 P.M. (number 399). Despite Stanton's earlier criticism that Nims was photographing too much scenery and not enough railroad route, Stanton chose to photograph the scenery here even though his railroad was to be along the opposite side of the canyon. The day was cloudy, and the low snow line in the background depicts the severe winter that Stanton's crew experienced in Grand Canyon.

another 18 species whose individuals did not survive that long (see table 2 in the appendix).

We used several methods to decide whether a plant belonged in the Century Club. Did the plant in the photograph seem to be the same species as the plant on the ground? Careful examination of the photograph with a magnifier revealed subtle twig and leaf details that verified the identity of most species. Was the base of an individual in the same position as that shown in the Stanton view? Neighboring rocks (as long as they had not been dislodged) could help answer this question. Was the base thick enough or woody enough to belong to a hundred-year-old plant? We concluded that the individual had lasted a century only if all other possible explanations, such as replacement by a younger plant, could be rejected.

The life-history strategies of these plants also

B. The view was replicated in bright sunlight by Tom Brownold on January 25, 1990, at 12:00 P.M. Amazingly, the walls of the ruin have changed more than the desert plants that surround it. Only one plant has died in the past century: the wolfberry next to the ruin in the 1890 view. Otis "Dock" Marston took a similar photograph of Cardenas Hilltop Ruin in 1957, and the wolfberry was alive in Marston's view. Ten individuals of Mormon tea and two other individuals of wolfberry persist.

make interpretation of repeat photography a risky business. Is that plant we see today the same plant as in the Stanton view, a different plant in a preferred spot, or a clone of the original? Usually, the photo crew could answer this question at the camera station by examining the plant or by looking at the relation of the plant to immovable objects in the view. One enduring lesson of the replication of Stanton views is that of preferred sites. In many views, a new individual, or even a different species, became established in a place where a plant was present in 1890. Methodological problems aside, one implication of preferred sites is immediate: perennial plants can become established in only a limited number of places. Perhaps "preferred sites" are just that: other sites could be used, but certain sites are more favorable for plant establishment.

Some species that made the list may strain credulity. For example, big galleta grass has no woody parts, yet we found forty-three individuals that passed our test of persistence for a century. As another example, shrub live oak, of which we observed

Figure 3.3. Crystal Creek

A. As Harry McDonald made preparations to hike out Crystal Creek to the North Rim, Stanton continued his documentation of the proposed railroad. Crystal Creek (mile 98.3) would have required a trestle of "not less than 80 foot span." The upstream side of the bridge would have been in the immediate foreground of this view (number 479), which was made February 8, 1890, at about 3:00 P.M.

only one persistent individual in one view, is unquestionably long-lived. In general, species determined to have persistent individuals in only one view are questionable members of the Century Club.

Shrubs

Shrubs are the ecological backbone of the desert in Grand Canyon. Their importance—as a stabilizer of slopes; as cover for birds, reptiles, and small mammals; as a food source for vertebrates and invertebrates; and as nurse plants for seedlings—cannot be

overstated. Yet ecologists know little about the life span of most desert shrubs.[23] We found that individuals of twenty-two species of shrubs had survived the past century. Only two species of widespread shrubs—brittlebush and snakeweed—did not have individuals that could live that long.

Mormon tea is the most common shrub throughout the river corridor from Glen Canyon Dam to Lake Mead. So named because the settlers of Utah (the "Mormons") made a medicinal drink from its stems, Mormon tea is found throughout the south-

B. Eleven individuals of three species are still alive in the foreground of this view. Nine individuals of Mormon tea, including one at lower center, remain, as do one catclaw tree near the creek bottom and one beavertail cactus in the outcrop at right center. Five new individuals of hedgehog cactus are present; none is apparent in the 1890 view. The riparian vegetation in Crystal Creek has been completely altered by the debris flow of 1966 and the subsequent establishment of non-native tamarisk. Robert Webb replicated Stanton's view on February 27, 1993, at 3:34 P.M.

western United States as several species.[24] Mormon tea is unusual because it produces cones instead of flowers. Individuals bear either male or female cones. The plants are leafless and use their green stems for photosynthesis. The family that includes Mormon tea is a relict of millions of years ago; in many ways, Mormon tea appears to be caught in an eddy on the river of plant evolution.

Four species of Mormon tea occur along the river corridor: *Ephedra nevadensis* and *E. torreyana* are common, and *Ephedra viridis*[25] and *E. fasciculata*

are rare. The four species are separated using the morphology of seeds and cones; they are difficult to distinguish in winter dormancy, which is how we viewed them. Where we could distinguish species, we concluded that several individuals of *Ephedra nevadensis* and *E. torreyana* and one individual of *E. fasciculata* had survived the century. Given the similarity of the four species, *E. viridis* probably could also persist for a century, but we could not confirm this premise with the Stanton views.[26]

Especially in sandy soils, Mormon tea propagates

by offshoots or the rooting of stems. This vegetative propagation does not seem to occur in Grand Canyon, probably because plants grow on rocky slopes. The single, aboveground stem makes individuals easy to count in photographs of Grand Canyon, whereas such a determination is difficult in other areas.[27] We identified 685 individuals of Mormon tea in 173 views that are at least a century old, by far the largest number for any species. Moreover, the mortality rate[28] is quite low—only 17 percent of the observed individuals per century.

Two common associates of Mormon tea—blackbrush and wolfberry—also are members of the Century Club. Blackbrush, which dominates many plant assemblages in northern Arizona and southern Nevada and Utah,[29] was observed in only three views, and those were in Glen Canyon. In those views, eighteen individuals had survived the century; none had died. Blackbrush lives considerably longer than a century; one shrub in Utah was estimated to be four hundred years old.[30] By contrast, biologists know little about the life span of wolfberry.[31] It is leafless in winter, exposing the divaricate, white stems that allow positive identification in photographs. In thirty-one views, seventy-seven wolfberry individuals had survived the century; the mortality rate for this species was only 13 percent per century.

Creosote bush is the archetypal shrub of the hot deserts of North America. Rainfall brings out the best in its pungent leaves as the aroma of its resins fills the air after a summer thunderstorm. Brief rain showers are all the encouragement creosote bush needs to produce a show of yellow flowers in winter, spring, summer, or fall. With its twin, waxy leaves that minimize water loss and its wandlike branches that emanate from a subterranean root crown, creosote bush is the epitome of a long-lived species.

To no ecologist's surprise, creosote bush can live for at least a century in Grand Canyon. That interval is a gross understatement; one ecologist has claimed that a creosote bush in the western Mojave Desert is nearly 12,000 years old.[32] This "individual" actually resulted when the center of the original plant died and clones, genetically identical to the original plant, remained alive. Whether creosote bushes in Grand Canyon have survived that long is uncertain,[33] but they can certainly live far longer than a century. In areas not subjected to grazing, of eighty-five individuals visible in seventeen Stanton views, only one creosote bush had died, a mortality rate of only 1 percent per century.

Two common associates of creosote bush also are long-lived. White bursage, with a previously reported life span of a third of a century,[34] is also a member of the Century Club; thirteen individuals appeared in the same positions in five photographs. Ocotillo, a semisucculent shrub that attains treelike dimensions in Grand Canyon, reportedly can live for several centuries.[35] In Grand Canyon, we found eight ocotillos in four views still alive after a century.

Several other species are surprising members of the Century Club. One is four-wing saltbush, a fast-growing shrub used to stabilize disturbed surfaces.[36] Fast-growing shrubs typically are short-lived, yet we found nine persistent individuals of four-wing saltbush in seven views, all of which were at or upstream of Nankoweap Creek. Shadscale, very common in the low-elevation deserts of the Great Basin, is a scrawny, thorny shrub that occurs in the first fourteen miles of Marble Canyon. In five views, we found thirteen individuals of shadscale that had survived the century.

Grasses

Until recently, perennial grasses generally were considered of value only as food for wildlife and livestock.[37] Biologists know little about the life expectancy of grasses, but conventional wisdom holds that perennial grasses should live only twenty years or less.[38] Analyses of the Stanton views suggest otherwise, because five perennial grasses are members of the Century Club.

Grasses inherently are difficult to define as individuals. Many grasses can reproduce by seeds or via underground stems called rhizomes. Rhizomatous cloning produces clusters of plants in which individuals cannot be differentiated with surety. Fortunately, few grasses reproduce vegetatively in Grand Canyon. Those that do elsewhere possibly are hindered from doing so here because the rocky substrate limits the propagation of underground rhizomes. All the grasses we observed in the Stanton views produced definite, solitary clumps, except bush muhly.

Big galleta grass is the most important of the long-lived grasses of the river corridor. This grass is the most common nurse plant for barrel cactus, agaves, and possibly other desert plants.[39] Forty-three individuals of big galleta grass in fifteen views appeared to be in the same spot after a century; I interpreted this to indicate that this species of grass can live at least a century. The mortality rate was 32 percent per century. We found only a few persistent individuals of four other grass species, largely because, except for big galleta grass, we tallied only those plants clearly visible in the foregrounds of Stanton views.

We cannot with certainty verify the longevity of perennial grasses. Unlike trees and shrubs, grasses do not have a central stem that expands laterally with growth rings; instead, they grow in clumps that enlarge or change shape with age. One is tempted to verify the age of a grass by the size of its basal clump, but clumps form quickly and are limited in size by rocks in soils. Although some perennial grasses of the river corridor seem long-lived, we have little evidence other than repeat photography to support these conclusions.

Cacti

More than shrubs or grasses, cacti epitomize the deserts of the Western Hemisphere. Along with other succulent species, cacti symbolize aridity because they have the ability to store water in their tissues, forestalling drought. They are not generally thought of as having long life spans, although the giant columnar cactus of the Sonoran Desert can live perhaps two centuries. But what of the ground-hugging cacti, like the ones along a Grand Canyon trail that leave a welter of spines in your leg if you brush up against them? In Grand Canyon, eight species (and two hybrids) of these cacti might live longer than you will.

Beavertail cactus is a prostrate, gray-green prickly pear, nondescript most of the year except in springtime, when its large, magenta flowers light up the talus slopes. Although beavertail has no large spines on its pads, beware its glochids. These tiny, needle-like spines are hard to see but easy to feel when hundreds of them become lodged in skin. Beavertail has no apparent defense other than these glochids; other prickly pears are grazed by livestock and wildlife despite their large spines.

In sixteen views, we found twenty-nine individuals of beavertail that had lived through the past century.[40] A close relative, Mojave prickly pear, also lives at least a century; we noted twenty-three persisting individuals in thirteen views. Unlike beavertail, Mojave prickly pear is covered with long, flexible spines that earn it a descriptive epithet: grizzly prickly pear. Both species have a white and gnarled root crown, massive compared to the size of the aboveground parts. Prickly pears may owe their longevity to these root crowns. Individual stem pads, definitive of prickly pears, probably remain on a plant for ten years or less. New pads are put on in good years, sometimes profusely, but old pads are shed during drought. Through it all, the root crown is the control center of the prickly pear's aboveground biomass.

Fine-leaf yucca, another succulent, lives longer than a century as well. We observed sixteen individuals of this species in the same position as the originals in four views. This yucca, common in sandy soils along the river corridor and throughout northeastern Arizona, produces stems from a root crown.

Figure 3.4. 128 Mile Canyon

A. The Stanton expedition had one of its hardest yet most successful days on February 22, 1890. At 128 Mile Rapid, while the boats were being lined to avoid "a very, very rocky" fall of eight to ten feet, Stanton climbed up to the top of the Tapeats Sandstone to make this upstream view (number 570) at about 9:30 A.M.

Although the stems may live a half-century or more, the root crown apparently persists for more than a hundred years in Grand Canyon.

Therein lies the crux of determining longevity in repeat photography. Fine-leaf yucca and the various long-lived cacti reproduce vegetatively. The offset clones they produce are genetic facsimiles of the parent; therefore, they can reasonably be considered persistent. Engelmann prickly pear literally creeps along the ground, forming roots where the pads touch the soil. The original root crown is left behind as chains of pads break away. The pads on the oldest end die, while new ones form on the other end or in the middle of the chain. Is this the persistence of an individual or the creation of a series of short-lived individuals? And when does one individual "die" and another "become established"? In wrestling with this issue on Engelmann prickly pear, I concluded that those creeping pads were indeed the same individual. The issue of definition of an individual plant remains, and the answer may be more difficult to attain than the design of Stanton's railroad.

B. This striking view was replicated by Robert Webb on February 23, 1992, at 10:30 A.M. Most of the plants in the foreground are either big galleta grass or Mormon tea. Of eleven clumps of big galleta grass that could be distinguished in the 1890 view, eight have survived. All eight individuals of Mormon tea that could be distinguished in the foreground also persist. Six barrel cactus are visible in the 1890 view; in the same area of the 1992 view, twenty barrel cactus are visible. The increase probably is the result of a decrease in the severity of frost in the past century.

Trees

From sturdy oaks to the ancient bristlecone pines, many species of trees are known to live for hundreds to thousands of years. Six species of trees in Grand Canyon belong to the Century Club—one is shrub live oak. Juniper would also have made the list, but neither Stanton nor Nims photographed the lone juniper under which they slept at 23½ Mile Rapid. The most common, persistent trees, however, are

neither oaks nor evergreens but legumes—mesquite and catclaw. These two are also the most common native trees along the river corridor.

Catclaw, a spreading shrub of the Sonoran and Chihuahuan Deserts reviled by hikers for its namesake thorns, has a kinder personality in Grand Canyon. Here, it is a small, spindly tree with few thorns. Catclaw is a facultative riparian species (that is, although it is most numerous along the old high-water line or along the bottoms of side canyons, it

Figure 3.5. Forster Canyon

A. The weather was rainy but warm on February 20, 1890. The expedition spent a rare day of running rapids instead of lining and portaging them. Stanton summed up the pleasures of river running with his description of 122 Mile Rapid: "We run [122 Mile Rapid] in fine style. High waves but we cut through on the left and miss them all. What beautiful rapids all day today." After running Forster Rapid (mile 122.6), he captured this downstream view (number 555) at about 3:45 P.M.

can and does survive in the desert). To say that it survives is an understatement: in parts of Grand Canyon, catclaw, along with Mormon tea, is one of the few woody perennials present.

Catclaw occurs throughout the river corridor from about mile 39 to Lake Mead. In the Inner Gorge, it grows in the old high-water zone and also on the slopes above. In ninety-eight views, we identified 240 catclaw trees that were more than a hundred years old. Of these trees, perhaps half had no obvious source of extra water. One may remove any doubt as to the longevity of catclaw by inspecting

the diameter of the trunk, which is typically four to six inches and increases with age. Moreover, recent work on annual rings in catclaw indicates the species may have a life span of one to two hundred years.[41]

Mesquite is less surprisingly a member of the Century Club.[42] This tree, long valued for its wood, is most common in the old high-water zone and is uncommon in narrow parts of the river corridor. Throughout the southwestern United States, mesquite is considered an invasive species that has benefited from the overgrazing of grasslands.[43] In Grand Canyon, it typically grows in dense stands, which

B. The fine-leaf yucca in the foreground (or rather its stems that arise from the persistent root crown) remains in the same place as the original plant stood a century before. This species reproduces vegetatively as well as through seeds. Dave Edwards replicated Stanton's view on February 16, 1991, at 10:41 A.M.

makes individual mesquites difficult to distinguish in most of the Stanton views. In fifty-eight views, however, we observed solitary mesquite trees that had survived the century.

Nonpersistent Species

Eighteen other desert plants were identified in the Stanton or replicate views. Several of these may be able to persist as individuals for more than a century, but we could not verify that persistence with the Stanton photography. One such species is the shrub Wright lippia, known to be long-lived in southern Arizona.[44]

Of the shorter-lived shrubs, the most widespread is brittlebush.[45] Although it had limited distribution in 1890, it now dominates much of the desert vegetation along the river corridor. It has increased sufficiently in the last century to become a diagnostic plant of several desert assemblages along the river corridor.[46] About twenty-five individuals of brittlebush could be identified in Stanton views, but none survived the century. Snakeweed, an indicator of overgrazed lands, also is relatively short-lived.

Perhaps the most notable species that cannot live a hundred years is Utah agave.[47] Although agaves generally are called "century plants," no agaves actu-

Figure 3.6. Doris Rapid

A. The Colorado River rose three feet during the night of February 23, 1890, although the heavy rains had ended several days before. The next day, Stanton and his crew reaped the benefits of higher water, which covered rocks and allowed rapids like 134 Mile and 135 Mile to be run in relative safety. After lunch, they arrived at Doris Rapid (mile 137.5), named for Doris Nevills, who inadvertently swam it in 1940. To Stanton, the rapid offered "high waves, a drop of 8 to 10 feet. Exciting river. Run it." Stanton exposed this downstream view (number 592) from the right side at about 1:00 P.M.

ally live this long. Instead, the typical life span is ten to twenty years.[48] In part, nonpersistence is built into their life-history strategy. Agaves reproduce either by offshoots from the parent plant or by germination of seeds. We observed what appeared to be offshoots in approximately the same position as the original plant in one Stanton view, but the parent had died and its remains had disintegrated. Because individu-

als die after they flower, agaves can ill afford a long life span; if flowering occurred at intervals of greater than a century, sexual reproduction of agaves would be ineffective and genetic diversity in the species would be limited.

Several species of cactus in Grand Canyon have life spans of much less than a century. Hedgehog cactus may live less than ten years.[49] One species of

B. Jane Bernard replicated this view on February 18, 1991, at 12:28 P.M. The rapid appears unchanged over the past century. Prominent catclaw trees at center and right center are more than a century old. Four other catclaws, three clumps of big galleta grass, and two individuals of Mormon tea also survived the century.

prickly pear (*Opuntia chlorotica*) also did not persist. Similarly, barrel cactus, the largest species of cactus in Grand Canyon, has a life span of less than a century.[50] In general, the cacti that survived the century were prostrate, closely hugging the ground or wrapped between rocks, whereas those species that did not persist were upright.[51]

Three species in particular illustrate different mechanisms contributing to the repopulation of preferred sites, wherein new plants become established where other plants have died. None of the 277 barrel cactus visible in Stanton photographs survived, although in several views, barrel cactus occupied approximately the same positions in the original and replicate views. In this case of preferred sites, a parent plant may have dropped its heavy seeds directly downward, producing a new barrel cactus in the same position. Spiny aster, by contrast, is abundant wherever it is present. This prolific woody-based perennial probably lives less than ten years; in the

Figure 3.7. Cryptobiotic crusts

A. February 19, 1890, began hard and ended easily. To start, Stanton's crew portaged their belongings around Waltenberg Rapid (mile 112.2); then they lined and portaged their boats. They lined 112½ Mile Rapid before lunch. In the afternoon, the cloudy sky of morning turned to sunshine, and the rough whitewater turned into a mostly quiet reach between cliffs of schist and granite. At mile 114.2, the expedition stopped, and Stanton climbed up the right bank to capture this upstream view (number 539) at 3:08 P.M.

span of a century, the probability of this type of a plant becoming reestablished where another one had previously lived and died is quite high. Similarly, fluff grass is a common, short-lived grass in Grand Canyon. Although it appeared in the foreground of at least one replicate view, its apparent "persistence" probably owes more to the fecundity of the species than to long life span.

Soils and Decomposition

Cryptobiotic Crusts

In less-visited parts of Grand Canyon, desert soils appear to be covered with a mat of black soot. But instead of being an inorganic mat of carbon, the black mat consists of living organisms in an assemblage

B. Stanton's view is not totally clear in the center foreground; few desert plants can be interpreted. But at the lower left, the dark black soil surface is a cryptobiotic crust, still in the same position and approximately the same size a century later. Careful examination of the edge nearest the camera indicates that the crust has retreated a maximum of about six inches; the edge farthest from the camera is nearly unchanged. Cursory examination of its surface indicated the crust contains mosses and lichens, suggesting an old, complex assemblage of organisms. Steve Tharnstrom replicated this view on March 1, 1993, at 12:21 P.M.

called a cryptobiotic crust.[52] Less conspicuous than shrubs, but equally important to the ecosystem, soil crusts along the river corridor are rarely appreciated for their beauty and function.

Cryptobiotic crusts are complex assemblages of cyanobacteria, fungi, lichens, and mosses. When one views the mixture of yellow, red, green, gray, and black life forms that combine to cover the soil,

one can easily imagine their diversity. Most crusts contain microscopic cyanobacteria, most notably the species *Microcoleus vaginatus*.[53] This cyanobacterium, the typical colonizer of new crusts, forms living sheaths that intertwine through soil, binding the surface of the soil.[54] As crusts age, they become more biologically complex. Macroscopic lichens and mosses become established and compete with the

Figure 3.8. Crystal Rapid

A. Before 1966, Crystal Rapid (mile 98.3) was a benign reach of whitewater, especially in comparison with the rapids a short distance upstream. Had the Stanton expedition not lost a boat upstream in Horn Creek Rapid, Stanton likely would have decided to run this rapid. Instead, the crew portaged their belongings and lined their boats on the right side. Immediately upon arriving at Crystal Creek on February 8, 1890, Stanton did what most modern river runners do: he walked up to the scout point on the debris-flow terrace overlooking the rapid. Instead of scouting the whitewater, Stanton documented his railroad route (across the right side) with this downstream view (number 478) at about 3:00 P.M.

cyanobacteria (formerly called blue-green algae). The presence of lichens and mosses in a cryptobiotic crust indicates its antiquity.

Biologists have only recently begun to define the functioning of cryptobiotic crusts in the deserts of the southwestern United States. Crusts increase infiltration and decrease water erosion and evaporation, and because crusts also increase roughness and strength, the soils bound by crusts are more resistant

to wind erosion. Crusts are well known for nitrogen fixation in desert ecosystems; in some deserts, they may be the principal nitrogen fixers in soils. Studies have not conclusively shown whether crusts promote or inhibit plant establishment, but crusts likely interact positively with many perennial plants.

Cryptobiotic crusts are very sensitive to disturbance. Although they mechanically bind soil surfaces, they are too brittle to resist trampling by

B. Stanton's view and its replicate illustrate a number of aspects of environmental change in the past century of Grand Canyon history. The change in the rapid, now one of the biggest in Grand Canyon, was caused by a debris flow on December 6, 1966. Tamarisk, a non-native tree, chokes the once-barren mouth and debris fan of Crystal Creek, a perennial stream. Five individuals of Mormon tea persist on the edge of the debris-flow deposit. More subtle is the change in the soil surface in the foreground. Stanton's view shows a rough, blackened surface characteristic of old cryptobiotic crust, which would have been very stable on this ancient debris-flow terrace. Now, trampling by river runners intent on scouting Crystal Rapid has destroyed the crust and removed about three inches of soil. Ralph Hopkins replicated Stanton's view on a rainy February 1, 1990, at 1:57 P.M.

wildlife, livestock, or people. Not surprisingly, the recovery of disturbed crusts begins with the reestablishment of cyanobacteria.[55] Crusts dominated by cyanobacteria return relatively quickly, but the restoration of their productivity lags. With the passage of time, usually decades, lichens and mosses also recover.[56] Once an old crust has been disturbed, it probably requires decades (if not centuries) to recover fully.[57]

Cryptobiotic crusts are so complex (and unphotogenic) that we could interpret aspects of this complex and important soil ecosystem in only eleven views. In general, we found that undisturbed crusts had changed only inches in diameter during the past century. In places, the impact of human footprints had reduced or destroyed the coverage of cryptobiotic crusts. Relatively thick crusts have become established in the new high-water zone, but these may

Figure 3.9. Tiger Wash Rapid

A. On their first clear day in a week, Stanton and his crew struggled through the last of the Roaring Twenties, a series of closely spaced rapids in Marble Canyon. The portaging and lining required every half-mile took its toll on boats and humans. Tiger Wash Rapid (mile 26.6) required yet another portage of goods and lining of boats. At noon, when most of the crew was resting in the sunshine, Stanton climbed onto a shady terrace on river left and made this downstream view (number 317). Dominating the center of his view is a juniper tree that appears to have died a long time before Stanton arrived.

consist only of cyanobacteria. More complex crusts may require many more decades to develop fully.

Decomposition

Even dead things last a long time in Grand Canyon. At Tiger Wash Rapid (mile 26.6), we climbed up a terrace on the left side of the rapid. The Stanton views we were to replicate appeared prosaic; the downstream view showed the trunk of a dead juniper in the center of the view. Unbelievably, the dead juniper was still present in 1991, albeit missing a few small branches and some bark. I cannot remember which one of us first said, "It's still dead!"

The following year, at Boulder Creek (mile 82.2), we climbed up a debris fan to replicate three views. What we saw in the downstream view was amazing: not only was a dead tree still present, but a piece of driftwood remained wedged between two boulders. Wondering how long the tree—a catclaw—had been dead, I collected the smallest twigs for radiocarbon dating. These twigs, about a quarter-inch in diameter, would yield a date of when the tree had last grown and therefore would approximate the age of death. To my surprise, the radiocarbon date was 370±60 years B.P.;[58] in other words, the tree had died about A.D. 1550. Encouraged by this finding, I re-

B. The dead juniper still dominates the downstream view at Tiger Wash Rapid. Small twigs collected from the tree and radiocarbon dated indicate that the tree died about 550 years ago. The new juniper on the terrace is one of the few present along the river corridor. None of the Utah agaves was still alive after a century, but many new ones occur throughout the foreground. Five individuals of Mormon tea and one of wolfberry survived the century; Apache plume has decreased on the left and increased on the right sides of the view. Liz Hymans replicated this view on February 2, 1991, at 4:42 P.M.

turned to the dead juniper at Tiger Wash and pulled the smallest branch from the snag. The date of last growth was 550±75 years B.P.,[59] which indicated that the juniper had died about A.D. 1400.

Dead trees still standing after hundreds of years; driftwood still wedged between rocks after at least a century: these seemed anomalies worthy of explanation. The persistence of driftwood is somewhat plausible, because driftwood on the Colorado River has been dated to 950 years old.[60] Certainly wood that old could persist for a century, wedged as it was above the soil between two rocks and generally free from moisture that would have contributed to its de-

composition. But the standing trees were puzzling: the roots had not rotted out or been eaten away by insects.

In Grand Canyon, decomposers such as termites preferentially attack dead wood depending on its hardness, density, and proximity to water and soil. Two species of termites live in the canyon, but they may prefer less dense woods than catclaw or juniper.[61] Termites require moisture to survive, and they build their nests in soil, which retains moisture; they attack wood that touches the ground, or they build tunnels through cracks in rocks to reach their food supplies.[62] The juniper and catclaw trees I observed were on rocky slopes where termites may be unable to build nests. Fungi also decompose wood, but in a dry climate like Grand Canyon, their efficiency is low.

Repeat photography has shown that the longevity of a species is related to the persistence of its dead wood. Short-lived species such as brittlebush decompose readily, whereas long-lived trees such as juniper and catclaw can persist for centuries as snags. Whereas the nutrients bound in the wood of short-lived species are cycled relatively quickly through the ecosystem, the nutrients bound in the wood of long-lived species may be tied up indefinitely, long after the individual has died. In Grand Canyon, where plant growth appears to be somewhat limited to preferred sites, the persistence of a dead snag not only ties up nutrients but also ties up a site where another plant could become established.

Stability in Isolation

Think of desert plants as individuals instead of as a group. They moved into Grand Canyon at different times thousands of years ago, and all are now well adapted to the arid climate. Using different life-history strategies, they compete with one another for limited resources. They also compete to get by in times of drought, to prosper in times of excess moisture, and to ensure reproduction of their species. In the sanctuary of the river corridor, many of them were alive when Stanton ran the Colorado River a century ago. Members of the Century Club form the stable backbone of the desert ecosystems in Grand Canyon.

These well-adapted plants can live for at least a century, but how long beyond that? The enduring image of Mormon tea in the Stanton views is a plant that has changed little in size over a century. Does that mean it can live for two centuries or even longer? The desert of Grand Canyon began to coalesce about 12,000 years ago; the current distribution of plants has been stable for perhaps 4,000 years. Could some of those plants in the Stanton views, perhaps the creosote bushes, be the pioneering individuals of their species in Grand Canyon, still alive after several millennia? The answer would be pure speculation, but the idea arises from an overwhelming sense that these plants are able to withstand whatever the climate of Grand Canyon can produce. Little wonder that "vegetational inertia" exists where these plants are the players.

Members of the Century Club have survived in different ways. During drought, shrubs drop their leaves, if they have any to start with. When drought is excessive, shrubs and trees may drop whole branches, and prickly pears may shed their pads. The essence of these desert plants lies underground in their roots. Several species appear capable of losing their aboveground growth only to return as separate, but genetically equal, clones.

With their tremendous ability to survive, the desert plants of Grand Canyon might seem unchanging, much like the cliffs. Many of the plant assemblages consist of individual shrubs that appear unbelievably stable. Isolated though the plant communities may be, Grand Canyon nevertheless is affected by the whims of the atmosphere overhead. Although most of the populations of dominant perennials have been stable over the past century, climate has varied. Some species were affected by climatic change, and the effects were captured on photographic emulsion, allowing further insights into the desert plants in Grand Canyon. One quickly learns that these plants are indeed individuals exhibiting different environmental tolerances.

Despite Stanton's belief (which was then commonly held and still lingers among some stock raisers) that desert vegetation serves a purpose only if consumed by livestock, most of Grand Canyon has been untouched by livestock grazing. Few wild grazers live in the canyon either. Bighorn sheep are few, and rabbits are absent in the bottom of Grand Canyon.[63] The largest herbivore in much of the river corridor is the packrat. This low level of herbivory may have contributed to the surprising longevity of individual shrubs, grasses, and cacti that populate the slopes next to the river.

Widely viewed as the product of extreme climatic conditions, North American deserts are also perceived to be unchanging vegetation communities.[64] Yet desert plants respond to many stresses, particularly those induced by climate and herbivory.[65] Large tracts of ungrazed desert are rare. Thanks to Robert Brewster Stanton, repeat photography provided an unprecedented way to evaluate many aspects of longevity and change in desert plant communities at the bottom of Grand Canyon.

CHAPTER 4

Herbivory

These days, passengers on river trips through Grand Canyon seldom fail to encounter wildlife. The river corridor teems with animals, whether flocks of migrating birds or an occasional beaver. It is difficult to pass through certain reaches without seeing bighorn sheep gazing back from the safety of some precarious perch in the rocks. Because of the dwindling amount of untamed land in the West, Grand Canyon is a wildlife refuge.

The canyon did not have a reputation for abundant wildlife a century ago. Early explorers painted a desolate portrait of wildlife along the river, particularly the dearth of large grazing animals, which they sought for food. By the middle of the twentieth century, such animals were common—in the case of burros, too common—along the river. Twenty of Stanton's photographs and our replicates show the effects of heavy grazing in areas of Grand Canyon. These heavily grazed areas contrast starkly with the rest of the canyon, where large grazing animals have been uncommon for millennia.

The Increase in Populations of Large Grazing Animals

During John Wesley Powell's first expedition in the summer of 1869, the men subsisted on meager rations. They keenly scanned the canyon walls for game, particularly bighorn sheep. They did not covet bighorn sheep as a treasured wildlife sighting; they wanted to kill large animals to supplement their rancid bacon and spoiled flour. On their second expedition, which enjoyed better provisions, Powell's men saw but could not kill two bighorn sheep in the vicinity of Tanner Rapid (mile 67).[1]

Stanton's crew saw more bighorn sheep than did Powell's men. During the three-month trip in the winter of 1890, they saw fifteen bighorn sheep on the left shore in the vicinity of Whitmore Wash (mile 185).[2] At Bright Angel Creek, they saw many tracks of bighorn sheep and coyotes.[3] Together the Powell and Stanton trips spanned 125 days, in winter and summer, but the explorers reported seeing only seventeen bighorn sheep and no other large animals.

Later river runners sought game for profit as well as for food. In 1896, for example, George Flavell wanted to trap beaver in Grand Canyon; he hunted large game to augment his food supply. He shot a bighorn sheep, which he called an ibex, near Fossil Canyon (mile 125) and saw others near Kanab Creek (mile 143.5).[4] In 1909, Julius Stone hired Nathaniel Galloway, a noted outdoorsman who wanted to assess the potential for hunting in Grand Canyon, as his head boatman. Stone and Galloway saw at least three bands of bighorn sheep in the vicinity of Matkatamiba Canyon (mile 148) and a solitary ram in the vicinity of National Canyon (mile 166.6).[5]

The experience of Charles Sheldon, a famed outdoorsman and big-game hunter, was different. Sheldon went to Havasu Canyon in 1912 to hunt bighorn sheep for museum specimens.[6] He quickly learned that whereas deer were found only above the rims, "most of the sheep . . . [were] along the Colorado River and the slopes of the big tributaries." In five days, Sheldon saw at least thirty-two bighorn sheep on both the left and right sides of the river; he shot and skinned several rams and packed them out of the canyon. Bighorn sheep may have kept a low profile in most of Grand Canyon, but at least one outdoorsman who looked carefully found them in abundance near Havasu.

Despite Sheldon's success, sightings of bighorn sheep along the river corridor remained uncommon in the first half of the twentieth century.[7] Other large herbivores, however, were seen more frequently along the river. Feral burros appeared in large numbers, particularly in western Grand Canyon. Mule deer occasionally drifted down to the mouths of major tributaries draining the North Rim but apparently did not permanently inhabit the river corridor. By the middle of the twentieth century, river runners consistently saw deer and burros along the river. Human intervention, through accidental and purposeful release of livestock and through wildlife management in the Grand Canyon Game Reserve, had changed the ecological balance of the canyon.

Populations of herbivores may increase rapidly, only to decrease just as precipitously later. These extreme population fluctuations are called irruptions.[8] In theory, irruptions result from some sort of release, such as the introduction of non-native animals into an unoccupied niche or the sudden removal of predators or diseases that controlled the population. During the rapid increase, forage is depleted; when the food supply is exhausted, the population crashes. The population after the crash may eventually stabilize (generally with fewer animals than before the irruption) as the seriously overgrazed range begins to recover. The archetypal irruption is the case of the mule deer herd on the Kaibab Plateau in the 1920s, which at one time graced ecological texts with its elegant simplicity.[9]

Another, less-recognized population irruption occurred in Grand Canyon at the same time: burros released in the late nineteenth century reproduced rapidly in isolated parts of Grand Canyon. Grazing by feral burros and to a lesser extent by domestic livestock has affected the desert plant assemblages shown in some of the Stanton views. Instead of light usage, like the browsing of bighorn sheep, heavy grazing by burros occurred for extended periods in parts of the river corridor. We captured the results of grazing on film as we replicated the views from the Stanton expedition.

The Herbivores

Burros

Early prospectors seeking gold and silver in northern Arizona were attracted by the spectacular geology of Grand Canyon.[10] The first documented prospecting occurred near areas of known geography and easy access. In 1776, a Spanish missionary priest, Francisco Tomás Garcés, was the first person of European descent to visit Havasu Canyon. His report, and those of subsequent visitors, made its location relatively well known. Prospectors discovered silver in Havasu Canyon in 1866 and lead deposits in 1879.[11]

The population of Arizona boomed in the 1870s and 1880s, and the promise of profitable ore lured many prospectors to Grand Canyon. Some, like S. S. Harper, tried to increase the accessibility of Grand Canyon through large-scale projects such as railroads. Others, like Seth Tanner, discovered, enlarged, and publicized trails into the canyon. John Hance pioneered the New Hance Trail in 1894 and mined asbestos downstream of Hance Rapid (mile 76.8) in the 1890s.[12] Beginning in 1890, William Bass guided tourists and mined a variety of deposits near Shinumo Creek (mile 108.6); the deposits were profitable enough that he built a cableway in 1908 to haul burros, horses, equipment, and ore across the Colorado River.[13] The new trails allowed access for many prospectors, among them Felix Lantier, whose activities in Grand Canyon might never have been known except for his chance encounter with Stanton's expedition.[14]

Although prospecting activities were extensive, mining operations in Grand Canyon were rarely profitable.[15] Mineral deposits were inevitably low grade, and transportation costs were high. In the absence of Stanton's railroad, pack animals—especially burros—carried freight on the tortuous trails of the canyon. Burros escaped or were deliberately released into the canyon; miners could capture members of wild herds when new animals were needed. Native to northwestern Africa, burros reproduced prolifically in the canyon, since their new environment had an ample food supply initially and few predators (even mountain lions could not consistently kill burros).[16] Grand Canyon became one of the major concentrations of burros in the western United States.[17]

Three distinct herds formed near the river corridor.[18] The Tonto Platform herd developed from burros that escaped from mining and tourist operations on the South Rim and Phantom Ranch; this herd mostly ranged a thousand feet above the river, reaching the river only at Red Canyon (mile 76) and Phantom Ranch. Burros released from Bass's mining operations in Shinumo Creek formed the Shinumo herd, which mostly ranged on flat terrain on the Tapeats Sandstone away from the river corridor but were common next to the right side of the river between about miles 122 and 125.[19] The Lower Canyon herd comprised animals released at various points; this herd ranged only on the right side of the river from about Parashant Canyon (mile 198) to 220 Mile Canyon.[20] Burros were also on the left side of the river corridor near Diamond Creek, but these animals did not range far up- or downstream.

"Wherever burros are concentrated, the native vegetation suffers."[21] This observation, typical of land managers, may well have been true in parts of the river corridor. Burros were not finicky; they ate or otherwise damaged trees, shrubs, forbs, and grasses in varying proportions, depending on the time of year.[22] Ecologists such as J. W. Jordan observed that burros would crop plants to the ground, then dig out the roots with their hooves; the burros may have extirpated grasses and some palatable shrubs in heavily grazed areas. They cut terrace trails across steep slopes, accelerating the rates of erosion. Springs, in particular, were fouled, prompting fears that bighorn sheep would not use their normal watering areas.

In the 1920s, the National Park Service concluded that burros were damaging perennial vegetation, polluting water sources, and degrading habitat for other wildlife. Attempting to stem the population growth, park rangers shot thousands of burros on the Tonto Platform. Between 1924 and 1931, 1,467 burros were killed by park rangers and left to decompose, reducing the population to between 50 and 75 animals.[23] Between 1932 and 1956, 370 more burros were eliminated. Between 1956 and 1968, 771 burros were destroyed, and an additional 252 were captured and removed. The introduction of burros had resulted in a population increase that apparently could not be stabilized without unacceptable changes to the habitat.

The Tonto Platform herd bore the brunt of park rangers' efforts to control the burro population; the Shinumo and Lower Canyon herds were generally left alone. The size of the Shinumo and Lower Canyon herds was much less than that of the Tonto Platform herd. For example, the herd in 209 Mile Canyon, considered one of the largest segments of the Lower Canyon herd, numbered only 8 to 15 individuals. Only 150 burros ranged between Parashant and Bridge Canyons, a distance of thirty-seven river miles, with use concentrated near water sources.[24] The size of these herds may well have been limited by the amount of available food and water.

Between 1965 and 1969, the National Park Service culled the Shinumo herd; rangers shot 28 burros in Bedrock Canyon. Another 18 animals were killed in 1976.[25] The Lower Canyon herd, which was not then within the boundaries of the national park, was not disturbed. Despite the large reductions in the size of two of the three herds, burros continued to reproduce with alarming speed.

With the merging of Grand Canyon National Park and Grand Canyon National Monument in 1975, the National Park Service issued an environmental impact statement on a proposed management plan for burros that was to be "a final solution." The management objective was "to restore conditions conducive to the perpetuation of the natural processes as they functioned before disruption by technological man or competition from non-native plants and animals."[26] Wildlife managers would accomplish this objective either by having park rangers use high-powered rifles to kill the burros or by having environmental groups transport the burros out of the canyon.

The goal was elimination of all burros within the park. The Lower Canyon herd, which had the highest population density of the three in the mid-1970s,[27] was the top priority. Between 1980 and 1981, 580 burros were removed by boat or by helicopter or were herded out of the canyon.[28] Park rangers shot the remainder. The Lower Canyon and Tonto Platform herds were eliminated; one burro is reported to remain in the former range of the Shinumo herd.[29]

The burro-reduction program caused considerable controversy among animal-rights groups, environmentalists, scientists, and land managers. The controversy swirled around three diverse perspectives. The National Park Service and environmentalists noted that burros were not native and claimed they were damaging the natural ecosystems of Grand Canyon National Park. Paleoecologists claimed the burros merely occupied a niche not used since the Pleistocene; presumably, burros and Pleistocene herbivores consumed the natural vegetation in much the same way. Animal-rights groups argued that burros, as well as feral horses, are naturalized elements of desert ecosystems and are part of our national heritage. The National Park Service, with its legal mandate of preservation, won the argument: the burros were eliminated.

Other Domestic Livestock

Other than burros, domestic livestock have grazed only on small reaches of the river corridor. At one time, horses, mules, and burros grazed desert plants in the vicinity of Phantom Ranch and Bass Camp (mile 108), but the grazing was light and seasonal. Rustlers are reputed to have used the Tanner Trail, then called the Horsethief Trail, to transport stolen stock from southern Utah to northern Arizona.[30] These horses probably grazed in the vicinity of Lava Canyon Rapid, but their tenure in Grand Canyon likely was brief.

The operators of Lees Ferry maintained small cattle herds at the mouth of the Paria River;[31] when the ferry service was discontinued in 1928, this grazing likely ceased. Navajos continue to run cattle, sheep, and perhaps even goats across from Lees Ferry. Their animals are confined to the left bank by cliffs from about three miles above Lees Ferry to mile 1 in Marble Canyon. Desperate for rangeland, one Navajo family lowered sheep and goats over the sandstone rim on ropes to the river ten miles upstream of Lees Ferry.[32] Sheep grazing, which apparently occurred before construction of Glen Canyon Dam, may have been brief; the animals were removed in some unknown manner. Their trails were still obvious in 1992.

Mule Deer

Before white settlers introduced grazing animals to northern Arizona, periodic fires kept the forest understory in check on the Kaibab Plateau. Abundant grass and browse provided considerable food for mule deer, and mountain lions, coyotes, wolves, and Paiutes culled the herds. A dynamic equilibrium must have existed among food supply, numbers of deer, and numbers of predators. In the 1870s, Mor-mon settlers turned the Kaibab Plateau into summer range for domestic livestock. The introduction of livestock changed the existing balance: livestock competed with the deer herd for food, and ranchers, to protect their stock, felt a need to control the populations of predators. By the end of the century, a few hundred thousand sheep and tens of thousands of cattle grazed on the Kaibab Plateau.[33] Early conservationists considered the excessive grazing a threat to the deer herd.

The Grand Canyon Game Reserve, primarily on the Kaibab Plateau, was established in 1906 to increase the size of the deer herd. The deer population skyrocketed in response to increased food supply (due to above-average precipitation, fire suppression, and reduced livestock grazing), fewer predators, and a ban on deer hunting.[34] The rate of increase startled wildlife managers. From an estimated 4,000 animals in 1906, the deer population doubled by 1912 and peaked between 30,000 and 100,000 deer in 1924.[35] The Kaibab Plateau was browsed too heavily, and many animals starved. The crash was swift; by the most conservative estimate, 60 percent of the herd died between 1924 and 1927, and the population declined to about 10,000 animals in the mid-1930s.

Once rarely seen along the river, deer are now common in wide reaches and at the mouths of large tributary canyons. Tame deer are common at Phantom Ranch and along major hiking trails. Rafters frequently see deer swimming in lower Marble Canyon, and deer are common in large side canyons that issue from the North Rim. At a few places—for example, the mouth of Saddle Canyon—deer have depleted the desert vegetation. Mostly, deer appear to browse riparian vegetation in side canyons and along the river.

Bighorn Sheep

In the middle part of this century, wildlife biologists thought burros competed for food with bighorn sheep, thus threatening the canyon populations of the native herbivore. Several decades later, careful studies found that the two species use different foraging areas and to a certain extent different watering areas.[36] For example, the highest density of bighorn sheep appears to be on the left side of the river corridor between about miles 120 and 160; burros grazed only on the right side of the river corridor in a small part of this area. Nevertheless, the population of bighorn sheep in Grand Canyon may have decreased while that of burros was increasing.

Estimates of the population of bighorn sheep appear contradictory. In the 1930s, 200 bighorn sheep were counted in the national park. By the late 1970s, before the final solution to the burro problem was enacted, only 50 bighorn sheep were reported to occupy the Tonto Platform between Red Canyon and Fossil Canyon (miles 77 to 125).[37] In 1987, 72 were observed along the river corridor and an additional 35 were seen from the rim.[38] Did the population of bighorn sheep increase, or did better observers count more sheep?

Evidence of an increase in the numbers of bighorn sheep along the river corridor is tantalizing but inconclusive. Despite the occasional kill by a mountain lion or eagle, bighorn sheep have only one main predator: humans. The Hualapai and Havasupai, and to a lesser extent the Paiutes, hunted bighorn sheep until the people were confined to reservations. Few people now hunt bighorn sheep in Grand Canyon.[39] Moreover, diseases borne by domestic livestock decimated herds of bighorn sheep[40] much like diseases borne by Europeans killed large numbers of Native Americans. Nor is it likely that populations of bighorn sheep would have increased in response to any other environmental factor; their food supply (mostly grasses, Mormon tea, and other shrubs)[41] has changed little over the past century. If bighorn sheep are increasing in number, the likely reasons are the control of human predation and isolation from livestock herds.[42]

Herbivores and Perennial Vegetation

Grazing by domestic livestock is considered one of the most important causes for modification of the natural environments of the western United States.[43] However, climatic change could have been responsible for many of the environmental transformations attributed to livestock.[44] Biologists have difficulty ascribing vegetational change conclusively to either of these two influences. Large tracts of ungrazed desert where long-term changes can be attributed to a climatic variation are rare.[45] One large area that has been mostly spared heavy grazing, having been only browsed by bighorn sheep, is the bottom of Grand Canyon. Here—thanks to the burro irruption, some isolated rangeland, and a man who wanted to build a railroad—the effects of livestock may be separated from those of climate.

Grazing and Plant Demography

In the canyon, grazed areas were segregated from ungrazed areas by impassable cliffs, in effect providing experimental areas that were captured in the Stanton views. I used the replicate views to compare the effects of heavy grazing by burros and domestic livestock to the effects of browsing (or light grazing) by bighorn sheep. In each old photograph, I counted the number of individuals of each plant species, estimating the total plant population and the proportion of each species in 1890; in the replicate photograph, I made the same counts but also counted the number of plants that had died and the number of plants that were new.

Demography is the calculation of statistics (including the rates of establishment and mortality) about a population or group. The Stanton views can be divided into two sets: views within the range of bighorn sheep and views within the range of burros or other livestock. (Only two views, too few

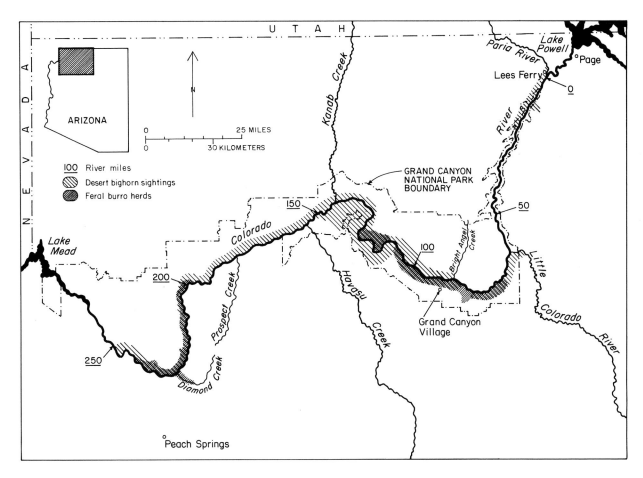

Figure 4.1. Areas used by burro herds before 1981 in Grand Canyon

to merit analysis, depict the effects of mule deer.) Cattle, domestic goats and sheep, horses, and burros differ in forage preference, amount of utilization, and severity of impacts. I considered these differences irrelevant to this type of comparison and combined the views of areas used by livestock into one group of comparison photographs. Livestock (including burros) prefer grasses; however, no grasses were visible in views of heavily grazed areas. Overutilization could have eliminated the grasses from these views; however, even the 1890 views, made before burros and other livestock were introduced, show too few grasses to yield meaningful results.

From the published distribution maps, I estimate that feral burros used about 13 percent of the river corridor. Most of the use—10 percent—was on the right side. Ten of Stanton's camera stations were in areas subsequently grazed on heavily by burros; all of these sites were in western Grand Canyon. Unfortunately, when Stanton took his photographs, he was across the river from where the Shinumo herd ranged, and views in other areas used by burros (for example, Diamond Creek) do not show desert vegetation.

I examined only a few common species: white bursage, Mormon tea, creosote bush, and beavertail prickly pear. In grazed areas, Mormon tea and beavertail occur in areas used by domestic livestock

Figure 4.2. Indian Canyon

A. March 1, 1890, was a busy day for the Stanton expedition. After launching from the bottom of 205 Mile Rapid, the crew made twenty miles and Stanton photographed twenty-three views. This downstream view (number 643), made at 8:00 A.M., was one of his first that day. His railroad likely would have passed through the foreground, a bench on top of the Tapeats Sandstone.

and feral burros, whereas creosote bush and white bursage occur in reaches grazed on only by burros. For each plant species, I calculated establishment and mortality rates. Fortunately for Grand Canyon, but unfortunately for this type of analysis, the number of views showing ungrazed vegetation (244) was twelve times greater than the number showing heavy use (20).

Burros heavily graze white bursage.[46] No individual white bursage plants in heavily grazed areas

lived through the past century; the mortality rate for white bursage is 100 percent, with no recruitment. In other words, heavy grazing by feral burros caused local extirpation of white bursage. In ungrazed sites, the establishment and mortality rates are 28 percent and 43 percent of the population per century, respectively, suggesting population decline even in the absence of burros.

Burros and livestock did not affect Mormon tea as heavily. Twenty-one individual Mormon tea plants in

B. The downstream view from above the mouth of Indian Canyon is one of twenty that show the effects of grazing on desert vegetation in Grand Canyon. This site had heavy burro grazing that ended ten years before this view was made; numerous burro trails crossed through the foreground of this view. Most of the perennial plants visible in the 1890 view are gone; only three ocotillos, a creosote bush, and five individuals of Mormon tea persist. The ocotillos in the view have scars at their base caused by burro grazing. The most abundant plant in the foreground of the 1890 view, interpreted to be white bursage, had twenty-nine individuals, all of which are now dead. Only one seedling of white bursage, which is not visible in the view, was found at the site. Four individuals of barrel cactus are visible in the 1890 view; thirty are visible in the 1991 view. The change may have resulted from a decrease in the frequency of severe frosts in Grand Canyon. Ray Turner photographed this view on February 23, 1991, at 8:03 A.M.

heavily utilized sites have persisted for the last hundred years. Nevertheless, the mortality rate is twice as great in heavily grazed areas as in ungrazed areas: 30 percent as opposed to 17 percent. Establishment also was higher in heavily grazed areas (30 percent) than in ungrazed areas (24 percent), which some-

what offsets the losses. Heavy grazing increased the turnover rate of Mormon tea; in other words, about the same number of individuals are present in each Stanton view as in the corresponding replicate view, and the average life span of the population was reduced by grazing.

Figure 4.3. Ungrazed desert vegetation at mile 215.2

A. Stanton and his crew were in a hurry to find Diamond Creek on March 1, 1890. Despite this, at 11:20 A.M. Stanton stopped above Three Springs Canyon on the left to photograph his proposed railroad route through a right-hand bend (number 651). The railroad would have traversed the right bank. Only by accident did Stanton include desert vegetation in his view. Only two barrel cactus appear in this view—the most obvious at the extreme left side. Several inconspicuous brittlebush appear in the midground at left and center of the view.

Creosote bush and beavertail cactus, which have a considerably different stature, share the common trait of low palatability. Burros eat these species primarily during extreme drought, when other food is scarce.[47] More likely burros affect these unpalatable plants by trampling them. Burros seek annual plants beneath the canopy of creosote bushes, breaking branches and damaging root crowns in the process. Soil erosion between shrubs also damages plants by exposing their roots. The result is substantial change; the mortality rate of creosote bush rises from 1 percent per century in ungrazed sites to 33 percent per century in grazed areas. The mortality rate of beavertail more than doubles between ungrazed and heavily grazed areas, from 26 to 60 percent per century. In both cases, recruitment increased by a similar amount, indicating an acceleration in population turnover.

B. This view upstream of Three Springs Canyon had the most persistent species of any view: eight. Although turnover has occurred in many species, particularly in the prickly pear and cholla, most of the shrubs are still alive after a century. These species are creosote bush (lower left), range ratany (midground center), Mormon tea (several individuals throughout the view), Fremont thornbush (midground at center), wolfberry (left foreground), beavertail (lower center), buckhorn cholla (lower right), and mesquite (midground at center). The density of plants in the view is much higher in 1991, but the increase is mostly in barrel cactus and brittlebush. Only two individuals of barrel cactus are visible in the 1890 view (one is at the extreme left center); twenty-two are visible in the 1990s view. Similarly, brittlebush, which was present here in 1890, has increased dramatically. This view, more than most, illustrates the framework of climatically insensitive species around the suite of frost-sensitive species. This site, nine miles downstream from Indian Canyon and on river left, was ungrazed by burros. As a result, long-lived species persist with little turnover compared with the relatively large turnover in grazed vegetation across the river. Dave Edwards replicated this remarkable view on February 24, 1991, at 1:17 P.M.

A Puzzling Plant Invasion

To most observers of range condition, snakeweed is an undesirable shrub that, being unpalatable, becomes more common under grazing. Dense stands of snakeweed are the symbol of overgrazing on western rangeland. Snakeweed has a wide distribution; it occurs in the sagebrush steppe of Idaho as well as the hot deserts of southern California. It also occurs in Grand Canyon and is one of the most common species observed in replicates of the Stanton views.

I cannot determine why snakeweed has become ubiquitous in Grand Canyon. It is not reported as common in the fossil records of the Pleistocene or Holocene,[48] and we observed snakeweed in only two Stanton views from 1890; both were on a sand dune near the mouth of Forster Canyon (mile 122). In 1938, Elzada Clover and Lois Jotter found snakeweed only at mile 26.5, at Tanner Rapid (where it was common), and in Havasu Canyon; they did not see any at Lees Ferry or President Harding Rapid, places where it is now common.[49] Snakeweed now occurs in parts of the Inner Gorge, even beyond the reach of bighorn sheep. The individuals in replicate views, with few exceptions, are small and suggestive of recent germination.

Several aspects of the life-history strategy of snakeweed invite speculation as to why this indicator of overgrazing has become more common along the river corridor. Snakeweed grows primarily in response to winter rain. Its seeds ripen in late June and early July. It is common in rangelands on the rims of Grand Canyon; its seeds likely blow into the river corridor during the frequent high winds. The individuals that become established do not replace existing plants; instead, snakeweed appears to occupy unfavorable (or empty) niches between long-established shrubs and grasses. Snakeweed may be exploiting over the short term a favorable climate that allows germination and establishment; drought may force it from its niche.

The Legacy of Paleoecology

Paleoecology provides a different perspective on the impact of grazing. During the last ice age, particularly between 13,000 and 22,000 years ago, Grand Canyon had a much richer assemblage of vertebrates than it has now.[50] Many small animals—such as squirrels, raccoons, marmots, and porcupines—lived at river level.[51] Shasta ground sloth was a large,

slow-moving creature that roamed parts of western Grand Canyon.[52] Harrington's mountain goat claimed the cliffs much like bighorn sheep do today.[53] The fossils tell us of the presence but not the density of the Pleistocene herbivores. One may presume that a stable population of Pleistocene herbivores required certain minimum numbers in the herds and that maximum numbers were regulated by food supply, predators, or both.

Carnivores and scavengers completed the food web. Coyotes, mountain lions, and perhaps even larger carnivores such as wolves hunted Pleistocene herbivores. Condors and an enormous vulture, Merriam's terratorn, scavenged the remains of herbivores killed by carnivores or through other causes. The sediment in Stanton's Cave preserved bones from seventy-five species of birds, fourteen of which are no longer present in the region.[54]

Fossilized dung tells us what some of these Pleistocene herbivores ate. Shasta ground sloths consumed mainly globe mallow (an herbaceous perennial) and Mormon tea.[55] Harrington's mountain goat had a diet of 75 percent desert herbs and shrubs and 25 percent grasses.[56] In theory, the diet of both species could easily be supplied by the current vegetation of the river corridor. Both species, as well as the other large Pleistocene herbivores, became extinct about 11,000 years ago;[57] once the carcasses of large herbivores were no longer available in abundance, some of the avian scavengers likely became extinct as well, at least in Grand Canyon.

Two competing theories explain why these and other large herbivores vanished from Grand Canyon as well as the rest of North America. The climate became warmer starting about 13,000 years ago, and plant distributions began to change. The habitat of large herbivores may have become unsuitable (although, as noted above, the plants they ate remain in the river corridor).[58] Alternatively, the extinctions coincided with the arrival of peoples from Asia, who crossed a land bridge through what is now the

Bering Sea and quickly migrated southward. These peoples were efficient hunters, perhaps too efficient; they may have extirpated the large fauna of Grand Canyon.[59] If humans did not kill off the large herbivores outright, they certainly contributed heavily to the demise of these animals.

The extinction of large herbivores left a niche open for other herbivores in and around Grand Canyon. Only one species exploited this niche: bighorn sheep arrived about 10,800 years ago, about the same time as the demise of Harrington's mountain goat.[60] The newly arrived bighorn sheep ate mostly herbs and shrubs.[61] Evidence of use of Stantons Cave (mile 31.6) by bighorn sheep ends about 2,000 years ago, although bighorn sheep have continuously occupied some parts of Grand Canyon: they were a staple in the diet of the Havasupai.[62] Other than bighorn sheep, the largest herbivores common during the prehistoric Holocene in Grand Canyon were packrats and ground squirrels.[63]

The Effects of Grazing and Management

When viewed in old photographs and new replicates, the desert plants of Grand Canyon illustrate the impact of heavy grazing. The mortality and recruitment rates of common species were greatly accelerated in grazed areas. Some species were locally extirpated. In a desert ecosystem that showed little turnover in response to browsing by bighorn sheep, grazing by burros and livestock had major impacts.

Let us assume that what happened in Grand Canyon is representative of what happened elsewhere in the West. Ignore the fact that burros use different forage than cattle or sheep; ignore any substrate-induced differences between plant assemblages in Grand Canyon and elsewhere. Release of herbivores, through the elimination of predators or the introduction of animals into an unoccupied niche, caused heavy grazing and other "damage" to the environment. Heavy grazing accelerated the rate of turnover

in desert plants; reduction of palatable vegetation either capped the number of animals or eventually caused catastrophic die-off. Humans upset whatever balance was present, if any, and the acceleration of change in plant demographics and an extreme oscillation in animal populations resulted.

What the "natural" state of affairs is depends on the length of your perspective. Biologists do not know whether populations of mule deer or other large herbivores underwent extreme fluctuations before this century. Perhaps Havasupai, Hualapai, Paiute, or even Anasazi or Basketmaker hunters endured irruptions in the populations of their prey that were similar to the problems faced by twentieth-century wildlife managers. In managing herbivory in national parks, or for that matter on any publicly owned lands, one must decide what perspective to take: a limited view based on a few generations of experience, or a longer view based on millennia. Whichever perspective one chooses, humans cannot easily be dismissed as an unnatural force in the environment.

Two major problems undercut the hypothesis that human intervention—whether in the Pleistocene or in the twentieth century—differs from natural changes. First, the notion that the empty niche left behind by the extinct large herbivores was somehow "unnatural" comes from the assumption that *Homo sapiens* is not a natural predator. The distribution of plants and animals shifted considerably at the end of the Pleistocene; why is the shift in the distribution of humans not deemed a natural consequence of climatic change? If *Homo sapiens* is considered a natural predator, the question of the missing herbivores is moot: their extinction was "natural." The second problem revolves around an unanswerable question: would Pleistocene herbivores have persisted into the Holocene if humans had not entered what is now North America? Dietary information derived from fossil dung suggests these herbivores ate plants that were similar to those found in the

Thinking Like a Canyon:
Wild Ideas and Wild Burros

PAUL S. MARTIN

Compared with the minor changes of the last 100 years that are seen in repeat photography, the changes of the last 40,000 years that are revealed through the fossil record were monumental. Grand Canyon is rich in dry caves, suitable shelters for the large herbivores of the Pleistocene and ideal tombs for their remains: not only their bones but also their droppings, horns, hair, and hooves. In these caves ecologists have found the remains of mountain sheep, deer, Harrington's mountain goats, ancient equids (relatives of the modern horse), and Shasta ground sloths. Also surprisingly common in some canyon caves was a giant scavenging bird, the California condor.[1]

Ancient dung deposits show that the native grasses, Mormon tea, globe mallow, prickly pear, saltbush, and other plants eaten in this century by mountain sheep, burros, deer, and cattle were eaten during the Pleistocene by ground sloths, mountain goats, and even Colombian mammoths.[2] Before the extinctions, mammoths, camels, and other large herbivores must have been numerous on the Kaibab Plateau, generating enough carcasses to sustain the nestling condors and their parents in their canyon aeries. Such clues from the fossil record suggest that the native plants of the New World were accustomed to being eaten, and not just by the deer and mountain sheep that have survived to the present.

Nevertheless, these days not all herbivores are granted equal rights to eat plants in national parks. A case in point is the controversy that decided the fate of burros in Grand Canyon National Park. As early as the days of Stanton's photographs, burros released from or escaped from mining camps were inadvertently boxed in by cliffs to populate some parts of the Inner Gorge. Occupying their range for a century did not guarantee usufruct. Guidelines written by highly regarded specialists recommended "that the biotic associations within each park be maintained, or where necessary recreated, as nearly as possible in the condition that prevailed when the area was first visited by the white man."[3] To guarantee action, the National Park Service provided funding for research on "the burro problem" leading to a final solution.

Counter-arguments from skeptics were ignored. No matter that many other alien species (such as tamarisk, red brome grass, camelthorn, house sparrows, houseflies, carp, and trout, to name a few) would not be purged because their eradication would be too difficult or too expensive. No matter that burros ate alien as well as native plants and that their carcasses might feed scavengers in a future restoration project for condors or wolves in Grand Canyon. No matter that the burros' genealogy could be traced to the evolution of horses (the Equidae) in western North America—beginning over 60 million years ago—and that the equid fossil record in the New World vastly exceeds that of mule deer and mountain sheep.[4] Resource managers ruled that only the deer and sheep enjoyed incumbency, making one concession: if the public objected to the killing of all the burros (it did) and could stand the expense (a private organization could), hundreds of wild burros would be (and were) rounded up and flown out by helicopter to be adopted by caring members of our species. The remnants, wily escapees that could not be captured, were hunted down and shot.

Early in this century many land managers, including rangers in Grand Canyon and other national parks, underwent a rebirth in consciousness. They had been "helping" nature, as they understood nature, by destroying coyotes, mountain lions, wolves, and other "bad" predators that killed the "good" deer, elk, and pronghorn. Then some perceptive biologists saw the profound error in this logic and reformulated their practice according to a new vision. Some, following Aldo Leopold, called the new policy "thinking like a mountain."[5] A mountain fears its deer (for overbrowsing) and loves its wolves (for keeping the deer in check). Although these ideas on natural regulation were also flawed, they at least served as something of a reprieve for the targeted predators.

Evidently, managerial protocols can suddenly change. The idea that wild burros may add value to the Inner Gorge, once rejected out of hand, deserves more thought.[6]

Surely management of national parks and other public lands is myopic if the goal is limited to preserving or re-creating what Spanish explorers and missionaries saw beginning in the sixteenth century. Arizona and the West were not "pristine wilderness" when Europeans arrived. America was already inhabited, in many places abundantly inhabited, by indigenous people. At least 11,000 years before Columbus, the first colonists arrived from Asia to witness and perhaps assist in the aforementioned extinctions.

The struggle to fathom nature and to manage it accordingly continually challenges bureaucrats, philosophers, advocates, scientists, and, not least, the public. Some turn to history to run ecological experiments. Robert Webb's research is one provocative example; it could mean that some desert plants will stop growing when not eaten! The presence of fossils of condors and other extinct species in Grand Canyon caves suggests another, even wilder, experiment for the future: restoration ecology. I call this view "thinking like a canyon." Canyons fear nothing, neither herbivores nor predators, neither native species nor aliens —only that alien human beings might sell a canyon short. What might the North American landscape and its inhabitants look like if the cast of large herbivores and carnivores included species equivalent not only to those seen by the first white explorers, but also those seen by the first Native Americans? Could wild burros provide a food supply for wolf restoration in or around Grand Canyon, as has been accomplished in Turkmenistan in the Commonwealth of Independent States? When people begin to think like a canyon, a brighter day for many more kinds of large animals—wolves, condors, and burros included—must lie ahead.

Feral Burros:
Old Arguments and New Twists

STEVEN W. CAROTHERS

In 1982 a colleague and I were kicking over 12,000-year-old sloth dung in a cave about ninety miles upstream of Glen Canyon Dam on Lake Powell. Because of my previous experience with the ecological impacts of feral domestic livestock (horses and burros) in Grand Canyon,[1] I had been asked to evaluate grazing-related impacts throughout Glen Canyon Recreation Area. The small herd of livestock that we had tracked into what became known as Bechan Cave[2] had thoroughly trashed not only the riparian habitat and adjacent upland terraces but paleontological and archaeological sites as well.

The terrain was too severe and the animals too wild for even the most experienced and dedicated cowboys to round up the escapees. I recommended that "direct reduction" be implemented immediately: a bureaucratic euphemism for "shoot them." Healing the damage wrought by those livestock would take years; the sooner recovery got underway, the better.

By some poetic twist, the fossil feces were later identified by Dr. Paul S. Martin. Dr. Martin and I had been arguing for several years—in the scientific literature, in the media, and virtually anywhere we could find an audience—over the appropriateness of feral animals in park ecosystems. Dr. Martin's position was that large herbivores, once a part of the ancient landscape, should be allowed to roam once again regardless of their domestic origins. My position was that domestic livestock gone wild cause intolerable damage to present-day ecosystems and should be removed.

Dr. Martin laments that the burros' century-long occupation of Grand Canyon "did not guarantee usufruct." I had to scramble for my dictionary on that one. Usufruct means "the right of using fruits of an estate belonging to another without impairing the substance." Burros were denied usufruct because they did impair the substance of the estate; they were overgrazing habitats and inflicting long-lasting damage to the ecosystem. Data gathered by our Grand Canyon research team in 1975 showed that where burros roamed, plant and small mammal populations were drastically reduced compared with similar areas where burros were absent.[3]

If empirical evidence were not enough, management policies demanded that burros be removed.[4] Preserving natural environments is inherent in the concept of setting aside and protecting tracts of land as national parks, and by "natural" we mean ecosystems unaltered by the activities of humankind. Burros in Grand Canyon were introduced by humans. By definition they are not a natural species but an exotic species, and a harmful one at that.

We physically cannot remove all exotic plants and animals from Grand Canyon, but we cannot give up on trying to restore it to as much of a natural ecosystem as possible. In the case of damage caused by feral burros, something could be done. We could, and did, find and remove all the burros from Grand Canyon in the late 1970s. Within only a few years after burro removal, signs of overgrazing began to disappear.[5]

The argument that burros should be tolerated in Grand

Canyon because their genealogy can be traced to the evolution of horses in western North America may have a romantic flavor, but it is belied by the fact that ecological systems of 12,000 and more years ago have no equivalent today. The climate is different, the habitats are different, and there exist no canyon predators capable of controlling rapidly expanding populations of wild horses and burros. Over the last several millennia, an array of desert plants, bighorn sheep, and a few large predators have coexisted within a viable inner canyon ecosystem—apparently without the need of equid grazers. Robert Webb's replicate photographs may indicate that desert plants almost stop growing when not eaten, but ample data also show that desert plants die when grazed beyond their ability to photosynthesize. Slow-growing desert vegetation hardly represents an argument for introducing or tolerating wild burros or horses (or cows) in our national parks.

Something interesting is afoot, however, down in Hualapai land. The Hualapai Tribe has submitted an unsolicited proposal to the U.S. Fish and Wildlife Service, the agency mandated to protect our endangered species. The Hualapais have proposed that the next batch of captive-bred California condors be released within their one-million-acre reservation bordering the lower Colorado River in Grand Canyon. The last of the free-flying condors was removed from the wild in 1989, mostly because the poisonous environmental soup of the Los Angeles Basin airshed where they once flourished was hazardous to their health. The Hualapais argue that the clear air, the fossil record, and historical data indicating a long prior occupation by condors in the area, combined with an abundance of food, all indicate that condors would find a healthy and peaceful home in lower Grand Canyon.

What is the abundant food? None other than the wild burros that continue to roam the Hualapai Indian Reservation. The Hualapais propose to manage the burro populations as a food source for California condors, a proposal which I find of incredible utility—for the Hualapais, for the California condors, and especially for the burros.

I still maintain that feral livestock has no place within our national parks. In some cases the parks were established specifically to protect the landscape from the ravages of "hoofed locusts," as John Muir once referred to domestic livestock. But on the Hualapai Indian Reservation, where the land is already managed for livestock production, what better use of the forage than to provide substance for an endangered species? Things are rarely as simple as they seem; where once I would have argued for the removal of wild burros from the entire region, not just from Grand Canyon National Park, I happily take a new position.

modern river corridor.[64] The river supplied a reliable water source. The predators that preyed on these animals remained (with the addition of humans). Indeed, paleoecologists do not know exactly what aspect of the changing environment would have made the river corridor unfavorable for survival. It could have been the increased summer heat, the change in seasonality of rainfall, the loss of tree cover—these changes may not have mattered to certain plants or predators, but they may have been fatal to the Pleistocene herbivores. Regardless, these reasons are only speculation. If we consider only the last 11,000 years, we need not contend with the issue of extinct herbivores; bighorn sheep were the only known herbivores in the Holocene. The introduction of domestic livestock and burros into this niche is indicted as "unnatural": the consequence was "damage." Once again, human influence, direct or indirect, is excluded as a natural process.

Humans of the twentieth century differ from those of 11,000 years ago in only two ways. The first is technology; high-powered rifles killed burros, and spears killed ground sloths. The second, and more profound, is intent. Miners purposefully introduced burros; park rangers intentionally eliminated them. We would have to guess whether the first Americans were purposeful in their intent to eradicate Pleistocene herbivores (if indeed that is what happened).

Missing from all this discussion is whether plants have intrinsic value. If a species is rare or endemic to a certain substrate, we value it as an endangered species. But what about Mormon tea and creosote bush? They are neither rare nor endangered, and their value is measured more as forage than as the anchor of ecosystems. If plants are not appreciated for their role, we are managing animals, not ecosystems.

The mandate of the National Park Service is to preserve and protect while allowing nonconsumptive uses. Theoretically this mandate unequivocally applies to the entire ecosystem; in practice, animals and human visitation are favored in park management.[65] In Grand Canyon, the natural grazing animals were not the overriding issue; the claims of competition between bighorn sheep and feral burros were contrived. At the time of Stanton's expedition, the vegetation of the river corridor was not under the pressures of a large population of herbivores. The plants in Stanton's views warranted protection and preservation through the establishment of Grand Canyon National Park not because burros were nonnative or bighorn sheep were threatened but because the prehistoric ecosystem did not contain large numbers of grazing animals. Sometimes humans in attempting to remove themselves from their environment make the right decisions for the wrong reasons.

CHAPTER 5

The Disaster of Frost

The bottom of Grand Canyon can be a hot place. During summer, when air temperatures often exceed 100°F, river passengers and guides alike seek shade or rejoice when a wave breaks over their boat, giving instant relief. To desert plants, high above the cold water released from Glen Canyon Dam, summer heat is something they are well adapted to—and even require—for survival.

Deserts are defined by climate that humans consider harsh. They occur in regions of low and highly variable rainfall, low humidity, and high, variable temperatures.[1] Growing in typically dry, rocky soils, desert plants endure intense summer heat (temperatures often exceed 120°F), are buffeted by winds sometimes greater than sixty miles per hour, and are battered by rocks loosened during intense rainfall. Despite these conditions, many individual plants in Grand Canyon have survived for a hundred years or more. Other plant species have increased considerably in the narrow strip of desert above the Colorado River. These species appear to have rebounded in the wake of a natural disaster—extreme cold—that affected Grand Canyon before Stanton's expedition.

Disasters are natural or human-induced events that decimate plant assemblages. Not all the plants are killed; instead, their ranks theoretically are

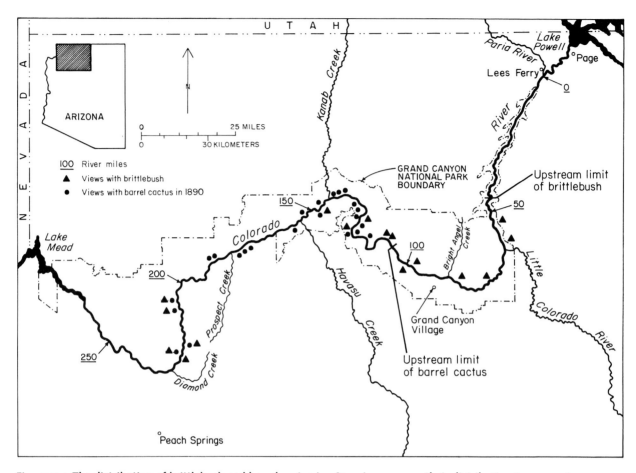

Figure 5.1. The distribution of brittlebush and barrel cactus in 1890 views versus their distribution in 1990s views

thinned of the old, diseased, or otherwise unfit individuals. Catastrophes, by contrast, eliminate most, if not all, plants; examples of catastrophes common in Grand Canyon include massive rockfalls, hot ground fires, or the episodic floods that occur in tributary canyons. When one thinks of natural disasters, such disasters as fires, insect outbreaks, or the spread of disease may be the first to come to mind. Fires are unlikely in the sparse vegetation of the desert in Grand Canyon, and biological disasters such as disease and insect outbreaks have not been reported. Nevertheless, the narrow strip of desert along the Colorado River may be prone to disasters such as droughts or extreme cold—these disasters are caused by fluctuations in climate.

Although deserts in general are not thought of in terms of cold weather, cold is a factor that dictates the limits of certain deserts. For example, the northern limit of the Sonoran Desert in Arizona is defined by freezing temperatures, because the columnar cacti and most leguminous shrubs and trees that characterize this desert are sensitive to frost.[2] The desert of Grand Canyon likewise is affected by cold. The depth of the relatively narrow canyon creates a subtle climatic effect. The river corridor is an ideal conduit for the drainage of cold air from higher elevations of the Kaibab Plateau to the north, the Colorado Plateau to the northeast and east, and the Coconino Plateau to the south. Sunlight rarely reaches river level along much of the river corridor, so daytime temperatures can remain low in winter. As a result, severe freezes occur in the upper parts of the river corridor in Grand Canyon; in general, the severity of freezing decreases downstream as the elevation decreases from 3,100 feet at Lees Ferry to 1,200 feet at the head of Lake Mead. The effect of microclimate is paramount: slopes facing south or southwest in relatively open sections of the canyon have higher temperatures in winter, while those facing north have lower temperatures.

Because some desert plants in Grand Canyon can be long-lived and well adapted to the climate, they might appear to have little reason to change, other than the ongoing cycle of death of the oldest plants and germination of replacements. However, the assemblages of desert plants in Grand Canyon comprise species of varying tolerances, and some of these species are less comfortable than others with even a slight variation in climate. As the Stanton views show, some species that now dominate the desert vegetation of Grand Canyon have greatly benefited by the warmer climate of the past century.[3]

Expansion of Frost-Sensitive Species

Brittlebush

Brittlebush is a common shrub of the Mojave and Sonoran Deserts, particularly on both sides of the valley of the lower Colorado River. In Grand Canyon, brittlebush occurs between mile 42.5 and Lake Mead,[4] although it is relatively uncommon in many parts of the Inner Gorge (miles 77 to 113). In many areas, this pretty, yellow-flowered shrub dominates the desert vegetation, and its bright, silvery leaves that persist in winter make it easy to identify in photographs. Individuals are short-lived but produce abundant seed, which allows brittlebush to become established rapidly after favorable winter rains. Brittlebush is sensitive to frost and extreme summer drought.[5]

Frost sensitivity in any plant is described both by the lowest temperature and by the number of hours of below-freezing temperatures that the plant can withstand. For brittlebush, damage to leaves and the growing tips of stems has been recorded at 25°F with below-freezing temperatures lasting about eighteen hours; serious damage to stems was recorded at 18°F, and stems were killed to the ground at 17°F.[6] In these cases, which apparently did not result in the death of numerous brittlebush individuals, temperatures did not remain below freezing for more than a day. Ecologists have not determined how low temperatures need to get, or how long freezing temperatures must last, to kill brittlebush, but near President Harding Rapid (mile 43.8)—near the upstream limit of brittlebush—70 percent of the individuals on north-facing slopes were killed by temperatures perhaps as low as 9°F between December 1990 and January 1991.[7]

By contrast, in 1890 brittlebush was uncommon along the river corridor. Stanton first captured an image of this shrub at mile 55.8, or approximately twelve miles downstream of its current limit.[8] Only seventeen Stanton views clearly show brittlebush, and five of these are downstream of mile 200. Of the seventeen sites, eleven faced the relatively warm directions between southeast and southwest. Many views show individuals cradled between or next to large boulders, some of which are black or covered with dark desert varnish. These boulders apparently provided enough additional warmth in comparison to other nearby sites to minimize frost damage and allow survival. The favorable microclimate associated with the boulders provided a refuge from extreme cold.

During the repeat photography trips made between 1990 and 1993, brittlebush was present at 137 camera stations and was clearly visible in eighty-one of our replicate views. Although sixteen views show brittlebush in both 1890 and the 1990s, only one camera station had brittlebush visible in 1890 and not visible in 1990. None of the individuals visible in 1890

Figure 5.2. Dutton's Depot Grounds at Bass Rapid

A. John Wesley Powell and his geologist, Clarence Dutton, had warned Stanton that he would not find a level place in Grand Canyon to serve as a switching yard. With a touch of sarcasm, Stanton called the place where he would have built such a yard "Dutton's Depot Grounds." After the crew lined Bass Rapid (mile 107.8) and stopped for lunch just below, Stanton climbed up about three hundred feet above the river to make one last view (number 518) of his proposed switching yard. The foreground shows ten individuals of Mormon tea, a few spiny asters, and a prickly pear.

views was able to survive for a century, although in many cases new plants were growing in nearly the same sites. The probability that chance alone could cause brittlebush to appear rarely in 1890 yet commonly in the 1990s is extremely low.[9] Perhaps even more striking is the large increase in the density of brittlebush; at many of the camera stations, brittlebush was the most common shrub.

Because brittlebush was present near its current upstream limit in 1890, its distribution probably became established at some prehistoric time, perhaps thousands of years ago. Brittlebush seeds were found in a 1,300-year-old packrat midden collected from the Chuar Valley at about mile 65.[10] Extreme cold possibly reduced the abundance of brittlebush in the decades before 1890, but individuals that were growing

B. Ted Melis replicated this view on February 20, 1992. Unfortunately, the bright sunlight in 1992 caused considerably deeper shadows than those caused by the cloudy conditions in 1890. Only three of the individuals of Mormon tea died during the century; all were in the center of the 1890 view. In contrast, brittlebush, shown here with its silvery leaves and hemispheric shape, dominates the assemblage, with about ten brittlebush now present. The prickly pear died, and spiny aster no longer appears in the foreground.

in warmer microhabitats survived. No dead brittle-bush are visible in 1890 views, which suggests either recurrent freezing episodes or a single severe freeze long enough before 1890 to allow decomposition of the woody remains. In other words, the increase in brittlebush between 1890 and 1990 is not the result of a species invading a favorable habitat for the first time; instead, brittlebush was killed back by a higher frequency of severe frost before 1890. When freez-ing temperatures became less severe sometime after 1890, the population of brittlebush greatly increased.

A case in point is the valley where Stanton wanted to build his switching yard and depot, which he would have named Dutton's Depot. Between miles 107.5 and 108.5, the canyon widens; the relatively flat area to the right of the river, where Dutton's Depot would have been built, faces southwest. Stan-ton made eight views of the proposed depot site,

Figure 5.3. Barrel cactus at Bedrock Rapid

A. At the end of Middle Granite Gorge (mile 130), diabase, a distinctive intrusive rock that is greenish black in Grand Canyon, forms a prominent ledge on both sides of the Colorado River. Before running Bedrock Rapid on February 22, 1890, Stanton climbed through a notch in the diabase at 9:00 A.M. to photograph his railroad route, which would have passed through the center of this downstream view (number 574). Six individuals of barrel cactus are scattered through the view. No brittlebush is visible.

but only one shows brittlebush. In this view, the leaves of individual brittlebush barely overtop the dark gray boulders that surround them. All eight of the replicate views clearly show brittlebush, which now dominates the plant population on the proposed depot grounds.

Because of its brief life span, sensitivity to frost, and prolific but episodic reproduction,[11] brittlebush populations probably have fluctuated considerably during the past century. Unfortunately, little photo-

graphic evidence is available that might be used to document these fluctuations. In views made during the U.S. Geological Survey expedition of 1923, full-grown brittlebush commonly appear at densities comparable to those in the 1990s at sites downstream of mile 200. Therefore, brittlebush may have become reestablished in less than thirty-three years. This rate of reestablishment suggests that freezes severe enough to kill brittlebush had ceased sometime before 1923. The fact that the plants were full-

B. On February 17, 1991, Liz Hymans replicated Stanton's view below Bedrock Rapid at about 1:30 P.M. under cloudy skies. Barrel cactus has increased in this view; eighteen are visible in 1991. None of the cactus in the 1991 view is the same as in the 1890 view. Brittlebush is now common in the foreground and midground.

grown indicates a decrease in the incidence of killing frosts well before 1923.

Barrel Cactus

Barrel cactus[12] occurs in drier and rockier parts of the Sonoran and Mojave Deserts and in foothills of the western Mojave Desert. Near the northern limit of its distribution in southern Nevada and southwestern Utah, barrel cactus commonly occurs only on warmer, south-facing slopes, a pattern that reveals its sensitivity to frost.[13] In Grand Canyon, it is common along the Colorado River between about mile 110 and Lake Mead.[14] It was present in western Grand Canyon more than 10,000 years ago.[15]

Stanton was particularly taken with barrel cactus; some of his views are closeups for which he used captions like "nail-keg cactus." This slender, columnar cactus is easy to identify in historic and modern views. When backlit, the dense spines at its top form a distinctive halo-like arc. Because of its distinctive appearance, barrel cactus could be recognized as far as nine hundred feet away from the camera station.

Like most columnar cacti, barrel cactus blooms during the summer rainy season and produces large seeds in yellow, fleshy fruits. The seeds provide food for a variety of animals, particularly packrats, which are the most common agent for dispersing the black seeds. In prehistoric times, Native Americans possibly collected the fruits for food or other purposes, thereby accidentally spreading the seeds.[16] Most seedlings that survive are sheltered by nurse plants, which reduce the effect of summer heat on the young cactus.[17] The most common nurse plant, big galleta grass, also provides some protection against frost damage.

Although barrel cactus is less sensitive to cold than are other columnar cacti, its northerly limit is similarly determined by frost.[18] Damage to photosynthetic cells in the thick skin of the cacti occurs at 17°F. Plants can be cold hardened, or slightly desensitized to freezing weather, if moderately low temperatures occur before the onset of severe cold.[19] Cold hardening may allow plants to withstand temperatures as much as 2°F lower than they could otherwise tolerate.

Frost damage is minimized by the dense spines that cover the growing tip, which lowers the minimum temperature the plant can withstand as it grows taller.[20] In other words, adult plants can tolerate colder temperatures than juvenile or seedling plants. Adult plants are probably damaged but are not at risk of death during extreme freezes, whereas seedling and juvenile individuals are killed.[21] The species could also be limited by prolonged drought, particularly in summer.[22] However, its occurrence in the western Mojave Desert, where rainfall predominantly occurs in winter, suggests adult barrel cactus probably can tolerate all but the most severe droughts.

In 1890, barrel cactus first appears in a view around mile 120, about ten miles below its current upstream limit.[23] Like brittlebush, barrel cactus has a low density in 1890 views. Most of the individuals present in 1890 views are tall, indicating that either the cactus were not reproducing or the seedlings and juveniles had been killed. The sites with barrel cactus present in 1890 had no preferred direction, such as south, or other characteristic that would suggest a warmer microhabitat. This photographic evidence also suggests that only seedlings and juveniles were killed, whereas adults were relatively unaffected. No dead barrel cactus are visible, which suggests that the reduction of an existing population must have occurred sometime before 1890.

In the 1990s views, the increase in the density of barrel cactus is striking throughout its current range. In forty-seven views, only six from 1890 show more individuals than the 1990s views. Many of the individuals visible in 1990s views are juveniles, which indicates that the population has recently been reproducing. On average, 128 percent more individuals are visible in the 1990s views than in the 1890 views, an average of 7.9 more in each view.[24]

Like brittlebush, barrel cactus was well established in its current range by 1890. The most striking change since 1890 is the increase in density and the filling in of its range. Although barrel cactus commonly appears in photographs taken in 1923, the density in the 1923 views is not as high as in the 1990s views. This comparison indicates that barrel cactus has been much slower than brittlebush in reclaiming its lost habitat.

The difference between reestablishment by brittlebush and reestablishment by barrel cactus may be caused by the two species' contrasting life-history strategies. These species have vastly different mechanisms of seed dispersal: brittlebush seeds are dispersed by wind, whereas the larger seeds of barrel cactus require transport by animals. Conditions favorable for the germination of brittlebush probably occur more frequently than do those for barrel cactus.[25] Brittlebush is well adapted to the colonization of recently disturbed or otherwise vacant spots, whereas barrel cactus has a better chance of survival if it grows under a nurse plant. Brittlebush is fast-growing and can reproduce at an early age, whereas barrel cactus grows only about a third of an inch per year.[26]

Other Cacti

We recorded increases in the populations of twelve other species of cactus that are visible in the Stanton views. In almost all views, the number of all cacti increased over the last century; in many cases, the increase was very large. Perhaps the most striking change was the expansion of prickly pear cacti, which increased at almost every site where they were present in 1890.[27] Although most species of prickly pear can withstand severe frost as an adult, cold conditions deter germination and establishment of seedlings.[28]

A second species of barrel cactus—cottontop—grows in Grand Canyon between about miles 25 and 110. Cottontop was visible in only three Stanton views; all three sites were between miles 48 and 70, which is the warmest part of Grand Canyon in winter. In the 1990s views, this species appears in fifteen views and exhibits a sixfold increase in the number of visible individuals. Cottontop in the 1990s views was visible in sections of canyon that are wide and as a result receive more direct sunlight in winter.

The Climate of a Century

The number of brittlebush and barrel cactus dramatically increased in the 1990s views compared to the 1890 views. Both species occupied most of their current range in 1890; therefore, the increase in the number of individuals represents mostly a filling in of the range, not an expansion of the range as was the case with snakeweed. What caused this change? I hypothesize that some phenomenon, probably climatic, suppressed these species before Stanton took his photographs. After 1890, another change occurred that allowed these species to reoccupy and

fill in their prehistoric ranges. The suppression and then increase in brittlebush and barrel cactus in Grand Canyon can be explained by two possible causes: extreme cold and drought before 1890, and more equable conditions after.

Precursor Conditions

Unfortunately, no continuous, long-term weather records exist for Grand Canyon in the decades preceding Stanton's expedition.[29] Thus, data from other regions and anecdotal evidence are the only information available to reconstruct any general climatic change that may have affected the desert plants of Grand Canyon.

A climatic period known as the Little Ice Age, characterized by extremely cold winters (especially in Europe) and changes in precipitation, peaked between about A.D. 1550 and 1750.[30] In the southwestern United States, atypically wet conditions occurred between A.D. 1609 and 1623 and again between A.D. 1835 and 1849.[31] Unusually large floods occurred in this period, and lakes that are now dry filled.[32] The increased precipitation during the Little Ice Age caused change in desert plant assemblages in southern Nevada.[33] The Little Ice Age also had severe winter temperatures. Glaciers in the western United States made small advances,[34] and severe freezes affected tree growth in the western United States. A series of five severe freezes between A.D. 1805 and 1837 was unprecedented in four hundred years.[35] The Little Ice Age ended in the mid-1800s, after which average temperatures increased in the continental United States.[36]

However, rainfall in the late 1800s remained mostly above normal. Particularly in the 1880s, abnormally large winter storms caused floods on most of the rivers in the southwestern United States,[37] and the years 1883 to 1885, just before Stanton's expedition, were unusually wet. Normal conditions or slight drought punctuated these periods of flooding. The unusually high rainfall of the last half of the nineteenth century may be related to anomalously frequent and severe storms, particularly notable between 1878 and 1891, that were caused by a general warming of the Pacific Ocean, called El Niño.[38]

The winters were cold during this same period in the southwestern United States.[39] Severe, protracted cold weather and excessive snowfall crippled Utah's cattle industry in the winter of 1880.[40] The winter of 1886 claimed at least 35 percent of the herds of rangeland cattle on the Great Plains during intense and frequent blizzards.[41] In northern Nevada, half the cattle died in the abnormally cold and snowy winter of 1889–90.[42] Stanton recorded this cold weather succinctly in his diary; one terse reference states, "I am almost frozen."[43]

Winters in Grand Canyon during the decades before Stanton took his photographs thus appear to have been wetter and colder than they are now. The above-average rainfall, particularly in winter, should have promoted the germination and establishment of brittlebush; yet only isolated individuals appear in Stanton's views. The severe freezes that likely occurred during the late nineteenth century would explain the low numbers of brittlebush and barrel cactus in 1890.

Precipitation

The century since Stanton's expedition has had highly variable climate with several notable extremes, especially in precipitation (see figure 1 in the appendix). The most severe historic drought in Arizona occurred between 1896 and 1904,[44] or just after Stanton's expedition. The excessively wet period of 1906 to the early 1920s immediately followed the drought; this combination was unprecedented in the last thousand years.[45]

In Arizona, normal to below-normal precipitation characterized the middle part of the twentieth century, with the exception of the wet years 1939 to 1941. The intensity of summer precipitation declined on the Colorado Plateau, leading to a decrease in flood-

ing.[46] The drought between about 1955 and 1963 was nearly as severe as the 1896–1904 event in northern Arizona. After the early 1960s, changes in atmospheric circulation and El Niño conditions caused changes in the seasonality of precipitation and flooding in southern Arizona.[47] In northern Arizona, precipitation increased between about 1978 and 1985 in response to the atmospheric changes.

In the century between the Stanton views and replicates, two droughts occurred that are among the five most severe in the last thousand years; yet despite the sensitivity of brittlebush and barrel cactus to drought, the populations of both species have increased in Grand Canyon. The increased precipitation of the decades before the 1990s may have encouraged the germination and establishment of these species, but the more likely explanation, as discussed earlier, is the decreased frequency of frost.

Frost

Extreme cold in Arizona results from a highly specific set of atmospheric conditions.[48] Mild winters typically occur when winds move mostly west to east and air masses originating near the Arctic Circle cannot be transported far enough south to affect Arizona; cold winters typically occur when the pattern of winds becomes highly sinuous over North America and air movement is mostly from north to south. Under this type of flow, Arctic air masses can move into Arizona in a matter of days. Before 1930, the north-south flow of air dominated the atmospheric circulation over North America.[49]

Because Grand Canyon acts as a cold-air conduit during the winter months, temperatures in the bottom of the canyon can be extremely low. At Phantom Ranch, the lowest temperature in the past twenty years is –9°F, measured in January 1971;[50] however, typical winter lows vary between 20°F and 40°F. At Lees Ferry, by contrast, the lowest temperature is 3°F, recorded in 1963—and in January 1971, Lees Ferry experienced a low of 6°F, which suggests the below-zero temperature downstream at Phantom Ranch was localized or a measurement error.

Cold weather occurred in the century after Stanton's expedition, but not as frequently as before (see figure 2 in the appendix). Seven outbreaks of cold weather severe enough to damage agricultural crops in Arizona occurred between 1894 and 1905; the frequency of similarly severe periods of cold weather then decreased to about once a decade.[51] One freeze in 1937, which reached -11°F at St. George, Utah, killed the aboveground parts of most nearby mesquites and creosote bushes.[52] This was the most recent severe frost in the Grand Canyon region.

The Frozen River

One indication of a lessening in the severity of winters from the late 1800s to the mid-1900s is the decreasing frequency of the freezing of the Colorado River at Lees Ferry.[53] The most severe freeze occurred in 1878, when the river was frozen from bank to bank below the Paria River for more than two weeks.[54] During this period, a Mormon missionary party passed through the area and crossed the river on the ice. They reported that all water sources were frozen and that they had to melt snow to water their teams. On reaching the Colorado River, the missionaries unhitched their heavily laden wagons and pulled the wagons across on ice that was two feet thick.

On December 31, 1879, a party of Mormons headed for southern Arizona reached the north bank of the Colorado River at Lees Ferry.[55] The ferry was not operational. The Mormon travelers, uncertain what to do, decided to camp and pray for guidance. Their options were few, because Lees Ferry was a considerable distance from the nearest settlement to the north and little feed was available around the ferry site for their stock. They had little choice but to cross the river. When they awoke the next day, the river was frozen; ice floating in the river (and backed up above Paria Riffle) likely had coalesced overnight into a continuous sheet. The colonists quickly took advantage of the situation and moved their animals and wagons across the three hundred feet of ice. The following morning the ice broke up.

On at least two other occasions, the ice was thick enough to allow animals to cross the Colorado. In January 1866, Navajo raiders drove a flock of sheep stolen from the Mormon settlement of Kanab, Utah, across the frozen Colorado River at Crossing of the Fathers, about thirty miles upstream of Lees Ferry. In January 1925, a Navajo trading party rode ponies and drove pack mules over the ice at Lees Ferry.[56]

Hydrologists meticulously recorded when river ice affected the Lees Ferry gaging station between 1921 (the date of its inception) and 1963. Since 1963, water released from Glen Canyon Dam at a uniform 50°F has been too warm to freeze at Lees Ferry. Records from the gaging station indicate that although ice periodically affected the measurement of flow in the Colorado River, January 1925 was the last time before the closure of Glen Canyon Dam that the river was completely frozen (see figure 3 in the appendix).[57]

The Effects of Frosts

Changes in the desert vegetation of Grand Canyon might be regarded as local and insignificant, perhaps relevant only to that deep chasm. But the types of ecological changes observed in Grand Canyon could have occurred elsewhere in the Southwest as well. If Grand Canyon is a microcosm of the southwestern United States, damage to or the death of certain desert plants (particularly cacti and succulents) in the canyon during unusually cold episodes should reflect ecological changes that occur, unmeasured, outside the canyon as well. Little ecological evidence exists to verify or refute the presence of any regional effects that may have occurred.

Numerous Stanton views we replicated show the effects of frost episodes in Grand Canyon. As discussed earlier, brittlebush, which was scarce in 1890, now dominates the desert vegetation of much of the river corridor; likewise, 60 percent fewer barrel cactus are visible in the Stanton views than in the replicate views. In the 1890 views, desert vegetation appears relatively sparse, with open space visible among the individuals—which in many cases are Mormon tea or wolfberry. In the 1990s, most of the individuals appearing in the 1890 view are still present, but the open space has been filled with shrubs (mostly brittlebush) and cacti. Long-lived shrubs such as Mormon tea provide a framework for plant communities that is little affected by the climatic fluctuations of a century, whereas the open patches in the communities are periodically filled with and emptied of species that fluctuate considerably in response to climate. Disaster, then, is a relative word. Despite the fluctuations of species that are sensitive to climate, the assemblage as a whole is very stable when viewed from the perspective of a century or more.

CHAPTER 6

Floods, Dams, and Riparian Vegetation

Elzada Clover of the University of Michigan had an ambitious goal: she wanted to make a botanical survey of the canyons of the Colorado River. In 1937, she met the person who could make her dream possible. Norm Nevills operated a fledgling whitewater business on the San Juan River in southeastern Utah. He was attempting to develop a commercial river-running business on the Colorado River and offered Clover the perfect vehicle for her ambitious survey. In June 1938, Nevills launched his business at Green River, Utah, with his first run through Cataract, Glen, and Grand Canyons. Two of his passengers were Clover and her assistant Lois Jotter, who made plant lists and collected specimens. Clover and Jotter were the first women to run all of the whitewater of the Colorado River; they also were the first scientists to systematically record observations on the flora of the river corridor.[1]

One of the habitats that Clover and Jotter described was the "margin of moist sand" at the river's edge. In 1890, the "margin of moist sand" was barren. Likewise, in 1938, most of this zone was devoid of plants because they could not survive the scouring and inundation by periodic floods.[2] The plants Clover and Jotter did find were typically native riparian species except for one non-native tree called tamarisk, or saltcedar, which occurred at only a few sites in Grand Canyon.[3]

In the late 1960s, Dr. Paul S. Martin of the University of Arizona reexamined the "margin of moist sand." He was studying fossil dung from Shasta ground sloth preserved in Rampart Cave in western Grand Canyon and plant fossils preserved in Stantons Cave (mile 31.6). Seeking a detailed description of the present-day vegetation to facilitate his interpretations of past distributions, he decided to make a more complete collection of the plants of the river corridor.[4] During his collecting, he found that something had changed: the "margin of moist sand" was no longer barren. Formerly swept clean by the annual floods, the banks had been colonized aggressively by riparian plants in the few years since Glen Canyon Dam had become operational in 1963.

Martin found tamarisk "abundantly distributed" along the river corridor. Although alarmed at its "explosive spread" through Grand Canyon, he also noted its usefulness as shade for campers.[5] Tamarisk was not the only species whose distribution had increased along the river: coyote willow, Goodding willow, cottonwood, and several species of shrubs were aggressively colonizing the newly available substrate. By the late 1970s, tamarisk was distributed throughout the river corridor, in many places choking the once-barren channel banks.[6]

The photographs of Franklin Nims and Robert Brewster Stanton well document the conditions seen by Clover and Jotter, showing a stark river corridor largely devoid of trees and riparian plants. The few trees present—honey mesquite and catclaw—mostly lined the river at the level that would be reached by floods of about 100,000 cubic feet per second (cfs), or about the two- to five-year flood level before the closure of Glen Canyon Dam. This line of mesquite and catclaw is now called the "old high-water zone," which denotes its perceived relictual status. Clover and Jotter's "margin of moist sand" is now occupied by thickets of tamarisk, two species of willows,

arrowweed, and other native shrubs. This "new high-water zone"—where the number of breeding birds is five to ten times greater than before[7]—is a critical resource of the river corridor in Grand Canyon.[8] Moreover, the new high-water zone is one of the few major riparian areas in the southwestern United States that has had an increase in vegetation this century.[9]

The old and new high-water zones represent the most visible change in Grand Canyon during the past century. What in 1890 was barren sand is now critical wildlife habitat. What once was a zone of vegetation dependent on extra water from annual floods may now be threatened with slow death from drought. The construction of Glen Canyon Dam has obviously changed this part of the riverine environment. What is not so obvious is the course of changes in the past century and what the future might hold for the riparian species that occupy the old and new high-water zones.

Damming the Colorado River

Floods on the Colorado River begin high in the mountains of Utah, Colorado, and Wyoming. Snowpack in the Rocky Mountains, the principal source of runoff, typically is deeper than normal during years in which El Niño conditions develop. El Niño, "the child," is the name for unusual phenomena that occur about Christmastime in the ocean off Peru. The phenomena, which arise from unusually warm waters and changes in wind direction, have their roots in the equatorial Pacific Ocean from Peru to Indonesia.[10] Warm seawater in the eastern North Pacific Ocean provides abundant moisture for storms moving toward the southwestern United States. Recurring every three to five years, El Niño conditions can cause significant changes in flow through the atmosphere over the Northern Hemisphere, leading to usually severe weather conditions;[11] in fact, all the largest floods in Arizona have occurred during times of El Niño.[12]

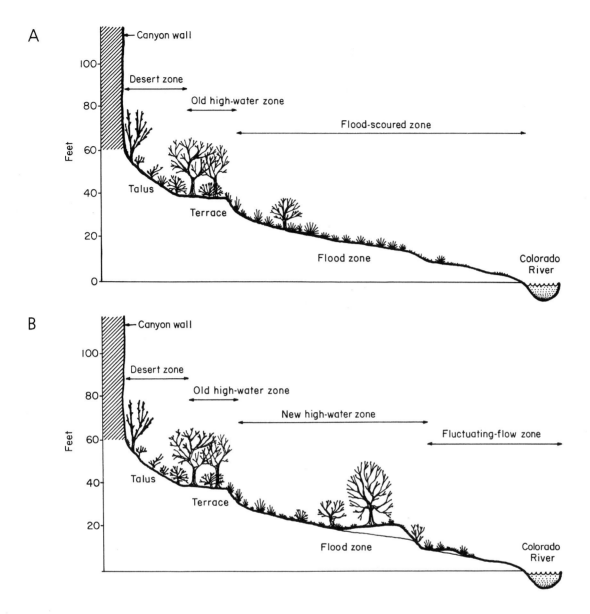

Figure 6.1. Relations between flow regulation in the Colorado River and the old and new high-water zones

A. Before the completion of Glen Canyon Dam, the old high-water zone lined the Colorado River at about the 10,000 cfs stage. This zone, which consists of plants that grow in drier settings in the southwestern United States, benefited from annual flooding. Plants received additional water in early summer, and inundation may have promoted seed germination. Below the old high-water zone, floods scoured the seedlings of perennial vegetation that attempted to become established. Stanton's views, which provide the most comprehensive information on conditions before the closure of the dam, show no perennial vegetation established below the old high-water zone. Modified from Johnson, "Historic Changes in Vegetation."

B. Flow regulation, particularly flood-control operations of Glen Canyon Dam, has allowed establishment of a new high-water zone and slow breakup of the old high-water line. Smaller floods and higher base flow in the river has created a more stable hydrologic environment that allows marshes and other wetlands. Conversely, the zone wetted by the river is lower, and plants in the old high-water zone do not receive as much water. Germination of mesquite in the old high-water zone is now infrequent. Modified from Johnson, "Historic Changes in Vegetation."

Observations have been made on flow in the Colorado River since the establishment of Lees Ferry in 1872. Reportedly, the largest flood in history occurred in 1884. Jerry Johnson, son of ferry operator Warren Johnson, rescued his cat from an apple tree that was surrounded by the floodwaters.[13] About a third of a century after the flood, the younger Johnson showed a surveyor from the U.S. Geological Survey the apple tree, and the surveyor estimated a stage for the 1884 flood.[14] The first discharge determined from the "cat-in-the-tree" evidence was 250,000 cfs, based on an extrapolation of the gaging station record at Lees Ferry; the estimate was increased to 300,000 cfs in the 1950s.[15] Other historic floods not included in the gaging record may have occurred in 1891, 1905, 1916, and 1917.

Systematic observation and measurement of discharge began at Lees Ferry in 1921 and near Phantom Ranch in 1923. Measurement began with the largest flood in the gaging record, which occurred on June 18, 1921. Estimated at 220,000 cfs, the 1921 flood was almost 100,000 cfs larger than the second-largest recorded flood, which peaked on July 1, 1927. Before completion of Glen Canyon Dam in 1963, the largest floods peaked between mid-May and early July; the flood of September 1923, which peaked at 112,000 cfs, is the only known annual peak in Grand Canyon before the construction of the dam that did not result from snowmelt (see figures 4 and 5 in the appendix).[16]

Most of the largest floods on the Colorado River occurred during El Niño years, including 1884, 1891, 1905, 1917, 1941, and 1957. The most severe El Niño storm of the twentieth century caused the large inflow to Lake Powell in 1983. However, floods also occurred during years without El Niño conditions, including 1921, 1927, 1952, and 1984. Although El Niño provides a compelling explanation for some high-runoff years, it does not explain all floods. El Niño

conditions increase the probability that large floods will occur on the Colorado River, but they are certainly not a necessary condition for floods.

Floods that passed through Grand Canyon, while beneficial to the old high-water zone, had devastating effects on settlements along the lower Colorado River. The call for flood control on the Colorado River began in earnest in 1905: the floods of 1904–1905 remain among the largest on record in the Southwest. Before being controlled by dams, the Colorado River downstream of Yuma was fickle in where it ran: although in most years, flow rushed southward to the Gulf of California, in other years, the river broke through its natural levees and rushed west and north into the California desert.[17]

Before 1905, humans inadvertently aided the Colorado in its long-standing attempt to maintain an inland sea in southern California. Potential farmland surrounded the Salton Sink, which was a small, salty lake; all that was required was irrigation water. Investors attained funding to divert water from the Colorado River into the natural depression. Agriculture began to thrive because of the long irrigation ditch. But years of drought had lulled the irrigators into complacency, and the flood of 1905 cut through the headgates of the canal with a vengeance. The Colorado River abandoned its delta and began to drain into the Imperial Valley, creating the Salton Sea and causing millions of dollars in damage to the fledgling agricultural industry.[18]

The U.S. Reclamation Service, which became the Bureau of Reclamation, decided that a comprehensive plan of dams for flood control and water supply was required on the Colorado River.[19] Such an expensive plan would necessarily involve the federal government, the states that would benefit from water development, and private utilities that saw the potential for generating hydroelectric power. The location of the first dam was predetermined.[20] The big economic interests, which wielded the greatest political power, were in southern California; the first dam would be built where irrigation water and hydroelectric power could be easily transported to southern California. The bill authorizing the Boulder Canyon Project near the tiny desert town of Las Vegas, Nevada, became law on December 14, 1928.

The construction of the 726-foot-high dam near Las Vegas is one of the greatest engineering feats of the twentieth century.[21] Boulder Dam, renamed Hoover Dam, was actually built in Black Canyon because the bedrock under its foundation was more favorable there than in Boulder Canyon. When the gates of Hoover Dam closed on February 1, 1935, the dam created a lake that at the time was the world's largest. Lake Mead extended into western Grand Canyon, flooding the last forty miles of river corridor. The still waters caught the awesome sediment load of the Colorado River, forming an extensive delta that stretched upriver beyond the Grand Wash Cliffs. With the addition of each ton of sediment from the Colorado River, the capacity of Lake Mead decreased.

Hoover Dam and Lake Mead were just the beginning of water projects on the Colorado River. By the early 1950s, small dams were built downstream of Hoover Dam to enable the transfer of water to California and to supply water to irrigation projects on both sides of the river. The massive water project in the Upper Basin, called the Colorado River Storage Project, was bitterly debated. The project, authorized on April 11, 1956, contained plans for numerous dams, including Flaming Gorge on the Green River, Navajo on the San Juan River, and Curecanti on the Gunnison River. It also authorized Glen Canyon Dam, to be built a mere fifteen miles upstream of the beginning of Marble Canyon.

Construction of Glen Canyon Dam took seven years, and the dam cost nearly $300 million.[22] At a height of 710 feet, the dam impounds Lake Powell, the world's longest lake. When the gates of Glen Canyon Dam were closed on March 13, 1963, the Colorado River was changed forever. The millions of tons of sediment that once coursed through the canyons and into Lake Mead were instead caught in Lake Powell. Glen Canyon Dam releases a long-term average of 8.2 million acre-feet of water per year; the dam's turbines generate power for much of the southwestern United States. The Bureau of Reclamation attempts to release water only through the dam's power plant, which has a maximum capacity of about 31,500 cfs. The releases fluctuated each twenty-four hours within a range of 3,000 to 31,500 cfs. The change from free-flowing river to measured releases profoundly changed the riparian vegetation in Grand Canyon.

The Old High-Water Zone

The old high-water zone consists of several distinct assemblages of plants. In the narrow gorges upstream of mile 40, the old high-water zone typically is indistinct and native trees are uncommon. Netleaf hackberry is abundant near Lees Ferry, and live oak occurs only upstream of Lees Ferry. Upstream of mile 40, redbud and juniper are rare; the most common species is Apache plume, a shrub. Downstream of mile 40, catclaw is the most common tree of the old high-water zone; in the narrow, steep Inner Gorge, where the zone is indistinct, catclaw typically is the only species. Reaches consisting mostly of catclaw are the most common in Grand Canyon. Between miles 40 to 77 and miles 167 to 225, mesquite joins catclaw to form another conspicuous assemblage of the old high-water zone.

These assemblages thrived under the annual hydrologic cycle of the unregulated Colorado River. The annual flood was greater than 50,000 cfs in

Figure 6.2. Glen Canyon Dam

A. For Stanton's crew, the objective on the morning of December 23, 1889, was not just to survey a railroad route but to reach Lees Ferry for Christmas. They had camped the previous night only a short distance above the current site of Glen Canyon Dam. At 8:30 A.M., Stanton stopped in a right-hand bend 14.7 miles upstream of Lees Ferry. While others surveyed the route, Nims captured this upstream view under cloudy skies (number 235).

80 percent of the years; in one-third of the years, the flood exceeded 100,000 cfs. High water lasted for weeks, allowing banks to become saturated. Plants could not establish low on the channel banks because floodwater would scour them away; those plants high on the slopes benefited too infrequently from the additional water. Along the old high-water zone, the seasonally plentiful water supply created an environment where trees and shrubs that ordinarily would be dispersed in desert settings crowded together in thickets.

Glen Canyon Dam radically altered the hydrologic regimen of the Colorado River.[23] Since the regulation of flow began, the Colorado River below the dam has not exceeded 100,000 cfs and exceeds 50,000 cfs less than 1 percent of the time (see figure 6 in the appendix).[24] Saturated substrate now occurs twenty to fifty feet below the old high-water zone. Despite long taproots, plants stranded on the old high-water zone cannot easily reach this saturated soil. The reduction in the availability of water is the major impetus for change in the old high-water line since 1963. Changes

B. In October 1956, the blasting began on the walls of Navajo Sandstone at this once obscure spot. In 1963, Glen Canyon Dam was completed and Lake Powell began to fill. At this point, about one-half mile downstream, a new horizonal stripe on the wall was created by seepage from the reservoir. The small sand bars that lined the banks of the Colorado River in 1889 have eroded away, although a large sand bar is present directly across the river from the camera station. Robert Webb photographed this view on October 29, 1992, at 10:39 A.M.

in the distribution of the species that populate the old high-water zone reveal the consequences of flow regulation.

Apache Plume

Apache plume typically occurs 3,000 feet higher than the elevation of Lees Ferry.[25] This shrub is not always riparian, but before the closure of Glen Canyon Dam, Apache plume thrived in the old high-water zone upstream of mile 40 and occurred only occasionally in the desert vegetation above. Such a

species is called a facultative riparian species because it benefits from but does not require a riparian setting. Apache plume propagates via seeds and sprouts arising from its roots; most of the plants in the old high-water zone are interconnected, making definition of individuals impossible.

Apache plume is visible in eleven views between Lees Ferry and mile 27. One view of desert vegetation at mile 30 shows two individuals of Apache plume, isolated from Colorado River water by bedrock, that had survived the century. The density of Apache

Figure 6.3. Apache plume in the Roaring Twenties

A. The Stanton expedition had trouble passing through the Roaring Twenties, a reach of frequent rapids between miles 20 and 27. Because of the drownings the previous summer, the crew lined and portaged most of the rapids in this reach. While a lining was underway around the rapid at mile 23.3, Stanton made this upstream view (number 301) on January 7, 1890, at 11:30 A.M. Apache plume forms the old high-water zone here.

plume decreases in six views, increases in one view, and remains about the same in four views. Although this part of the old high-water zone appears to be relictual, Apache plume is not likely to disappear soon. As the two individuals at mile 30 show, Apache plume can survive without supplemental water.

Mesquite

Although mesquite grows in dry sites throughout most of the southwestern United States, mesquite in Grand Canyon is a facultative riparian species. Few desert sites along the river corridor have significant amounts of mesquite; the notable exceptions are in

Furnace Flats (miles 65 to 72) and at the mouth of Nankoweap Creek (mile 52). In Furnace Flats, wind-blown sand is deposited in mounds around the bases of individual trees, rendering the false appearance of an interconnected system of plants. Even in these seemingly dry settings, the extremely long taproots of this species may connect these mesquites to the shallow water table fed by the Colorado River.

In comparing the fifty-eight original and replicate views in which mesquite could be positively identified, I did not find an unequivocal decrease in the density of mesquite over the past century as I had anticipated from the reported effects of Glen Can-

B. Apache plume has decreased in more replicate views than it has remained the same or increased. It has decreased in this view for two reasons: a debris flow from the unnamed canyon at right has destroyed many plants, and operation of Glen Canyon Dam has reduced the amount of water available for remaining vegetation. The future of this type of old high-water zone may well be illustrated in this view; the prominent line of Apache plume may decay into scattered individual plants to limit competition for water. In addition to persistent individuals of Apache plume, three individuals of Mormon tea and three of wolfberry around the rock at right center have survived the past century. The sand bar at left center has increased in size. Ted Melis replicated this view on November 16, 1990, at 3:33 P.M.

yon Dam. Comparison of the 1890 and 1990s views indicates that 51 percent of the views show an increase in the density of mesquite, 21 percent appear to be about the same, and 28 percent show a decrease. Surprisingly, 10 percent of the views show an increase in density but a decrease in the canopy size of individual mesquite trees.[26] The size decrease likely is the result of drought pruning brought on by the operation of Glen Canyon Dam, rather than true meteorologic drought.

These unexpected findings could have two interrelated causes. First, mesquite is sensitive to frost:[27] individuals may either die or have most of their aboveground biomass killed during extreme freezes.[28] Possibly less severe freezes, which allowed an expansion of brittlebush and cacti in desert settings after 1890, may also have created an environment favorable for the establishment of additional mesquite in the old high-water zone. Second, unusually high runoff in the Colorado River occurred between about 1906 and 1930.[29] More frequent wetting of the old high-water zone may have spurred additional ger-

Figure 6.4. Mesquite in lower Marble Canyon

A. After camping within sight of the mouth of the Little Colorado River, which was an expedition milestone, the Stanton expedition eagerly started downstream on the morning of January 20, 1890. Photographs took priority over milestones, however, and Stanton stopped on the left bank at mile 59.0 to make this downstream view (number 368) at 9:30 A.M. Stanton's image includes an apparently healthy mesquite thicket in the right foreground and several scattered mesquite trees in the center.

mination of mesquite. In both scenarios, individuals would have died back once floods no longer irrigated their roots.

Mesquite is not likely to die out soon. Individual plants may receive sufficient rainfall to survive, and in any case, rainwater would supplement the groundwater that individual plants probably attain through extremely long taproots. The predominant effect of Glen Canyon Dam may be to decrease or even eliminate the establishment of seedlings.[30] Without recruitment of new individuals, which is extremely slow in the desert setting of the old high-water zone, mesquite may be sentenced to a slow extirpation, not because of drought but because old individuals will die and not be replaced.

The plant assemblages of the old high-water zone may eventually become more typical of the desert than of the river corridor. As old individuals die, the once-dense thickets will thin in the face of decreased water supply, thus providing openings that may allow limited recruitment of nonriparian species. Before flow regulation, mesquites functioned as

B. At mile 59, mesquite trees show the obvious effects of decreased water availability over the past century. Trees that were obviously larger in the past are still alive but have died back. Less obvious is the increase in the density of mesquite, which occurred at some time during the past century before the closure of Glen Canyon Dam. Individuals of Mormon tea (fifteen), catclaw (one), and beavertail cactus (two) persist throughout the left side of the view; in addition, several brittlebush appear at left center. The prominent sand bar in the midground has changed shape but is about the same volume. Robert Webb replicated this view on January 5, 1992, at 11:17 A.M.

quasi-riparian trees; existing plants must now adapt to their newly arid environment. Instead of emphasizing growth and reproduction in a water-rich environment, these trees must reserve their limited resources just to stay alive. Part of this adaptation is drought pruning of extraneous branches, which is amply documented in replicate Stanton views.

Catclaw

Of the three most common trees and shrubs in the old high-water zone, catclaw is the least affected by Glen Canyon Dam. Catclaw thrives in the desert vegetation of the river corridor and is fully capable of surviving without supplementary floodwater. Like mesquite, catclaw grows in dense thickets that make the interpretation of longevity of individuals difficult. In observations of about 360 individuals in dry sites, however, the density of catclaw has increased 17 percent since 1890. Because of catclaw's ability to thrive in the desert, this tree has not suffered from regulation of the Colorado River.

Indeed, unlike mesquite, catclaw in the old high-

Figure 6.5. Mesquite at Awatubi Canyon

A. Stanton and his crew rowed through "a beautiful bay of still water" before reaching the mouth of Awatubi Canyon (mile 58.1). After landing on the right and climbing up a sand dune, Stanton made this upstream view (number 365) on January 20, 1890, at about 9:15 A.M.

water zone may become increasingly common.[31] Reduction of mesquite may provide openings for the establishment of catclaw. Although catclaw may come to dominate the old high-water zone, the vegetation pattern in the zone will probably be reduced from a dense thicket to scattered individuals as regulation of floods continues.

The New High-Water Zone

The "margin of moist sand" no longer has the characteristics it had before construction of Glen Can-

yon Dam. Operation of the dam limits the inundation of channel banks to stages between 30,000 and 100,000 cfs. Moreover, large releases have scoured away most of the silt-rich deposits that had built up in the canyon before the dam's construction; the amount of sand along the river corridor has been greatly reduced. Newly deposited sand, where it occurs, is well sorted and coarser grained than the sediments that once were deposited by the river. The new deposits have fewer nutrients and a lower capacity to retain water; consequently, fewer seedlings can become established.[32] The once-barren channel

B. A mesquite thicket, prominent in the right foreground of this view, has decreased in density in the past century. Dead treetops at right center show this decrease vividly; once-tall trees have died back for the lack of the extra water that had once been provided by the unregulated Colorado River. The camera station is difficult to reoccupy; the dune Stanton stood on has increased in height. Nonetheless, abundant unchanged rocks in the left midground allow interpretation of changes in some desert plants. Five individuals of Mormon tea persist on the slope at left, and several clumps of Mojave prickly pear appear to be in the same places a century later. Liz Hymans replicated this view on February 5, 1991, at 11:11 A.M.

banks range from saturated deposits of silt and clay, to relatively dry and well-sorted bar sand, to boulders and bedrock.

The different substrates of the river corridor create disparate assemblages of native and non-native trees, shrubs, grasses, and forbs in a variety of habitats. The presence of these plants depends on the regulation of flow in the Colorado River; the existence of the new high-water zone is completely controlled by humans. Benefits accrue from these species, native and non-native alike, because they provide food and habitat for wildlife.[33]

Initially, plant colonization must have been a contest among seeds. The competitors would have come by air and water. Seeds had long rained onto this barren strip, but the spring floods used to wash away the seedlings and kill any adults that had gained a roothold. With regulation of the annual floods, individual plants quickly became established; a race began that would determine which species, or groups of species, would survive. But the species in the race for colonization had different starting points; the seeds did not come from plants along the Colorado River.

The Stanton photographs show no perennial riparian vegetation below the old high-water zone. A few views show native species in the old high-water zone that occupy the once-barren banks. Most of these species require the extra water provided by the river: they are obligate riparian species. The native species so abundant along the river corridor today, including arrowweed, coyote willow, and seep willow, were abundant in the tributary canyons. Stands of these plants along the perennial streams (such as Bright Angel, Shinumo, Tapeats, and Deer Creeks) were probably the source of seeds for the plants that colonized the new high-water zone. Seeds from mesquite and catclaw, which have colonized parts of the new high-water line, came from the nearby old high-water zone.

Either accidentally or purposefully, settlers introduced the non-native species into the southwestern United States during the past century. Many of these species were expanding their ranges at the time of the closure of Glen Canyon Dam. Wind or floodwaters transported the seeds of these "invader" species into Grand Canyon, where they spread—slowly at first and then much faster after the dam was built.

One invasive non-native species is camelthorn. A particularly despicable weed native to Asia, camelthorn entered California accidentally in contaminated alfalfa seed sometime before the 1930s. It appeared in Arizona along the Gila and Little Colorado Rivers in the mid-1930s.[34] Seeds or rhizomes swept down the Little Colorado River to the Colorado River in Grand Canyon, where camelthorn was first reported in 1970.[35] The species prefers loose sand and spreads via seeds or rhizomes; the spiny plants, which are a nuisance on camping beaches, are now widespread below the mouth of the Little Colorado River.

The invasion of Bermuda grass is an example of humans introducing a species purposefully, only to have it spread accidentally. The Office of Indian Af-

fairs provided Bermuda grass seed to the Havasupai in Havasu Canyon in the early 1900s; two sacks of those seeds were washed down Havasu Creek in the flood of 1910.[36] In 1938, Bermuda grass was abundant from the village of Supai in Havasu Canyon down to the Colorado River, was common at Separation Rapid (mile 239, at the head of Lake Mead), and was common along Bright Angel Creek near where it had been planted at Phantom Ranch.[37] Now, Bermuda grass is abundant from the mouth of Havasu Canyon downstream to Lake Mead, and other patches occur just downstream of Phantom Ranch.[38]

Tamarisk

Tamarisk has become naturalized along all the major rivers in the Southwest, reproducing prolifically and establishing dense stands. Considered a problem species by those who irrigate or manage water supplies, tamarisk also poses a problem for botanists; several species, all quite difficult to distinguish, were introduced into the Southwest, and only one is invasive.[39]

Tamarisk, also known as saltcedar, was introduced into the United States from Eurasia in the early 1800s.[40] It arrived in California in the mid-1850s; the best evidence indicates that it escaped from cultivation in the 1870s.[41] George Adair, pioneer of the short-lived town of Adairville, Utah, on the Paria River, reportedly planted tamarisk around his house in 1870. A botanist first collected tamarisk from the region at Kanab, Utah, in 1909. A 1925 flora of Utah noted that tamarisk grew along the Virgin River.[42] It expanded rapidly throughout the western United States in the 1920s and 1930s.[43] A lover of water, especially saline water, tamarisk rapidly became established in dense thickets adjacent to irrigation canals, in and around reservoirs, and along stream channels, particularly those downstream of dams.

Despite its presence in the region, and despite its fecundity, tamarisk did not immediately overwhelm Grand Canyon. The first documented tamarisk along the Colorado River was at the mouth of the San Juan River in southern Utah, where it was observed in biological surveys between 1933 and 1938.[44] By 1936, tamarisk grew along the river between Nankoweap Creek and Tanner Rapid (miles 52 to 69) and was present near the mouth of Bright Angel Creek (mile 87).[45] The patchy distribution of tamarisk in the 1930s and its presence at the mouths of major tributaries suggest that its seed came down major tributaries, not up the river corridor from the lower end of the river as has been reported.[46]

Along the untamed Colorado River, the annual floods limited the establishment of tamarisk. Tamarisk typically grows behind obstructions that provide protection from the full force of floods.[47] In the whitewater reaches of Cataract Canyon, for example, tamarisk is found largely in backwater areas where flow velocities are low.[48] When the frequency of floods decreases, the probability that tamarisk will survive increases.

In Grand Canyon, the density and distribution of tamarisk increased abruptly after 1963. Tamarisk colonized the new high-water zone before most other species. It was abundant by 1970; by 1977, it occurred throughout the river corridor with few significant gaps.[49] Releases from Glen Canyon Dam greater than 31,500 cfs provided ideal conditions for the establishment of tamarisk, which germinates rapidly in the wet sand left after a flood subsides.[50] The lack of additional flooding allowed seedlings to mature into trees. The rate of the invasion slowed as the new high-water zone filled with plants.[51] The flood of 1983 destroyed large numbers of tamarisk;[52] continued high water in the mid-1980s kept it from reestablishing, at least temporarily.[53]

The life-history strategy of tamarisk explains a great deal of its invasiveness and ability to dominate riparian zones. A mature tamarisk can produce more than a billion seeds per year.[54] Tamarisk reportedly can withstand inundation for as long as seventy days,[55] although many individuals were killed by extended inundation along the Colorado River between 1983 and 1986.[56] Tamarisk trees have long, downward-branching taproots that extend into the saturated zone.[57] Tamarisk does not compete strongly with other, more shallow-rooted species. Because of its deep, isolated roots and preference for sandy substrates,[58] it may be more vulnerable to being ripped from the ground by floodwaters than are species like Apache plume that have interconnected root systems.

To measure the abundance of tamarisk, we examined each replicate photograph. Tamarisk is visible in 71 percent of the 1990s views of the river corridor, but its distribution is uneven. Reaches without tamarisk in replicate views typically have little sandy substrate.[59] In most cases, vertical walls, bouldery banks, or solid bedrock limit the establishment of tamarisk. Most of the reaches without tamarisk also appear to have high-velocity currents near the shoreline.

Other species have become established in tamarisk stands and may eventually replace it. Coyote willow does not compete directly with tamarisk, but the interrelation between the two species may result in increased numbers of native willow and decreased numbers of tamarisk.[60] Because of dense shade and large amounts of leaf accumulations under tamarisk trees, seedling establishment is decreased within mature stands. These trees produce resins and other chemicals that decrease infiltration and the water-holding capacities of soils under tamarisk. These changes may limit the reproduction of tamarisk, but coyote willow, which rarely produces seedlings in Grand Canyon, may benefit. Coyote willow, which reproduces vegetatively, is shade tolerant and can become established under mature tamarisk trees. As old tamarisk trees die, they may be replaced by this native willow.[61]

Marshes

Visitors to the bottom of Grand Canyon frequently are delighted with the large population of birds

Figure 6.6. Tamarisk and sand bars at Salt Creek

A. Stanton, faced with passage around Horn Creek Rapid, purposefully allowed one of his boats to drift into the rapid without oarsmen. The *Marie* was smashed to pieces against a rock near the bottom of the rapid. The eleven men of the expedition crowded into the remaining two boats, and the stop for photographs at Salt Creek (mile 92.5) was no doubt welcome. Stanton made this upstream view (number 460) on February 7, 1890, at 11:30 A.M.

and other wildlife. This abundance of wildlife is due partly to the presence of marshes, which occur mostly in wide sections of canyon where large eddies have formed. Wildlife tends to be concentrated in these wide reaches. The seemingly impenetrable vegetation of marshes forms a protective cover for many species of nesting birds and other animals,[62] some of which are not native to Grand Canyon. Native species, such as beaver, have prospered in the dam-controlled river, largely because the new high-water zone provides more food.

Before Glen Canyon Dam, marshes were well developed in spring-fed areas above the old high-water zone. Examples of small, marshy areas shown in the Stanton views include Vaseys Paradise, the springs at Deer Creek Falls, and the marsh around the warm springs at the base of Lava Falls Rapid. These marshes are still present and look very much like they did in 1890. However, other marshes have since developed.

Marshes that are now present below the old high-water zone owe their existence entirely to Glen Can-

B. Tamarisk is now the most common riparian plant in Grand Canyon. Its colonization of Grand Canyon accelerated after the closure of Glen Canyon Dam. Tamarisk is beneficial to sand bars; as is apparent at left, tamarisk traps sand that might otherwise be washed downstream during periodic high releases. It also provides shade against the relentless summer sun. As the original view at Salt Creek shows, tamarisk was not present in Grand Canyon in 1890. Glenn Rink replicated this view on January 29, 1990, at 11:35 A.M.

yon Dam. Before regulation, flow in the Colorado River varied too much to allow the establishment of marshes with perennial vegetation. Before the closure of Glen Canyon Dam, the base flow of the Colorado River was much lower and more variable, which meant that obligate riparian species could not depend on sufficient water in all seasons of the year. Floods once tore through areas that now support marshes, scouring sediment and ripping out any vegetation that might have become established in the short interval between floods. Moreover, these

areas were inundated for long periods during late spring and early summer, when many marsh plants would germinate.

Marsh plants need abundant water around their roots but cannot withstand scouring or lengthy inundation of their canopies. The 1983 flood, which peaked at 96,200 cfs,[63] caused widespread damage to or even killed plants in the new high-water zone. Half of the riparian plants below the 50,000 cfs stage were killed by drowning, burial, or erosion during this flood,[64] which was small compared to those be-

Figure 6.7. The marsh at Cardenas Creek

A. Late on the afternoon of January 23, 1890, Stanton and his crew noticed a structure on the top of a promontory hill above Cardenas Creek (mile 71). Stanton took this upstream view (number 396) at 3:00 P.M. during the climb to what is now called Cardenas Hilltop Ruin. Except for scattered mesquite and what appear to be clumps of willows, little riparian vegetation is present along the Colorado River.

fore the closure of the dam and contained only a fraction of the sediment load that the unregulated river once carried. Despite the damage, seedlings became established within several years of the cessation of the high releases from the dam.[65] These seedlings would have been eliminated quickly on an unregulated Colorado River.

Marshes require hydrologic stability:[66] they develop where changes in river stages are minimal and flow velocities are low. Dense vegetation slows flow velocities even further, and sediment is deposited around the plants. The trapped sediment supports even more vegetation. Yet hydrologic stability in a riverine environment does not mean a lack of variation in discharge rates or the absence of erosive flows. Occasionally, marshes need scouring flows to open the waterways, which become clogged with sediment. In the era of flow regulation, this scouring occurs during the highest of the daily fluctuating flows.

Plants in marshes are adapted to flood-prone environments and have some ability to withstand the

B. Marshes, prime riparian habitat in Grand Canyon and elsewhere, provide habitat for native fishes and wildlife, particularly birds. Young native fish use the backwaters as protection from predators, and birds frequently nest in the dense vegetation. The marsh at Cardenas Creek, for example, is nesting habitat for southwestern willow flycatchers, an endangered species. But marshes were not present in 1890; they exist solely because of the flood control by Glen Canyon Dam. Most of the increased riparian vegetation in the view is tamarisk, although willow, arrowweed, and other native species also have increased. In the desert vegetation of the foreground, five individuals of Mormon tea, seven of wolfberry, and three big galleta grass persist. Tom Wise replicated this view on February 26, 1993, at 10:06 A.M.

force of water. For example, arrowweed has numerous interconnected lateral roots that spread out above the water table.[67] This root system binds the soil and makes the removal of plants during small floods difficult, like pulling up a blanket of sod. During a large flood, however, the substrate of marshes typically is saturated, and even these extensive root systems do not have enough strength to resist being torn out.

Other Species in the New High-Water Zone

Many predominantly rocky parts of the new high-water zone have been colonized by trees and shrubs that are, at best, facultative riparian species. Long-leaf brickellbush is commonly found upstream of mile 180 in the new high-water zone. This species now dominates many boulder-covered parts of the channel upstream of mile 170,[68] but it is not visible

Figure 6.8. New desert vegetation at 217 Mile Rapid

A. While his crew scouted 217 Mile Rapid, Stanton walked to a high sand terrace to expose this upstream view (number 654) on March 1, 1890, at 1:27 P.M. His camera station is very close to the highest flood level on the modern Colorado River, as indicated by the driftwood at right.

below the old high-water zone in any 1890 views. Clover and Jotter noted long-leaf brickellbush only at Vaseys Paradise (mile 32) and in Conquistador Aisle (miles 120 to 125); it was not mentioned in general descriptions of plants of the riparian zone.[69]

This shrub commonly lines the channel margins and grows on terraces of tributary canyons. Long-leaf brickellbush is well adapted to floods of short duration, like the ones that occur almost every year in side canyons, but is very susceptible to drowning in prolonged dam releases.[70]

In some reaches, elements of the old high-water zone are slowly encroaching on the new high-water zone. Mesquite seeds do not readily germinate in the old high-water zone, but they have germinated in parts of the new high-water zone, leading to the establishment of young plants there.[71] Catclaw is expanding more slowly into this newly available habitat. As the old high-water line degenerates, a new line of mesquite and catclaw may eventually become established downslope. Given the slow establishment and growth rates of these trees, their ma-

B. Desert vegetation dominates this once-barren terrace. The most conspicuous plant is buckhorn cholla. The sandy surface is blackened by cryptobiotic crust, mostly likely cyanobacteria, which commonly colonizes barren surfaces in preparation for the ascendancy of algae, fungi, and lichens. New desert assemblages and cryptobiotic soils also colonize the new high-water zone throughout Grand Canyon. Out of the view to the right is a pile of driftwood that represents the highest flood in the past century. This driftwood, which includes railroad ties, is at a higher elevation than the driftwood shown in Stanton's view, which probably was deposited in the 1884 flood. Jim Hasbargen replicated this view on February 26, 1991, at 2:41 P.M.

turation in the new high-water zone will require decades if not centuries.

New Desert Vegetation

Desert vegetation has invaded the drier parts of the new high-water zone, particularly in western Grand Canyon. In wide reaches, the area formerly inundated during the annual flood included debris fans and talus cones that had only small amounts of fine-grained substrate. In narrow parts of the Inner Gorge, sheets of bedrock that formerly were barren now provide at least scant habitat for plants. Bedrock and coarse-grained substrate limit the storage of groundwater, so these sites are dry despite their occurrence below the old high-water line. These parts of the new high-water zone actually represent a downslope encroachment of desert vegetation on the river corridor.

Common species in the new desert vegetation include desert broom, snakeweed, various species

Figure 6.9. The new high-water zone below Three Springs Canyon

A. Although Stanton was determined to make it to Diamond Creek on March 1, 1890, photography took precedence over his desire to reach civilization. Stanton stopped on river right at mile 216.5 to make this upstream view (number 652) at noon.

of cacti, and Mormon tea. Grasses and herbaceous perennials constitute much of the vegetation cover in this zone. Because desert vegetation becomes established much more slowly than riparian vegetation, colonization of these parts of the new high-water zone may require decades to centuries.

Desert broom is not an obligate riparian species throughout its range,[72] but it requires extra water in Grand Canyon. After the closure of Glen Canyon Dam, desert broom in the old high-water zone appeared to become water stressed.[73] In Stanton views, desert broom is uncommon in the old high-water zone and is present in the old high-water

zone between miles 166 and 213; in replicate views, the species is absent from the old high-water zone. Desert broom has, however, invaded the new high-water zone, particularly in wide reaches. Of the species in the new high-water zone, it has one of the lowest tolerances of flooding.[74]

A Dilemma for Environmental Management

The river corridor that Stanton saw and photographed was desolate in comparison to the verdant channel banks of today. Now, most river runners hardly notice the old high-water zone; their view is

B. In the lower Grand Canyon, desert broom and other species commonly occupy the new high-water zone. At this site, the upper end of a now heavily used camping beach, desert broom and sweet bebbia are the dominants. These species do not require a riparian habitat but will thrive in one. Jane Bernard replicated this view on February 26, 1991, at 11:13 A.M.

blocked by the lush riparian vegetation that grows lower on the banks. Operation of Glen Canyon Dam has increased the amount of riparian habitat in Grand Canyon. The channel banks are now biologically productive and are a more attractive place for recreationists.

Where does one draw the line between welcome and unwelcome change in a national park? Of all the changes during the past century, perhaps none is more disturbing to the aesthetic of wilderness and preservation of natural environments than the new high-water zone in Grand Canyon. It is not the

zone itself that constitutes the dilemma—it is tamarisk, the most common occupant of the new high-water zone. Tamarisk is a non-native invader of the national park, as are camelthorn and Bermuda grass.

Yet instead of being universally reviled, non-native plants in this setting are appreciated by many biologists and river runners. Some biologists like tamarisk because it creates wildlife habitat. Some river runners say that because tamarisk and Bermuda grass bind loose sand, they should be planted on the edges of camping beaches to reduce erosion.[75] Wetland habitat is dwindling so in the Southwest

Managing the New Riparian Zone for Its Naturalized Values

BRYAN T. BROWN

My first raft trip down the Colorado River through Grand Canyon, in 1976, was an eye-opener. I was simultaneously inspired and overwhelmed by every aspect of the journey, an experience that profoundly changed my view of the natural world and how it worked. In particular, I was mesmerized by the cool, green stands of tamarisk growing down to the river's edge in seemingly impossible contrast to the nearby arid desert slopes and rocky cliffs. Since I was in a national park that had a mandate to preserve the natural environment, I naively reasoned that the river must have always looked like this.

My initial impressions were dashed a short time after the trip ended at Pearce Ferry. Patient new colleagues and friends pointed out how the dense stands of tamarisk at the water's edge had developed only recently due to the elimination of scouring floods, an unanticipated side effect of Glen Canyon Dam.

In the early 1980s I again had the opportunity to make several raft trips down the river, this time as a graduate student intent on studying habitat use by breeding birds. Aware of recent scientific findings indicating that tamarisk was poor habitat for birds,[1] I suspected that my study would show similar results. I even went so far as to suggest in my research proposal that fieldwork would focus on patches of native vegetation because nesting birds were more likely to be concentrated in these areas.

Again, my preconceived notions were put to rest before the end of the first field season. Not only were birds significantly more abundant in tamarisk-dominated areas

than in areas of native vegetation, but birds within the new high-water zone were selectively nesting in tamarisk.[2] The density of nesting birds in some well-developed patches of vegetation in the new high-water zone was comparable to the highest densities ever reported for non-colonial birds in North America.[3] The diversity of birds in the new high-water zone was similar to that of the old high-water zone, but tamarisk-dominated habitats were home to the vast majority of obligate riparian birds nesting in the river corridor.[4]

The riparian community of the new high-water zone, including everything from plants and birds to reptiles and small mammals, is an unanticipated gift and should be managed as such. While the overall extent of riparian habitat across the Southwest has greatly decreased in the last several decades, the abundance of riparian habitat in Grand Canyon has actually increased. The tamarisk-dominated new high-water zone is not displacing native plant communities, because virtually no vegetation existed there before the scouring floods were limited in frequency and size. The unique combination of native and introduced species interacting in a productive manner identifies the new high-water zone as a naturalized community.

However, appreciation of the new high-water zone and its resources is far from universal. Several years of extraordinary high-water releases from Glen Canyon Dam between 1983 and 1986 caused widespread erosion of beaches, loss of tamarisk habitat, and subsequent reductions in the overall abundance of birds downstream in Grand Canyon. Very large fluctuations in water levels, if they continue to occur, may reduce or even eliminate vegetation in the new high-water zone, resulting in a less diverse population of birds.[5]

The National Park Service has yet to articulate a coherent policy regarding the new high-water zone,[6] perhaps because interpretation of its mandate to maintain naturally regulated ecosystems miscarries in the face of the new artificial environment. Resource management options for the new high-water zone more often than not consist of either trying to eradicate tamarisk or encouraging native plants to assume dominance. Managers should consider the second option only after identifying its influence on birds and other vertebrates presently dependent on the new high-water zone.

For example, the willow flycatcher is an obligate riparian species that nests exclusively in the new high-water zone, making extensive use of tamarisk.[7] It is legally designated as endangered in the Southwest, so modifications to its nesting habitat in the river corridor are subject to the terms of the Endangered Species Act of 1973. How should managers respond when an endangered native bird is nesting in exotic vegetation in an artificial environment and is threatened with human-caused changes to its habitat?

Regardless of how the Colorado River through Grand Canyon is managed, changes will continue to occur in the community of the new high-water zone. Some of these changes will be unanticipated, but most can be controlled or directed by the manner and quality of water released from Glen Canyon Dam. A goal of future resource management should be to maintain as much of the naturalized value of the new high-water zone as is compatible with the conflicting needs of other resources in the river corridor.

that *any* wetland is valued, even if it is created by water-development projects or dominated by non-native species. River runners appreciate tamarisk for a more prosaic reason—shade from the inhospitable summer sun.

For those wishing to get rid of tamarisk, the "solution" is clear: release large floods more frequently from Glen Canyon Dam in winter, when tamarisk does not germinate.[76] Decrease river discharges during the summer months to dry out the saturated banks. The distribution of tamarisk in Grand Canyon would, after some time, look like that of the nearly barren whitewater reaches of Cataract Canyon. But this "solution" would cause problems of its own. The new ecosystem of marshes, nesting birds, and other mammals attracted to the riparian setting might be eliminated. Clearly, the interaction of river flow, substrate, riparian vegetation, and dam operations is a complex problem, one not easily solved. The trade-off is the aesthetic of wilderness preservation set against the value of rapidly dwindling riparian habitats.

An interesting alternative may be to do nothing. Native riparian species such as coyote willow may replace tamarisk without any change in the flow regime.[77] Tamarisk may defeat itself: adult plants may impede the establishment of their own seedlings. However, the conversion, if not thwarted by some as-yet-unforeseen biological process,[78] may be extremely slow.

The old high-water zone does not offer such a dilemma. Nothing short of restoration of the historic flood regime—effectively, the elimination of flood control by Glen Canyon Dam—would return this zone to its original condition. The species of the old high-water zone may now be jeopardized more by climate than by river flow. Although species like mesquite may have sufficient water at present, a sustained drought could result in significant mortality of many individuals of the species that still cling to survival in this zone. Such a drought might spur the breakup of the thickets in this zone into clumps of individuals that could better compete for the scarce resource of water in a desert.

With its mandate to preserve and protect, the National Park Service constantly faces a contradictory mission. In Glen Canyon and Lake Mead National Recreation Areas, which bracket Grand Canyon National Park, all riparian habitat along the Colorado River was destroyed before the National Park Service began to manage them for recreation. The shorelines and deltas of Lakes Mead and Powell can be managed for biological productivity or for aesthetic values, but the riparian zones created by these lakes did not exist before the construction of the dams. Grand Canyon was a national park *before* Glen Canyon Dam was built; the species composition and structure of the riverine environment within the canyon is relatively well known. The management question here is not restoration to a pre-Columbian condition that can be only vaguely ascertained; instead, the question could be whether to attempt to manage the river corridor to regain some form of the condition that existed when Congress designated Grand Canyon National Park.

CHAPTER 7

Streams of Mud and Rock

In early July 1889, Robert Brewster Stanton watched helplessly as three members of his expedition drowned; even that experience did not prepare him for what happened on the morning of July 18. Crew members had stashed their remaining gear in what is now called Stantons Cave and began hiking up nearby South Canyon (mile 31.5). Midmorning, they rested and watched a large storm blow across the cliffs. Stanton described the resulting runoff vividly:

> As the rain commenced to fall we heard some rocks roll down the slope behind us, when we looked up, and it seemed as if the whole slopes of the gorge had begun to move at the top. Little streams of water came over the top, and in a moment they changed into streams of mud; and as they came down they gathered strength and turned to streams of mud and rock, undermining larger rocks; and starting them they plunged ahead, and in a few moments the whole sides of the canyon seemed to be moving down upon us with a roar and awful rumbling noise; and as the larger rocks plunged ahead of the streams, they crashed against other rocks, breaking into pieces; and the fragments flew into the air in every direction, hundreds of feet above our heads; and as these came nearer the bottom where we were, it seemed as if we were to be buried in an avalanche of rock and mud. But the rain soon ceased, and the whole

canyon resumed its deathlike stillness except for the noise of the little stream of muddy water running in the creek bed at our feet.[1]

This debris flow in South Canyon was probably similar to ones that occur every year in a few small drainages of Grand Canyon. During intense summer thunderstorms, rocks and debris falling from the steep slopes and cliffs mix with storm runoff, forming a slurry that races down the steep, unchannelized surfaces. Typically, these debris flows do not have much energy and stop on the more gentle slopes of the major channels. Debris flows that reach the Colorado River require more energy, which typically means they occur during larger, more infrequent storms and involve relatively large failures of bedrock or slopes, like the one in Diamond Creek in 1984.

On any summer day, the mouth of Diamond Creek (mile 225.5) is a busy place as river runners leave the Colorado River. On July 20, 1984, crews from o.a.r.s, Incorporated, and Outdoors Unlimited (ou) had already packed up and were ready to begin the long drive back to Flagstaff, Arizona.[2] At 3:30 p.m., the guides began the bumpy trip up the Diamond Creek road, which follows the channel of Diamond Creek.

Guides are keenly aware of meteorology and watch storms closely. Failure to do so could mean a stranding, or even injury or death, during hikes up side canyons. July 20 began clear and hot with no tangible sign of a severe storm. Up in the headwaters of Diamond Creek, however, a severe thunderstorm was brewing. The storm appeared severe enough to the Hualapais, whose land includes Diamond Creek, that they ordered the evacuation of a road crew. Nevertheless, the ten guides who were attempting to drive up the road were not aware of the distant storm.

The two-truck caravan laden with river gear was stopped only one-half mile up Diamond Creek from the river. The ou truck, an old Dodge Power Wagon,

stalled in wet gravel in the middle of the channel. Diamond Creek normally has perennial flow, and a small flood the previous day had left the road more treacherous than usual. Dennis Silva, head guide for ou, and Mike Walker with o.a.r.s got out to free the disabled vehicle. Steve Mahan, a guide for ou, began hiking up Diamond Creek to ask the road crew for help.

Mahan saw it first; "it" was the proverbial "wall of water." He climbed up the canyon walls to safety and watched as the flood spread out over the floodplain of Diamond Creek, knocking over trees like they were matchsticks. Downstream in the constricted reach where the trucks were stalled, the other guides heard a roar that sounded like a bulldozer coming downstream, but it was moving too quickly for a bulldozer. They looked upstream to see a massive brown wave bearing down on them. With only a minute to spare, they scrambled up nearby slopes and watched as the torrent smashed into their trucks.

According to Silva, a small surge of water was followed several seconds later by a front at least five feet higher. The front appeared to be a dark slurry of sediment containing lots of wood; no boulders were visible. The ou truck, stalled upstream of the o.a.r.s truck, was hit first. The old Dodge was not overtopped; instead, the front forced the truck to rise and pirouette into the flow. Silva distinctly remembers hearing the breaking of glass when the front hit the truck; any air trapped in the vehicles was quickly exhausted and replaced with mud. Similarly, the two-ton gmc truck containing o.a.r.s equipment rose with the flood, pirouetted, and floated upside down with the flow. Walker recalled that the front of the flow appeared to be higher than the cab of the o.a.r.s truck. Silva last saw both vehicles floating upside down with their wheels sticking out of the flood.

At the Colorado River, guides with Arizona Raft Adventures were beginning a takeout. As the flood hit the Colorado River they looked up, startled, in time to see the vehicles floating by, wheels sticking out of the surface of the flow. Estimates of the size of the flood vary, but some witnesses reported that the wave formed when slurry met river was twenty-five to thirty feet high, and the vehicles reportedly rose on the wave. A few months later, the vehicles were found about a thousand feet downstream on the right side of Diamond Creek Rapid.[3] Up Diamond Creek, the main flow lasted twenty to thirty minutes, then dropped about five feet. After six hours, Diamond Creek could be safely waded.

The debris flow witnessed in Diamond Creek illustrates many aspects of this spectacular type of flash flood. That the flood was a debris flow is substantiated by eyewitnesses' observations about the wave front and the behavior of the trucks. The small, preceding surge probably was the perennial flow of Diamond Creek being pushed along in front of the debris flow; this phenomenon is common because the two types of fluids—slurry and muddy water—do not mix readily. The main front, with a sharp crest that evokes the image of a "wall of water," is typical of the snout of a debris flow. The boulders in the snout were probably obscured by a mixture of water and mud combined with floating wood. The trucks were not overtopped and rolled down Diamond Creek; instead, they rose on the surface of the flood wave and floated upside down in the torrent. This could have happened only in a high-density slurry, which commonly can suspend boulders weighing many tons as if they were corks.

Debris flows, natural flash floods that occur in Grand Canyon and in other steep terrains of the world, are slurries of water, mud, and rock that often move with spectacular swiftness.[4] The colorful, sculptured cliffs that attract millions of tourists every year combine with intense summer thunderstorms to provide conditions ideal for debris flows. The steep exposures of unstable bedrock, containing abundant clay, are ideal for the initiation of debris

flows.[5] This fascinating sediment-transport process, which is responsible for many of the qualities that attract people to the Colorado River, is one of the best subjects for study using repeat photography.

The Process of Debris Flow

To visualize a debris flow, consider what is required to make concrete. You start with a mixture of sand, gravel, and cement, which contains particles the size of silt and clay. Such a mixture is what a sedimentologist would call "poorly sorted": many different-sized particles mixed together. The idea is to keep those particles mixed when the concrete is poured into place. Add water to the mixture, but measure carefully! Any mason knows that if not enough water is added, the concrete will not flow; if too much is added, the particles will segregate when the concrete is poured. Thus, the amount of water added to concrete must be exact. Typically, wet concrete contains only 6 to 7 percent water (by weight).

The concrete in your wheelbarrow has some interesting properties. If you shake the wheelbarrow, the slurry moves somewhat like a liquid, but if you put a large rock on the surface, it does not sink out of sight. Tip the wheelbarrow onto a slope, and watch the concrete flow. The center of the mass moves, while the edges stop and form levees. If enough concrete is poured, the levees act as channel banks, allowing the center of the slurry to continue flowing. The particles do not segregate; the flowing concrete and the large rock move as a plug of material. Consider what happens when a truck dumps yards of concrete at a construction site. From nearly the highest point on the truck, the concrete flows continuously down a metal chute, which acts as a confining channel, and the concrete slowly spreads out and stops upon reaching a flat surface.

A thunderstorm is brewing in Grand Canyon. Intense rain pelts a slope of Hermit Shale, creating a fast-moving slurry of red mud and water. Below, a large block in the Supai Group gives way, mixing with the slurry as it plunges over a thousand-foot cliff of Redwall Limestone. At the base of the cliff, the mixture of boulders, ground-up rock, and muddy water has enough energy to flow down the gentler slopes of a channel. Boulders and other sediment from the bottom and sides of the channel are picked up as the debris flow speeds down the channel through the layers of bedrock. Here and there, where the channel widens slightly, small amounts of the slurry are deposited as the flow seeks to maintain its confined channel. At the Colorado River, the slurry no longer is confined by bedrock. Most of the sediment and water slows and spreads out over a debris fan, where it stops. The leading edge of the debris flow, however, has enough momentum to enter the Colorado River, and large boulders deposited at the leading edge as it slows partially divert flow in the river.

Debris flows in Grand Canyon have three distinct phases that are similar to the mixing and pouring of concrete: initiation, confinement, and deposition. First, water, mud, and boulders must be mixed with sufficient energy to produce flow. Second, the slurry must be confined, either in a bedrock channel or between self-formed levees. And finally, deposition must occur either on a debris fan or in the river. The entire process, from initiation to deposition, occurs quickly.

Initiation

Debris flows require two processes before they can mobilize. Intense rainfall, common during the summer months, provides the water. Slope failures provide the necessary sediment—from clay to boulders—for the slurry. Both must occur simultaneously, which is why debris flows are relatively uncommon.

The intense, sometimes protracted thunderstorms of July through September initiate most debris flows. These storms are either widespread, affecting numerous tributaries, or concentrated over one canyon. The intensity typically is greater than an inch per hour, and rainfall may last several hours. Certain types of regional storms also cause debris flows. For example, thunderstorms from dissipating tropical cyclones caused debris flows in Prospect Canyon in 1939 and 1963.[6] The Crystal Creek flood of December 1966 resulted from a warm winter storm,[7] but this type of storm rarely affects Grand Canyon. In fact, the December 1966 debris flow is the only one known to have been caused by a winter storm in the past century.

Where rockfalls occur is somewhat indicative of where the slope failures that cause debris flows begin. The wall across from the mouth of Nankoweap Creek, for instance, is almost guaranteed to produce rockfalls after a storm.[8] Rockfalls and debris flows are related: the same lithologies that produce rockfalls at river level also yield slope failures that mobilize into debris flows. Intense rainfall is the difference between these two processes of mass wasting. Debris flows require a slope failure; that failure might be merely a rockfall if it occurs during light rain or in the absence of rain.

Certain rockfalls are legendary to river runners. For example, in 1974, a group of scientists from the Museum of Northern Arizona rowed through Tiger Wash Rapid (mile 26.6), the final rapid of the Roaring Twenties. Or so they thought. Right in front of them hung a pall of dust from a rockfall that had just occurred on the right side of the channel, creating a new rapid. This rapid, informally named "MNA Rapid," had been created.[9] Sinyala (mile 153.3) and MNA Rapids are the only sizeable ones in Grand Canyon that are controlled by rockfalls.

Rockfalls can be individual stones, loosened by rain or ice heaving, or larger avalanches involving parts of cliffs. Most previously documented rockfalls in Grand Canyon were avalanches; most originated

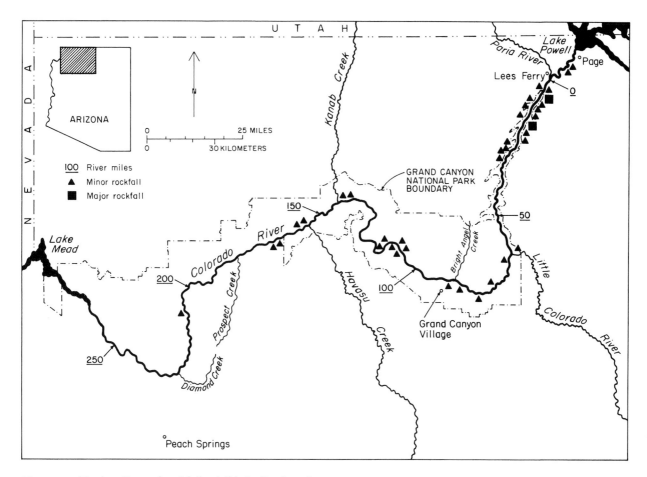

Figure 7.1. The locations of rockfalls visible in Stanton views

in the cliff-forming limestones.[10] But the limestones are the most stable rock formations. Cliffs of Redwall Limestone reportedly erode, by rockfall and dissolution, at a rate of a foot and a half per thousand years.[11] At that rate of retreat, Redwall Limestone is not a prolific producer of rockfalls or debris flows.

In the replicates of Stanton views, rockfalls typically produce white streaks on distant slopes; alternatively, new boulders, angular and broken, may appear in the foreground. Rockfalls can easily be distinguished from debris flows because there is no coherence in the deposit and only a little fine sediment is mixed with the boulders. Instead, scattered boulders, smashed rocks, and broken trees mark re-

cent rockfalls. Fresh-looking scars on Redwall Limestone cliffs typically are deceptive, some having occurred more than a century ago, as shown in the Stanton views.

Rockfalls along the river corridor have not occurred randomly in the past century. They are most common in upper Marble Canyon, particularly where Hermit Shale and the Supai Group are at river level. Where Redwall Limestone lines the river, rockfalls do not appear in Stanton views. Rockfalls are common in Muav Limestone, which underlies Redwall Limestone, and in fractured granite, diabase, and Dox Sandstone of Precambrian age. Not all of these units can produce debris flows, but most do.

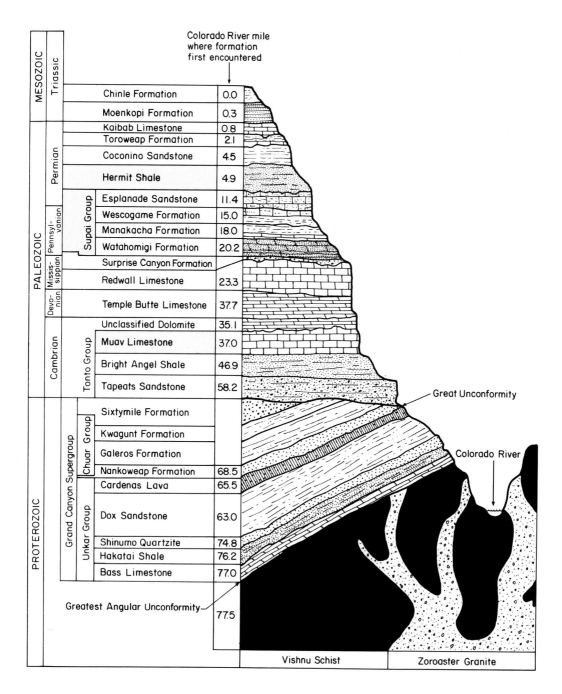

Figure 7.2 area labels:

MESOZOIC — Triassic
Chinle Formation — 0.0
Moenkopi Formation — 0.3

PALEOZOIC
Permian
Kaibab Limestone — 0.8
Toroweap Formation — 2.1
Coconino Sandstone — 4.5
Hermit Shale — 4.9

Supai Group — Pennsylvanian
Esplanade Sandstone — 11.4
Wescogame Formation — 15.0
Manakacha Formation — 18.0
Watahomigi Formation — 20.2

Mississippian
Surprise Canyon Formation
Redwall Limestone — 23.3

Devonian
Temple Butte Limestone — 37.7

Cambrian — Tonto Group
Unclassified Dolomite — 35.1
Muav Limestone — 37.0
Bright Angel Shale — 46.9
Tapeats Sandstone — 58.2

Great Unconformity

PROTEROZOIC — Grand Canyon Supergroup
Chuar Group
Sixtymile Formation
Kwagunt Formation
Galeros Formation
Nankoweap Formation — 68.5

Unkar Group
Cardenas Lava — 65.5
Dox Sandstone — 63.0
Shinumo Quartzite — 74.8
Hakatai Shale — 76.2
Bass Limestone — 77.0

Greatest Angular Unconformity — 77.5

Colorado River mile where formation first encountered

Colorado River

Vishnu Schist   Zoroaster Granite

Figure 7.2. The bedrock geology of Grand Canyon

Debris flows typically are initiated by failures of Hermit Shale, Supai Group rocks, or Muav Limestone.

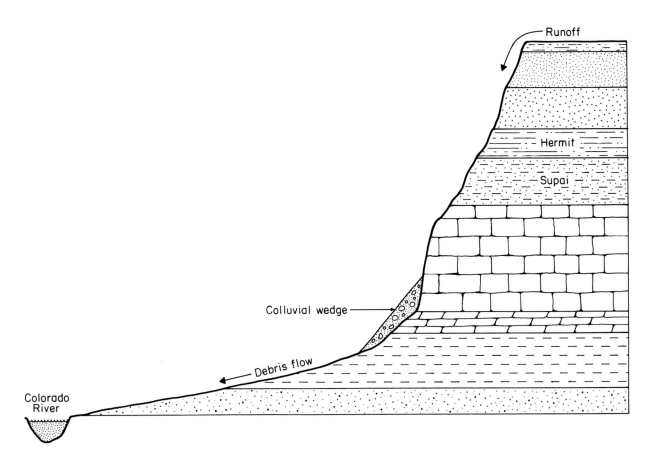

Figure 7.3. Grand Canyon cliff

Diagram showing colluvial wedges against a cliff in a geological formation that is typical of Grand Canyon. Intense rainfall causes the failure of colluvial wedges and the initiation of debris flows.

It is easy to understand how debris flows in Grand Canyon become mobilized. Intense rainfall and height above the river are the sources of energy; slope failure and runoff from the storm are the key ingredients. Slope failures can occur in bedrock or on loose slopes. Certain types of bedrock in Grand Canyon are more susceptible to failure than others, and as a general rule, slopes fail more frequently than cliffs. Bedrock units that form slopes are mostly shales, whereas units that form cliffs typically are limestones or sandstones. Massive, uniform rock layers like most of the Redwall Limestone are very stable, whereas formations composed of alternating limestone, sandstone, and shale layers—such

as the Supai Group—are unstable and more susceptible to failure. Susceptibility has little to do with the "hardness" or "softness" of units: sandstones from the Supai Group may equal or exceed Redwall Limestone in resistance. Layering produces the critical instability because resistant but thin layers are rapidly undercut by erosion of the weaker layers.

Abundant quantities of silt and clay increase the propensity for bedrock failure and debris-flow mobilization. A mixture of silt, clay, and water (called the matrix) fills the spaces between larger particles and raises the density of the fluid. Formations containing significant amounts of clay (Hermit Shale, for instance) are the most important units for the ini-

Figure 7.4. Diamond Peak

A. When Stanton and his crew saw Diamond Peak, at the center of this downstream view at mile 222.6, they knew their goal of Diamond Creek was within reach. Stanton wanted badly to hike out to the railroad and telegraph at Peach Springs to find out whether the negatives he had sent out for development were exposed correctly. Despite his eagerness, documentation of the railroad came first. Stanton made this view (number 660) on March 1, 1890, at 3:30 P.M.

tiation of debris flows; failures in Hermit Shale have contributed to most large debris flows in Grand Canyon. Muav Limestone, a silty dolomite that grades downward into Bright Angel Shale, is another important producer of slope failures. Many units of the Precambrian Grand Canyon Supergroup, particularly Dox Sandstone, contain enough fine particles to produce debris flows.

Even the most failure-prone units fail less often when they are close to river level. In the first twenty miles of river downstream of Lees Ferry, only five rapids are present. Only two of these—Badger Creek and Soap Creek Rapids—are significant. The debris flows that created these rapids came from the Chinle

Formation at the base of the Vermilion Cliffs.[12] At mile 20, Hermit Shale, which first appeared at river level at mile 5, is 1,000 feet above the river. With elevation comes potential energy to mobilize falling debris into slurries. Seven rapids and numerous riffles are present between miles 20 and 27, and the slopes above the river appear to be piles of loose boulders.

Raise certain bedrock units high above the Colorado River, add intense rainfall, and debris flows will result. Failures in these units are responsible for many of the largest debris flows of the past century in Grand Canyon. In December 1966, eleven slope failures in Hermit Shale, the Supai Group, and Muav Limestone contributed to the debris flow in Crys-

B. Raymond Turner replicated this view on February 26, 1991, at 2:41 P.M. A debris flow that occurred sometime before 1965 deposited numerous boulders and cobbles on the dune. Despite the deposition, several of the creosote bushes persist. Just over the foreground bushes, a new sand bar is visible on the left side of the Colorado River. This bar, now covered with tamarisk and willows, resulted from a change in river flow around the enlarged debris fan at the mouth of the channel, which drains an unnamed tributary.

tal Creek.[13] These failures took place 4,000 to 6,000 feet above river level and thirteen miles up a side canyon from the river. Of ninety-three slope failures throughout Grand Canyon in 1966, 70 percent were in Hermit Shale and the Supai Group.[14] The 1984 debris flow in Monument Creek began as an avalanche from the Esplanade Sandstone of the Supai Group and flowed nearly three miles while descending 3,000 feet.[15]

More common than bedrock failure is failure of the unconsolidated piles of rockfall detritus. These piles, called colluvial wedges, are wedge-shaped in cross section: thin at the top and thick at the bottom. They are common at the base of Redwall Lime-

stone cliffs; their boulders and cobbles are mostly Redwall and Kaibab Limestones and Supai Group sandstones, while sand, silt, and clay are contributed by Hermit Shale and fine-grained strata of the Supai Group. This poorly sorted mixture makes an ideal source for debris flows.

Failures of colluvial wedges can be classified into three types. In the first, runoff from intense rainfall erodes gullies into the wedges. As the runoff moves down extremely steep slopes, more and more material is entrained until a slurry forms. In the second, a mass of saturated colluvium fails and falls downslope into a channel. Like an avalanche from bedrock, the falling colluvium mixes with rainfall and

Figure 7.5. Boucher Rapid

A. At Boucher Rapid (mile 96.7), Harry McDonald and Stanton decided to line the boats down the left side and portage the supplies around yet another rapid of the Inner Gorge. After the boats were safely below this "long rocky" rapid on February 8, 1890, Stanton made this view (number 475) at 1:30 P.M. The gravel in the channel of Boucher Creek suggests that a flash flood, but probably not a debris flow, had occurred some time before Stanton reached the site.

runoff to form a debris flow. The third type of failure involves water pouring off cliffs onto colluvial wedges. This mechanism, called the "firehose effect," is highly erosive.

Debris flows that begin in colluvial wedges tend to be small and flow only short distances, except in the case of failures caused by the firehose effect. The 1987 flow in 18 Mile Wash was caused by a flash flood pouring over a 300-foot cliff of Kaibab Limestone and falling on an unstable slope in Hermit Shale and the Supai Group. In 1990, debris flows between

miles 62 and 64 resulted from water falling over the Redwall Limestone onto colluvial wedges that accumulated on slopes of Muav Limestone. Prospect Canyon, which enters the Colorado River at Lava Falls Rapid, experienced four major debris flows between 1939 and 1963, all of which were mobilized by the firehose effect. Floodwaters in Prospect Creek, a large drainage, fall over a 1,000-foot cliff onto a scree slope of loose basalt boulders and other colluvium, which then mobilize and flow only one mile to the Colorado River.

B. Boucher Rapid is not considered a very formidable reach of whitewater today. The debris flow of 1966 at Crystal Rapid, only a mile and a half downstream, raised the river level sufficiently to drown out the tailwaves of Boucher Rapid. Boucher Creek had its own debris flow in 1951 that is one of the largest in the history of Grand Canyon. This flow, which caused deposition of boulders on practically the entire debris fan, moved boulders four to six feet in diameter from the 1890 view and deposited new ones of about the same size. It is not known whether the rapid was more or less difficult to navigate after the debris flow, but no river expedition had significant problems here. Tom Wise replicated this view on February 18, 1992, at 2:37 P.M.

Flow

Where the canyon reaches its full depth near the South Rim, the source areas for debris flows are 3,000 to 4,000 feet above and many miles from the Colorado River. Resistant formations, such as Redwall Limestone, play a role in the process of flow from the cliffs to the river. The Redwall forms canyons in bedrock that confine moving debris and sustain long-distance transport. Most of these side canyons preserve little evidence of past debris flows. Debris flows are not infinite in size; instead, they typically carry a relatively small volume of material delivered in a large pulse. If confining channels were not present, debris flows would lose most of their volume simply by depositing material in levees. The

Figure 7.6. 75 Mile Canyon

A. As Stanton and his crew approached 75 Mile Canyon, they watched the rising walls of Shinumo Quartzite with concern. The narrow canyon meant the rapids ahead would be more severe. While the crew lined what is now called Nevills Rapid, Stanton made this upstream view (number 407) at 8:15 A.M. The fresh-looking deposit in the midground, which does not have any overlying sand from the Colorado River, indicates that a debris flow had occurred the previous summer. The large boulder at right center is approximately twelve feet in diameter.

narrow tributary canyons thus serve the same purpose as the cement truck's chute, transporting the slurry to the river in a confined flow.

And flow they do. The 1966 debris flow in Crystal Creek flowed thirteen miles from initiation points to the Colorado River.[16] Prehistoric debris flows, which have left depositional evidence in Shinumo and Kanab Creeks, could have flowed as far as twenty-five miles. Most debris flows travel shorter distances, primarily because most tributary canyons are only a few miles long; more typical debris flows, like the 1984 flood in Monument Creek and the 1987 flood in 75 Mile Canyon, travel two to four miles.

How debris flows can travel such distances is not well understood.[17] To estimate magnitudes of debris flows in the absence of a mechanistic theory,

B. 75 Mile Canyon has produced numerous debris flows in the past century. Changes in the foreground boulders are evidence of one of these debris flows; scars in catclaw trees indicate that this flow occurred in 1959. The extensive deposition at the main part of the debris fan occurred during a debris flow in August 1987; note the burial of the large boulder that was more distinct in 1890. The view was replicated by Ralph Hopkins on January 27, 1990, at 12:00 P.M. In September 1990, another debris flow occurred in 75 Mile Canyon.

most researchers resort to simple energy and mass balances. One conception, called "runup," uses the height reached on a wall configured at a 90° angle to a flow to estimate velocity. The assumption is that the kinetic energy of flow is entirely converted to the potential energy of height. Another conception equates movement around bends with centrifugal force on a mass moving in an arc. The flow superelevates on the outside of the bend as a function of the radius of curvature of the bend, the channel width, and the velocity of the flow. Like the runup concept, superelevation is a measure of the flow's kinetic energy. Neither method requires an understanding of how debris moves; consequently, neither is very accurate. But they are the only techniques we have.

In the absence of a better method, one has no

choice but to use runup and superelevation to estimate the magnitude of debris flows in Grand Canyon.[18] Peak velocities for debris flows range from 8 to 20 feet per second.[19] The magnitude of the Crystal Creek debris flow of 1966, for example, lies within the known realm of debris-flow size, with velocities ranging from 10 to 17 feet per second. Other small debris flows in steep angled chutes moved closer to 20 feet per second. Another measure, the peak discharges of debris flows, can be comparable to that of the flow in the Colorado River itself after regulation by Glen Canyon Dam. The discharge of the 1939 debris flow in Prospect Creek may have exceeded 30,000 cubic feet per second (cfs).[20] The peak discharge for the 1966 Crystal Creek debris flow was about 10,000 cfs; other debris flows from smaller tributaries have also reached this size.[21] More typical debris flows range in size from 2,000 to 5,000 cfs, although high-angle chutes can certainly yield smaller debris flows.

Debris flows are mostly sediment. The water content of the 1966 debris flow in Crystal Creek was about 30 percent by weight; therefore, the discharge was about 7,000 cfs of sediment. We have estimated water content of more than twenty debris flows by collecting sediment samples from levees and adding water until we observed a slurry.[22] Water content typically ranged among the debris flows from 5 to nearly 40 percent, depending on the amount of fine material in the debris flow.

Some of the boulders are enormous. One boulder transported into the river in 1990 at mile 62.5 weighs 280 tons. In Crystal Creek, a boulder weighing 49 tons did not reach the Colorado River in 1966; larger ones deposited in the river increased the severity of Crystal Rapid. The size of boulders transported is not necessarily related to the discharge of debris flows; boulder size varies tremendously among debris flows of about the same size.[23]

As yet, the exact mechanism for transport of huge boulders has not been determined, but we do know many of the circumstances. Transport of boulders is partly explained by buoyancy, or more specifically the difference in density between fluid and rock. "Typical" rocks in Grand Canyon have a density of 2.60–2.70 grams per cubic centimeter; water has a density of 1.0 gram per cubic centimeter. Drop a rock in water, and the difference in density is large enough that the rock sinks immediately. But a slurry of 20 percent water and 80 percent sediment has a density of about 2.3 grams per cubic centimeter, much closer to that of the rock. Still, the rock should sink, albeit slowly. Some upward force is needed to balance the downward force of the rock's mass against the fluid's density.

One of those forces is the "traffic jam" created by all the particles in a slurry. Particles get in the way of others trying to sink. There is a jostling among all those buoyant boulders, collisions that may cause a sinking particle to move upward or an ascending particle to sink. In pure water, forces are transmitted only in the fluid; in debris flows, forces are transmitted in the fluid and by particle-to-particle collisions.

Another force helps to support those boulders. High-frequency fluctuations in pressure, on the order of one cycle per second, occurred in the interstitial fluid at the base of landslides created in a flume.[24] These pressures could have occurred for many reasons; they have resulted from flow over a rough bed like the bottom of a typical Colorado River tributary. The pressures generated were of sufficient magnitude to support the media; in other words, transient pressures generated within the fluid could provide the supporting forces for boulders.

Research on debris-flow mechanics continues at the same time as debris flows recur naturally in Grand Canyon. Slurries are a complicated phenomenon that are not easy to describe or model. But every year they occur somewhere in Grand Canyon, and they speed down side canyons aimed at the Colorado River. When they arrive, they leave a messy pile of mud and debris and, perhaps, an altered Colorado River.

Deposition

The hike down 75 Mile Canyon is pure pleasure. Within a mile of the Colorado River, the channel winds between walls of lavender Shinumo Quartzite several hundred feet high. Beautiful dry waterfalls form drops in the bed of the ephemeral stream. The bed of the channel is mostly well-sorted gravel with only small amounts of fine sediment, suggesting that only streamflows (and not debris flows) have passed between these walls. The quartzite is polished: not a grain of sand clings to the sides. Occasionally splatters of mud are visible under an overhang, and here and there small catclaw trees grow from clumps of mud and boulders clinging impossibly to the wall. Debris flows have indeed been down this canyon, but they have not left an obvious mark.

At the terminus of the canyon, a pile of loose boulders extends down to the familiar roar of a Grand Canyon rapid. Small terraces of mud and boulders with catclaw trees growing out of them line both sides of the channel. Not much is growing on the broad fan, which appears at first glance to be a chaotic pile of boulders, many of which are more than three feet across, with some being as big as automobiles.

Yet there is pattern in the chaos and there is order among the piles of boulders on the debris fan. The channel is still confined, not by quartzite but by levees of mud and boulders. Higher parts of the debris fan, untouched by the Colorado River in recent years, clearly exhibit their origin in a debris flow: they are frozen piles of mud and boulders jumbled together. The presence of boulders seems incongruous, since the canyon of quartzite had few boulders. Near the edge of the river, a fan-shaped lobe of boulders, larger than most, was pushed out of the canyon,

depositing the bouldery face of a snout. Some of the biggest boulders on the fan are found in the snout.

This is the pattern of deposition of small debris flows from 75 Mile Canyon, which is similar to deposition on more than five hundred debris fans along the Colorado River. Most debris flows lack sufficient mass and energy to reach the Colorado River; instead, they expend mass and dissipate energy in creating the levees on the fan. Debris flows traverse bedrock-lined canyons without depositing much material, but they are forced to decelerate when they reach the debris fan. Small debris flows, shedding their mass to sustain flow down the fan, typically stop short of the river.

Larger debris flows make it to the river but not much farther. Although many have constricted rapids and changed the course of the Colorado River, none has turned and flowed downstream in the river. Debris flows lose too much energy and mass in the wide river corridor. In addition, the turbulent water of rapids dilutes the slurry—extra water works into the interstices, and boulders can no longer be supported in the flow. In most Grand Canyon rapids, the largest boulders are at the head, which is also the closest point to the mouth of the tributary canyon. Boulders near the bottom of rapids are generally pushed there by the force of the Colorado River.

Debris fans are a jumble of all the colors of Grand Canyon. Steely gray boulders of Redwall Limestone[25] mix with red sandstones from the Supai Group; here and there are yellow slabs of Coconino Sandstone and gray boulders of Kaibab Limestone. Some of the colors are fresh, but others are dull as if they had been laying on the fan for a long time. Many are sharpened from long exposure to rain and river water. The Colorado River before its taming by Glen Canyon Dam worked to erode these boulders.

Debris fans along the Colorado River are the cumulative deposition of many debris flows. The finer sediments were washed away or reworked by floods in the Colorado River. Debris flows deposit poorly sorted sediments; before the river was dammed, it would wash away as much sediment as it could entrain and carry. Debris fans, particularly the parts that extend beneath the river and create the drop through rapids, are a measure of the frequency of sediment production by tributaries and the river's ability to entrain large boulders before regulation. Since completion of Glen Canyon Dam in 1963, the delicate balance between tributaries and the river has shifted: debris fans are getting larger and rapids are getting narrower.[26]

Frequency of Debris Flows

Determining how often debris flows recur in Grand Canyon is problematic. In some tributaries, like 75 Mile Canyon and Prospect Creek, they appear to occur frequently; other tributaries have not had a debris flow in the past century. Because no one has recorded the occurrence of debris flows or other floods in most of Grand Canyon, the history must be reconstructed from deposits left by the floods.

Likewise, determining when debris flows occurred in the past is not easy. Several methods are available, but no one tool is entirely sufficient. For example, radiocarbon dating of organic materials is the standard way to determine the age of sediments deposited in the last 40,000 years. But debris flows occur in ephemeral streams with little plant life; very little organic material is deposited with the mud and boulders. Only under certain rare circumstances can debris flows be dated using radiocarbon analysis.[27]

Dendrochronology, the study of tree rings, is another method for dating floods. Trees typically add wood to their girth every year. These annual increments are usually distinct as rings when viewed in the cross section of a tree trunk. If trees grow close enough to a stream channel, a debris flow will abrade the upstream sides, leaving scars on the tree. With time, the scars heal and preserve evidence of the

passage of the debris flow. Unfortunately, trees are sparse in Grand Canyon, and their rings generally are difficult to count or cross-date.[28] Nonetheless, catclaw trees in a few tributaries have scars that indicate debris flows may recur every thirty to forty years, on average.

Repeat photography reveals facets of the debris-flow story. New boulders on debris fans, a sure sign of recent debris flows, are striking in repeat photographs. Before the closure of Glen Canyon Dam in 1963, floods on the Colorado River eroded away most of the newly deposited debris, but nevertheless some boulders remained; the residual deposits that formed after 1890 are obvious in repeat photographs. Repeat photography can also reveal the number of debris flows from a tributary in the past century, but only under certain special conditions: for example, multiple historic photographs can be used to reconstruct a history of debris-flow activity, such as in Prospect Canyon at Lava Falls Rapid. A single historic view, such as one of Stanton's, can also be used if it was taken from a vantage point that looks down on a debris fan. In this case, changes in the patterns of debris flow deposition may reveal many past debris flows.

The definition of a tributary that can produce debris flows is somewhat arbitrary. One can examine the squiggly lines on the topographic maps and delineate drainages, but debris fans and rapids are the important evidence of debris flows. Innumerable chutes and gullies that drain minuscule areas can also produce debris flows. We have identified 529 tributaries of the Colorado River that yield debris flows periodically.[29] The debris fans of 130 of these tributaries are visible in Stanton views. By examining changes in the arrays of boulders on the debris fans, we found 87 tributaries that had one or more debris flows during the past century; in other words, roughly two-thirds of all debris fans visible in the Stanton views showed evidence of debris flows. Two-thirds of the largest tributaries (greater than four square miles) had at least one debris flow in the past century.[30] In addition, we observed debris flows in 17 small chutes or gullies.

The average frequency of debris flows in Grand Canyon varies greatly. Some tributaries had no debris flows during the past century; others had four or more (see table 3 in the appendix). Careful study suggests that debris flows are clustered in time, four having occurred in Prospect Creek between 1939 and 1963, none in the preceding half-century, and none after 1963. A large flow may destabilize enough sediment to supply further debris flows until the supply is exhausted. Another major slope failure occurs, perhaps a half-century later, perhaps centuries later, and the cycle repeats itself. In this way, debris flows beget debris flows.

Parts of Grand Canyon appear to have had more frequent debris flows than other parts, at least during the past century. The highest frequency of debris flows has occurred between the Little Colorado River and Hance Rapid (miles 61.5 to 77). Of seventeen tributary debris fans in this reach recorded in Stanton views, sixteen had deposition from at least one flow in the past century. Some tributaries have had more than one debris flow in the past century; for example, 75 Mile Canyon had three debris flows between 1959 and 1990, and Palisades Creek (mile 65.5) had perhaps five flows between 1965 and 1990.

The reach between Havasu Creek and Lower Granite Gorge, which encompasses river miles 157 to 213, had the lowest percentage of tributaries with debris flows.[31] Some tributaries, such as 217 Mile Canyon, do not appear to have experienced a debris flow for perhaps several centuries. Whereas these tributaries have small floods on a frequent basis, debris flows are rare. The notable exception is Prospect Creek, one of the most active producers of debris flows in Grand Canyon.

Repeat photography indicates that debris flows occur on average every twenty to fifty years in tributaries of the Colorado River. Some tributaries may not have had a debris flow for centuries, but that lack of debris flows does not indicate they will not occur in the near future. If one does occur next year, or the year after, many may occur in a relatively short period. Conversely, consider Prospect Canyon and its propensity for debris flows at midcentury. Is another "big one" overdue? Prospect Creek had at least a half-century of quiescence before 1963; such quiescence after 1963 ended in 1995.

The Geomorphic Framework of the Colorado River

The routine is all too common in Grand Canyon. It's late afternoon and time to find a campsite. Let's assume you aren't a professional river guide who knows the camps and arranges days in advance for their use. Instead, you're looking for a patch of sand where you and your companions can spread out and spend a comfortable night. Where do you look?

You row a few miles on quiet water; the only sand you see supports a dense thicket of tamarisk and willow. A cleft appears in the canyon walls ahead, and the familiar roar of whitewater is heard. A debris fan has forced the river to one side, and large boulders are on the banks and in the shallow water of the rapid. A large patch of sand lies just upstream of the rapid, but it has been taken by another river party. You run the rapid and pull your boat into an eddy below. There it is, camp for the night: a large sand bar that begins where the boulders end at the bottom of the rapid.

The boats are unloaded, and you look around as dinner is prepared. The rapid just upstream of camp flows in a curving pattern around the debris issuing forth from a tributary canyon. Some rocks show through the water, indicating the reason for the arrangement of waves in the whitewater. On shore, sand begins where boulders end; the sand that lines the eddy will provide a comfortable camp. The waves dissipate into a pool of quiet water below the rapid;

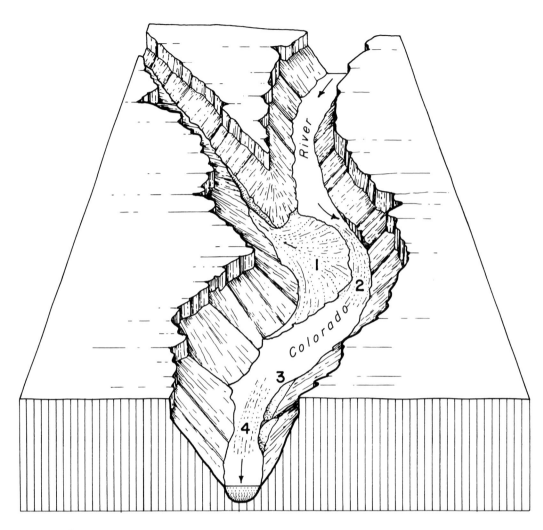

Figure 7.7. Mouth of a typical tributary

At a typical tributary juncture in Grand Canyon, debris-flow deposition creates a debris fan (1) in the Colorado River, which forces the river against the opposite wall of the canyon. A rapid (2) forms as water flows over boulders deposited in the river. An eddy (3) forms downstream as a result of the expansion of the river. Boulders eroded from the debris fan by floods in the river are redeposited downstream in a debris bar (4), also known as an island, rock garden, or boulder field. A secondary riffle or rapid forms around this debris bar. The presence of the debris bar constrains the size of the eddy and backs up water below the rapid, forming a pool.

a line of turbulent water, called an eddy fence, separates the calm water at your camp from the bottom of the rapid. Looking downstream, you see another riffle, this time flowing around an island of rocks on the opposite side of the river from the debris fan. Then it clicks: this arrangement of boulders, whitewater, and sand is all related.

River runners and scientists have long recognized parts of the association between tributary canyons, whitewater, and sand bars.[32] John Wesley Powell was the first to comprehend that the boulders in rapids were deposited during tributary floods;[33] Stanton and other early explorers also noticed the close association of tributaries and rapids. But Powell believed that differential erosion of bedrock somehow affected the river; his crew learned to dread the appearance of granite and limestone along the river because it indicated, so they thought, intense rapids ahead. They were wrong. The geology at river level affects only channel width, not slope.[34]

Debris flows, rapids, and sand bars make up the geomorphic framework of the Colorado River, the same framework that Stanton saw in 1890. To truly appreciate this framework, and to fully understand its rate of change, one must step out of the perspective of a human lifetime. An event that may appear rare to most people may seem frequent to a geologist.

Most observers recognized that rapids are created by flash floods in tributary canyons. An early river guide states, "It should be remembered, however, that influx of sediments by tributary streams is a very intermittent process. It is usually accomplished only during major flash floods, at which time great quantities of debris are transported and dumped into the Colorado River in a matter of *a few hours*. . . . [I]magine the force of *water* necessary to bring this material down side canyons to the debris fans" [emphasis added].[35] In the broad perspective, this interpretation is correct. What is missing is an understanding of the process of debris flow and its frequency. A debris flow takes not hours but minutes to deposit boulders. The force of water is irrelevant to the process of boulder transport out of tributaries. Although debris flows are a type of flash flood, the similarity between water flow and debris flow ends with that commonality. Only extremely rare streamflow floods could move boulders as large as the ones moved by debris flows every year in Grand Canyon.

Rapids exist because the Colorado River lacks sufficient power to remove all boulders deposited during debris flows. Most of the sediment deposited by debris flows is removed; typically, the river will erode all mud and sand whenever the debris fan is inundated and will also transport most of the cobbles and small boulders. Whereas clay, silt, and sand may be transported a long distance from the source debris fan, the eroded cobbles and boulders are transported only a short distance downstream. Just below the rapid, the cobbles and small boulders accumulate in neatly sorted piles. These deposits, called debris bars[36] and informally called "islands" and "rock gardens," form secondary riffles and rapids. These stretches of whitewater are known informally as the "Son of . . ." rapids (for example, Son of Hance) in recognition of their link to the parent rapid.

Between this secondary riffle and its upstream rapid is a pool of water that appears to move endlessly in a circle. These eddies are zones of flow separation that generally have velocities low enough to allow sand deposition. Most of the sand is underwater; camping beaches are the tip of the pile that is exposed after high flows subside. What constrains the size of most eddies are boulders at the upstream end and cobbles and boulders downstream. Debris flows deposit the upstream boulders; reworking by the Colorado River moves others downstream onto debris bars. The eddy spins between piles of boulders that are the result, directly and indirectly, of debris flows from a tributary.

Debris fans, rapids, and sand bars are all controlled, directly or indirectly, by the process of debris flows. Debris fans that are reworked remain remarkably unchanged until the next debris flow. Rapids change—in terms of their navigation by river runners—with each change in water level of the river, but the underlying configuration of boulders that create the waves and holes changes little until the next debris flow. Rock gardens and islands remain until the next debris flow and reworking flood. Finally, the sand bar, the least stable element of this geomorphic framework, can change with fluctuations in flow or the pattern of flow release from the dam. But the locations of most sand bars are fixed between piles of boulders, and the general configuration of sand bars is dependent on when the last debris flow occurred.

Debris Flows and the
Downcutting of the Canyon

Viewed from the rims, Grand Canyon is a maze of spires and canyons, of mesas and benches. Everything appears ageless, frozen in time, as rocks interfinger with air. But what seems a mad jumble of topography nevertheless exhibits order: all slopes eventually end at the Colorado River. The exposed layers in the canyon's walls alternate in slopes and cliffs that are consistent with the type of bedrock. Every cliff has a cone of rubble at its base, every indentation in the rim yields a water course. Yet the canyon is defined not so much by what is there as what is absent. The theme is space: missing rock.

Evidence of the geomorphic processes that created these empty spaces is on display everywhere. White scars on red cliffs, with fresh-looking piles of debris below, are sure signs of recent avalanches or other slope failures. The base of every cliff accumulates a pile of colluvium; some of these accumulations appear recent, some appear old. The accumulations of rubble do not account for the vast openness, all that missing rock. During five million years of history, those accumulating piles of rubble must have been moved in debris flows from the bottoms of cliffs to the Colorado River, which then transported the material out of Grand Canyon.

We are taught that mountains erode to the sea uniformly, grain by grain, a little at a time during each rainfall. The bottoms of the deep canyons leading to the Colorado River reveal the real mechanism of erosion. Many appear streaked with the red trail of debris flows, as if the canyons were painted with mud. Follow the snaking channel up to its source, and you will find a rockfall, a gully, or a scar in a cliff. Then follow the channel down to its juncture with the Colorado River, and you typically will see a rapid flowing over and around a debris fan. Debris flow, the most pervasive sediment-transport process in Grand

Canyon, is not routine but catastrophic: debris flows move entire slopes, not just individual grains of sand.

Grand Canyon has existed for 4 to 6 million years and has been at its current depth for perhaps 2 million years.[37] During this time, no downcutting has occurred. The last of the lava dams, which are presumed to have controlled base level for the river, formed 140,000 years ago. These dams controlled base level approximately two-thirds of the way through Grand Canyon; downcutting still could have occurred at the Grand Wash Cliffs and propagated upstream through the remnant lava dams, but it did not.

The mere presence of debris fans and rapids has broad implications concerning whether a bedrock canyon is downcutting. The rapids account for about 10 percent of the distance while causing 50 percent of the fall in the Colorado River through Grand Canyon.[38] In the relatively warm and dry climate of the present, the Colorado River is expending its erosive energy on removing boulders from the rapids instead of eroding downward through bedrock.

The depth of Grand Canyon is not controlled by resistant bedrock; at least it has not been so controlled during the last ten thousand years. Instead, the more than five hundred debris fans along the length of the river corridor inhibit further downcutting. The river is expending its energy on removing the massive boulders thrown into it by minuscule tributaries, not on eroding the underlying bedrock. It is a titanic struggle between small and large: tributaries push boulders in, and the river tries to transport them downstream or dissolve them. The tributaries are winning for now. The presence of rapids indicates that the bed of the Colorado River is rising, not downcutting. Now, operation of Glen Canyon Dam is allowing the buildup of boulders and cobbles to accelerate. Because of human intervention, the natural process of debris flow is overwhelming the unnatural pattern of river flow.

CHAPTER 8

Crystal and Lava

It [Hermit Rapid] was about the same as all rapids. I may be wrong but it seems to me that if one keeps one's eyes open and exercises caution, these rapids are nothing more than a little fast work plus a good dunking. . . . I have come to believe that if one forgets the ominous roar of these rapids and the fact that people have built a halo of awesomeness around them, . . . they present nothing but a physical problem that can be easily overcome.   *Barry M. Goldwater*[1]

Crystal and Lava Falls Rapids are reputed to be the most difficult reaches of navigable water in the western United States.[2] They are, at most water levels, the most difficult whitewater in Grand Canyon.[3] These two rapids have instilled fear and inspiration in a generation of river guides and whitewater enthusiasts, most of whom well remember "Crystal Day" and "Lava Day" from their Grand Canyon river trips.

With respect and fear comes mythology. Crystal and Lava Falls Rapids are the subjects of tales that transcend reality. Crystal Rapid (mile 98.3) is alleged to have formed overnight during a storm with "at least a one-thousand year rating;"[4] Lava Falls Rapid (mile 179.3) purports to be the unchanging remnant of an ancient lava dam that once stood thousands of feet high.[5] These perceptions do not have foundations in fact. In reality, Crystal Rapid was greatly

Figure 8.1. Crystal Rapid

A. Stanton photographed this view of Crystal Rapid (number 481) at about 11:45 A.M. on Sunday, February 9, 1890, a day off for the expedition. This view is one of four photographs that document changes in Crystal Rapid. Flow through the rapid is left to right, and the deepest part of the rapid appears at the bottom of the view.

enlarged during a debris flow in December 1966, but that debris flow was not an unprecedented event in Crystal Creek. The lava dams at Lava Falls Rapid have long since eroded away, and changes in the rapid, the most unstable in Grand Canyon over the past century, reveal the true cause of this awesome reach of whitewater.[6]

The Stanton photographs illustrate that both Crystal and Lava Falls Rapids are controlled by the same debris-flow processes that control other rapids in Grand Canyon. The rapids' current sizes reflect an ongoing struggle between the Colorado River and its tributaries. In effect, the conflict is between two sediment-transport processes: debris flows from tributaries and streamflow in the Colorado River. The Stanton views, combined with historical records and geologic and hydrologic information, can be used to evaluate the true geomorphic significance of these awe-inspiring rapids. Moreover, knowledge of changes in these rapids over the past century allows a guess as to their potential size on a dam-regulated Colorado River.

B. The repeat view was made in a light rainstorm by Tom Brownold on February 1, 1990, at 12:20 P.M.; the background cliffs are partially obscured by low clouds. The deepest part of the rapid in 1890 has been filled in with large boulders, many of which are greater than twelve feet in diameter. The constriction of the channel, which forced flow to the left, changed Crystal Rapid from a negligible rapid to the primary obstacle to navigation in the Inner Gorge. The lack of changes in rocks that line the left, or Slate Creek, side of Crystal Rapid indicates that the 1966 debris flow did not cross and dam the Colorado River.

Myths and Rapids

Stanton's crew were disgruntled when they pulled in at the head of Crystal Rapid in early February 1890. The expedition had lost one of its three boats just two days earlier in Horn Creek Rapid, and on Saturday, February 8, the crew had lined Hermit and Boucher Rapids before reaching Crystal Rapid.

Stanton wanted to climb to Point Sublime on the North Rim; Crystal Creek looked large enough that a route to the rim might be found up its channel. The expedition camped on a beach above the rapid, and Stanton climbed up a nearby terrace. This terrace, a crucial scout point, is now familiar to every Grand Canyon river runner. Stanton was interested only in photographing the views upstream and downstream before dark, not scouting Crystal Rapid. The rapid did not appear to be a serious impediment to downstream travel, especially compared to others they had passed that day.

Stanton explored the mouth of Crystal Creek. He found the place to be photogenic and took eight photographs. Included in these were two pictures of his cook, James Hogue, sitting on the wall of an Anasazi ruin perched on the downstream side of the terrace. Also, he photographed the bed of Crystal Creek, the head of the rapid, and some fast-moving water just downstream of the mouth. On Monday, Stanton and two others climbed toward the rim, stopping to make an additional image of Crystal Rapid from a vantage point high above the gorge.[7] Stanton's reasons for photographing Crystal Rapid so extensively are a mystery: the rapid was singularly unimpressive in 1890.

After his climb, Stanton and his crew easily lined boats down the right side of the wide, long rapid. They lined Crystal Rapid not because they feared its severity but because they were still cautious after having lost a boat upstream. A mile downstream, they reached Tuna Creek and found a "bad rocky rapid," which was "a worse rapid than last."[8] A river runner would be unlikely to make a similar comparison between Tuna Creek and Crystal Rapids today.

Crystal Rapid changed little for eight decades after Stanton saw it. Navigational difficulties were rare, except for the Tadje-Russell expedition of 1914–1915. Charles Russell had bumbled his way through the Colorado's canyons in 1907, and he achieved a remarkable level of poor leadership and bad luck on his second trip. Hardly a model for a well-planned expedition, Russell had more than his share of troubles in Crystal Rapid.[9] He rammed his boat immovably into the island of rocks that jammed the left center of the rapid. The crew hiked out Slate Creek, which enters the left side of Crystal Rapid, to the rim and returned with a block and tackle. They rescued the boat, then sank it on another rock a short distance downstream.

Photographs of Crystal Rapid taken before 1966 show a very stable rapid with a number of notable features. The main flow of water coursed down the right side of the river, next to the mouth of Crystal Creek. An arcuate island of boulders, apparently the remnant of a debris-flow snout, surrounded the mouth of Slate Creek. Crystal itself was a long rapid with a respectable fall of seventeen feet.[10] It was remarkably free of boulders if one stayed to the right; the lower part had easily run waves and fast water. In July 1941 Norm Nevills may have summed up the opinion of early river runners: "This stretch through here is real sport and goes like the dickens over these small rapids. Hardly a place in the canyon more fun to run than these."[11] One of the first river guides rated Crystal Rapid a 4 on a scale of 10.[12]

Then, in 1966, something happened that has become legendary in Grand Canyon history. What once was a very wide and easily run rapid became, perhaps in a span of only several minutes, the greatest obstacle to whitewater navigation in the Inner Gorge. The story of the 1966 debris flow in Crystal Creek, and the subsequent response of the Colorado River, describes the largest change in a rapid during the past century. Although no one witnessed the 1966 debris flow, enough is known of the circumstances to challenge many of its myths.

Unusual, but not particularly rare, meteorological conditions developed over the western United States in early December 1966 as a cutoff low-pressure system formed in the upper atmosphere over the Pacific Ocean.[13] Although cutoff lows are common in the winter months, this swirling air mass off the California coast packed an extra punch of moisture. Cutoff lows are typically adrift in a largely stagnant atmosphere, much like driftwood floating in an eddy; it is difficult to predict exactly where or how fast one will travel over the southwestern United States. In this case, the storm moved to the north and stalled over the mountain ranges of eastern California, southern

Nevada and Utah, and northern Arizona. The storm brought widespread flooding to those states.[14] The Virgin River, in southern Utah to the north and west of Grand Canyon, had its third-largest flood in a little more than a century. Of more importance to Crystal Rapid, a series of storm cells slammed into the Kaibab Plateau on the north side of Grand Canyon between December 4 and 6, and large amounts of rain fell throughout the drainages of the North Rim.

The first myth—or exaggeration—concerns the amount of rain that fell during the December 1966 storm. Popularized accounts imply or state that 14 inches of rain fell in two days over the entire watershed (forty-three square miles).[15] Actually, this amount was estimated in only one rainfall gage, at 8,700 feet at the North Rim Entrance Station to Grand Canyon National Park.[16] Winter storms in the western United States have a strong orographic effect; in other words, the amount of precipitation during storms generally increases with elevation. The December 1966 storm was no exception. Phantom Ranch, at 2,570 feet (an elevation comparable to that of the mouth of Crystal Creek), received 2.08 inches of rainfall during the storm, or less than a quarter of its annual precipitation. Other gages at elevations between Phantom Ranch and the North Rim recorded 4 to 6 inches of rainfall. A contour map of the rainfall[17] suggests that the drainage of Crystal Creek received an average of about 5 inches. This is still substantial rainfall, although not unprecedented for a winter storm in the mountainous regions of Arizona.

The unusual aspect of this storm was the lack of snowfall at higher elevations. Because the storm was intensified with moisture from the warm tropical latitudes, it was relatively warm and able to deliver bursts of high-intensity rainfall. In most of the drainages affected by the storm, the runoff was concentrated in channels as streamflow.[18] In the Crystal Creek drainage, however, slopes in Hermit Shale, the

Supai Group, and Muav Limestone failed at nineteen sites. In Dragon Creek, the major tributary of Crystal Creek, eleven slope failures mobilized into debris flows on the steep slopes.

Maurice Cooley and Byron Aldridge of the U.S. Geological Survey, along with Robert Euler, archaeologist at Grand Canyon National Park, examined the canyon of Dragon Creek in March 1967. Using a standard technique for estimating the size of streamflow floods (the slope-area method),[19] they estimated a peak discharge of 29,000 cubic feet per second (cfs) for the debris flow at a site about six miles from the Colorado River. (Aldridge and Cooley recognized the inappropriateness of using equations designed for streamflow estimation on a debris flow, but the technique was the only one available in 1967.) The debris flow was followed by streamflow of about 1,000 cfs, which caused substantial channel erosion.

In March 1986, Pat Pringle, Glenn Rink, and I reexamined the magnitude and frequency of the Crystal Creek debris flow.[20] Using photographs taken by Cooley and Euler, we were able to locate the mud line preserved twenty years earlier at a number of sites. Estimating velocity by superelevation and runup evidence,[21] we estimated a discharge range of 9,200 to 14,000 cfs for the peak discharge. Given the uncertainties in the technique, the most appropriate estimate of discharge for the debris flow is about 10,000 cfs. At least three-quarters of this discharge was sediment ranging in size from clay to boulders.

Most popularized accounts contain the imagery of a wall of mud and boulders racing through Crystal Creek to the Colorado River. The velocity of the debris flow is the second myth of the 1966 debris flow and Crystal Rapid. Cooley and Aldridge estimated a velocity of 16 miles per hour (mph) using equations that are not appropriate to the phenomenon of debris flows. Our 1986 estimates range from 10 to 12 mph, which are reasonable estimates of velocity for typical debris flows.[22] In a popular account, however, the flow velocity was 50 mph (73 feet per second),[23] the speed of a fast-moving train.

Euler had examined and mapped some archaeological sites in Dragon Creek only a year before the 1966 debris flow. He found two roasting pits that had been abandoned by the Anasazi about nine hundred years ago.[24] When Euler returned in March 1967, he found that one roasting pit had been obliterated by the debris flow, and mud from the peak of the flow had lapped up onto the second roasting pit. Cooley, Aldridge, and Euler concluded, based on this evidence, that the debris flow had "a recurrence interval of only once in several centuries."[25] The relation between the 1966 debris flow and the "obliterated" roasting pit fired people's imaginations. The recurrence interval for the 1966 debris flow is commonly reported in popular accounts as five hundred to one thousand years;[26] one account inflates it to millennia.[27] This, the third myth about Crystal Rapid, appears to be based more on a need to explain or exaggerate the increased navigational difficulty of the rapid than on additional physical evidence from Crystal Creek.

Recurrence interval is an easily misunderstood concept. A hundred-year flood has a probability of 1 in 100 of occurring in a given year; it may occur more than once per century. Strictly speaking, the largest flood that occurs in a given century is not necessarily a hundred-year flood. Moreover, a hundred-year rainstorm does not necessarily cause a hundred-year flood, because watershed conditions before the storm begins may either enhance or decrease the amount of runoff.

The true recurrence interval for the storm and debris flow of 1966 may never be known. Given the difficulties in estimating precipitation in an isolated drainage, combined with the uncertainty of when major failures might occur in the cliffs, one cannot say with certainty when another debris flow of similar size might occur. Estimation of frequency from debris-flow deposits along Crystal Creek is also prob-

lematic, because some debris flows may not have left deposits. However, physical and circumstantial evidence suggests a recurrence interval shorter than a thousand years for this spectacular debris flow.

No hydrologists or meteorologists who have studied the 1966 storm have estimated a recurrence interval for the precipitation amounts, yet a popular account gives a recurrence interval of a thousand years.[28] The National Weather Service, in a review of the largest storms affecting the Colorado River drainage, does not even mention the 1966 storm in its list of "important rainstorms" that was used to estimate probable maximum precipitation in the region.[29] In fact, the largest one-day precipitation for December at Phantom Ranch and Bright Angel Ranger Station occurred in 1978 and 1951, respectively.[30] Although more extreme precipitation was localized over Crystal Creek, no rainfall data exist to suggest that the storm was even the largest in the twentieth century.

The December 1966 storm caused a flood on Bright Angel Creek that devastated structures at Phantom Ranch and damaged a newly installed pipeline. The flood was the second largest in a fifty-year record. The estimated frequency for this flood is about fifty years, based on a statistical analysis;[31] the frequency of the 1966 flood on the Virgin River is similar.[32] Therefore, the only streamflow gaging data of relevance indicate a recurrence interval of less than a century for floods caused by the 1966 storm. However, a mine shaft built between 1893 and 1916 near the bed of Crystal Creek[33] was filled by the 1966 debris flow. This fact suggests that no other debris flow in Crystal Creek of the same magnitude had occurred in the preceding half-century.

However, stratigraphic evidence indicates that debris flows in Crystal Creek may be considerably more frequent than one per thousand years.[34] Wood entrained in a debris flow had a radiocarbon age of 180±70 years B.P., or sometime between A.D. 1650 and A.D. 1950.[35] Two other debris-flow deposits—including the 1966 flow—overlie the dated deposit; all three reached the Colorado River, and the older two may be presumed to have affected Crystal Rapid. If the original debris flow occurred three hundred years ago, a recurrence interval of one per century is suggested by the stratigraphic evidence.

The archaeological evidence of the "obliterated" roasting pit might seem to indicate a longer recurrence interval for the 1966 debris flow. Yet the Anasazi may not have been the last aboriginals to build or use roasting pits. Paiute Indians from southern Utah used drainages emanating from the North Rim after the Anasazi abandoned Grand Canyon in A.D. 1150.[36] A roasting pit in Tuna Creek, west of Crystal Creek, was reused by the Paiutes.[37] In this roasting pit a debris-flow deposit separated a lower stratum bearing Anasazi artifacts and dated at A.D. 1100 from an upper stratum bearing Paiute artifacts and dated at A.D. 1320–1425.[38] The roasting pits in Dragon Creek could likewise be younger than A.D. 1100.

In March 1986, I found other roasting pits along Dragon Creek that had been untouched by the 1966 debris flow. Because both roasting pits affected in 1966 were on the outside of bends in Dragon Creek, the rise in stage associated with flow around the bends (superelevation) caused material to leave the channel and be deposited on the pits. Instead of having been obliterated, the one roasting pit instead was buried under about a foot of sediment. I observed two other roasting pits in the near-vertical channel walls about a half-mile downstream of the "obliterated" pit. Like the roasting pit observed by Euler, these pits had also been buried—by an older and considerably larger debris flow than the 1966 event. Sometime before 1966, the channel shifted laterally and the pits were cut in half. Presumably these pits were also used about nine hundred years ago, although they could have been built by Paiutes much later. Archaeological evidence in Dragon Creek is thus inadequate for determining the frequency of debris flows.

Estimates of the frequency of flow based on the

evidence of damage to roasting pits are thus highly questionable. The fact that roasting pits were buried by a previous debris flow in Dragon Creek, combined with direct radiocarbon dating of preserved debris-flow deposits, suggests a recurrence interval of perhaps several centuries for debris flows that reach the Colorado River from Crystal Creek. Not surprisingly, this is the same conclusion reached by Cooley, Aldridge, and Euler for the recurrence interval of the 1966 debris flow.

What happened when the debris flow reached the Colorado River is also conjectural. No one observed the contact between debris flow and streamflow; it may have occurred during the night of December 5–6. The deepest part of the river channel was near the right bank at the mouth of Crystal Creek; the debris flow must have created tremendous waves and a gargantuan splash when the bouldery snout entered the deep and swiftly flowing rapid. When the peak flow ended—it could not have persisted for more than several minutes—the Colorado River had been severely constricted. Formerly about three hundred feet wide, Crystal Rapid had been reduced to a width of one hundred feet when first observed in 1967.[39]

The prevailing myth is that the 1966 debris flow in Crystal Creek dammed the Colorado River.[40] One account holds that the debris flow "hit the opposite wall,"[41] which implies that considerable energy remained after the hypothetical damming. Perhaps these accounts are correct, but because no observers saw the collision between slurry and rapid, one can only look at the physical evidence and circumstances and speculate about what might have happened.

The mean discharge in the Colorado River was about 10,000 cfs on December 5, 1966.[42] The gage record shows that the river rose several thousand cubic feet per second over the next few days in response to the storm runoff. It may therefore be fair to assume that 10,000 cfs of water, boulders, and mud emanating from Crystal Creek hit 10,000 cfs of water flowing in Crystal Rapid. While confined to the bedrock reaches of Crystal Creek, the debris flow may not have decreased substantially in velocity. When the debris flow reached the river, however, it would have decelerated on the unconfined and wide debris fan, whereas water in the river would have been accelerating into the rapid. By virtue of its greater density, the debris flow may have had more momentum, but was that momentum enough to carry boulders across the river?

Comparison of the Stanton photographs with 1990 conditions indicates that if the debris flow did cross the river, it did not cause substantial deposition on the Slate Creek side. In other words, it could not have "hit the opposite wall" because if it had, at least some depositional evidence of the slurry would have remained on the Slate Creek side. A more realistic scenario would be deposition of a new debris fan that possibly extended to within fifty feet of the left bank. Interaction between streamflow in the Colorado River and the moving debris flow probably diluted the front sufficiently to prevent a full damming of the river.

In one sense, severe constriction of the river is a "dam," but this definition is more in the sense of a weir in a canal than a structure that forms a lake. The 1966 debris flow increased the bed elevation of the Colorado River substantially. Crystal Rapid now falls about thirty-three feet,[43] or an increase in fall of sixteen feet as a result of the 1966 debris flow. This increase in the elevation of the riverbed was sufficient to enhance "Lake Crystal," a two-mile reach of quiescent water that marks the current approach to Crystal Rapid. The increased bed elevation backed up enough water to drown out the tailwaves of Boucher Rapid, one and a half miles upstream.[44] After the 1966 debris flow, the rating for Boucher dropped from a 6 to a 3–4.

Newly enlarged, Crystal Rapid was a tricky bit of navigation. Between 1966 and 1983, it had a steep tongue that swept boats into a nasty array of boulders, waves, and holes. Most of the drop in the rapid occurred below the mouth of Slate Creek.[45] The largest hazard was the Crystal Hole, which was triggered by flow over a large piece of Vishnu Schist. This rock may be either bedrock or a large boulder that was transported out of Slate Creek or had fallen off the left wall.[46] Below the Crystal Hole, scattered boulders made navigation seem like bumper pool.

Just ask Martin Litton. Litton's first run of the Colorado was in 1955 with P. T. Reilly. Later, he founded Grand Canyon Dories and is the oldest living person to have rowed the Grand Canyon. Just after the 1966 debris flow, he inspected Crystal Rapid and did not like what he saw.[47] As owner of the company, he assumed responsibility for the equipment and decided to run all four dories through, one by one. The first boat flipped in the big hole and floated upside down through the Rock Garden, tearing off the decks, bow, and stern. The second flipped in the hole and was torn up along the cliffs along the left side. The third and fourth dories met the same fates.

If the 1966 debris flow had occurred in an unregulated Colorado River, Crystal Rapid might not have persisted as a major navigational hazard. However, until 1983, flood-control operations of Glen Canyon Dam precluded large discharges that might have dislodged the troublesome boulders from their positions. The combination of high spring runoff and a nearly full Lake Powell forced spillway releases from the dam that peaked at 96,200 cfs on June 29. The flood changed Crystal Rapid again.[48] The boulders that littered Crystal Rapid began moving perhaps when the rising water first exceeded 40,000 to 50,000 cfs. When the discharge reached 70,000 cfs, witnesses reported hearing a low rumbling that was interpreted as boulders rolling along the bed. Although releases remained high for several years, most of the reworking of the debris fan at Crystal Rapid occurred right before or during the peak of the 1983 flood.

The severity of the rapid increased as a result of the 1983 flood. The steepest part of the rapid shifted from about the mouth of Slate Creek to 250 feet upstream. At normal dam releases, a severe hole lies at the base of the tongue of glassy water entering the rapid. River runners typically avoid this hole by keeping to the right, although a strong lateral wave forces the unwary boater directly into the hole. This lateral wave has decreased in strength since 1983, presumably by the reworking of smaller boulders.

The legacy of the 1983 flood, at least until the next large release from Glen Canyon Dam, is a debris bar at the base of the rapid that is called the Rock Garden. Unlike many other rapids, such as Granite Rapid, Crystal Rapid did not have a debris bar before 1966. Outwash during deposition of the new debris fan and reworking by dam releases had previously scattered some boulders downstream, but these boulders were not a continuous, emergent island at low water. Only after the 1983 flood did a sufficient quantity of boulders accumulate to form something that appears as an island at typical dam releases.

For all the mythology that has grown up around the 1966 Crystal Creek debris flow, one issue has been overlooked. The debris flow did not affect the nearest downstream rapid: Tuna Creek Rapid, Stanton's "bad, rocky rapid," is the same as it was in 1890. No large rocks were transported the mile downstream from Crystal Rapid. Rapids on the Colorado River are influenced only by a nearby source of boulders, whether delivered by debris flow or rockfalls. In Grand Canyon, no evidence suggests that major rapids are formed or are affected by deposition of river-transported boulders in the manner of pool-riffle sequences typical of other rivers in the United States.

Remnant of a Lava Dam?

Every river runner has a strong visceral reaction to Lava Falls Rapid. Depending on how and when you view it, Lava Falls is either ugly or beautiful: ugly while a route through the massive waves is being scouted, and beautiful when viewed safely from the eddies downstream after a successful run. This reach of whitewater is rated as the standard 10 against which other rapids in Grand Canyon are judged in severity. And because it is the only remaining large rapid in western Grand Canyon, it stands out in the context of otherwise calm waters.

Like Crystal Rapid, Lava Falls Rapid has inspired many myths among river guides.[49] The first myth of Lava Falls Rapid is the amount of drop; published guides commonly report a fall of thirty-seven feet over a short distance.[50] The actual water-surface fall through Lava Falls Rapid is only about twelve feet through the main part of the rapid,[51] but one gets the impression from the turbulent waves that the drop is immediate and mostly vertical. As with any rapid, the difficulty in running Lava Falls Rapid arises from a unique geometry of waves and holes that result from flow over and around boulders.

The landmarks of Lava Falls Rapid all have names that are familiar to modern river guides. The Ledge Hole, or Ledge Wave, is in a class by itself as a navigational hazard. At typical water levels, the Ledge Hole spans a quarter of the river at the top left center of the rapid. Water appears to pour over a straight edge into the hole or crashing wave below, which has led to speculation that a ledge or dike of ancient basalt forms the hydraulic feature. At higher water, a run opens perilously close to the left side of the Ledge Hole. At intermediate water levels, the "slot run" just to the right of the Ledge Hole is an option that requires a precise entry at the right center of the rapid. Now, since Glen Canyon Dam, flows are generally low enough that the Ledge Hole can be avoided by running far right.

The run at far right at Lava Falls Rapid is the sensible route at lower water levels. It is by no means easy—as many guides put it, you line up and then you eat it. Lining up a rowing boat consists of entering right and determining how you want your boat

Figure 8.2. Lava Falls Rapid

A. The night of February 26–27, 1890, was the coldest experienced during the Stanton expedition. Stanton and his crew had decided to portage goods and line boats on the left side of Lava Falls Rapid (mile 179.3), but the weather was frigid on the morning of the 27th. To keep warm, John Hislop decided to set fire to the dry vegetation that surrounds the warm springs at the base of the rapid. Stanton waited until 11:00 A.M. for the smoke to clear to get a better view of the rapid (number 621). Note the chaotic appearance of the rapid and the large rock (about fifteen feet across) at right center in the rapid (the "missing rock").

aligned for the V waves, a pair of laterals that meet in the middle of the run. These waves tend to fold over on one another, which adds an element of suspense as to which wave will crash on the boat first when you arrive at the apex of the V. Once through the V waves, and presumably still upright and in your boat, you must keep the boat facing square into the major waves below. Failure to keep the boat straight can result in a flip in waves that are the biggest in

Grand Canyon. On the right at the bottom of the rapid is a large basalt boulder called the Black Rock; just upstream of this rock is a large wave appropriately called the Big Wave. Depending on the surges at this point, a boat can run safely, be flipped in a crash of the Big Wave, or be surfed right and onto the Black Rock.

Running Lava Falls Rapid did not appear to be a good idea to Stanton in 1890. The expedition had

B. The repeat view was made by Raymond M. Turner on February 11, 1990, at 11:37 A.M. The rapid has changed considerably in the century between the views because of debris flows from Prospect Canyon on the left. A debris flow that occurred in 1939 deposited the prominent low terrace at left center; subsequent debris flows in 1954, 1955, and 1963 contributed to changing the upper left of the rapid from a relatively quiescent area to whitewater choked with boulders. As a result of the 1939 debris flow, flow through the rapid was forced to the right and the "missing rock" rolled downstream and was submerged. This rock is the cause for what is now called the "Big Wave," a formidable obstacle to navigation on the right side of the rapid. The "Ledge Hole," which appears at lower right, formed after the 1955 debris flow and gained its full width after the 1963 debris flow.

camped "at the head of the great cataract formed by the lava dike."[52] Stanton exposed three negatives from a position that he had marked with a cairn on the left terrace. The downstream view provides important insights into the navigability of the rapid Stanton opted to portage.

The run to the right may not have been the obvious option in 1890. No tongue then extended down

the right side; instead, a series of waves and pourovers formed the top of the rapid. A large boulder in the channel perhaps fifty feet upstream of the Black Rock partially blocked what is now the right run. James Fennemore and Jack Hillers of the second Powell expedition stood on this rock in 1872 to photograph the rapid.[53] Perhaps the right run was not as necessary in 1890, because the Ledge Hole

C. At about 1:30 A.M. on March 6, 1995, a large debris flow from Prospect Canyon constricted the Colorado River by about one-half. This view, taken by Robert Webb at 11:00 A.M., shows the enlarged debris fan, recessional flow in Prospect Creek, and an unrunnable Lava Falls Rapid. Subsequent reworking resulted in a rapid that is easier to run than before.

did not resemble its modern configuration. Fennemore and Hillers's views of the rapid show a large, pyramid-shaped pile of boulders where now glassy water enters the rapid above the modern Ledge Hole. This rock is faintly visible in Stanton's view of the rapid made eighteen years later.

The left run was absent as well. However, relatively slow-moving water abruptly fell over a line of pourovers in the middle of the rapid. The slow water and abrupt fall offered a relatively easy alternative to running the rapid. Boats were lined through the slow water until the pourovers, where boatmen skidded their watercraft over some very large boulders.[54] Frequently, boats were damaged more in portaging than they might have been if the rapid had been run.

A second myth about Lava Falls Rapid (besides the amount of fall in the rapid) concerns the relation between local geology and the cause of the rapid. The setting would be impressive without the massive whitewater; ancient lava flows still visible after having poured over the canyon walls catch one's attention as a major change in the geology of the canyon. Although inconspicuous outcrops of basalt are present as far as two miles upstream, the really impressive lava flows begin about a half-mile above the rapid. These flows, which originated more than a million years ago, formed dams across the Colorado River with lakes that are reported to have stretched back to Lees Ferry and beyond.[55] One lava flow extended at least eighty-five miles down the Colorado River. The most recent lava dam formed 140,000 years ago.

These lava flows that poured over the 3,000-foot canyon walls, not the rapid itself, were the inspiration for John Wesley Powell's naming the site "Lava Falls."[56] Powell was the first to suggest that the rapid was somehow controlled by intact remnants of the lava flows,[57] and later observers repeated the error. Even Stanton, generally an astute observer, referred to the rapid's being formed by a "lava dike." Basaltic dikes do occur about a mile upstream at Vulcans Anvil, but nothing at the rapid suggests any subterranean injection of volcanic rock. The explanation has been embellished to the point that the rapid is said to be controlled by "rocks and ledges under water"[58] that presumably are remnants of the lava dams. Perhaps the grand spectacle of impressive lava flows and a massive rapid distracts observers from the real evidence of the rapid's origin, which is the massive terraces of debris-flow deposits that line both sides of Prospect Creek. Even accounts that acknowledge debris flows from Prospect Creek as the origin[59] attribute to ancient or prehistoric debris flows the formation of spectacular hydraulic features like the Ledge Hole.

Most Grand Canyon river runners, past and present, recognize the association of rapids with tributaries. Because tributaries are typically small in Grand Canyon, their signature at river level is a debris fan. But Prospect Creek is an exception, and the fan at the mouth of the creek is likewise in a class by itself; only the one at the mouth of Nankoweap Creek, reputed to have been formed by a massive landslide, is larger.[60] The debris fan that forms Lava Falls Rapid looms more than seventy feet above the river. Abundant vertical exposures cut into the fan by Prospect Creek and the Colorado River show numerous boulders in a matrix of gravel, sand, and mud that could have been emplaced only by debris flows from Prospect Creek.

This unusual fan is at the mouth of an unusual tributary. Prospect Creek is large in comparison with typical Grand Canyon tributaries; it drains ninety-seven square miles of high desert south of Grand Canyon. Most of this watercourse is typical of desert rivers that mostly transport sand, silt, and clay in floods down gentle grades. One mile from its mouth, however, Prospect Creek is anything but typical, for there its canyon was filled by the lava flows that dammed the Colorado River over a million years ago.[61] Unlike the Colorado River, which had the flow necessary to erode its lava dams, Prospect Creek is still trying to erode the blockage.

The result of the blockage is a spectacular thousand-foot cliff over which floods plunge en route to the Colorado River. Immense piles of loose rubble at the base of the cliff can be entrained into the falling water, mobilizing debris flows. The plug of basalt had provided a continuous source of material for debris flows, which probably began soon after the last lava dam across the Colorado River was eroded away. After traveling the short distance through the cliffs, one flow after another deposited the enormous debris fan in the Colorado River, forming the rapid. Any residual influence of intact basalt would have inconsequential effects compared to the substantial deposition of boulders in the river.

One might assume that any tributary that can deliver the volume of debris like that stored in the debris fan of Prospect Creek must do so frequently. Repeat photography can be used to test this assumption. Fortunately, numerous photographs and movies have been made of Lava Falls Rapid, beginning with stereoscopic views made by Fennemore and Hillers in April 1872. Every expedition that brought a camera photographed Lava Falls Rapid, and these views have been preserved. In addition, the spectacular view downstream from Toroweap Point, high above the rapid on the northwestern rim, has also been popular with photographers. By closely examining these photographs,[62] we can create a detailed history of change in Lava Falls Rapid that belies its image as ancient and unchanging.

Before 1939, four features characterized the rapid. At low water, no definite tongue was present; instead, a line of drops perpendicular to the channel occurred across the top of the rapid. At discharges below about 18,000 cfs, a group of boulders in the center of this line appeared as a pyramid when viewed from several angles. Flow on the right side was deflected by a large basalt boulder just above the Black Rock; this boulder is prominent in photographs, even in those taken from Toroweap Point, and could be seen at water levels less than about 30,000 cfs. Deflection of the flow pushed water away from the Black Rock, and the tailwaves appeared to follow a straight path to the bottom of the rapid at all water levels. Flow immediately adjacent to the Black Rock was relatively calm, suggesting that perhaps river runners could intentionally eddy out just upstream in low water.[63]

The rapid did not change between 1872 and 1939 despite floods in excess of 200,000 cfs in 1884 and 1921 and possibly in 1891, 1905, and 1916. Low-water views, such as the one made by Emery Kolb on January 1, 1912, indicate that the bottom of Lava Falls Rapid was composed of boulders more than ten feet in diameter. These large boulders appeared to be wedged together into piles. Water flowing over these piles would have formed treacherous holes and waves; this bed configuration probably accounts for the early descriptions of the rapid being full of holes and rocks even at high discharges.

Only George Flavell in 1896, Buzz Holmstrom in 1938, and Don Harris and Bert Loper in 1939 are known to have run Lava Falls Rapid before it changed. No one knows how Flavell ran the rapid, but it "put about eight inches of water in the boat."[64]

Amos Burg filmed Holmstrom running the rapid in 1938: Holmstrom went right. Harris and Loper ran right at a river level of about 7,600 cfs and "lightly touched a rock."[65] Only hours before his successful run of Lava Falls Rapid, Loper had carelessly flipped his boat in Gateway Rapid, which is now rated a 3 compared to the 10 of Lava Falls Rapid.[66] Another river runner, Norm Nevills, chose to line Lava Falls on the left in 1938, but he speculated that a right run was risky but possible at the water level he saw (20,000 cfs).[67]

The period during which the rapid apparently remained unchanged, from some unknown time before 1872 to September 1939, contrasts dramatically with the events of the mid-twentieth century. The likely date for the first twentieth-century debris flow is September 6, 1939.[68] This debris flow, the largest in our experience in Grand Canyon, had a discharge of about 30,000 cfs.[69] The net effect is clear in views made after 1941. The pyramid of rocks at the top of the rapid was removed, possibly by the force of the impact when the debris flow met the Colorado River. The big rock probably was dislodged at the same time and rolled a short distance downstream. Water flowing over the newly submerged rock created the hydraulic conditions necessary for the Big Wave, just downstream.[70] The right run had been softened, but the river extracted a toll for passage—the Big Wave.

On his next trip in 1940, Norm Nevills became the first boatman to face the new Lava Falls Rapid. As Barry Goldwater (who later became Arizona's most influential senator) looked on impatiently, Nevills pondered the run on water at a level of less than 3,000 cfs. In his diary, Goldwater notes, "At Lava Falls most of the water flows over to the right bank where it plunges over a fall that seems to be twelve or fifteen feet high. That of course left only the left side to consider as a possibility of running, and, if that possibility didn't show itself, we faced a portage."[71] Nevills chose to run the rapid, but the diary does not indicate whether he took Goldwater's advice and ran left. In 1941, Nevills decided that lining was the obvious way to traverse the rapid.[72]

River running was a luxury during World War II, and few river runners encountered Lava Falls Rapid between 1941 and 1947. By the mid-1940s, the 1939 debris fan had been partially eroded by Colorado River floods, starting with the 1941 discharge of 120,000 cfs. Few changes in the rapid are visible in photographs taken by passengers on Nevills's trips in 1942 and 1947 from approximately the same position on the left side.

The axiom that "debris flows beget debris flows" applies to Prospect Creek. After a long hiatus, Prospect Creek came alive in the 1950s with a succession of debris flows that further altered the shape and flow patterns of Lava Falls Rapid.

P. T. Reilly, who ran the Colorado River in the 1950s, reflects that the largest change he knew of in Lava Falls Rapid occurred in 1954. John Riffey, who was formerly a long-time ranger at Tuweep, also observed that a flood occurred in Prospect Wash in the summer of 1954.[73] Indeed, aerial photographs Reilly took in 1955 show an enlarged debris fan at the mouth of Prospect Creek. In his opinion, the flood of 1954 made the rapid much easier to run: the spaces between the large boulders were filled in and the flow became less turbulent with fewer holes scattered around the rapid. The debris flow of 1954 and the ones that followed filled in the once-open left side of the rapid, which forced the main flow down the right side. The tailwaves that previously ran straight began to curve to the left at the bottom of the rapid. Of more significance to the spectacular nature of the rapid, the Ledge Hole began to form.

The 1955 debris flow was probably the second largest of the century, exceeded only by the debris flow of 1939. The 1955 flow, which occurred between March and mid-July,[74] effectively constricted the rapid by two-thirds, forcing all flow at low water to the right. All but the largest boulders present on the left side of the river before March 1955 were re-

placed or buried by this debris flow, including the rocks that formed the incipient Ledge Hole. The geomorphic effects of this debris flow, and perhaps the 1939 debris flow, too, were at least as spectacular as the 1966 debris flow at Crystal Rapid. The difference is that Lava Falls Rapid has always been large, and the effects of the debris flows could be eradicated by Colorado River floods.

The mid-1950s were low-water years on the Colorado River. Several years of winter drought affected much of the United States, particularly in New Mexico, Colorado, and Texas.[75] The low discharges of the river[76] were insufficient to budge the large boulders that choked the left side of Lava Falls Rapid. The droughts were broken rather dramatically in the winter of 1956–57. El Niño conditions once again arose, causing intensified winter storms. The result was abundant snowpack in the Rocky Mountains, a quick spring thaw, and one of the last floods that could be considered "natural" on the Colorado River.

The 1957 flood peaked at 125,000 cfs on June 13. The floodwaters had the power to pluck large boulders out of the recently formed debris fan of Prospect Creek and move them downstream. When the flood receded, only the largest boulders, with diameters in excess of five feet, remained on the left side of the rapid. The debris fan, which had withstood two years of smaller floods during the drought years, had been reworked back to a configuration similar to the one that existed before 1954. But with the addition of new large boulders into the middle of the rapid, the Ledge Hole had formed and the V waves marked the run to the right.[77]

The last major change occurred in the summer of 1963. A debris flow that probably occurred in early September[78] created a debris fan similar in size to the one formed in 1955. However, this debris fan was composed of notably smaller boulders about three feet in diameter. This debris fan persisted until the release of 58,400 cfs from Glen Canyon Dam on June 15, 1965. The reworked debris fan did not appear to differ greatly from the one present before 1963. Further changes in Lava Falls Rapid occurred during the 96,200 cfs flood of 1983, but these changes were relatively minor and probably consisted of re-arrangement of boulders deposited in 1963.

Lava Falls Rapid is thus not a direct remnant of a lava dam but instead the premier example of a Grand Canyon rapid that was formed and is maintained by debris flows. All the major rapids in Grand Canyon are controlled by debris flows,[79] and Lava Falls Rapid is no exception. The intense and violent energy of water in the rapid is not caused by flow over im-movable bedrock; the Colorado River, given enough flow, is able to alter the arrangement of waves, holes, and rocks at Lava Falls. In the era of flow regulation, the issue of what constitutes sufficient discharge is critical. Whereas debris flows will continue to occur in Prospect Creek, the runoff energy resulting from the melting of a deep snowpack or a large storm can no longer be directed against the boulders that form Lava Falls Rapid—unless people let it happen.

A Study in Contrasts

Many striking contrasts are apparent in the historic changes of Crystal and Lava Falls Rapids. The only real similarity between Crystal and Lava Falls Rapids in the late twentieth century is that both are severe obstacles to navigation. However, Crystal Rapid has been a violent rapid for only the latter third of the century, whereas Lava Falls Rapid has become easier to run.[80] Crystal Rapid may owe its severity more to the presence of a dam upstream of Lees Ferry than to a long-term propensity for debris-flow activity in Crystal Creek; in contrast, the largest debris flows that changed Lava Falls Rapid occurred before the regulation of the Colorado River, and unimpeded floods reworked its aggraded debris fans. Debris flows may reach the Colorado River at Crystal Rapid only once per century; in contrast, debris flows fre-quently reached the river at Lava Falls Rapid.

Lava Falls illustrates the long-term struggle be-tween frequent debris-flow deposition and stream-flow processes, particularly before the closure of the dam. As in prehistoric Crystal Rapid, all but the largest boulders were washed downstream and out of Lava Falls Rapid, creating a rapid that remained stable for at least a third of a century. Between 1939 and 1955, the amount of boulders pushed into the unregulated river by debris flows was too much for floods to transport. Although the river had enough power to widen itself and remove most of the con-striction, residual boulders resisted the largest dis-charges. Boulders were added that displaced some of the boulders that littered the rapid before 1939, but, if anything, the fall through the rapid is steeper than when Stanton viewed Lava Falls in 1890.

Debris flows constricted both rapids after the clo-sure of Glen Canyon Dam, but the interaction of river and debris fan was different. The 1963 debris flow at Lava Falls Rapid was largely removed by dam releases of 58,000 cfs in 1965, and minor reworking occurred during the higher 1983 high releases. The debris fan at Crystal Rapid, enlarged in 1966, was first reworked by releases of about 38,000 cfs in 1973, but major changes occurred only when dam releases ex-ceeded 50,000 cfs in 1983. The difference is explained largely by the size of boulders that composed the ag-graded debris fans; whereas the 1963 debris flow was possibly the smallest and had the smallest boulders of any in the twentieth century at Lava Falls Rapid, the 1966 debris flow at Crystal Rapid had very large boulders.

It is interesting to speculate what might have been the result if debris flows at Crystal and Lava Falls Rapids had occurred earlier or later. For ex-ample, if the 1966 debris flow in Crystal Creek had occurred in 1939, Crystal Rapid might not have been as severe an obstacle to navigation as it is currently. Floods in the quarter-century before the closure of Glen Canyon Dam likely would have removed many of the boulders that currently litter the top of Crystal Rapid, and the particular sequence of waves and holes that give Crystal Rapid its fearsome character might have been completely different. Crystal Rapid would probably still be a more difficult rapid than the one Stanton viewed in 1890 but perhaps would not have the reputation it has enjoyed in the latter part of the twentieth century.

What if the debris flow in Prospect Creek had occurred in 1966 instead of 1939? Little evidence remains of the 1939 debris flow in Lava Falls Rapid, but its discharge and effects on an otherwise stable rapid indicate it was larger than the Crystal Creek debris flow of 1966. Lava Falls Rapid probably would have persisted in a highly constricted state until the 1983 high flows, with an uncertain potential for navigation in the intervening seventeen years. Apparently, a discharge of 120,000 cfs in the Colorado River was required to remove much of the deposition of the 1939 debris flow—the river's discharge of 96,000 cfs in 1983 would have removed far less.

In the era of regulation by Glen Canyon Dam, understanding the recurrence interval of debris flows is fundamental to predicting future changes in these rapids. There is no reason to assume that the frequency of debris flows that maintain these rapids will change in the future, because humans do not affect the generation of debris flows in Grand Canyon. The infrequency with which debris flows reach the river at Crystal Rapid suggests that changes in the near future might be restricted to occasional downstream movement of boulders, especially if another large release occurs from Glen Canyon Dam. The potential for change at Lava Falls Rapid is much greater. Debris flows affected the rapid about every ten years in the mid-twentieth century; an extrapolation of this frequency would mean the potential for another large debris flow at Lava Falls Rapid is extremely high despite the hiatus of thirty-two years.

Debris flows will undeniably continue to occur at both Crystal and Lava Falls Rapids. Unlike the recurrence interval for debris flows, the recurrence inter-

val for boulder-removing floods has been greatly reduced by the closure of Glen Canyon Dam. Should a debris flow occur at either of these rapids, humans would have to decide whether to make a large release from the dam in an attempt to transport downstream the boulders that obstruct the river. In light of this possibility, the largest change over the past century at Crystal and Lava Falls Rapids was caused not by debris flows but by the construction of a dam upstream of Grand Canyon.

Coda

During the night of March 5–6, 1995, debris flows occurred in Crystal Creek and Prospect Canyon during a major winter storm. Only minor changes occurred in Crystal Rapid, but Lava Falls changed significantly. As chance would have it, my crew and I were camped above Lava Falls Rapid the night of the debris flow. A microburst of rainfall at midnight capped a storm that had been continuous for twenty-six hours. At about 1:30 A.M., we heard a loud roaring sound from Prospect Canyon that lasted three to five minutes. We did not comprehend what had happened until the next morning when we inspected the rapid.

Although the rapid was initially constricted by about 50 percent, reworking by the Colorado River eroded the face of the enlarged debris fan to about a 33 percent constriction. When we first saw the rapid, it was unrunnable; reworking during the three days we observed and measured the debris fan actually made the rapid easier to run (although at higher velocities) than before. The debris flow is the largest in Prospect Creek since 1955 and the largest in Grand Canyon since the Crystal Creek debris flow of 1966. Its occurrence underscores the need for large releases from Glen Canyon Dam—larger than power plant releases but much smaller than floods before the closure of the dam—to rework deposits left by recent debris flows.

CHAPTER 9

Water Running over Boulders

Just ask any experienced Grand Canyon river guide, and he or she will tell you how to run any rapid at any level of flow. The runs sound rote. At Badger Creek Rapid, you run the center tongue most of the time, avoiding the pile of rocks at the upper left and the pourovers on the right. At House Rock, you have to pull right—*hard* right to avoid the hole on the bottom left. But wait before you start pulling, because the right side is the "rumble run" through shallow pourovers. At Horn Creek, you must know the water level; the rapid is a seething caldron of holes at low water but it washes out at high water. Dubendorff is "bony" at low water, so you have to pull right behind the "whale rock" or "stickiup" just upstream of the "table rock." Most of the time, the only rapids that should be scouted are Hance, Crystal, and Lava Falls Rapids. Even these rapids are so familiar that some professional guides are comfortable running them "wide open," without scouting.

Although familiarity with a rapid can lead to cockiness, experienced guides (ones who have run Grand Canyon for twenty years or more) will also tell stories about changes in some rapids, that in some places riffles now exist where flat water used to be, and that the hole in 209 Mile Rapid formed sometime in the late 1970s. They might even tell you that they read somewhere that President Harding

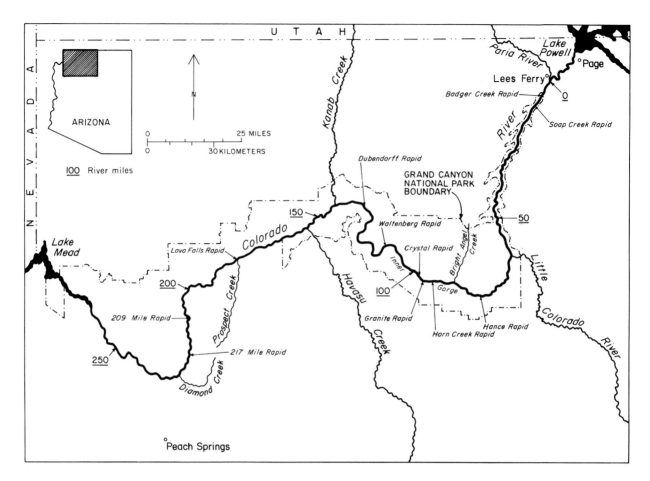

Figure 9.1. Locations of some of the major rapids in Grand Canyon

Rapid did not exist in 1911, that the large boulder in the channel fell off the right wall sometime before 1923. Other guides who know the intricacies of the river will mention possible long-ago changes in Soap Creek Rapid, for example.

One approach to the question of whether rapids have changed in Grand Canyon is to read the accounts of the first expeditions down the Colorado River. The first river runners in Grand Canyon faced an unknown river and were challenged by the rapids. They described their difficulties, real or perceived, in their navigation. John Wesley Powell was the first to describe the rapids, but his crew portaged most of them. Powell's exaggerated account of the size and

difficulty of rapids confused those who followed and used his writings as a guide.[1]

The descriptions are tantalizing. Robert Brewster Stanton summed up Fishtail Rapid (mile 139.1) tersely: "One immense wave in it."[2] Most modern river runners would agree that the hole in Fishtail Rapid is awesome and is the only interesting feature of the rapid. But Stanton experienced low water on most of his expedition, and he describes many rapids, and even riffles, only as "rocky." Many of the succinct descriptions of rapids by the early expeditions could apply to any Grand Canyon rapid.

But fear and respect for Grand Canyon rapids led the early river runners to do something besides write down their impressions of the whitewater: most river expeditions photographed rapids that appeared difficult to run, producing a thorough collection of views, from different angles and water levels, of Grand Canyon whitewater. Several rapids, such as Badger Creek, Soap Creek, Hance, Sockdolager, and Lava Falls Rapids, were photographed extensively. Others were recorded only by Stanton's camera.

By my reckoning, fifty-seven major rapids occur on the Colorado River in Grand Canyon.[3] Stanton secured images of thirty-eight of these. Most of the photographs are clear enough to show gross changes and their cause. Because Nims and Stanton made long exposures, only fixed waves are visible in the whitewater, but the locations of above-water boulders and the sizes of debris fans can be readily evaluated. To discuss changes, or lack of changes, in all thirty-eight rapids would be of interest only to serious river historians. Some of these rapids have a mystique or a checkered history of navigation, however, that can be explained by changes in the physical condition of the rapid. What follows is a description of how certain key rapids have changed during the past century and how others have remained in approximately the same condition as they were in 1890 (see tables 4 and 5 in the appendix).

The Last Rapid Run

Soap Creek Rapid—the very name struck fear into the hearts of early explorers. They were not concerned about House Rock Rapid, and 24½ Mile was just another rapid, but they were on the lookout for Soap Creek Rapid (mile 11.2). They did not want to run this fearsome rapid by mistake. The mystique of Soap Creek Rapid was passed down from river runner to river runner. This was the rapid, after all, that had wrecked a raft carrying ten prospectors in 1872.[4] This rapid was alleged to have claimed the life of Frank Brown in 1889.[5] It is not surprising, then, that

the first run of Soap Creek Rapid was unintentional.

Powell took one look at Soap Creek Rapid and ordered a portage of the fifteen-foot fall in 1869. He did not bother to look in 1872; the crew knew they would portage the rapid. The Brown-Stanton expedition portaged Soap Creek Rapid on July 9, 1889; at the time Stanton noted that "the fall at its head [was the] greatest of any we have passed."[6] After Frank Brown's death the following day, Stanton had bad memories of Soap Creek Rapid. When his second expedition reached it on December 30, he ordered an immediate portage.

In the fall of 1896, George Flavell and Ramon Montéz were running the Colorado River essentially for fun and for the potential profits from trapping.[7] They were the first river runners to follow Stanton and used one of his popular accounts as a river guide.[8] Flavell was an experienced outdoorsman, and lining or portaging rapids was not his idea of fun. On October 17, Flavell got a scare with a bumpy ride through Badger Creek Rapid, the first one in Marble Canyon. A short distance downstream, he scouted Soap Creek Rapid. Flavell read Stanton's description, but Flavell was also a fearless boatman and had run rapids that both Stanton and Powell had portaged. Yet Flavell found that Soap Creek was not an ordinary rapid:

> We viewed something to impress us for some time to come. It was some four or five hundred yards in length, the first 50 yards having about 12 feet of fall. It was rocky and seemed to be lashed into one mass of lather. We sat and gazed on it for two or three hours before our eyes had got their fill. The spray bounced 10 or 12 feet high, and as I was looking I noticed some 20 feet high, a dim mist of spray which puffed up like smoke. And it flashed across my mind, "If you have any doubt where that smoke comes from, just try to run it!" Still, I could of run it with an empty boat, but it would have been too far to carry the stuff and it was decided best to make a portage.[9]

Figure 9.2. Soap Creek Rapid

A. On July 9, 1889, Frank Brown and Stanton camped on the sand bar below Soap Creek Rapid (mile 11.0). The following morning, Brown was thrown from his boat and drowned in Salt Water Riffle, which is around the bend at the center of this view. The return, on December 30, was a sad one for Stanton and his crew. While supplies were being portaged on the right side, Stanton crossed to the left for surveying work on his railroad route. Sometime during the afternoon, Nims made this downstream view (number 283). Although his view does not show the large boulder at the head of the rapid, it does show the two lines of waves that Ellsworth Kolb described in 1911.

Except for the length, Flavell might have been describing Lava Falls Rapid, which inspires similar feelings today. With his portage and lining of Soap Creek Rapid, Flavell met his only match in Grand Canyon. He successfully ran every other rapid, including Lava Falls, Separation, and Lava Cliff Rapids.[10]

George Wharton James explored the Grand Canyon region during the decade after Stanton's success-

ful run. In 1897, while visiting Lees Ferry, James met Nathaniel Galloway, who had run Grand Canyon the preceding year. James had heard the stories about Soap Creek Rapid, and he convinced Galloway, who had a boat, to take him down to see it. Galloway knew its name but apparently did not know its location: the rapid Galloway instead showed James was Badger Creek Rapid.[11] Even Galloway, who revolutionized river running, had immense respect for Soap Creek

B. Few river runners scout Soap Creek Rapid now. Where Kolb saw two tongues at the head of the rapid, divided by a large boulder, the run now is down the center. The slope of Hermit Shale at left is unstable; few rocks, including those in the prominent ledges, are recognizable a century later. Moreover, the sand bar Stanton camped on twice is no longer usable by river parties; the former camping beach is now littered with rocks that create a difficult mooring. Ralph Hopkins replicated this view on January 18, 1990, at 3:10 P.M.

Rapid (even if he did not know exactly where it was).

Emery and Ellsworth Kolb were neither experienced river runners nor outdoorsmen of note: they were photographers. In 1911, the two brothers decided to replicate Powell's 1868 trip and film a movie of their adventures.[12] They had gained experience and confidence running whitewater in the canyons of the Green River and in Cataract Canyon of the Colorado River. When they reached Soap Creek Rapid in late afternoon, they found that

the rapid had a fall of twenty-five feet, and was a quarter of a mile long. Most of the fall occurred in the first fifty yards. . . . On the very brink or edge of the first fall, there was a submerged rock in the centre of the channel, making an eight-foot fall over the rock. A violent current, deflected from the left shore, shot into this centre and added to the confusion. Twelve-foot waves, from the conflicting currents, played leap-frog, jumping over or through each other alternately. . . . Soap Creek rapid in many ways was not as bad as some we had gone over in Cataract Canyon, but there were so many complications that we hesitated a long time before coming to a decision.[13]

The Kolbs were duly impressed by the rapid, particularly the haystack waves, but they were determined to be the first to run it.

Ellsworth rowed; Emery filmed. Although Ellsworth pulled with all his strength, the stern of his boat caught on a rock and he was thrown from the boat as it tipped on its side. He retained a grip on the gunwale, however, and climbed back into the boat after it righted. Reaching the shore below the rapid, Ellsworth wanted to try again despite the fading daylight. On his second attempt, he went over the large rock at the top of the rapid. The boat flipped in the succeeding waves, and Ellsworth had a long swim beside the overturned boat. When his wild afternoon and evening was over, he noted, "Somehow I had lost all desire to successfully navigate the Soap Creek Rapid."[14]

Most of the river trips or expeditions in the first third of the century chose to portage Soap Creek Rapid. In 1923, the U.S. Geological Survey expedition portaged on the right. With ten men, five boats, and one and a half tons of equipment, the expedition took all day to get past the dangers of Soap Creek Rapid.[15] More photographs exist of this portage than of any other place or event experienced by the 1923 expedition.

To portage or to line appeared to be the choice at Soap Creek Rapid. But in 1927, Clyde Eddy did neither, thus earning the distinction of being the first to successfully, albeit unintentionally, run Soap Creek Rapid.[16] Eddy was an adventurer, not a boatman, and had dreamed of running the Colorado River for many years. He used Powell's book as a river guide and had no intention of running Soap Creek Rapid. However, after entering Marble Can-

yon, Eddy mistook Badger Creek Rapid for Soap Creek Rapid and lined the less formidable rapid. Soap Creek Rapid looked like just another reach of whitewater, and Parley Galloway (Nathaniel's son) had a thrilling ride with Eddy as his passenger. The historic run of Soap Creek Rapid, the last rapid to be run in Grand Canyon, was uneventful compared to the rest of Eddy's trip; he lost a boat in Dubendorff Rapid and lined and portaged many other rapids.[17]

Sometime in the 1930s, though, Soap Creek Rapid lost much of its mystique. The rapid had changed. River runners encountered fewer of the violent waves that had impressed Flavell and others. The Frazier-Hatch expedition of 1934 portaged the rapid,[18] but Buzz Holmstrom ran it solo in 1937 and again in 1938.[19] Don Harris and Bert Loper ran it in 1939.[20] Norman D. Nevills, the first commercial boatman to run Grand Canyon, was generally so cautious that he drew criticism.[21] Although he lined or portaged many of the largest rapids, even he did not feel that Soap Creek Rapid was particularly difficult: he ran it in 1938. His journal entry for the 1941 trip states, "We land on right, and a glance suffices to show that it is easily run."[22] This reaction contrasts strikingly with that of Flavell in 1896.

What happened between 1896 and 1941 at Soap Creek Rapid? The wave formed by the rock Kolb so carefully described, and then accidentally rowed his boat over, is visible in 1935 aerial photography of Grand Canyon[23] but not in modern aerial photographs, even when the water level is low. Evidently, a flash flood or debris flow came down Soap Creek in the mid-1930s.[24] The large rock may have been washed downstream or buried under new debris. Unfortunately, none of the four views at Soap Creek taken by Stanton shows that particular rock. I think the boulder is still present but that deposition of new boulders downstream during a tributary flood has smoothed the topography of the bed of the rapid. As a result, the water flowing through the center of the rapid has less turbulence than it once had. I can guess all I want at what changed, but the certainty of the matter is that the rapid is easier to run because the boulder no longer affects navigation.

Conventional wisdom holds that flash floods and debris flows make rapids more difficult, as illustrated by the 1966 debris flow in Crystal Creek. Sometimes, as in the case of Soap Creek Rapid, a flood from a side canyon can make a rapid easier to run. That is the nature of water flowing over a pile of boulders: move a critical one, and the rapid's navigability changes. Whether it gets easier or harder depends on the specific arrangement of boulders in a rapid and the type of boat one uses.

Other Rapids with Significant Change

House Rock Rapid

House Rock Rapid (mile 16.7) has taken the place of Soap Creek Rapid as the most respected rapid in Marble Canyon. In House Rock Rapid, the river makes a sharp turn to the right around a large but low debris fan. At high water, the debris fan is submerged and the rapid is washed out, but at low water much of the current flows through a large hole on the bottom left of the rapid. Guides must keep their boats moving to the right in House Rock Rapid to avoid that hole. The maneuver required to navigate House Rock Rapid successfully is the most difficult in the first seventy-six miles of navigation at low to moderate flows.

Navigation of the rapid was not always so difficult. In the 1950s, Otis "Dock" Marston wrote to all the boatmen he knew requesting their opinions on the severity of rapids in Grand Canyon.[25] Emery Kolb wrote back listing Soap Creek Rapid as a 10, equivalent to Hance, Horn Creek, Granite, Hermit, and Lava Falls Rapids. He did not list House Rock as a major rapid. Other boatmen responded similarly. But by the 1960s, river guides rated House Rock

Rapid as slightly less severe than Soap Creek Rapid and equal to Badger Creek Rapid.[26] The change resulted from a large debris flow from Rider Canyon that occurred sometime between 1966 and 1971.[27]

Granite Rapid

Running Granite Rapid (mile 93.5) feels somewhat like a sleigh ride down a steep hill. There is little choice in running a raft through Granite: minute adjustments are possible at the top, but a boat must inevitably go through the largest waves. Skillful boaters will be able to make a few maneuvers to keep out of the waves dashing along the cliff on the right, but mostly the run is barely under control. The goal is to keep the boat pointed downstream and perpendicular to the waves.

Granite Rapid has changed more than most rapids in Grand Canyon. When Jack Hillers of the second Powell expedition photographed it in 1872, Granite Rapid was wide and rocky. The rapid had narrowed sometime before Hal Stephens replicated Hillers's photograph in 1968.[28] The reason for this constriction was that at least one debris flow had occurred in Monument Creek, which enters on the south side of the river and creates the rapid. The debris flow that shows prominently in Stephens's view occurred in the summer of 1968.

The best-known debris flow in Monument Creek occurred in July 1984.[29] This debris flow, which peaked at about 4,000 cubic feet per second (cfs) of water, mud, and boulders, caused extensive deposition on the debris fan. Flow in Granite Rapid was forced farther right, and for several years the rapid was relatively narrow. High releases from Glen Canyon Dam in the mid-1980s eroded much of the newly deposited material, and Granite Rapid is now similar to its condition before the debris flow of 1984.

209 Mile Rapid

Stanton ran 209 Mile Rapid in 1890 with little fan-

Figure 9.3. Granite Rapid

A. John Wesley Powell used a drawing of Granite Rapid (mile 93.5) to illustrate how his crew ran rapids in 1869. Ironically, Powell's crew portaged this rapid, as did Stanton's twenty-one years later. Stanton made this upstream view (number 464) of the head of Granite Rapid and the mouth of Monument Creek on February 7, 1890, at 1:15 P.M.

fare. He saw little need for concern because the rapid was more like a long riffle. The rapid is unusual for Grand Canyon; the river flows around an island, not over a debris fan. The island, however, is formed from the outwash from debris fans from three canyons that reach the river here.

In 1978, a commercial river trip reached 209 Mile Rapid and noticed dust hanging in the air. The rapid was changed. A spectacular hole was present on the right side, formed by a large block of basalt that had fallen from an ancient debris fan on the right side of the channel. In 1890, Stanton made an upstream

view from the bottom of 209 Mile Rapid that shows the basalt boulder poised in the debris fan above the head of the rapid. The replicated view shows the cavity left by the fallen rock.

Rapids with Little or No Change

The Pinball Run

Hance Rapid is big, wide, and nasty. It has changed little if at all since Stanton lined it in 1890. The rapid is filled with boulders that either snag boats at low water or form haystacks that can flip boats at high

B. Granite Rapid is one of the biggest rapids in the Inner Gorge. It cannot be cheated at most water levels experienced in the 1990s; river runners usually run the largest waves in the rapid. The rapid has changed considerably in the past century because of debris flows out of Monument Creek (at right). The last major debris flow, in 1984, pushed the flow of the Colorado River farther right and changed the rapid from a wide, rocky channel to a narrow, swift chute. Tom Brownold replicated this view on January 29, 1990, at 10:30 A.M.

water. At least one rock in Hance Rapid (mile 76.8) is named for a guide who was unlucky enough to park a boat on it. One of the three most difficult rapids at all water levels, Hance Rapid is of sufficient size to cause even the most experienced guides to scout it.

Hance Rapid is so difficult that many Colorado River expeditions lined or portaged it. The exception was Flavell, who in 1896 was the first to run it. The water was low, probably less than 5,000 cfs, and the run was not pretty:

After going some 10 miles we came to a very bad rapid. Tying up the boat, we went down to investigate. It was one mass of boulders. The water entered by two channels at the head. It was perhaps as bad [as] or worse than any we had struck, and the show for running it was very slim. . . . [T]o our surprise three mounted men came up, dismounted, and tied their horses. . . . They were anxious to see us get over the rapid. . . . I decided to run the rapid (though I would not if they had not been there) and pushed off.

Figure 9.4. Hance Rapid

A. Stanton's camera captured this view (number 412) of Hance Rapid (mile 76.8) on January 27, 1890, at about 11:30 A.M. Stanton and his crew decided to portage; rocks block the rapid, leaving little possibility of a run in which a boat would hit none of them. If a similar water level occurred today, professional guides, particularly those with motorboats, would face the choice of waiting for higher releases from Glen Canyon Dam or making the very difficult run, which might end with the boat wrapped around a rock.

We had to make exact points to get through, which we failed to do, and in the flash of an eye an oar was broke, a rowlock tore out, and the *Panthon* was piled up in the boulders. We were not yet in the main part. . . . I pried her off. Twenty feet more and we came up again. Again we pried her loose. This time we whirled out in the main rapid. . . . We went down sideways, endways, and every way, the three spectators standing on the rocks. . . . If we had bad luck in breaking the oar and rowlocks, we had good in getting through the rapid.[30]

Flavell nearly paid dearly for his showmanship. Bouncing a rubber raft like a pinball off rocks is relatively forgiving, but to do so in a wooden boat was little short of suicidal. A more prudent boatmen would not have considered running Hance Rapid in such low water.

Despite the reputation of Hance Rapid among modern river runners, many early river runners had

B. Tom Brownold replicated Stanton's view on January 27, 1990, at 12:20 P.M. The water level in 1990 was much higher than in the view made a century before, but the major rocks that make Hance Rapid difficult are still present. Although some rocks have been rotated by Colorado River floods, the foreground rocks on the debris fan have not changed significantly.

fewer difficulties here than in other rapids. For example, Nevills, who rowed wooden cataract boats in the 1930s and 1940s, usually ran Hance Rapid.[31] One reason for the occasional relative ease of navigability is the width of the river at Hance Rapid: river runners have room to maneuver. Moreover, at low water, flow through the rapid is relatively slow. A small boat can enter at far right and still have room and time to row left, left, left to miss the maze of rocks that can make Hance Rapid a pinball run. Miss the right-to-left run, and there are some hateful pourovers to navigate.

Big rapids inspire big speculation as to their origins. At Hance Rapid, for example, a dike of black

basalt, which cuts through the red Hakatai Shale, enters on the right. Some have used it to explain the fierceness of the whitewater at Hance Rapid;[32] the resistant dike is alleged to underlie the rapid, forcing the Colorado River to erode the surrounding Hakatai Shale "like sugar." But the all-controlling dike does not appear to cross to the left side of the river, and it is only ten to twenty feet thick.

Like all other large rapids in Grand Canyon, Hance Rapid is created and maintained by debris flows. The tributary that controls Hance Rapid is Red Canyon, which enters on the top left of the rapid. Red Canyon contains the largest area of de-

Figure 9.5. Ruby Rapid

A. Stanton and his crew believed they could have run Ruby Rapid (mile 104.8) if the low water of February 15, 1890, had not exposed two rocks at the foot of the rapid. They lined and portaged the rapid on the left, or Ruby Canyon, side. Remarkably, they lined two boats and portaged gear 450 feet in a mere forty minutes. After a lunch rest, Stanton made this upstream view (number 503) across the debris fan at 1:00 P.M. The lack of sand in the canyon mouth and the presence of fresh-looking gravels all the way to the river indicate that a flash flood had recently occurred in Ruby Canyon, probably in the summer of 1889.

posits created by landslides and avalanches in Grand Canyon.[33] These landslides and avalanches in Red Canyon would have occurred in prehistoric times and could have coincided with intense rainfall, creating the conditions for large debris flows. Evidence for such prehistoric debris flows is abundant in the terraces of mud and boulders that line Red Canyon.

Horn Creek

When the Colorado River flows between 3,000 and 9,000 cfs, Horn Creek Rapid (mile 90.2) is the most difficult in the Inner Gorge, if not the entire canyon.[34] Two prominent rocks stick out of the middle and left side of the rapid, which spawn rooster-tail waves at moderate water levels. These waves, which look like

B. Ted Melis replicated the view of Ruby Rapid on February 14, 1991, at 2:11 P.M. Despite the higher water level in 1991, the rapid and debris fan are unchanged after a century. Erosion and deposition by the Colorado River have caused the only changes in the debris fan. Instead of fresh-looking gravels at the mouth of the canyon, cobbles and boulders are now exposed. A large sand bar has been deposited at right center, obscuring a clear view of the channel mouth.

horns, are not the source of the rapid's name; instead, the rapid is named for Tom Horn, an infamous figure in western history.[35]

Horn Creek Rapid requires finesse at low water. The right side is a maelstrom of waves and nasty holes, and large boulders block entry on the left side. A good run in a rowing boat requires entry at the right side, careful maneuvering around waves and holes, and movement to the left side. Miss the run, and the price might be a flipped boat. At the bottom right, the current impinges on a black ledge of schist that looks like a gigantic mace. Drift too far right, and the ledge will do serious damage to your boat, especially if the boat is wooden.

The prettiest run I have seen of any rapid was made by Liz Hymans in Horn Creek Rapid. With flow a bit less than 10,000 cfs, and without first scouting the rapid, Liz started her run hugging the right shore with her eighteen-foot raft perpendicular to the current. As her boat entered the rapid, the holes just downstream on the right side looked truly menacing. But Hymans pulled steadily, and not hard, to the left. She carefully controlled the momentum of her boat to miss hole after hole, and when she finished we were on the left side of the river. She made it look easy, and the raft had less water in it than in many lesser rapids. Such is the skill of a twenty-year veteran of Grand Canyon river running.

Stanton could have used a guide like Hymans in 1890. Faced with Horn Creek Rapid at low water, Stanton mistakenly thought that Powell's crew had released an unmanned boat in a rapid to avoid the labors of portaging. He therefore ordered the *Marie*, which had just been rebuilt after the accident in Grapevine Rapid, to be pushed out into the head of the rapid. The boat was flushed to the right and flipped several times in those nasty waves and holes before hitting the piece of schist at the bottom—where the *Marie* was smashed to pieces.[36]

Horn Creek Rapid has not changed since Stanton's "first real disaster" in the winter of 1890. No debris flows have occurred in the small drainage that enters the rapid on the left. The black piece of schist is still waiting; boats are still smashed onto it. The rocks that form the rooster-tail waves are still at the head, and violent waves and holes still appear on the right side at low water. What has changed is the competence and experience of professional river runners, who now view Horn Creek Rapid as a challenge that can be overcome.

The Jewels

The stretch of whitewater known as "the Jewels" actually starts at Crystal Rapid (mile 98.3), but to most river runners, the Jewels start at mile 100. Over the next seven miles, the whitewater comes fast and furious. The rapids—Agate, Sapphire, Turquoise, 104 Mile (Emerald Canyon), Ruby, and Serpentine Rapids—look so similar that whenever you do not know where you are on the Colorado River, you are "lost in the Jewels."[37]

Stanton's crew took three and a half days to move the eight miles through the Jewels. Perhaps because of the low water or because the sturdy Harry McDonald had left the expedition several days before, the Jewels as a whole were the expedition's most difficult stretch of whitewater. During the repeated linings and portages, Stanton photographed most of these rapids. None of them appears to have changed significantly in the past century.

Waltenberg Rapid

At low water, rocks in Waltenberg Rapid[38] (mile 112.2) may knock holes in wooden boats. Stanton thought it was "full of rocks to the surface." Lying just beneath the surface, these boulders have claimed many victims. Flavell was lucky; he ran it first in 1896 with little trouble. The Kolbs did not run it as easily. On Christmas Eve of 1911, Ellsworth Kolb entered the rapid first with his brother, Emery, just behind. Emery's boat lodged on some rocks at the head of the rapid, and Ellsworth flipped in a vicious hole in the middle of the rapid. Working rapidly in an attempt to rescue his brother, Emery pried his boat off the rocks and launched into the rapid. He then knocked a huge hole in his boat on an unseen boulder.[39]

Waltenberg Rapid was likewise Buzz Holmstrom's bane. On his solo run in 1937, Holmstrom struck several rocks hard but nevertheless got through. The next year, he again hit rocks on the right side that punched a hole in the bow of his boat.[40] In 1938, Holmstrom became the first river runner to navigate all the whitewater in Grand Canyon during one trip. Of all the rapids he ran, Waltenberg Rapid gave him the most difficulty.

Holmstrom might still find Waltenberg Rapid difficult to navigate; it has changed only slightly in the past century. At least one debris flow has occurred in Waltenberg Canyon in the past century, and the aggradation of the debris fan on the right side has created a slightly narrower and probably deeper channel. The rocks that plagued many early river runners may be just slightly deeper now, making the rapid less hazardous to run.

Dubendorff Rapid

At low or high water, Dubendorff Rapid (mile 131.8) is formidable. In 1909, Seymour Dubendorff[41] accompanied Julius Stone and Nathaniel Galloway on the first pleasure run of Grand Canyon. Dubendorff flipped his boat on the first big wave in the rapid. He had to swim a miserable three hundred yards without his boat as Galloway and Stone retrieved the flotsam. After pulling himself out of the water, his face streaked with blood, Dubendorff uttered the ultimate line of self-assurance in the face of defeat: "I'd like to try that again. I *know* I can run it!"[42] To commemorate his accident, the rapid was named for Dubendorff, and the two tributaries that enter nearby are named Galloway Canyon and Stone Creek.

At high water, Dubendorff Rapid is a mass of angry waves. At low water, successful navigation requires a vigorous move to the right about a quarter of the way through the rapid to avoid a pile of sharp, angular limestone boulders on the lower left. Those boulders fell from the cliffs sometime in the past century. Much of the low-water flow moves through this pile, forming a rock garden at low discharges. No debris flows have emanated from either Galloway Canyon or Stone Creek in the past century. The line of boulders at the top of the rapid forces a left-to-right run at low water; they were present when Stanton photographed the rapid in 1890.

The Cheese Grater

Stanton named this distinctive passage of whitewater Boulder Rapid for the obstacle in its center. The U.S. Geological Survey expedition of 1923 renamed it President Harding Rapid because the crew stayed at mile 43.5 for an extra day to mourn the president's death. Perhaps the most descriptive name is "the Cheese Grater," a phrase used by Bill Beer to describe the boulder in 1955.[43] Beer and John Daggett have been the only people to swim the entire Colorado River through Grand Canyon, and President Harding Rapid caused their most severe accident: the current drew Daggett under the boulder and held him there. "The Cheese Grater" left him bleeding from cuts on his head and hands.

President Harding Rapid seems benign (it is rated a 4), but many boating accidents have occurred because of the boulder. Unwary or careless river runners underestimate the pull of current directly toward the boulder and the unfortunate encounter with its razor-sharp edges. As Daggett found, the boulder is undercut and can trap a swimmer. At high water, rare now on the dam-regulated river, the boulder is the cause of a huge wave that can flip (and has flipped) boats, including thirty-three-foot motorized rafts.

Controversy over the origin of the rapid (and when the boulder was emplaced) began during the 1923 U.S. Geological Survey expedition. Emery Kolb, the head boatman of the trip, could not remember seeing the boulder during his 1911 trip.[44] Powell does not mention seeing it in 1869 or 1872. The crew of the 1923 U.S. Geological Survey expedition speculated that the rock had fallen into the river recently from the right wall of the canyon. Scanning the talus slope, one can almost imagine the cavity from which it might have fallen.

Stanton's photographs indicate that the boulder was probably thrown into the river during a debris flow from Tatahoysa Wash on the left side of river. In 1984, a debris flow from this canyon deposited a fourteen-foot-wide boulder on the debris fan; boulders of similar size appear on many debris fans in Grand Canyon. But the limestone boulder that Beer and Daggett encountered in 1955 has been undercut, abraded, and dissolved by the river. The undercutting and the development of sharp flutes that earned it the comparison to a cheese grater suggest that the boulder has been in President Harding Rapid for a very long time.

Figure 9.6. Waltenberg Rapid

A. Waltenberg Rapid (mile 112.2) was the site of many boating accidents among the early river expeditions. To avoid the dangerous whitewater, Stanton's crew lined their boats down the left side and then portaged the boats over the rocks in the center of the view (number 531). At midmorning on February 19, 1890, Stanton photographed two members of his crew standing at the bottom of the rapid.

Sutured Rocks and Stable Rapids

The key for Colorado River guides is the day-to-day stability of the bed of rapids. Knowing the water level tells them where a run will be, and most of the time, their memory and skills serve them well. Maybe once in a career a guide will come around a corner and see a pall of dust in the air or see a debris fan both larger than remembered and covered with mud—and the rapid is changed.

The rapids of the Colorado River are merely water flowing over piles of boulders. Those piles of boulders can increase in size or be reduced by the river. None of the rapids in Grand Canyon is created by underwater ledges of bedrock. Only one major rapid —Bedrock Rapid (mile 130.5)—is significantly affected by bedrock in the channel. Even in the case of Bedrock Rapid, the river's flow is forced against an island of schist by a debris fan issuing from Bedrock Canyon. The navigational difficulty of Bedrock Rapid changes with each debris flow and subsequent

B. Jane Bernard replicated this view on February 15, 1991, at a slightly higher water level. The rapid has changed slightly during the past century. Large boulders that were on the left bank (right center) have been moved downstream by the Colorado River. Several debris flows from Waltenberg Canyon (left center) have aggraded the debris fan on the right side of the rapid. Despite these changes, the waves appear to be roughly the same.

reworking of deposits by the river.

Before completion of Glen Canyon Dam, the river transported most boulders downstream during spring floods. But piles of boulders, unmoved by the floods of the recent geologic past, remain in some rapids. In the absence of new boulders, such rapids have remained the same for a century. Remarkably, the boulders that formed them have withstood flows of at least 220,000 cfs without being displaced. Part of the reason for this resistance is the extreme weight of boulders in the rapids. But yet another process in rapids can render the boulders essentially immobile. To see evidence of this process, climb among the rocks on the old, stable part of a debris fan—ones that come to mind immediately include those at Soap Creek (away from the 1930s deposition), Hance, and 217 Mile Rapids—and look at the contacts between the largest boulders. On many debris fans, boulders fit together like pieces of a jigsaw puzzle. When water pushes on these boulders, they no longer respond as individual particles. Instead, the interlocking boulders take the force of running water like a sheet of bedrock. Sand may abrade them, water may dissolve them, but they will not be moved from their position by the force of water during a typical flood on the Colorado River.

Frederick S. Dellenbaugh, who accompanied the second Powell expedition in 1871–1872, was the first to recognize that boulders in rapids could become interlocked, a process termed "suturing":

> An interesting feature of this canyon [Cataract Canyon, Utah] was the manner in which huge masses of rock lying in the river had been ground into each other by the force of the current. One block of sandstone, weighing not less than six hundred tons, being thirty or forty feet long by twenty feet square, had been oscillated till the limestone boulders on which it rested had ground into it at least two feet, fitting closely. Another enormous piece was slowly and regularly rocking as the furious current beat upon it, and one could feel the movement distinctly.[45]

Members of the U.S. Geological Survey expedition of 1923 were also impressed with this process, which they observed between driftwood logs and boulders: they photographed a log worn into a piece of Muav Limestone just downstream of Havasu Creek.[46]

One can envision what happens to a boulder when the discharge through a Grand Canyon rapid is high. At some great force, the boulder begins to vibrate and then oscillates on its contact points, which typically are in the configuration of a tripod. If the boulder is not entrained into the flow and moved downstream, the grinding continues as long as the vibration continues. During flood after flood on the Colorado River, the boulder grinds at its points of contact with the other boulders; indeed, most sutured boulders appear to have been ground to fit the contact surfaces of other boulders. Abrasion clearly is an important process leading to sutured boulders and stable rapids.

Another, more subtle process also contributes to suturing. Pressure dissolution, a chemical process, contributes to suturing when calcareous rocks (such as limestone and to some extent calcite) are present —these rocks are soluble in water. At normal pres-sures, the rate of dissolution is low; limestone boulders lying in the Colorado River for a century would not dissolve much. But when pressure is added, the rate of dissolution of calcite rises dramatically. High pressures occur at the contact points between boulders, partly because their weight is distributed over a small area and partly because the force of water against the upstream side of a rock is transmitted to the bed of the rapid through the contact. When limestones or other calcareous rocks are involved, the rock dissolves more readily under pressure.

Thus grinding and dissolution, separately and in combination, cause suturing, and significant interlocking can occur in a century.[47] The suturing of newly deposited boulders begins immediately after a debris flow occurs and the boulders that cannot be transported out of the rapid become lodged in stable sites. With the passage of centuries or the recurrence of many floods on the Colorado River, boulders in the rapids become sutured together, forming an irregular pavement that would require floods of unimaginably large velocities and discharges to dislodge.

Sutured rocks are a river runner's dream. A rapid composed of sutured rock wears down only through abrasion or dissolution of the constituent boulders—long-term processes that would require millennia to cause rapids to change. Such a rapid would certainly have runs that change only with water level, and guides could rely on their memories for navigation. If stability is the dream, then debris flows are the nightmare. Rapids change immediately when large debris flows dump their boulders into the Colorado River. The loose, unsutured boulders are rearranged immediately by flow through the rapid; rearrangement continues whenever higher discharges occur. Flow through the rapid thus changes with each move of a boulder, making it prudent to scout a rapid before attempting to run it. At some point, however, the arrangement of boulders on the bed of rapids stabilizes and suturing starts.

The evolution of Grand Canyon rapids is an endless cycle, the constant struggle between the Colorado River and its tributaries for control of its gradient. In the short term, the closure of Glen Canyon Dam has allowed the tributaries to gain the upper hand. How rapids enlarged by debris flows will change in the future depends on several interrelated factors. First, rapids with frequent additions of boulders from debris flows will probably become larger and possibly more difficult to navigate in the absence of large releases from Glen Canyon Dam. The potential for large releases is related to the fickle nature of climate—specifically, the amount of fluctuation between wet and dry periods—and the more fickle nature of humans, who would have to be willing to operate the dam in a manner that mimics the natural process of boulder movement out of rapids. In some rapids, the rate of suturing versus the recurrence interval of floods down the Colorado River may determine long-term stability.

CHAPTER 10

Sand Bars and Glen Canyon Dam

During the railroad survey of 1890, Robert Brewster Stanton and his crew took advantage of the numerous sand bars as comfortable places to camp. The most miserable nights the Stanton expedition endured were at rocky camps such as the middle of Grapevine Rapid (mile 81.5), where sand bars were not to be found. Other early river runners used sand bars too, particularly because the driftwood that accumulated on them was one of the few sources of firewood near the river.

But Stanton and head boatman Harry McDonald had a greater interest in sand bars than mere comfort: those bars contained flakes of gold. The largest gold rush in Grand Canyon history occurred at the mouth of Kanab Creek, where members of the resupply party for John Wesley Powell's second expedition panned "colors" on the Colorado River sand bars.[1] As many as five hundred prospectors attempted to strike it rich at the mouth of Kanab Creek in the fall and winter of 1872. The rush soon ended because the gold was sparse. Still, the idea that gold dust could be mined from Colorado River sands was valid.

In the mid-1890s, Stanton and McDonald worked for Julius Stone, an Ohio industrialist, to dredge for gold in Glen Canyon.[2] Stone's operation, although not the first, was the largest attempt at placer mining along the upper Colorado River. Many placer mines were developed in the sand bars of Glen Canyon, but few were profitable, and no large operations persisted into the twentieth century. Prospecting in Grand Canyon, and the subsequent development of mining operations, was seriously limited by poor accessibility; one goal of Stanton's railroad was to open the region for mining.

The advent of commercial river running and construction of Glen Canyon Dam in 1963 caused a different value to be placed on sand bars. For nightly accommodations, river parties sought the comfort of large sand bars as camping beaches. The elimination of annual floods by Glen Canyon Dam allowed riparian plants to colonize sand deposits below the old high-water zone; some sand bars hosted a newly developing ecosystem within Grand Canyon. However, sand bars began eroding after the closure of the dam, prompting concern that the resource of sand was disappearing from Grand Canyon.

Degradation Downstream of Dams

Clear-water releases from dams affect the amount of sand stored in downstream river channels. To determine the status of sand and other sediment, hydrologists calculate a sediment mass balance. A mass balance is similar to calculating cash flow through a bank account. Simply stated, the change in storage of sediment in a reach of river is equal to the difference between the amount that enters the reach from all sources and the amount that is transported out. Sediment may be stored either on the bed of the river or in deposits—sand bars—that line its margins.

The Unregulated River

Before the closure of Glen Canyon Dam, the amount of sediment in the Colorado River at Lees Ferry averaged 66 million tons per year,[3] mostly sand, silt,

and clay. The Paria and Little Colorado Rivers, the largest tributaries in Grand Canyon, contributed a total of 3 and 9 million tons per year, respectively; an additional 9 million tons was contributed by other, smaller side canyons.[4] The total amount of sediment input to Grand Canyon measured near Phantom Ranch averaged about 86 million tons per year. If we assume that the long-term storage of sediment in the channel was approximately constant, the amount of sediment that left Grand Canyon was also about 86 million tons per year.

The amount of sediment in the Colorado River varied seasonally as well as from year to year. Although the entire drainage area upstream of Lees Ferry is 111,800 square miles, the source area for most of the runoff is the 40 percent of the drainage basin at relatively high elevations in Colorado, southern Wyoming, and central Utah.[5] Runoff from this area, which occurs during spring snowmelt, had sediment concentrations of less than 10,000 parts per million (ppm), most of it sand. Sediment concentrations of this magnitude are normal for western rivers. Snowmelt floods thus carried little sediment from the high-elevation source areas; the sand in the spring floods in Grand Canyon was largely picked up from the bed of the river. Most of the sediment that entered the river to be stored in the bed came from lower-elevation, semiarid basins in southeastern Utah and northern Arizona. During the summer floods from these basins, which result from intense thunderstorms, sediment concentrations were higher than 20,000 ppm, and much of the sediment was silt and clay. The sand contained in the summer floods from the tributaries was stored in the channel of the Colorado River and could be entrained by the snowmelt floods of the following spring.

The fate of all this sediment depended on the size of sediment and flow in the Colorado River. Coarse sediment, mostly sand, either was stored or was moved gradually through Grand Canyon, whereas fine sediment, mostly silt and clay, was transported through with the flow. Sediment was either transported downstream and into Lake Mead or stored on the bed or along the banks of the Colorado River. The amount of sediment stored in or along the Colorado River varied only slightly from year to year.

The rate of sediment addition to Grand Canyon was not constant even before the construction of Glen Canyon Dam. Settlers of the Colorado Plateau found broad alluvial valleys with small perennial streams or barely discernible channels. Between 1862 and 1909, the small streams throughout the Colorado Plateau eroded dramatically in a series of large floods, carving out deeply incised channels called arroyos. The floods eroded large quantities of sediment from these valleys and transported it into the Colorado River.[6] After about 1940, flooding became less severe in most tributaries in central Utah and northern Arizona because of climatic change.[7] As a result, sediment began to be stored on floodplains along tributary channels,[8] and less sediment reached the Colorado River at the river's junctures with major tributaries.

Fluctuations in sediment yield from tributaries caused a decrease in the amount of sediment carried by the Colorado River after about 1940. As erosion ceased in the tributaries, the sediment load decreased an average of 44 percent at the Grand Canyon gaging station after 1942,[9] and the channel bottom at Lees Ferry eroded (albeit almost imperceptibly) because of the decreased amount of sediment transported in the river.[10] Sediment storage in the bed and margins of the Colorado River thus was probably decreasing even before the closure of Glen Canyon Dam.

Releases from Glen Canyon Dam

The dam dramatically altered the hydrology of the Colorado River in Grand Canyon. Releases from the dam are considerably different from the previous discharges in the unregulated Colorado River. Instead of mostly steady flow with abrupt rises to 100,000 cfs or greater during spring floods, releases from Glen Canyon Dam vary only slightly over the seasons but typically fluctuate daily. During weekdays, dam operators produce power to follow electrical needs in the southwestern United States. On weekends, releases typically are low but steady. Daily operations of the dam vary weekly and monthly. Until recent changes in the dam's operation, on days when power demand was high, releases typically ranged from 3,000 to 30,000 cfs (see figure 7 in the appendix).[11] These releases have lower capacities for transporting sediment than did the floods that once passed through the canyon, and dam releases (with the exception of 1983) have been too low to move much sediment.

The sediment mass balance of the Colorado River had to change. The 66 million tons per year of sediment that used to pass Lees Ferry now is trapped in Lake Powell; only 0.4 million tons per year, most of it sand, passes Lees Ferry.[12] The only other additions of sediment to the river come from the tributaries, large and small. Large tributaries, like the Paria and Little Colorado Rivers, contribute 2.9 million tons per year of sand;[13] an unknown amount is also added by Bright Angel and Havasu Creeks and 528 other small tributaries.[14] Sediment continues to be transported out of Grand Canyon and into Lake Mead. To balance the budget, the river has tapped its account of stored sand on the bed and in the bars.

The Bureau of Reclamation knew that the reach just downstream of Glen Canyon Dam was going to erode; in an attempt to predict the amount of erosion, the bureau began monitoring bed elevations in the reach between the dam site and Lees Ferry in 1956.[15] Immediately after the Colorado River was diverted around the dam site in 1959, the channel began eroding. By 1963, when the dam's gates were closed, the zone of erosion extended seven miles downstream. After a release that peaked at 58,100 cfs in May 1965, erosion extended for the entire fifteen miles between the dam and Lees Ferry, and the river-bed, which had been mostly covered with sand before the dam was built, was becoming armored with cobbles. At Lees Ferry, the 1965 flood scoured twenty-seven feet from the bed, but after 1967, subsequent deposition stabilized the bed at about fifteen feet below the level measured by the bureau before 1963.[16] Erosion slowed by 1975, but nearly 300 million cubic feet of sediment, most of which was sand, had been eroded from the fifteen-mile reach.

The pattern of erosion just downstream of Glen Canyon Dam was completely expected and typical of what happens after construction of a dam on a river with an erodible channel and no other sources for sediment.[17] The clear water released from large reservoirs, referred to as "hungry water," is capable of entraining considerable amounts of sand from the channel. In the absence of sediment added to the river, erosion progresses downstream after closure of a dam. At any given location, once erosion begins, it progresses quickly. Erosion slows with time because larger particles, which cannot be moved by the releases, are concentrated on the bed and armor it against further degradation. All the while, the point of maximum erosion continues to move farther downstream. Erosion of sand bars downstream of Lees Ferry prompted a prediction in 1975; extrapolating from the known erosion rates, Emmett Laursen estimated that sand bars would persist for only two hundred years along the regulated river.[18]

But sediment is added to the Colorado River by tributaries, which complicates this otherwise straightforward story of erosion. As part of a 1973 beach inventory, Alan Howard and Robert Dolan from the University of Virginia calculated the sediment mass balance of the Colorado River.[19] To their surprise, they found a net increase in sediment stored between the gaging stations at Lees Ferry and Grand Canyon between 1965 and 1977. Barring large releases from Glen Canyon Dam, Laursen and others also concluded that sediment would be stored in the reach between Lees Ferry and Phantom Ranch (mile 87). Apparently, the sand eroded from the camping beaches was stored in the channel instead of transported out of Grand Canyon.

In 1973, the National Park Service, concerned that sand bars were eroding because of the clear-water releases from Glen Canyon Dam and that resources in Grand Canyon were deteriorating through overuse by river runners, contracted with Yates Borden of Pennsylvania State University to determine the visitor-use carrying capacity of the river corridor. Borden's team identified and classified 443 potential camping beaches in 1973.[20] Because this was the first inventory, the research team made no definite conclusions about the fate of the sand bars. However, the researchers emphasized the importance of sand as a recreational resource.

The 1983 Flood and Sand Bars

In the fall of 1982, El Niño conditions were developing in the equatorial Pacific Ocean. The pool of warm water that had formed earlier in the year off the coast of Peru expanded westward, and flow in the upper atmosphere over the Northern Hemisphere intensified. The winter of 1982–83 had the most severe weather of the past century.[21] By early winter, the effects of El Niño were felt on the West Coast of the United States. Storms dipped far to the south, gaining moisture and energy from the abnormally warm tropical ocean. The intensified storms moved northeastward over the western United States, repeatedly pounding the California coastline in the process.

Storm after storm dropped snow in the Rocky Mountains, creating an unusually deep snowpack in the headwaters of the Colorado River. The Bureau of Reclamation began 1983 with a plan of operations for Glen Canyon Dam based on a forecast of 112 percent of normal runoff; as a result, they left

Lake Powell nearly full.[22] Because the forecast gave the bureau little cause for alarm, releases from Glen Canyon Dam were normal in the early spring. But snows continued late into the spring, and the snowpack (and potential runoff) increased with each additional storm. Spring came late to the Rockies, and the sudden increase in temperatures caused rapid snowmelt.

Throughout the western United States, rivers flooded at record levels. Runoff in the Green and Colorado Rivers, which began rising rapidly in early June, was very high; the Colorado River in Cataract Canyon peaked at about 107,000 cfs on June 27.[23] The San Juan River had peaked at about 8,800 cfs the previous day. Lake Powell filled too rapidly; the Bureau of Reclamation had not planned for this large inflow into the already full reservoir. Releases from the dam had to be increased through the month of June to prevent the lake from overtopping Glen Canyon Dam.

Before completion of the dam, the annual flood had followed snowmelt in late May or early June, bringing large volumes of water and sediment down the Colorado River into Grand Canyon. The dam releases in the spring and early summer of 1983, although lacking the sediment load, somewhat mimicked the floods to which the river had been subject before the construction of the dam. Releases in late May to early June ranged from 22,000 to 28,000 cfs, but these releases did not offset the large volume of water entering Lake Powell. Discharge was increased to 31,500 cfs, the maximum discharge capacity of the power plant; after this discharge proved insufficient, the river outlet works were opened to release a total of 48,000 cfs (see figure 8 in the appendix). After a few days, it became clear that not enough water could be released through the generators and outlet works to stop the lake's rise. In desperation, the bureau opened the dam's spillways. When the spillways showed signs of erosion, plywood boards were attached to the top of the spillway gates to allow the level of the lake to rise above its maximum-pool elevation.

On June 29, the outflow from Glen Canyon Dam peaked at 97,300 cfs, or about the size of the typical flood in the unregulated river.[24] But this flood initially transported only a small amount of sediment in the form of concrete and sandstone eroded from the walls of the spillway tunnels into Grand Canyon.[25] The emergency measures taken by the Bureau of Reclamation were successful in preventing the overtopping of Glen Canyon Dam, but the large, clear-water releases were of serious concern to the National Park Service and river runners. Most feared the camping beaches in Grand Canyon would be severely eroded.

As this artificial flood subsided, river runners were astonished at the changes in Grand Canyon. Many sand bars used for camping had completely eroded away, as expected; unexpectedly, huge new sand bars had been built elsewhere. Dense riparian vegetation had been buried or cleared away from many sand bars, increasing their usable size as camping beaches. The data did not fit the preconceptions; a release from Glen Canyon Dam had, for the first time since dam closure, caused some sand bars to increase in size. The 1983 flood scoured this stored sand from the bed and deposited it along the channel margins, forming new or greatly enlarged camping beaches.

The 1983 flood brought the issue of sand bars back to the forefront. In light of changes caused by the floodwaters, the National Park Service decided to re-examine camping beaches. Nancy Brian and John Thomas, experienced river runners and National Park Service employees, visually examined sand bars during October 1983.[26] They found only 227 were comparable to the 443 campsites identified ten years earlier.[27] Erosion after 1973 but before the 1983 releases had claimed 26 campsites, mostly in narrow reaches. Of the comparable camping beaches, 28 percent had decreased in size, 30 percent had increased in size, and 42 percent appeared to be unchanged. The 1983 flood completely eroded away 24 beaches, but 50 new ones were created, mostly in the western part of Grand Canyon. Some of these were unstable and rapidly eroded away between 1984 and 1986, but many persisted.

Brian and Thomas were surprised by what they had found. Releases from Glen Canyon Dam were expected to erode sand bars, not create new ones. Yet of the sand bars that had been previously inventoried, 72 percent were either unchanged or had increased in size. Sand bars in narrow reaches were severely eroded; ones in wide reaches generally had gained sand. Of more importance, the 1983 releases from Glen Canyon Dam had changed sand bars in a systematic fashion; most sand bars in Marble Canyon, especially those nearest to the dam, were eroded severely, but many sand bars in western Grand Canyon had increased in size.

The pattern of change caused by the 1983 high flows has implications for what the future might hold for camping beaches in Grand Canyon. Change in sand bars is related to their distance downstream from Glen Canyon Dam and the width of the river corridor. Despite the capture of sediment behind Glen Canyon Dam, and despite the erosive effects of the dam's daily flow releases, enough sand had been stored in the bed of the river before 1983 to replenish many camping beaches. The 1983 flood provided clues as to what may happen to camping beaches during future large releases from Glen Canyon Dam and how sand bars are controlled on a dam-regulated river.

A Classification of Sand Bars

Deposits of sand along the Colorado River are classified according to their mode of transport, depositional site, and human use. The term *sand bar* refers to sand deposited along the banks of a river, as opposed to deposits of windblown sand. Brian and Thomas in their survey defined a camping beach as a sand bar on which at least six people can camp and that has a safe mooring for boats. Identification of camping beaches is important for recreational use, but many sand bars may not be suitable for camping because of dense riparian vegetation or poor mooring. Therefore, "sand bar" is a better classification than "camping beach" for interpreting changes in sand storage along the Colorado River.

Sand bars may be classified by their depositional site, which is related to flow patterns in the Colorado River.[28] Most sand bars, particularly large ones, occur in association with debris fans and rapids. Debris fans are built by debris flows from tributary canyons; these fans constrict the river and typically form riffles or rapids. River flow through the upper part of constrictions is completely downstream. Immediately downstream of the debris fan, the flow typically expands into a pool, and flow is divided into slow water moving upstream in eddies and fast water moving downstream in the tailwaves of the rapid. The farthest-upstream point along the bank where water moving downstream is no longer adjacent to the bank is called the point of flow separation. The point on the downstream side of the eddy where all flow is again moving downstream is called the point of flow reattachment.

The separation and reattachment points are not always at the same locations. As water levels rise, these points shift in a manner related to the geometry of the debris fan, pool, and nearest downstream debris bar or fan: in most cases, the separation point moves upstream on the debris fan until the fan is overtopped by water; the reattachment point moves downstream and is typically constrained by either a projection of bedrock, a second debris fan, or a debris bar or island.[29]

Sand bars that form on debris fans and close to the point of flow separation are called separation

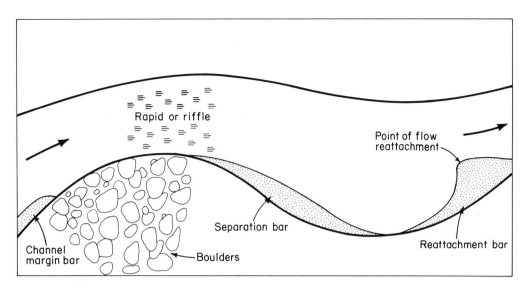

Figure 10.1. Features of a typical rapid

A typical rapid on the Colorado River consists of a debris fan, the rapid, and an eddy just downstream of the rapid in the expansion zone. Separation, reattachment, and channel-margin bars are deposited around the margins of the debris fan and eddy.

bars. Likewise, bars that form near the point of flow reattachment are called reattachment bars. In many cases, where sediment is abundant, separation and reattachment bars are continuous, although some of the sand may be underwater in the eddy at most water levels. Because flow conditions over reattachment bars change significantly as the water level rises at the reattachment point, reattachment bars are considered less stable than separation bars.[30]

A third type of sand bar is ubiquitous in Grand Canyon. Called channel-margin bars, these small sand deposits occur along the sides of the Colorado River and have the form of terraces. Channel-margin bars are not directly associated with large eddies; instead, they typically form in small eddies related to some sort of flow obstruction, such as a large boulder or a clump of riparian vegetation. These bars are seldom used for camping beaches, except in reaches with few separation or reattachment bars. Channel-margin bars, however, provide much of the substrate for riparian vegetation along the river corridor.

Patterns of Change

Sand bars are a major, although inadvertent, subject in 300 views taken by the Stanton expedition. The expedition typically experienced low water, which appeared to range from perhaps 3,000 to 6,000 cfs, except during the small flood that overtook the expedition in the vicinity of Upset Rapid (mile 149.8).[31] Stanton and his photographer, Franklin Nims, usually climbed well above the high-water level to make their negatives, which allowed a downward perspective on sand bars. Moreover, Stanton photographed many of the rapids, and separation and reattachment bars commonly appear in these views.

We interpreted change in sand bars by comparing the sizes of bars visible in Stanton views with those at the same sites a century later. Our goal was to determine whether any effects of Glen Canyon Dam had systematically altered the storage of sand along the Colorado River. Because of the association of sand bars with debris fans and, to a lesser extent,

Figure 10.2. Badger Creek Rapid

A. Badger Creek Rapid (mile 7.9) is the first major rapid encountered in Grand Canyon. Nims made this view on December 28, 1889 (number 277). We estimated the time of Nims's view to be about 12:30 P.M. from the shadows on the left side of the river. Nims's view shows the entire rapid: Jackass Canyon, a sand bar, and a debris fan on the middle right and Badger Canyon, a debris fan, and a sand bar in the middle.

with talus slopes, large boulders are typically present either in or adjacent to sand bars. We used boulders that did not change position in the intervening century as reference elevations to compare the size of sand bars in 1889 and 1890 with those between 1990 and 1993. We did not estimate the actual amount of change but instead interpreted the size of sand bars as having either decreased, increased, or remained

about the same over a century.

Other caveats bear mention here. The changes we interpreted were net effects, because sand bars have certainly fluctuated in size over the years as a result of floods and other erosional or depositional processes. Sand bars hidden by vegetation (mostly non-native Bermuda grass) in 1990–1993 views were not interpreted for changes. Some sand bars, viewed

B. The repeat view was made by Dave Edwards on January 30, 1991, at 12:36 P.M.; the river is several feet higher than in the 1889 view. The camping beaches at Badger Creek Rapid are affected significantly by dam operations because they are only twenty-three miles downstream of Glen Canyon Dam. The sand bar on the Jackass Canyon side has been studied for many years to determine processes of deposition and erosion. Several exposed rocks show that the sand bar downstream of Jackass Canyon has lost five feet of sand since 1889. The sand bar on the Badger Canyon side (lower center) has been severely eroded. Although river-level photographs show substantial amounts of change in boulders on both sides of the river, from this distance the rapid does not appear to have changed significantly. However, examination of historic views including Nims's has shown that a debris flow occurred between 1897 and 1909 in Badger Canyon. This debris flow deposited rocks that form a navigation obstacle at the upper right center of the rapid. Before a small debris flow in August 1994, only streamflow floods occurred in Jackass Canyon during the past century. Robert Webb reoccupied the site of Stanton's assistant.

from extreme angles, could not be classified as separation, reattachment, or channel-margin bars. These too were eliminated from the analysis.

The use of photographs taken a century apart to evaluate changes in a specific sand bar may be misleading. Sand bars may change size over periods of hours, days, or weeks, depending on flow conditions and the stability of the bar. Bars typically eroded during floods (before regulation of the river) as the water rose and aggraded as the flood receded; the use of repeat photography requires the assumption of little net change in the size of sand bars over the period of successive floods. Erosion or deposition might not have been uniform on a sand bar, with one part having eroded and a different part having aggraded over the past century. Sand bars may have fluctuated substantially in size before the closure of Glen Canyon Dam, as a recent study has shown.[32] However, many sand bars appear to be substantially smaller now as a result of erosion caused by Glen Canyon Dam.

Sand bars also may have eroded because of factors other than the operation of Glen Canyon Dam. High winds that periodically sweep the canyon cause severe erosion. Many large sand bars observed in 1990–1993 were topped by eolian dunes, which suggests that the sand deposited by the river has been partially removed by wind action. Sand bars on debris fans may be affected by debris flows or tributary flash floods that occurred in the past century. Even boaters walking to and from boats cause erosion.[33] Erosion by natural processes is indirectly related to dam operation, because releases from Glen Canyon Dam may not achieve a level sufficient to replenish the sand that is lost from sand bars that formed during floods before the closure of the dam.

To compensate for many of these problems, I defined nine reaches of the river, each with an average length of twenty-eight miles.[34] I evaluated changes in sand bars within each reach according to the discharges that would inundate them (see figures 9A and 9B in the appendix). Bars were separated into three categories of inundation: less than 30,000 cfs (called low-water bars), 30,000 to 70,000 cfs (high-water bars), and greater than 70,000 cfs. Sand bars inundated by less than 30,000 cfs are frequently affected by the fluctuating flows that are released from the power plant of Glen Canyon Dam, whereas the higher sand bars are affected only by releases greater than the capacity of the power plant. I evaluated 442 low-water bars and 149 high-water bars in the Stanton views. In addition, I evaluated 19 sand bars inundated by discharges greater than 70,000 cfs, but the small number of such bars precluded meaningful interpretation.

Throughout Grand Canyon, depositional sites for sand have not changed over the past century. Depositional sites are controlled at the mouths of tributaries by a combination of bedrock geometry and debris fans, although some of the "tributaries" are nothing more than high-angle chutes cut into vertical cliffs. Large-scale changes in sand bars on a river like the Colorado, where the depositional sites are fixed, reflect change in the total amount of sand stored in the river. In this sense, evaluating the size of a sand bar, even in a qualitative sense, is like reading the balance of the bank account of sediment storage. The inventory of sand bars yielded by the Stanton views reflects long-term change in sediment storage in the Colorado River.

In a few cases, we found new sand bars where the controlling debris fan had been altered, either through erosion of boulders by the Colorado River or through deposition by debris flows. In a few other places, particularly in upper Marble Canyon, sand bars had been completely removed. At some sites, debris flows had obliterated or substantially eroded separation bars on the downstream sides of debris fans. However, analyses of Stanton's views reveal that reaches with few sand bars in the 1980s had few sand bars in 1890, although the size of the sand bars may be considerably different. Conversely, reaches with many sand bars in 1890 still had many sand bars in the 1990s.[35]

The fifteen miles between Glen Canyon Dam and Lees Ferry show the clearest example of erosion of sand bars caused by Glen Canyon Dam. Of the sand bars inundated by less than 30,000 cfs, 94 percent were smaller. Few debris fans or eddies occur upstream of Lees Ferry; consequently, most of the sand bars in this reach are channel-margin bars with a few separation bars caused by rockfalls or debris bars. Erosion of sand bars is striking in Marble Canyon and Upper Granite Gorge. Few were completely removed, but between miles 0 and 35.9, 83 percent of the low-water sand bars had decreased in size. Many did not extend as far into the channel and appeared to be lower in elevation at their highest points. In the upstream half of Grand Canyon (miles 0 to 125.5), 72 percent of the low-water sand bars decreased in size. Wide reaches had slightly fewer eroded beaches than did narrow reaches. This erosion has significant effects on river running in Grand Canyon, because narrow reaches upstream of mile 125.5 had few camping beaches even before the construction of Glen Canyon Dam.

In western Grand Canyon, downstream of about mile 125.5, a higher percentage of sand bars have remained about the same size or have increased in size. For the low-water sand bars, the percentage of eroded bars decreases with distance from Glen Canyon Dam; in one reach 213.9 to 236 miles downstream of Lees Ferry, the percentages of bars that have eroded (49 percent) and those that have aggraded or remained about the same size (51 percent) are about equal. However, for the high-water sand bars, the percentage of bars that have aggraded (50 percent) is the largest of the three categories downstream of mile 160.0.

I categorized the 610 sand bars visible in the Stanton views as separation, reattachment, or channel-margin bars and then evaluated change in the bars by category (see figure 10 in the appendix). Roughly the same number of sand bars are in each category. Regardless of category, 61 percent of all sand bars were eroded (this result reflects the bias that more replicated views were in the eastern half of the river corridor, where most of the erosion had occurred). However, one-quarter of all reattachment bars had aggraded in the past century, compared with less than one-fifth and one-tenth for separation and channel-margin bars, respectively. Moreover, the percentage of reattachment bars remaining about the same size was one-half that of the other two types. This result suggests that reattachment bars may be the least stable type of bar in Grand Canyon. Conversely, 65 percent of all channel-margin bars had eroded in the past century, which suggests that channel-margin bars may be the type of sand bar most sensitive to the effects of the operations of Glen Canyon Dam.

Hypotheses and Caveats

Sand bars have changed in a definite pattern over the past century in Grand Canyon, and the pattern is related to distance downstream from Glen Canyon Dam. The pattern of erosion and aggradation is a signature of the cumulative operations of a dam and cannot be explained by other causes, such as an uneven distribution of sand in the river corridor of 1890. Several processes related to the presence and operation of Glen Canyon Dam may have worked in concert or individually to create this pattern. The eventual fate of sand bars in Grand Canyon depends on which of these processes dominates.

The first hypothesis is that the pattern of change in sand bars could be the result of progressive degradation downstream of Glen Canyon Dam. In this conceptual model, erosion proceeds downstream from the dam, moving progressively farther with time. The farthest downstream point of erosion, which was only 6 miles downstream of Glen Canyon Dam by 1959 and at least 15 miles downstream by 1965, may

Figure 10.3. Upstream of Elves Chasm

A. On the morning of February 20, 1890, after camping on a sand bar at mile 115, Stanton decided to "take it easy" while waiting for the sun to illuminate this view (number 542). As Stanton exposed the negative at 8:00 A.M., the crew loaded the last of the equipment and supplies onto the twenty-two-foot boats.

still be moving downstream. Erosion had progressed about 125 miles downstream from the dam by 1993, and if we assume that significant erosion had not occurred before the closure of Glen Canyon Dam in 1963, the rate of movement of the point of erosion may have been about 5 miles per year. Extrapolating this value forward in time, sand bars in Grand Canyon might be completely removed by A.D. 2014.

This conceptual model of downstream degradation is unrealistic and should not be used to predict the rate of removal of sand bars in Grand Canyon. The model does not account for the additions of sand

from tributaries such as the Paria and Little Colorado Rivers, the largest sources of sand. Numerous other tributaries also supply sediment during flash floods and debris flows. Moreover, eddies that trap sand may release it only above certain discharges, which links the fate of sand with the operations of Glen Canyon Dam.

Because the cumulative amount of drainage area that contributes sediment increases with distance downstream from Glen Canyon Dam, the second hypothesis is that at some point, additions of sand by tributaries are enough to make up for the amount

B. Steve Tharnstrom replicated this upstream view on February 22, 1992, at 9:00 A.M. Because of considerable erosion, the sand bar could be used only with considerable difficulty by modern river runners. Eight members of our crew posed in the approximate positions as Stanton's crew to illustrate the difference in the amount of sand between 1890 and 1992. The sand bars in this view, which was also replicated in 1976, 1983, 1984, and 1990, have steadily decreased in size over the sixteen years of photographic replication. However, the higher sand bar at extreme right center has increased in size.

of sediment trapped behind Glen Canyon Dam. Repeat photography of Stanton views suggests that this point may occur between miles 120 and 160; a more reasonable description would be that the point is somewhere downstream of the Little Colorado River.

It perhaps strains the imagination that tributary additions might be able to make up the sediment deficit in the Colorado River, which before the construction of Glen Canyon Dam was thick with mil-lions of tons of clay, silt, and sand. However, most of the sediment load in the unregulated river was silt and clay, and little of it was stored in Grand Canyon. After the closure of Glen Canyon Dam, the capacity of the river to transport sand decreased because flow releases were typically less than 31,500 cfs. Tributary additions and the change in flow regime of the Colorado River (floods before the dam were as high as 220,000 cfs, whereas releases from the dam typically

Figure 10.4. 119 Mile Rapid

A. Reaches where Tapeats Sandstone is at river level tend to have only small rapids and calm water. In this upstream view at mile 119.0 (number 548), several small riffles and quiescent eddies reflect the typical conditions. On February 20, 1890, Stanton had his crew stop at 10:23 A.M. to make this upstream view of 119 Mile Rapid. An insignificant reattachment bar appears at left center.

are less than 31,500 cfs) probably explain why the bed of the river aggraded downstream of the Paria River between 1965 and 1980.

If additions from tributaries are sufficient to balance the removal of sand from Grand Canyon, and if the broad-scale adjustment in sediment distribution is complete, one might conclude that the pattern of erosion and deposition may fluctuate only slightly in the future. Sand bars in Marble Canyon may continue to erode, but the sand bars downstream of about mile 125 may not change much or may even aggrade in the future. Several other processes complicate this possible scenario for sand bars. For example, climatic fluctuations may change the amount of sediment additions from the Paria and Little Colorado Rivers: significant decreases in precipitation, particularly in summer, would reduce the amount of sediment entering the Colorado River. Conversely, if the frequency of floods on the Colorado Plateau increases again, sediment additions might increase significantly.

Natural erosional processes may be more impor-

B. Ralph Hopkins replicated Stanton's views on February 3, 1990, at 3:36 P.M. It is startling how little change has occurred in the desert plants of the left foreground; catclaw trees and Mormon tea persist and appear strikingly similar. The sand bars have changed more; the reattachment bar is considerably larger.

tant than climatic fluctuations in determining the future of sand bars in Grand Canyon. Sand bars that are not subject to inundation by releases from Glen Canyon Dam are continually eroded by wind and the effects of camping. Floods from tributary canyons may bury or completely erode sand bars. High releases from Glen Canyon Dam are necessary to replenish the eroded deposits, assuming that sufficient sediment is stored in the channel and can be transported into eddies. In other words, limiting releases from Glen Canyon Dam to less than 31,500 cfs will result in the natural erosion of high sand bars

regardless of tributary additions of sediment. Those tributary additions will simply aggrade the bed of the river, in a manner similar to what happened between 1965 and 1980, and the stored sand cannot be deposited on the high camping beaches.

Large releases from Glen Canyon Dam are a mixed blessing,[36] particularly to sand bars. The pattern of change in sand bars observed between 1973 and 1983 is not unlike the general pattern of change over the past century: that is, mostly erosion upstream of mile 125 and mostly stasis or deposition downstream. One may presume that this pattern was enhanced

Figure 10.5. The bottom of 209 Mile Rapid

A. Stanton and his crew were in a hurry to reach Diamond Creek on the day this view was made, but an observer would not recognize their haste by the position of boatman Elmer Kane, reclining on a sandy beach at the bottom of 209 Mile Rapid. Stanton took this photograph (number 647) on March 1, 1890, at 9:10 A.M.

by the high releases from the dam between 1983 and 1986. If high releases are necessary to replenish sand bars, the effects of these releases may be detrimental to sand bars in the upper half of Grand Canyon, particularly in narrow reaches, and may also be detrimental to the recently developed ecosystem below the old high-water line.[37]

A final hypothesis is that the high releases of 1983 may have had the greatest influence in creating the pattern of erosion and deposition observed in the replicate views. Although sand bars may have been

eroding throughout Grand Canyon before 1983, the amount of sand stored in the bed increased with distance from Glen Canyon Dam. The 1983 flood scoured sand from the bed, but the amount of stored sand was insufficient to replenish many of the sand bars upstream of about mile 125. Downstream, however, sufficient sand was available—partly by the erosion of upstream sand bars and partly by the entrainment of sand stored in the channel—and many sand bars were greatly enlarged. If we had replicated the Stanton views before 1983, we might have seen

B. Erosion of sand bars is one of the major problems caused by clear-water releases from Glen Canyon Dam. Where Elmer Kane rested on sand in 1890, Tom Wise had to lie on rocks in 1990. In general, the erosion of sand bars decreased downstream of about river mile 120, and this site is no exception. The sand bar on river right (at right center) has significantly aggraded between 1890 and 1990. Although many of the rocks in the foreground are still present after a century, some, including the one serving as a backrest at lower right, have been rotated. Glenn Rink appears at lower right leaning against this rock. The repeat view was made by Ralph Hopkins on February 14, 1990, at 11:07 A.M.

less erosion upstream of Phantom Ranch and more erosion in western Grand Canyon.

Although the pattern of change in sand bars along the Colorado River indicates that Glen Canyon Dam was the most important factor affecting sand bars, repeat photography involving a comparison of only two points in time cannot be used to predict trends at any single sand bar. Those predictions must be made using sediment-transport modeling, mass-balance studies, and careful measurements of the effects of specific flows on sand bars. However, photographs taken a century apart show the large-scale pattern: erosion is not uniform throughout the river corridor in Grand Canyon. Erosion is severe in the eastern half of the river corridor, especially where camping beaches were rare even before the closure of Glen

Canyon Dam. However, the effect of Glen Canyon Dam on the western half of Grand Canyon is ambiguous at best.

The real value of the Stanton photography for interpreting the status of sand bars lies not in ascertaining the pattern of change but in demonstrating that sand bars persist in specific sites. This persistence in bedrock canyons allows a long-term evaluation of the stability of these bars, despite the fact that the interval between replicate photographs may be orders of magnitude greater than the rate of change of each bar. Evaluation of long-term change in sand bars using repeat photography probably works because the size of sand bars is not arbitrary. Instead, these bars are the most visible sign of the storage of sediment within a river: they represent the sediment health of a river. Repeat photography, particularly systematic photography like that done by the Stanton expedition, provides a means for producing a long-term inventory of sediment health.

CHAPTER 11

Stasis and Change

Grand Canyon changes people's lives. Robert Brewster Stanton succumbed to the force of Grand Canyon. His diary begins with descriptions of how he would dynamite the top off that cliff, tunnel through this point. All the wasted rock would be thrown into the river; in places, he would have stolen space from the river to construct his railroad in a bad section. Stanton criticized his photographer, Franklin Nims, for climbing to dangerous spots merely to take better photographs. Just document the proposed route, Stanton insisted. Then two events changed Stanton's attitude: he succeeded Nims as trip photographer, and his expedition penetrated deeper into Grand Canyon.

The changes are noticeable first in the photographs. In the upper reaches of Marble Canyon, the photographs are repetitious upstream-downstream views from the same types of places. At South Canyon, Stanton noticed the ruins of an Anasazi settlement, but he did not photograph them. Then he photographed lush Vaseys Paradise; when he reached Nankoweap, he photographed the prehistoric granaries high in the cliffs. *The proposed railroad route was not in either photograph.* Moreover, he began experimenting with different lenses to capture the same view. This was a bold move for an engineer whose

Figure 11.1. Lower Granite Gorge

A. By the time Stanton and his crew reached western Grand Canyon, they had developed sufficient boating skills to run what are now considered large rapids. These included 231 Mile and 232 Mile Rapids, which they ran on March 13, 1890, with little note. Below 232 Mile Rapid, Stanton stopped at 9:15 A.M. to capture this upstream view (number 684). He placed his camera only a short distance from his boat, which is uncharacteristic of his other views.

primary purpose was to photograph a railroad route using a limited amount of film.

Stanton's diary also shows the changes in his attitude about the canyon. At first he stuck to documenting his railroad route and telling of tragedies and hardships that befell his crew. Then, spliced between descriptions of trestle lengths and widths of overhead drains, he allowed bursts of enthusiasm. This passage, which describes sunrise near mile 36, is typical: "While the boats were loading I took photos. I hope . . . [they] will turn out well as . . . [this location] has the most beautiful reflection of the rising sun and cliffs in the still water that I have ever seen."[1] Business before pleasure was the order of the diary, but occasionally Stanton would launch into rhapsodies about how beautiful the colors were in the cliffs, how wonderfully warm the sunshine was. The crew even sang an air from a Gilbert and Sullivan operetta when they saw flowers and heard birds at Saddle Canyon.[2]

B. Now, 232 Mile Rapid is the last whitewater of note in Grand Canyon. The river flows freely for another four miles, depending on the level of Lake Mead. The reaches through gorges of schist and granite are well known for boils and whirlpools; both the original and replicate views artistically show this turbulence. Steve Tharnstrom matched the view on March 15, 1993, at 12:07 P.M.

Stanton's transformation continued as the expedition moved downstream. When Stanton made the difficult climb to the top of the Tower of Ra, more than four thousand feet above the Colorado River, he took the camera. He exposed more film on the sunrise from the Tower of Ra than on any other view in Grand Canyon; the railroad route is nowhere to be seen in these photographs. He was smitten. Near the end of his expedition, Stanton became nostalgic for eastern Grand Canyon, but he appreciated the more open grandeur of the western canyon. While his final descriptions of Grand Canyon complain of the lack of bright colors, he lauds the polished rocks and high banks of white travertine.

Although Stanton continued his engineering career overseas and in Glen Canyon, his love affair with Grand Canyon endured. He became the first serious historian of the Colorado River, although Frederick Dellenbaugh of the second Powell expedition published first.[3] Stanton was objective, whereas Dellen-

Figure 11.2. Upstream from Travertine Canyon

A. Stanton's diary assumes a decidedly engineering tone downstream of Diamond Creek. For example, in describing this upstream view (number 673), made March 12, 1890, at 4:00 P.M., Stanton states: "Broken up into a general slope, though the slope is not so flat as above, with points of harder rock standing up over the general slope. These must be cut very heavy in order to give a good line. But it will make a magnificent roadway."

baugh idolized Powell above all other explorers.[4] Stanton sought interviews with as many of the first explorers as possible and collected photographs and other memorabilia. By the time of Stanton's death in 1922, his writings had set the stage for a continuing debate on Grand Canyon history.[5]

Grand Canyon changes people, including those who would have changed Grand Canyon. Prospectors worked lonely years in its depths; hermits found havens in its side canyons. Those promoting tourism built cableways, bridges, and camps—most of which, unlike the surrounding plants and cliffs, could not endure the test of time. Engineers sought to dam the canyon's architect, the Colorado River, and submerge most of the enduring rocks under still waters, but after the river had been regulated and forty-five miles of the western canyon had been inundated by Lake Mead, the unworthiness of such an endeavor was recognized and the threat was ended.

Yes, the river now runs clear and green most of

B. Travertine Canyon (mile 229.0) has perennial flow and is a popular stop for river trips that extend below Diamond Creek. The view upstream from its mouth mostly shows Vishnu Schist and granite in walls that appear unchanged over the past century. Tom Wise replicated this view on February 29, 1992, at 4:05 P.M.

the year, instead of muddy brown, and many camping beaches are smaller. Yes, an exotic tree and some noxious weeds grow on banks that previously were barren. Yes, the annual flood has been harnessed, and some rapids may grow larger in the coming years. Yes, burros released by prospectors shortened the life expectancy of desert plants and scarred some hillslopes. Some people might think these changes are good, some might think they are bad—but fundamentally the canyon is little changed.

There is resistance in isolation, stubbornness in inaccessibility, and redemption in wild beauty. Some

plants in Grand Canyon have lived for a century and much longer; if they could talk, they might remind you that they are enduring whereas you are transitory. Debris flows continue to rumble through the tributaries, and boulders thrown into the river centuries ago still force water into waves.

The history of Grand Canyon is not about the attempted destruction of a sacred natural place, nor is it an unblemished success story of isolation thwarting development. The past century is instead an intertwined story of stasis and of change, of human attempts to tame the forces that made Grand Canyon and of natural forces acting much as they have for millennia. The interplay of force and resistance, whether biologic or geologic, is the history of Grand Canyon. The ramifications of that history have been masked by our preconceived ideas about what Grand Canyon was, is, and should be.

Uniformitarianism and Catastrophism

In eighteenth-century Europe, religion dominated scientific thought. Christian principles held that the world was only six thousand years old and that Noah's flood had reshaped its surface. Rocks and landforms were explained as remnants of flood deposition and erosion that occurred simultaneously; the earth had no history of its own before the arrival of man. The idea of catastrophism was born of religion: the processes that shaped the earth were thought to be brief, violent, and not of the same scale as the processes that act today. Moreover, it was believed that the cataclysms occurred only in a brief interval, when God created the earth.

Careful observation held otherwise. In 1785, James Hutton startled the world with his ideas of uniformitarianism;[6] he reported that the surface of the earth had been shaped not by catastrophic processes but by gradual forces of erosion and deposition—as viewed in rivers, in lakes, or in oceans—that sculpted the mountains and deposited the strata. Grain by grain, mountains were washed to the sea. Uniformitarianism holds that the earth is very old, that the processes that shaped it required extremely long periods of time, far longer than six thousand years.

As scientific favor shifted toward uniformitarianism, the paradigm of catastrophism was discredited for a time. The tide shifted: all explanation of landforms must be explained by uniformitarian processes. Then the idea of catastrophism, stripped of its religious overtones, was reintroduced in the early twentieth century by J. Harlan Bretz, who invoked immense catastrophic floods to explain the

Channeled Scablands, unusual landforms in eastern Washington.[7] Bretz fought a lonely thirty-year battle against the tide of science for acceptance of his catastrophic flood theory and with it the idea that catastrophic processes can shape the earth.[8]

Scientists now use the concept of catastrophism to explain landforms that result from high-magnitude, low-frequency events such as enormous floods, meteorite impacts, or extreme earthquakes. Events need not rival Noah's flood; instead, processes that are unusual in human life spans but more frequent when viewed from the perspective of geologic time are considered catastrophic. Catastrophism can be broadly viewed as stasis and change: long periods of uniform processes interrupted by an extreme metamorphosis.

Grand Canyon well illustrates the concepts of both uniformitarianism and catastrophism. The Paleozoic rocks, from Tapeats Sandstone up to Kaibab Limestone, gradually accumulated and turned to stone over hundreds of millions of years. Without torrential rainfall, removal of those rocks might also require millions of years. Yet most erosion in Grand Canyon results from catastrophic processes. Rockfalls drop tons of debris on the slopes below, instantly moving sections of cliffs. Debris flows are infrequent, high-magnitude floods that transport large quantities of sediment; they are at present the principal means of conveyance of coarse-grained sediment from the cliffs to the river. One-third of the side canyons have not had a debris flow in the past century, yet we know from the debris fans at their mouths that these tributaries had big ones in the past and will undoubtedly have others in the future.

Rapids are the cumulative results of catastrophic and uniformitarian processes. Debris flows dump boulders in, and only an unusually large flood in the Colorado River can transport the largest boulders out. Rapids in Grand Canyon do not appear to change much in the time that elapses between a debris flow and a large flood. Some boulders, rocking to the force of current, become sutured together, forming an interlocking mat on the floor of a rapid that probably cannot be changed by any conceivable Colorado River flood; instead, the ancient rapids made up of sutured boulders will wear down through dissolution or abrasion of the boulder mat.

The desert plant assemblages of Grand Canyon are also the product of uniformitarian and catastrophic processes. Uniformity shows a framework of species whose individuals are long-lived; shrubs such as Mormon tea appear to be able to live for centuries. Although there is no apparent reason why these plants should die (other than "old age"), about one-fifth of the population is replaced every century. Without disturbance, most of the desert plants in Grand Canyon behave as if controlled by some regular process of death and replacement. Moreover, most of the replacements occupy the space vacated by the deceased; the location and number of these preferred sites regulate this uniform process.

Catastrophic processes also regulate desert plant assemblages. Severe cold is fatal to brittlebush and certain cacti. With the cessation of the severe frost that was common in the nineteenth century, cacti and brittlebush have become common, even dominant, in parts of the river corridor. Rockfalls periodically obliterate desert plants on talus slopes; debris flows can scour plants from the terraces and hillsides of side canyons. Even the scouring of the new high-water zone in the days before Glen Canyon Dam was catastrophic to colonizing plants.

Other processes that operate on the environment of Grand Canyon are difficult to categorize by magnitude and frequency. Sand bars are affected by too many different processes operating over too many time scales to be categorized as uniform or catastrophic. Grazing accelerates turnover in the populations of some desert plants and as such is speeding up what normally is a gradual process. Some effects of heavy grazing are catastrophic: local extirpation of certain species threatens the future integrity and

stability of plant assemblages. On the whole, the effects of herbivory are too complex to be categorized simplistically.

The ideas of uniformitarianism and catastrophism are intimately linked to our perceptions of the world. For example, our view of natural landscapes is biased by our inability to look beyond our short lives. To many people interested in the canyon, the Crystal Creek debris flow of 1966 was a catastrophe because Crystal Rapid is now a ferocious reach of whitewater whereas before 1966 it was essentially a riffle. A larger debris flow occurred at Prospect Canyon in 1939; this flow also altered a rapid (Lava Falls), but it occurred before almost all of the living river runners first ran the river. When a debris flow causes spectacular change, we exaggerate its singularity: it becomes the "thousand-year flood." What causes us to judge such infrequency given our limited experience with Grand Canyon? Old photographs help; nevertheless, we still cannot appreciate the significance of debris flows like the ones in Crystal Creek and Prospect Canyon.

We betray our short perspectives by evaluating change as good or bad. In 1990, a flood tore through Havasu Canyon, devastating what for many was a paradise. I remember that while talking with a long-time river guide I maintained that floods were natural, that Havasu Canyon would recover, and that ultimately the flood was beneficial. The response, unshakable, was that Havasu Creek was damaged and would "never be the same." And perhaps it would not. We label change, particularly swift change, as bad; we like environments that are stable, at least in our lifetimes. We rarely value natural processes for what they are.

We value change on the basis of whether it occurs slowly or quickly. Many of the key processes in Grand Canyon act slowly, with effects too protracted for us to detect them without a tool like repeat photography. The most important processes that affect the geomorphology and ecology of Grand Canyon indeed act so slowly that we can just begin to appreciate them from the perspective of a century. But appreciate them we must, because we now exert a heavy influence on the environment of Grand Canyon. The conflict between the values cited in the creation of Grand Canyon National Park and the benefits of Glen Canyon Dam are at the core of future change along the Colorado River.

Establishment of a National Park

Explorers in the nineteenth century unfailingly recognized the pristine beauty of Grand Canyon. Stanton and others—John Hance and William W. Bass, to name two of the most prominent Grand Canyon figures—recognized the potential for tourism. Several popular books promoted tourism at the turn of the century, particularly after the completion of rail access.[9] Calls for preservation came with the increased visitation.

Establishment of Grand Canyon National Park was controversial among early residents of the region. Miners and ranchers opposed any change that would threaten their access to public lands, whereas others involved in the fledgling tourism industry welcomed the potential increase in visitation. Despite the objections of a reluctant Congress and outraged miners and ranchers, President Theodore Roosevelt established Grand Canyon National Monument on January 11, 1908. The argument over the land-use status persisted for more than a decade, but the tourist appeal and scenic wonders of the canyon prevailed over special interests. On February 26, 1919, Congress created Grand Canyon National Park.

The popularity of the new park can be gauged by the increase in visitation. In 1919, the year the park was created, 44,000 people visited Grand Canyon; a decade later, more than 200,000 visitors came; more than 300,000 in 1937;[10] a million in 1956; two million in 1969; and three million in 1976. Pressures on the park increased, and one of the largest problems was the patchwork of jurisdictions of managing agen-

cies in the region.[11] As a means of simplifying land-use management, the boundaries of Grand Canyon National Park were expanded by President Gerald Ford on January 3, 1975. The Grand Canyon Enlargement Act of 1975 placed the entire river corridor through Marble and Grand Canyons under the management of the National Park Service.

Visitation along the river corridor exploded with the proliferation of commercial river companies. After the completion of the second Stanton expedition, only thirteen people had successfully gone through Grand Canyon. The hundredth person to accomplish that feat did it in 1949. By 1954, two hundred people had run the canyon; the one-thousandth river runner went through in the early 1960s. Twenty-one commercial river outfitters had permits in 1990, taking between fifteen thousand and twenty thousand people per year through Grand Canyon.[12] More than three hundred thousand people had run the river through the national park by 1990.

Despite all the protections and regulations, the National Park Service and river runners perceived undesirable change in the river corridor. Sand bars continued to erode; populations of native fish continued to dwindle. Glen Canyon Dam, which was operated without consideration of downstream environmental impacts, was blamed for the changes. Scientists conducted intensive studies;[13] the Department of the Interior instituted temporary changes in the way the dam is operated. Environmentalists, convinced the management changes were neither permanent nor sufficient to protect the canyon, called for protective legislation. In 1992, Congress passed the Grand Canyon Protection Act, which has as a general goal the operation of "Glen Canyon Dam . . . in such a manner as to protect, mitigate adverse impacts to, and improve the values for which Grand Canyon National Park and Glen Canyon National Recreation Area were established."[14]

Taken literally, the values sought in the Grand Canyon Protection Act are those that were present when the park was established in 1919. The photographs of Robert Brewster Stanton are the best evidence of what the river corridor looked like at that time and may help answer questions such as whether tamarisk should be eliminated and whether sediment should be injected into the river. These questions would lead to proactive management based once again on our short human life spans and fear of change.

Dams and Other Human Controls

The most crucial change in the geomorphology and ecology of Grand Canyon during the past century occurred in 1963. The closure of Glen Canyon Dam ended any pretense of a natural riverine environment in Grand Canyon. The second most important change was the closure of Hoover Dam below the canyon in 1935, which caused the last forty miles of free-flowing river in Grand Canyon to become the delta of what was at that time the largest reservoir in the world, Lake Mead. Now, with the turn of some valves, humans can manipulate, among other things, sand bars, rapids, riparian vegetation, and wildlife habitat.

The litany of human-induced change is, on the surface, staggering when set against our pristine image of Grand Canyon. Sand bars have been eroded for at least 120 miles into the canyon; future dam releases control the fate of the remaining sand bars. Tamarisk, introduced as a decorative landscape plant, is now the most common tree along the river corridor. The size of the annual flood has been decreased by at least one-third, inadvertently facilitating the invasion of tamarisk. Burros, after helping to transport ores and people, were released to reproduce naturally in a large part of the canyon.

Humans exert the largest influence on the environment of Grand Canyon. We can pretend that the gorge between the rims is wilderness, but it no longer has the qualities that Robert Brewster Stan-

ton was privileged to see and photograph in 1890. Nor does our control stop with dams; after all, we first introduced burros to the canyon and then eliminated them. We mark trails and delineate them to limit erosion; we protect some beaches by building rock walls and planting vegetation. We may even be inadvertently controlling severe freezes by polluting the atmosphere.[15] Our control of Grand Canyon is limited by the priorities we place on specific actions, not by our lack of ability to use technology.

Indeed, we have the technology to manipulate Grand Canyon in fundamental ways. Build intake towers behind Glen Canyon Dam, and the water temperature of the Colorado River could be controlled as if it were bathwater. Sand, silt, and clay could be dumped into the river, giving it back the red color that originally inspired its name and the sediment that created its sand bars. We could, if we wanted, find every tamarisk, camelthorn, and clump of Bermuda grass and pull them out by the roots. Better still, we could release some insects or microbial pathogens that specifically attack these plants, or we could genetically alter non-native plants and animals so that they cannot reproduce. After a century of intervention, we have become more important to the future of Grand Canyon than most of the natural processes.

Some lucky hiker was staying at Monument Creek camp on July 27, 1984, when the debris flow roared by on its way to the Colorado River. Another person noticed a dead creosote bush in some remote canyon. Those people witnessed two of the last processes of change in Grand Canyon that we cannot directly control. Wilderness is almost an abstract concept between the rims. Sure, there are no roads for miles and it is easy to get away from people in some of the most beautiful terrain on earth, but we can—and do—manipulate the "wilderness" along the river.

Stanton's railroad, had it been completed, would have carved great scars into the revered cliffs that flank the Colorado River. Worse yet, Stanton

Figure 11.3. Elves Chasm

A. Like modern river runners, Stanton appreciated the beauty of the Inner Gorge, particularly near its end at mile 116.4. He made this upstream view (number 544) at 8:30 A.M. on February 20, 1890, and vividly described this reach: "The long stretch of river . . . is wonderfully beautiful, grand, and picturesque. The regular form of the inner granite gorge, capped with the 'beaded' [Tapeats] sandstone. The beautiful stretch of smooth but swift water. The rich green coloring of the grass, bushes, and the flowers among the granite breaks, and the shiny sparkling black granite. The marble cliffs on left coming close to the river in great frowning buttresses. On the right, the marble cliffs running almost parallel with river; broken into smaller buttresses of every imaginable shape, capped with several benches of the upper red sandstone, all a flaming red."

envisioned chalets in which tourists could enjoy their overnight visits. We would all recognize these changes as human-caused and intentional: they would catch our attention as catastrophic. What we do not see are the much larger scars in the environment along the river corridor, those human-caused changes that were mostly unintentional. To the untrained eye, the river corridor looks as untrammeled and wild as it might have appeared to John Wesley Powell. Our perceptions deceive us.

The debate about what Grand Canyon is and what it should be will continue as long as we affirm its status as a national park. We could manage it as an amusement park with minimum flows greater than 8,000 cubic feet per second (cfs) so the rocks are hidden in Hance Rapid and maximum flows less than 45,000 cfs to avoid that nasty hole in Crystal Rapid. We could manage the park to hide our influence,

B. Other than some eroded patches of sand and a few new plants, little has changed in this view over the past century. The qualities that Stanton admired in this view are still admired by river runners. Ted Melis replicated Stanton's view on February 15, 1991, at 3:40 P.M.

sweeping away footprints and picking up litter. Or we could set a more difficult goal that recognizes our power. We could attempt to mimic natural processes and return the river corridor to some semblance of its condition before human intervention. We need to make that choice, because the future of Grand Canyon is firmly in our hands.

Grand Canyon in 2090

Another century passes, and in our wisdom we continue to preserve Grand Canyon as a national park. Someone decides to go back to the camera stations and repeat 445 Stanton views and our replicates of the river corridor. What could we of the twentieth century reasonably expect that person to find?

Much depends on how we choose to manage the Colorado River and the national park. We cannot predict what the new high-water zone or the sand bars will look like, because too much depends on how the dam will be operated. It is highly unlikely that Glen Canyon Dam will be used as a tool to reproduce conditions on the unregulated river. The old high-water zone will probably continue to fragment and look less like a line of vegetation and more like scattered trees and bushes. Attrition will take its toll;

Figure 11.4. 241 Mile Rapid and Lake Mead

A. The Stanton expedition had trouble with the notorious Separation Rapid on March 13, 1890. Stanton's boat struck a rock, smashing a hole in the side of the boat and pinning it temporarily in rough water near the bottom of the rapid. Stanton was thrown from the boat; his life jacket kept him afloat through the remainder of the rapid. Exhausted from their exertions, the crew camped at the head of 241 Mile Rapid. The following morning, Stanton photographed this view (number 697) at 8:30 A.M.

there likely will be more catclaw and less mesquite and Apache plume. In 2090, the old high-water zone may be only a memory, an image preserved in old photographs.

Chances are the rapids on the river will be much larger in 2090. The vision some people had in the 1960s of the regulated river—a series of large drops separated by pools—is possible. A more likely scenario is a continuation of what has already hap-

pened: some rapids will be larger, some will be less difficult, and some will be unchanged. We might reasonably expect a hundred or more new debris flows by 2090 but cannot predict their effects: a high dam release, unexpected or intentional, could rework aggraded debris fans. The river likely will still be runnable; river guides will always find a way to run dangerous rapids.

The desert shrubs and grasses will continue to die

B. We had no such trial and tribulation in reaching or leaving the place where Stanton took his photograph. Lake Mead now reaches above mile 237, drowning out Separation Rapid. Whereas Stanton's view showed 241 Mile Rapid, our view shows a lake with a water level about fifty feet higher than that of the free-flowing river. The deep shadows in Stanton's view, caused by overexposure of the film in the early morning light, were not replicated; we arrived about an hour, two days, and 103 years after Stanton was here. Robert Webb replicated Stanton's view on March 16, 1993, at 9:45 A.M.

and be replaced, probably at the rates observed in the last century. Long-lived plants—exemplified by Mormon tea, creosote bush, and big galleta grass—are not likely to be affected by humans but may be affected by the expansion of the ranges of frost-sensitive plants such as brittlebush and cacti. We have no way of knowing whether killing frosts will occur in the next century, since global warming might eliminate serious cold. Grazing by non-native herbivores will not be a factor. Areas affected by

twentieth-century grazing will recover somewhat, but the repeat photographer of the future will recognize the residual effects.

As a society in the twenty-first century, we will continue to be concerned about the future of Grand Canyon. Lake Powell will not yet be full of sediment, and Glen Canyon Dam will still be operating. People will flock to the North and South Rims, seeking something that is missing from their daily lives. River trips will continue—we will not lose our desire for an adrenaline rush or an outdoor adventure—but the quality of those trips cannot be imagined. Our priorities will change, and we still may struggle with knowing what wilderness is or what we expect from it.

The Last Stanton Photograph

It had to end sometime. On March 15, 1993—three years and four river trips after our rephotography project began—we replicated the farthest downstream Stanton photograph. We camped at Travertine Falls (mile 230.5) in anticipation of working the next day with Stanton photographs above and at the top of Lake Mead. This was alien territory. Many of us knew Grand Canyon well, but only a couple of crew members had been below Diamond Creek far enough to know what this part of the canyon looked like. No one could identify the camera stations in advance; we had to trust the accuracy of Stanton's diary to guess where the photographs were taken. If we passed a camera station, another trip would be required to replicate that view. The next day we would not only replicate Stanton views, we would be doing so on the same day of the Stanton expedition.

We launched at 7:10 A.M., a very early start for a winter river trip. I was in an advance motorboat and quickly located the camera stations; one by one, the camera crews pulled out of the current. The photographers found the same light that Stanton had found when he had stood at his camera stations 103 years earlier, and by midafternoon they had replicated nineteen Stanton views, the most ever in one day.

Liz Hymans had a problem at the last camera station (near what once was 241 Mile Rapid), where she had to climb two hundred feet above Lake Mead on a granite cliff. She tried to replicate the photograph exactly, but she needed to be higher on the cliff. To do so meant climbing through a crack in the cliff carrying a pile of camera gear, and the sun was going down. In camp that evening, she explained that she had approximately matched the view but that she

wanted to match it exactly. We would have to return to that camera station.

The next morning, we arrived at the base of the camera station, a steep slope leading up to a cliff. I hate rock climbing, but I easily attained the exposed point of granite and called for the photographic equipment. I became depressed as I stared at the view—the last photograph showed a lake where 241 Mile Rapid had once boomed. Sand deposited under still waters appeared where desert vegetation had once struggled to survive. Why were we replicating this view?

We passed cameras, a tripod, film, and packs through the cleft and the others climbed through. The setup was easy; we had done it hundreds of times before. We finished a half-hour after we arrived. Kenton Grua and Hymans interpreted the photograph and found creosote bush and Mormon tea in the same spots as in the Stanton view. Grua compared the lake level with the rapid shown in Stanton's view; 241 Mile Rapid was beneath fifty feet of water and sediment.

As we stood there above the grave of 241 Mile Rapid, I knew this would be the last Stanton photograph I would replicate in Grand Canyon. The project had run its course; it was over. We had spent a hundred days on river trips replicating photographs that would have been used to justify a railroad. This was a decidedly low-tech, low-budget project with high-knowledge payoffs. There is no more basic scientific technique than interpreting old photographs. We discovered changes in Grand Canyon that could not have been determined any other way.

As we stood there on the cliff, someone wondered what the future would be for our photographs. Would someone want to replicate our views, say, ten years later? We were planning to store our negatives and prints archivally and keep high-quality notes so that someone could come along and have an easier time locating the camera stations than we had. But observational science is passé these days;

"real science" now requires high-speed computers or sophisticated chemical analyses. Researchers have to make measurements or test theories; some of my colleagues tell me that observation alone, unless it is done by satellite, is insufficient.

I learned the real value of repeat photography by replicating the Stanton views in Grand Canyon. Repeat photographs can tell you what measurements to make where theory is insufficient. Interpreting old photographs makes you look at the landscape, makes you look hard. Changes you see usually do not explain themselves. For me, this means additional careful measurement or examination of existing theories, some sleuthing to discover why certain changes might have occurred and others did not. We do not understand why changes occur in the landscape over long periods of time; our best theories work only over short periods.

Too much of our concept of the real world is based on our perception of stasis, an unchanging world. We live only a short while; even the history of world civilizations is insufficient to interpret environmental change that spans centuries. When it comes to our perspectives of wilderness, we usually assume that the conditions we see today were also present in the imaginable past. Our management policies sometimes reflect this short-sighted perspective. Repeat photography is one means of obtaining an objective and holistic perspective on environmental change.

We need such a perspective, in concert with satellites and high-speed computers, to understand the extent and causes of change and to manage wilderness.

The Stanton photographs changed the way I look at landscapes and my perception of time. I now want to find "new" old photographs and search continually for another view that might yield another piece of that puzzle called environmental change. I remember standing in the National Archives holding one of Stanton's negatives and realizing that although Stanton and his crew are dead and their equipment is gone, those fragile rectangles of emulsion *were there* on his expedition. I was holding history in my hands. I also was holding a powerful tool that can change our perception of the natural world.

I will always use old photographs; they provide a reality check on scientific theories about what forces of change are important. In the case of the Stanton photographs, the views became an end unto themselves—old photographs are scientific data. I have no doubt that our attempts to understand a century of environmental change along the Colorado River are enriched by old photographs. The original photographs, our rephotography project, and each rephotography project that might be conducted in the future add to our understanding of how nature works and at the same time enrich our appreciation of Grand Canyon.

Appendix

Table 1 Species in Grand Canyon That Can Live More Than 100 Years

Common Name	Species	Number of Individuals	Number of Photographs
SHRUBS			
White bursage	*Ambrosia dumosa*	13	5
Four-wing saltbush	*Atriplex canescens*	9	7
Shadscale	*Atriplex confertifolia*	13	5
Waterweed	*Baccharis sergiloides**	1	1
—	*Bernardia incana*	5	1
Spiny brickellbush	*Brickellia atractyloides*	5	3
Rabbitbush	*Chrysothamnus nauseosus**	1	1
Blackbrush	*Coleogyne ramosissima*	18	3
Mormon tea, joint fir	*Ephedra fasciculata*	**	1
Mormon tea, joint fir	*Ephedra nevadensis*	**	7
Mormon tea, joint fir	*Ephedra torreyana*	**	3
—	*Ephedra* sp.	685	173
Apache plume	*Fallugia paradoxa*	***	11
Ocotillo	*Fouquieria splendens*	8	4
Desert bedstraw	*Galium stellatum*	7	6
—	*Haplopappus salicinus*	1	1
Range ratany	*Krameria parvifolia*	3	1
Creosote bush	*Larrea tridentata*	104	21
Wolfberry, Anderson thornbush	*Lycium andersonii*	77	31
Fremont thornbush	*Lycium fremontii**	1	1
Rock mat	*Petrophytum caespitosum*	3	1
Trixis	*Trixis californica**	1	1
Greythorn	*Ziziphus obtusifolia*	3	3
GRASS			
Three-awn	*Aristida purpurea* var *nealleyii*	5	4
Big galleta grass	*Hilaria rigida*	43	15
Bush muhly	*Muhlenbergia porteri*	***	3
Indian rice grass	*Oryzopsis hymenoides**	1	1
Mesa dropseed	*Sporobolus flexuosus*	5	4
CACTI AND OTHER SUCCULENTS			
Cottontop cactus	*Echinocactus polycephalus**	1	1
Claretcup cactus	*Echinocereus triglochidiatus*	6	5
Buckhorn cholla	*Opuntia acanthocarpa*	6	4
Beavertail	*Opuntia basilaris*	29	16
Mojave prickly pear	*Opuntia erinacea*	23	13
Engelmann prickly pear	*Opuntia engelmannii*	12	6
Hybrid prickly pear	*Opuntia basilaris × erinacea**	1	1

Table 1 continued

Common Name	Species	Number of Individuals	Number of Photographs
Hybrid prickly pear	Opuntia engelmannii × erinacea*	1	1
Whipple cholla	Opuntia whipplei	4	3
Fine-leaf yucca	Yucca angustissima	16	4
TREES			
Catclaw	Acacia greggii	240	98
Net-leaf hackberry	Celtis reticulata	5	5
California redbud	Cercis occidentalis*	1	1
Birchleaf buckthorn	Rhamnus betulaefolia*	1	1
Honey mesquite	Prosopis glandulosa	***	58
Shrub live oak	Quercus turbinella*	1	1

*Questionable member of the Century Club; only one persistent individual was observed.
**Included under *Ephedra* sp. because the species could not be determined in all views.
***We could not determine the number of individuals for this species.

Table 2 Perennial Species That Were in Either the Stanton or the 1990s Views Whose Individuals Apparently Cannot Live for a Century

Common Name	Species	Common Name	Species
Utah agave	Agave utahensis	Snakeweed	Gutierrezia sarothrae
Wright lippia	Aloysia wrightii	Spiny aster	Haplopappus spinulosus
Desert broom	Baccharis sarothroides	Beargrass	Nolina microcarpa
Sweetbush	Bebbia juncea	Pancake pear	Opuntia chlorotica
Engelmann hedgehog	Echinocereus engelmannii	Indigo bush	Psorothamnus fremontii
Fendler hedgehog	Echinocereus fendleri	Tamarisk	Tamarix chinensis
Brittlebush	Encelia farinosa	Arrowweed	Tessaria sericea
California buckwheat	Eriogonum fasciculatum	Turpentine bush	Thamnosma montana
Fluff grass	Erioneuron pulchellum	Shrubby coldenia	Tiquilia canescens
Barrel cactus	Ferocactus cylindraceus		

Table 3 Major Debris Flows of the Past Century in Grand Canyon

Tributary Canyon	Rapid	Mile	Side	Year(s) of Debris Flow(s)
Badger Creek	Badger Creek	7.9	R	1897–1909
Soap Creek	Soap Creek	11.2	R	1930s
Rider Canyon	House Rock	16.8	R	1966–1971
22 Mile Wash	22 Mile	21.4	L	unknown
Unnamed canyon	24 Mile	24.1	L	1989
Tiger Wash	Tiger Wash	26.6	L	1890–1990
Unnamed canyon	none	30.2	R	1989
South Canyon	unnamed	31.6	R	1940–1965
Tatahoysa Wash	President Harding	43.7	L	1984
Unnamed canyon	new	62.5	R	1990
Lava Creek	Lava Canyon	65.5	R	1966
Palisades Creek	Lava Canyon	65.5	L	late 1970s
75 Mile Creek	Nevills	75.5	L	before 1935, 1987, 1990
Hance Creek	Sockdolager	78.7	L	1890–1990
Monument Creek	Granite	93.5	L	1984
Boucher Creek	Boucher	96.7	L	1951
Crystal Creek	Crystal	98.3	R	1966
Waltenberg Canyon	Waltenberg	112.2	R	1890–1923
Unnamed canyon	new	127.6	L	1989
128 Mile Creek	128 Mile	128.5	R	1890–1923
Unnamed canyon	unnamed	133.0	L	1890–1990
Kanab Canyon	Kanab	143.5	R	1923–1942
Prospect Canyon	Lava Falls	179.3	L	1939, 1954, 1955, 1963, 1966, 1995
205 Mile Canyon	205 Mile	205.4	L	1937–1956
Diamond Creek	Diamond Creek	225.5	L	1984
231 Mile Canyon	231 Mile	230.8	R	1890–1990

Table 4 Changes to Rapids of the Colorado River Visible in Stanton Views

River Mile	Rapid Name	Summary of Changes
11.2	Soap Creek	flood or debris flow from Soap Creek in the 1930s
14.5	Sheer Wall	debris flow from Tanner Canyon; fan eroded and rocks moved
16.7	House Rock	debris flow from Rider Canyon between 1966 and 1971
26.7	Tiger Wash	debris flows from both sides of river
26.9	MNA	rockfall from high-angle chute in 1974
62.5	unnamed	debris flow from unnamed tributary
65.5	Lava Creek	multiple debris flows from Palisades and Lava Creeks
78.7	Sockdolager	debris flow from Hance Creek deposited new rocks on left
93.5	Granite	multiple debris flows from Monument Creek
98.3	Crystal	debris flow from Crystal Creek in 1966
179.3	Lava Falls	multiple debris flows from Prospect Creek
205.4	205 Mile	rockfall from right; debris flow from 205 Mile Creek
208.8	209 Mile	rock created major hydraulic wave in 1979
230.9	231 Mile	debris flow and river erosion have changed rapid

Table 5 Rapids with Little or No Change over the Past Century

River Mile	Rapid Name	Summary of Changes
7.9	Badger	debris flow from Badger Canyon deposited rocks at upper right
43.5	President Harding	debris fan eroded, left run enlarged
75.5	Nevills	multiple debris flows from 75 Mile Canyon, but little effect
76.8	Hance	few changes
81.5	Grapevine	rocks moved from center of channel
87.9	Bright Angel	debris fan eroded at lower right
88.9	Pipe Springs	few changes
90.2	Horn Creek	few changes
95.0	Hermit	few changes
99.2	Tuna Creek	few changes
101.2	Sapphire	few changes
103.9	104 Mile	few changes
104.5	Ruby	few changes
105.9	Serpentine	few changes
108.5	Shinumo	few changes
112.2	Waltenberg	aggradation on right, boulders moved from left

Table 5 continued

River Mile	Rapid Name	Summary of Changes
118.8	119 Mile	few changes
131.8	Dubendorff	new rock garden at lower left
133.7	Tapeats	few changes
143.5	Kanab	debris flow from side, but few changes to rapid
164.5	164 Mile	few changes
217.4	217 Mile	few changes

Figure 1.

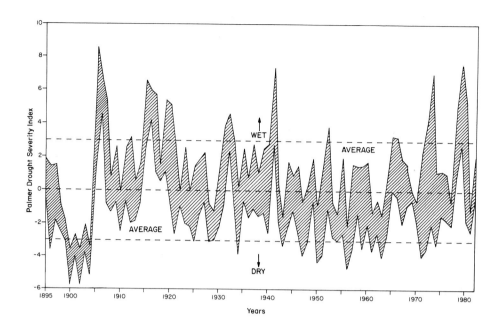

Figure 1.

The Palmer drought-severity index, which is based on temperature and precipitation, shows the effect of climate on growing conditions in a region. Values of the index less than −3 indicate drought; values greater than +3 indicate excess moisture. The drought of 1900–1905 is the most severe in the history of Arizona; the wet period of 1906–1928 also is prominent. A sustained period of drought in the mid-1950s was followed by erratic but generally above-average conditions in the 1970s and 1980s.

Figure 2.

The annual temperature curve for Arizona generally reflects the trend toward decreasing severe freezes in the state. Between about 1900 and 1920, Arizona had its most sustained period of severe freezes in history, with one severe frost every two to three years; annual temperatures dipped through this period. Warming occurred in the middle part of the century, between about 1930 and 1960, but severe freezes still occurred. During the past forty years, severe freezes have been rare, recurring at intervals of about one per ten years.

Figure 3.

The number of days that ice affected the gaging station on the Colorado River at Lees Ferry, Arizona, between 1923 and 1963. The closure of Glen Canyon Dam in March 1963 ended this unique record. The dam releases water at a nearly constant 50°F, which is too warm to freeze under any conceivable weather conditions at Lees Ferry.

Figure 2.

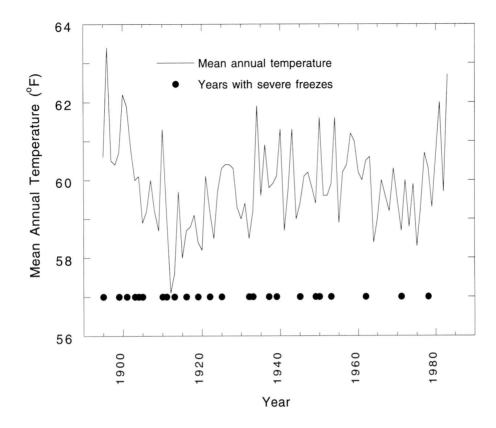

Figure 3.

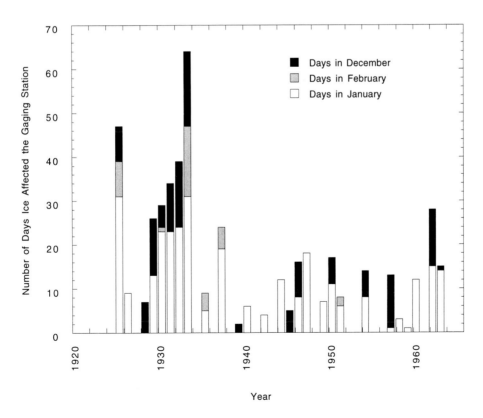

Figure 4.

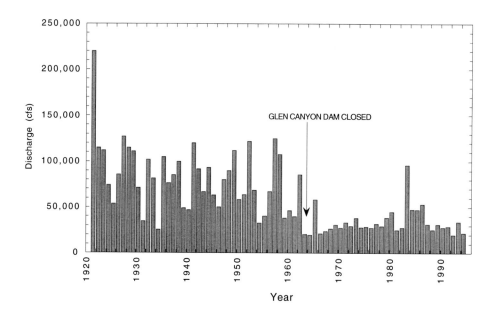

Figure 5.

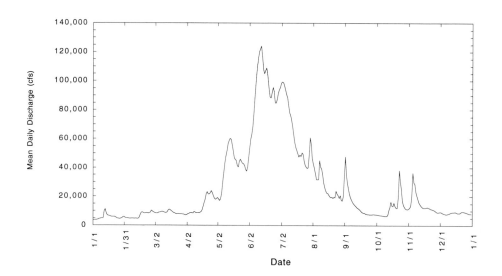

Figure 6.

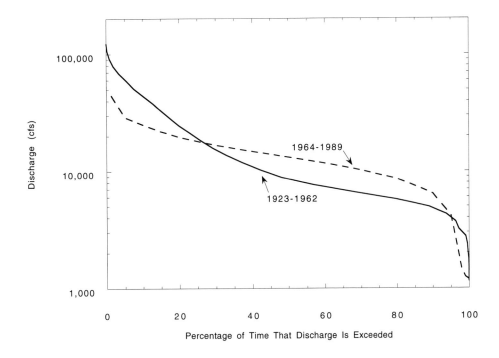

Discharge (cfs)

1964-1989

1923-1962

Percentage of Time That Discharge Is Exceeded

Figure 4.

Annual floods between 1921 and 1990 for the Colorado River near Grand Canyon, Arizona. The gaging station is located just upstream of the mouth of Bright Angel Creek (mile 87). Flow regulation by Glen Canyon Dam has reduced the two-year flood from about 100,000 cfs to about 31,000 cfs. In the thirty years of operation of Glen Canyon Dam, the old high-water line benefited from flooding only once—in 1983.

Figure 5.

During a typical year before the completion of Glen Canyon Dam, discharges for the Colorado River were low in winter and early spring, and flow rose rapidly in May and peaked in June. Sudden rises in discharge during the summer and fall were caused by tributary runoff after thunderstorms. This hydrograph for 1957 illustrates the seasonality of flow in the unregulated Colorado River measured at the Grand Canyon gaging station.

Figure 6.

Duration of daily average discharge, shown here for the Colorado River near Grand Canyon for the periods 1923-1962 and 1964-1989, is an important hydrologic measure that illustrates why marshes now form in wide reaches of Grand Canyon. Before flow regulation in 1963, a daily discharge of 10,000 cfs was exceeded only 35 percent of the time; now, 10,000 cfs is exceeded about 80 percent of the time. In contrast, a daily discharge of 30,000 cfs was exceeded nearly 20 percent of the time in the unregulated river; now, 30,000 cfs is exceeded less than 1 percent of the time. The relation of discharge duration for the regulated river is much flatter than for the unregulated river; low flows are now higher, providing dependable water during all seasons, and the floods that once scoured away riparian plants below the 100,000 cfs stage are now rare.

Figure 7.

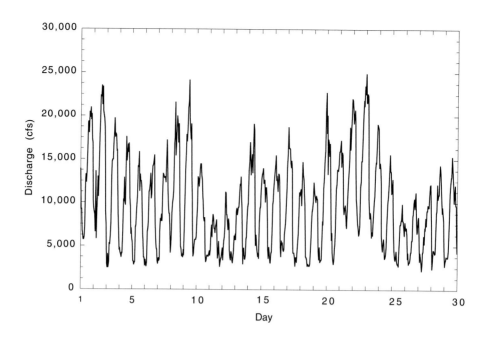

Figure 7.

Hydrograph of discharges for the Colorado River at Lees Ferry in September 1982. In 1982, Glen Canyon Dam had a release schedule that was typical of the first two decades of its operation. Flows fluctuated daily in response to power demands, and weekend releases were low. Change occurred in blocks of weeks or months as operators anticipated power consumption in the southwestern United States.

Figure 8.

Hydrograph of discharges for the Colorado River at Lees Ferry from 1983 until about the end of 1985. During this time, releases from Glen Canyon Dam were unusually high. High inflows to Lake Powell, which began the period nearly full, forced high releases. Back-to-back high inflows in 1983 and 1984, and subsequent sustained releases to lower the reservoir, accounted for the unusual pattern of dam releases.

Figure 9.

Pattern of change in sand bars along the Colorado River from Glen Canyon Dam to Lake Mead between 1889–1890 and 1990–1993. From the position of stable rocks or other features, sand bars visible in Stanton photographs were determined to have decreased in size, remained about the same size, or increased in size over the past century. The results of this size evaluation are grouped according to nine geomorphically based reaches.

A. Change in 442 sand bars that are inundated at less than 30,000 cfs (low-water case).

B. Change in 149 sand bars that are inundated by discharges between 30,000 and 70,000 cfs (high-water case).

Figure 8.

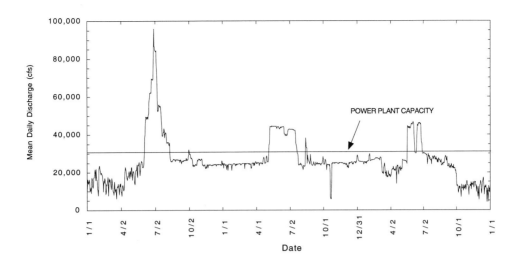

Figure 9.

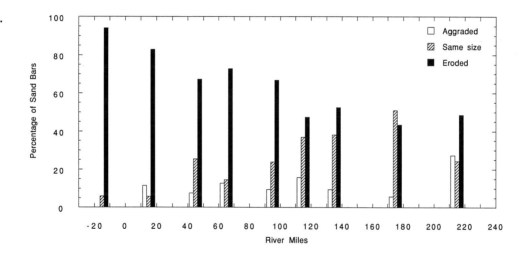

A.

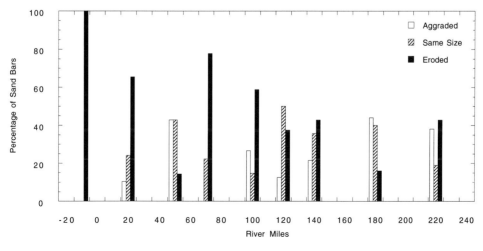

B.

Figure 10.

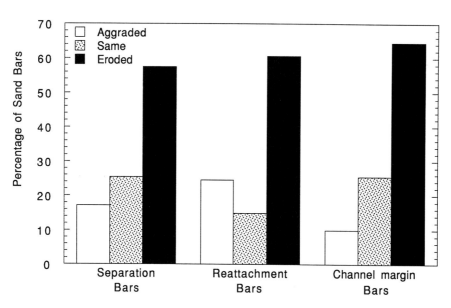

Figure 10.

Changes between 1889–1890 and 1990–1993 in 610 separation, reattachment, and channel-margin bars along the Colorado River interpreted in 300 Stanton photographs.

Notes

Introduction

1. D. L. Smith and C. G. Crampton, *The Colorado River Survey* (Salt Lake City: Howe Brothers, 1987).

2. R. H. Webb, P. T. Pringle, and G. R. Rink, *Debris Flows from Tributaries of the Colorado River, Grand Canyon National Park, Arizona* (Washington, D.C.: U.S. Geological Survey Professional Paper 1492, 1989), 39.

3. R. M. Turner and M. Karpiscak, *Recent Vegetation Changes along the Colorado River between Glen Canyon Dam and Lake Mead, Arizona* (Washington, D.C.: U.S. Geological Survey Professional Paper 1132, 1980), 125.

4. W. L. Minckley, "Native Fishes of the Grand Canyon Region: An Obituary?" in *Colorado River Ecology and Dam Management* (Washington, D.C.: National Academy Press, 1991), 124–177.

Chapter 1

1. Lieutenant Joseph C. Ives had reached this point in 1857 and had mapped it. J. C. Ives, *Report upon the Colorado River of the West, Explored in 1857 and 1858*, 36th Cong., 1861, House Executive Document 90. The Wheeler Survey had towed boats upriver to Diamond Creek in 1871 and had photographed its mouth. Tourists were regularly visiting Diamond Creek by 1883, which enabled the construction of a

hotel at its mouth in 1884. The hotel closed in 1889. J. D. Hughes, *In the House of Stone and Light* (Grand Canyon Natural History Association, 1978), 44–46.

2. Details of Stanton's life and expeditions are derived from two sources. Stanton's account of the expeditions in 1889 and 1889–1890 is published as Robert B. Stanton, *Down the Colorado*, edited by D. L. Smith (Norman: University of Oklahoma Press, 1965), 237. Stanton's diary of the two expeditions is published in Smith and Crampton, *Colorado River Survey*.

3. Letter published in *Engineering News and American Railway Journal*, March 22, 1890, 276. Stanton mailed this letter from Peach Springs, Arizona.

4. Smith and Crampton, *Colorado River Survey*, 238.

5. R. A. Bartlett, *Great Surveys of the American West* (Norman: University of Oklahoma Press, 1962), 408.

6. J. W. Powell, *Exploration of the Colorado River of the West and Its Tributaries* (Washington, D.C.: GPO, 1875), 400. Powell probably had not intended to write an accurate history of his 1869 expedition; instead, he was keenly interested in securing additional funding for his survey. His account mixes events from the 1869 and 1871–1872 expeditions into a single account. Frederick S. Dellenbaugh, a member of the 1871–1872 expedition, documented the second expedition in *A Canyon Voyage* (New Haven: Yale University Press, 1908), 277. The events in Powell's published diaries and accounts have been arranged chronologically in J. Cooley, *The Great Unknown* (Flagstaff, Arizona: Northland Publishing, 1988), 207. Cooley's work was criticized by R. C. Euler in "Adrift on the Colorado," *Journal of the Southwest* 33 (1991): 204–209 and Drifter Smith in "The Great Unknown: Adrift on the Colorado," *Journal of the Southwest* 33 (1991): 211–216. An excellent example of the products of Powell's project is C. E. Dutton, *Tertiary History of the Grand Cañon District* (Washington, D.C.: GPO, Monographs of the U.S. Geological Survey, Vol. 2, 1882), 264.

7. For a concise history of mining in Grand Canyon, see G. H. Billingsley, "Mining in Grand Canyon," in W. J. Breed and E. C. Roat, editors, *Geology of the Grand Canyon* (Grand Canyon Natural History Association, 1974), 170–178.

8. Stanton, *Down the Colorado*, 24.

9. For a complete description of the economic arguments for the railroad, see D. L. Smith, "Robert B. Stanton's Plan for the Southwest," *Arizona and the West* 4 (1962): 369–380.

10. Harper had not even seen Powell's report and had only been to the Colorado River at Lees Ferry. Stanton, *Down the Colorado*, 23–26.

11. The interview of Powell, which appeared in the *New York Tribune* on August 18, 1889, contained Powell's version of a conversation with Brown. Stanton discussed Powell's criticisms in *Engineering News and American Railway Journal*, September 21, 1889, 269–272.

12. Stanton, *Down the Colorado*, xiv–xv.

13. Ibid., 36.

14. Powell, *Exploration*, 249–251. Powell stated that Sockdolager Rapid could not be lined or portaged. On January 28, 1890, Stanton and his crew, who did not recognize Sockdolager Rapid from Powell's description, lined the rapid on the left.

15. Stanton, *Down the Colorado*, 34.

16. F. A. Nims, *The Photographer and the River, 1889–90*, edited by D. L. Smith (Santa Fe: Stagecoach Press, 1967), 75. Nims is recorded in the Colorado Directories as being a photographer in Colorado Springs in 1882 and in a partnership in photographic work with a Clark (or Clarke) in 1886. Other details of Nims's life were obtained from correspondence in the Marston Collection at the Huntington Library, San Marino, California, between Otis "Dock" Marston and Bess Nims, who was Franklin Nims's daughter-in-law.

17. Nims's diaries were in shorthand. Nims, *Photographer*, 18.

18. D. Baars, *A River Runner's Guide to Cataract Canyon and Approaches* (Evergreen, Colorado: Cañon Publishers, 1987), 80. Only sixteen miles of Cataract Canyon's rapids remain after the construction of Glen Canyon Dam and the filling of Lake Powell. Although this rapid is now called Brown Betty, the

Brown Betty was destroyed the next day in what is now called Rapid 10 lower in Cataract Canyon.

19. Jim Braggs, head river ranger at Canyonlands National Park, examined Nims's photographs of Cataract Canyon in June 1993. He estimated that the Stanton expedition had experienced discharges between 40,000 and 50,000 cfs.

20. River miles are measured upstream or downstream of Lees Ferry. L. Stevens, *The Colorado River in Grand Canyon: A Guide* (Flagstaff, Arizona: Red Lake Books, 1990), 115.

21. Stanton may not have stored equipment and supplies in the cave that today bears his name. William Edwards, who was present when the cache was retrieved, reports that the crew entered a second cave downstream. W. H. Edwards, "Diary of Wm H. Edwards, Boatman on the D.C.C.&P.R.R. Survey of 1889 and 1890," New York Public Library, Rare Books Section, unpublished typescript, 1890, 42. That night, they slept in the downstream cave, which was a balmy 70°F. The downstream cave better fits the description of what is now called Stantons Cave. However, on July 14, 1942, Norman Nevills wrote in his diary that a note signed by two of Stanton's boatmen (including Edwards) and dated January 14, 1890, was found in Stantons Cave.

22. Powell criticized the project in an interview in the *New York Tribune* on August 27, 1889. Stanton later rebutted Powell's criticisms (Stanton, 1889, letter, *New York Tribune*). Stanton had discovered the first of Powell's exaggerations on June 13, when Stanton measured the fall through the Big Drops of Cataract Canyon at fifty-five feet in two miles; Powell's account placed the figure at seventy-five feet in three-quarters of a mile. The actual drop between the top of Rapid 21 and the bottom of Rapid 23 is twenty-eight feet in three-quarters of a mile as measured in 1921 by the U.S. Geological Survey.

23. After the second trip ended, the promises were forgotten and Stanton paid the remaining debt of $12,500.

24. Unfortunately, Stanton chose to emulate the design of boats used on the Powell expedition, which re-

quired two oarsmen and one steersman. Improvements in boating technique began on the next two successful expeditions in 1896 and 1897. George Flavell faced downstream as he rowed the Green and Colorado Rivers in 1896. N. B. Carmony and D. E. Brown, *The Log of the Panthon* (Boulder, Colorado: Pruett Publishing, 1987), 109. Nathaniel Galloway is credited with having developed this technique, which he perfected during his trip with William Richmond in the winter of 1896–97. D. Lavender, *River Runners of the Grand Canyon* (Grand Canyon Natural History Association, 1985), 147. Flavell went bow first; Galloway went stern first.

25. William H. Edwards had considerable experience as a carpenter but no previous experience running rivers. His diary adds details to Stanton's account.

26. Modern river runners recognize the effect of water level on the severity of rapids and occasionally time their arrival at certain rapids to coincide with expected discharges in the dam-controlled Colorado River.

27. Stanton, *Down the Colorado*, 116–117.

28. Nims, *Photographer*, 16.

29. In St. George, Utah, the lows for January 7 and 8, 1890, were 18°F, decreasing to 15°F on January 12 and 14°F on January 16. At Fort Mojave, Arizona, located in a relatively open valley of the lower Colorado River, a low of 26°F was reached on January 14, 15, 17, 20, and 21. Today, the average low temperature in the vicinity of Fort Mojave for days in January is about 41°F.

30. The Tanner Trail originally was used by Native Americans. Seth Tanner was credited with its first use as a prospecting trail in the 1880s. Hughes, *House*, 53.

31. Smith and Crampton, *Colorado River Survey*, 162.

32. In the 1890s, McDonald worked for Stanton in Glen Canyon, which indicates that the parting at Crystal Creek was not the result of ill feelings between the two men. To quote Stanton's opinion of McDonald: "In after years McDonald was in my employ for a number of seasons, and was a capable and faithful man" (Stanton, *Down the Colorado*, 163). Edwards,

33. Stanton, *Down the Colorado*, 169–170.

34. The flood experienced during the Stanton expedition occurred at the same time as a large flood on the Verde River. W. D. Sellers, R. H. Hill, and M. Sanderson-Rae, *Arizona Climate: The First Hundred Years* (Tucson: University of Arizona Press, 1985), 9. After the trip, Stanton learned that the flood had come down the Little Colorado River and had been compounded by dam failures along that river. Stanton, *Down the Colorado*, 195n.

35. Smith and Crampton in *Colorado River Survey*, 215, explain the waves observed by the Stanton expedition above Havasu Creek as "sand waves." Sand waves result from shallow flow over sand dunes on the bed of the river and are common on southwestern rivers, particularly the San Juan River in southern Utah. The sand wave interpretation is controversial because the Colorado River is too deep and narrow in this reach to lead one to expect sand dunes. Stanton suggested the alternative explanation of a hydraulic jump (Stanton, *Down the Colorado*, 195).

36. The experience of Stanton's expedition at Lava Falls Rapid illustrates an important climatic difference between the bottom of Grand Canyon and sites in nearby valleys. The crew complained about the cold weather, and Edwards in his diary (p. 35) reported a low of 29°F. However, the minimum temperatures recorded at St. George and Fort Mojave were well above freezing. Sunlight does not reach the river at Lava Falls Rapid in February until about 11:00 A.M., or about the time the Stanton expedition moved downstream.

37. Smoke from the fire at Lava Falls Rapid could be seen three hundred miles away. Ibid., 35.

38. During Powell's 1869 expedition, the Howland brothers and William Dunn left the group at Separation Rapid (mile 239). They attempted to hike to the settlements in southern Utah but were reported to have been killed by a band of Shivwits who were enraged over an assault alleged to have been made on a Shivwits woman. F. S. Dellenbaugh, *Romance of the Colorado River* (New York: C. P. Putnam's Sons, 1902), 170–171. Some inconclusive evidence suggests the men may have been killed by Mormon settlers who mistakenly thought they were federal agents attempting to arrest those responsible for the Mountain Meadow Massacre. W. P. Larsen, "The 'Letter,' or Were the Powell Men Really Killed by Indians?" *Canyon Legacy* 17 (1993): 12–19. The details of this incident intrigued Stanton. A chance meeting in Glen Canyon with Jack Sumner on December 13, 1889, led Stanton to question the accuracy of Powell's account of what had happened at Separation Rapid. R. B. Stanton, *Colorado River Controversies*, edited by J. M. Chalfant (Boulder City, Nevada: Westwater Books, 1932), 261.

39. Powell greatly exaggerated the difficulty and lack of choices at Separation Rapid. O. Marston, "Separation Marks, Notes on 'The Worst Rapid' in the Grand Canyon," *Journal of Arizona History* 17 (1976): 1–20. For example, the Wheeler Survey lined boats up the rapid in 1871. George Flavell claimed to have run all three rapids in 1896, and the only rapid he discussed in detail was Lava Cliff Rapid. Carmony and Brown, *Panthon*, 69–70.

40. Ives, *Report*, 110.

41. R. B. Stanton, "Engineering in the Depths of the Grand Canyon," in Passenger Department of the Santa Fe, *The Grand Canyon of Arizona* (Chicago: Poole Brothers, 1902), 43–53. Stanton was not the only employer of Hislop's who appreciated his hardiness and work ethic; Hislop's wilderness skills became legendary during his work in Alaska. S. H. Graves, 1970, *On the "White Pass" Pay-roll* (New York: Paladin Press), 43–55.

42. Nims, *Photographer*, 54.

43. Nims's account of his participation in the second expedition is fictitious. One account (F. A. Nims, "Through the Colorado River," *The Commonwealth* 3 [1890]: 257–272) contains conversations among the crew that occurred when he was not present. Other articles pertaining to the second expedition (F. A. Nims, "Through the Mysterious Canyons of the Colorado," *The Overland Monthly* 19 [1892]:

253–270; idem, "Profile Negatives Canned," *Wilson's Photographic Magazine* 33 [1896]: 73–78) place Nims on the river after he had been evacuated.

44. Dellenbaugh wrote a critical and inaccurate account of the two railroad expeditions (*Romance*, 342–369), which may have inspired Stanton to write *Colorado River Controversies*.

45. Stanton, *Controversies*, 3–93. Stanton believed that White's interviewers had greatly embellished his story and had prompted him to increase his estimates of the distance he had traveled down the Colorado River. William Bass, however, believed White's river-run story more than the alternative explanation that White had traveled overland several hundred miles before entering the Colorado River at the mouth of the Grand Wash Cliffs. W. W. Bass, *Adventures in the Canyons of the Colorado* (Grand Canyon, Arizona: privately published, 1920), 17–29. Few modern-day historians believe White's story. See Lavender, *River Runners*.

46. This incident has attracted considerable historical interest, but it cannot be extracted from the controversy concerning the general accuracy of Powell's 1875 account (notes 6 and 38). Stanton believed that the Howlands and Dunn had left Powell's 1869 expedition because of Powell's dictatorial behavior, not because of the difficulty of Separation Rapid.

47. The head boatman for this trip was Bus Hatch, who later founded one of the first commercial river-running companies in the western United States. Roy Webb, *Riverman: The Story of Bus Hatch* (Rock Springs, Wyoming: Labyrinth Publishing, 1989), 39–54.

48. Lavender, *River Runners*, 76.

The Climb to the Tower of Ra

1. Smith and Crampton, *Colorado River Survey*, 185.

2. R. B. Stanton, "Engineering with a Camera in the Cañons of the Colorado," *The Cosmopolitan* 15 (1893): 298–303; idem, *Down the Colorado*, 166–172.

3. H. Butchart, *Grand Canyon Treks III: Inner Canyon Journals* (Glendale, California: La Siesta Press, 1984), 30–31.

4. Stanton, *Down the Colorado*, 169.

5. D. G. Davis, "Rim to 'Olla Vieja Cave' and Tower of Ra, May 29 to June 2, 1966," unpublished trip notes in the possession of R. C. Euler; idem, interviewed by R. C. Euler, 1985.

6. These two vessels are in the archaeological collections at Grand Canyon National Park and are recorded as site Ariz. B:16:58.

7. Davis, interviewed by Euler. The ground-glass fragments were collected as "archaeological" specimens and are now housed with the collections at Grand Canyon National Park as site Ariz. B:16:119.

8. Information from George Eastman House, Rochester, New York. P. L. Condax, interviewed by R. C. Euler, 1985.

9. Smith and Crampton, *Colorado River Survey*, 97.

Chapter 2

1. The information on repeat photography comes from G. F. Rogers, H. E. Malde, and R. M. Turner, *Bibliography of Repeat Photography for Evaluating Landscape Change* (Salt Lake City: University of Utah Press, 1984), 179. For a description of Finsterwalder's pioneering efforts and their effect on the field of glaciology, see G. Hattersley-Smith, "The Symposium on Glacier Mapping," *Canadian Journal of Earth Sciences* 3 (1966): 737–743.

2. Exemplary studies include J. R. Hastings and R. M. Turner, *The Changing Mile* (Tucson: University of Arizona Press, 1965), 317; and W. L. Graf, "Mining and Channel Responses," *Annals of the Association of American Geographers* 69 (1979): 262–275.

3. Vegetation changes revealed by repeat photography are reported by G. Rogers, *Then and Now: A Photographic History of Vegetation Change in the Central Great Basin* (Salt Lake City: University of Utah Press, 1982), 152; W. J. McGinnies, H. L. Shantz, and W. G. McGinnies, *Changes in Vegetation and Land Use in Eastern Colorado* (Washington, D.C.: U.S. Department of Agriculture, Agricultural Research Service Publication ARS-85, 1991), 165; T. T. Veblen and D. C. Lorenz, *The Colorado Front Range: A Century of Ecological Change* (Salt Lake City:

University of Utah Press, 1991), 186; and B. R. Gordon, G. P. Parrott, and J. B. Smith, "Vegetation Changes in Northern Arizona: The Alexander Gardner Photos," *Rangelands* 14 (1992): 308–320. A rather superficial treatment of vegetation change throughout the western United States, based on repeat photography of Timothy O'Sullivan views, is given in P. J. Salamun, "An Interpretation of Vegetational Changes along the Fortieth Parallel in Nevada and Utah, 1867–1981," in E. M. Murphy and J. M. Knapp, editors, *Kaleidoscope of History, Photographic Collections in the Golda Meir Library* (Milwaukee: University of Wisconsin, American Geographical Society Collection Special Publication No. 1, 1990), 73–86. An interesting repeat photography project documenting the recovery of rivers that were severely disturbed by mining activities in the Sierra Nevada of California is given in J. H. Turner, *Charles L. Weed Historic Photographs of Middle Fork American River Mining Activities* (Sacramento, California: U.S. Bureau of Reclamation Report, 1983), 47.

4. Turner and Karpiscak, *Vegetation Changes;* H. G. Stephens and E. M. Shoemaker, *In the Footsteps of John Wesley Powell* (Boulder, Colorado: Johnson Books, 1987), 286.

5. Many photographers have inadvertently replicated historic views at popular scenic sites in Grand Canyon, including the left rim overlook of Badger Creek Rapid, the downstream view from the granaries at Nankoweap, and the overlook at Toroweap Point. Otis "Dock" Marston, a river runner and historian whose first trip was in 1942, compiled the largest archive of historical photographs of Grand Canyon. The collection, housed in the Huntington Library in San Marino, California, contains thousands of prints organized by river mile. As far as I can determine, Marston did not purposefully replicate the views of other photographers except in Cataract Canyon.

6. Stephens and Shoemaker, *Footsteps.*

7. Turner and Karpiscak, *Vegetation Changes.* Eugene C. LaRue documented potential dam sites. He mostly used a panoramic camera, which produces views that are difficult to replicate with a typical modern camera. LaRue either did not climb high above water level or settled into precarious positions on cliffs. As a result, many of his low camera positions are now blocked by riparian vegetation, which became dense after the closure of Glen Canyon Dam. His views contain less information than Stanton's.

8. Stanton, "Engineering with a Camera," 296.

9. Smith and Crampton, *Colorado River Survey,* 97.

10. H. and H. T. Anthony and Company, *Illustrated Catalogue of Photographic Equipment and Materials for Amateurs* (New York: H. and H. T. Anthony and Company, 1891), 52–55. Of the Dallmeyer lenses available, these lenses best match the characteristics of Nims's camera. The author acknowledges Robert C. Euler for sending a copy of this catalog.

11. Robert Taft, *Photography and the American Scene* (New York: MacMillan Company, 1938), 385–387.

12. For a description of this camera, see M. Auer, *The Illustrated History of the Camera* (Boston: Little, Brown, and Company, 1987), 118–120.

13. Nims, *Photographer,* 32.

14. Ibid., 37.

15. Stanton, *Down the Colorado,* 101. Smith and Crampton, *Colorado River Survey,* 97, gives a list of photographic supplies for the second trip.

16. Stanton's knowledge of exposure times was limited to his experience with Nims's exposures on bright or partly cloudy days in the deep canyons. With heavy cloud cover or during late-afternoon or early-morning exposures, Stanton typically underexposed his negatives. Also, he notes that he overexposed negatives in the bright light and open country downstream of Needles, California. Smith and Crampton, *Colorado River Survey,* 277.

17. Number 615, a double exposure of the up- and down-canyon views at mile 176, was included in the album of prints in the National Archives. Its inclusion with other, normal views raises the question whether Stanton recognized the negative for what it was.

18. A list of Stanton's photographs is given in T. S. Melis, R. H. Webb, P. G. Griffiths, and T. J. Wise, *Magnitude and Frequency Data for Historic Debris Flows in Grand Canyon National Park and Vicinity, Arizona* (Tucson, Arizona: U.S. Geological Survey Water Resources Investigations Report 94-4125), appendix 4.

19. Stanton published many, but not all, of the photographs taken during the expeditions. Stanton, letters in 1889 and 1890 *Engineering News and Railway Journal,* and idem, "Engineering with a Camera."

20. Stanton, letter, *Engineering News and American Railway Journal,* September 21, 1889, 269–272.

21. E. A. Reynolds, "In the Whirlpools of the Grand Cañon of the Colorado," *Cosmopolitan* 11 (November 1889): 25–34.

22. The photographic album was exhibit number 176 in a case (*Utah v United States,* 284 US 534) that concerned fraudulent ownership of mineral rights in Utah. All of the early river runners still living testified in the case as to the navigability of the Green and Colorado Rivers. Nims's and Stanton's photographs, along with those of the U.S. Geological Survey expeditions of 1921 and 1923, were the best means of showing what the canyons looked like.

23. The U.S. Geological Survey expedition of 1923 is one of the most documented Grand Canyon traverses, described in C. E. Birdseye and R. Moore, "A Boat Voyage through the Grand Canyon of the Colorado," *Geographical Review* (April 1924): 177–196; L. R. Freeman, "Surveying the Grand Canyon of the Colorado: An Account of the 1923 Boating Expedition of the United States Geological Survey," *National Geographic Magazine* 45 (1924): 524–530; idem, *Down the Grand Canyon* (New York: Dodd, Mead, and Company, 1924), 299–371; and Lavender, *River Runners,* 58–65. In addition, Birdseye and LaRue kept diaries during the expedition that are unpublished. The story is told from the perspective of one of the boatmen, Elwyn Blake, in R. E. Westwood, *Rough-Water Man: Elwyn Blake's Colorado River Expeditions* (Reno: University of Nevada Press, 1992), 259.

24. Letter from Birdseye to Burchard, July 26, 1924, USGS Field Records Library, Denver.

25. Letter from Birdseye to Burchard, July 8, 1924, USGS Field Records.

26. Dossier on transfer transaction 449-170, accession no. 3075, dated June 29, 1949, Still Picture Branch, National Archives and Record Service, Washington, D.C.

Preservation of the Stanton Negatives

1. Taft, *Photography,* 385–386. American Film came in rolls of twelve or twenty-four exposures.

2. Paper negatives from the Stanton expedition exposed between miles 115 and 130 were accidentally cut in half by W. H. Jackson and Company during processing.

3. Collodion is a viscous solution of cellulose nitrate dissolved in alcohol and ether. When coated on the gelatin film it forms a protective layer.

4. Hannibal Goodwin is credited with having developed the first film of this type in 1887 (Taft, *Photography,* 325), although the Eastman Kodak Company was the first to make transparent film available to the general public. Kodak's version first became available on August 27, 1889; the patent was filed September 12, 1889, and was issued December 10, 1889 (Patent number 417,202) to Henry M. Reichenbach, an employee of Eastman Kodak. The Goodwin Film and Camera Company later sued Kodak for infringement of Goodwin's patent, which had been filed May 2, 1887. The settlement was made in favor of the plaintiffs in March 1914 (Taft, *Photography,* 391–403).

5. L. Clark, "The New Rollable Film of the Eastman Company," *British Journal of Photography* 37, no. 1551 (1890): 51–52.

Chapter 3

1. The most common species in Grand Canyon is probably the desert wood rat (*Neotoma lepida*). D. F. Hoffmeister, *Mammals of Grand Canyon* (Chicago:

University of Illinois Press, 1971), 87–92; E. L. Cockrum, "Recent Mammals of Arizona," in C. H. Lowe, editor, *The Vertebrates of Arizona* (Tucson: University of Arizona Press, 1980), 256.

2. The Pleistocene occurred between 2 million and 11,000 years ago. The Late Pleistocene, which represents the last glacial epoch, occurred between 70,000 and 11,000 years ago. The last glacial epoch is generally considered to have peaked at 18,000 years ago.

3. K. L. Cole, "Late Quaternary Vegetation Gradients through the Grand Canyon," in J. L. Betancourt, T. R. Van Devender, and P. S. Martin, editors, *Packrat Middens: The Last 40,000 Years of Biotic Change* (Tucson: University of Arizona Press, 1990), 240–258; idem, "Reconstruction of Past Desert Vegetation along the Colorado River Using Packrat Middens," *Palaeogeography, Palaeoclimatology, and Palaeoecology* 76 (1990): 349–366.

4. Scientific opinion is divided as to the nature of Pleistocene climate in the Southwest. One perspective calls for cooler climate with about the same precipitation (T. R. Van Devender and W. G. Spaulding, "Development of Vegetation and Climate in the Southwestern United States," *Science* 204 [1979]: 701–710). In contrast, Cole, in "Vegetation Gradients," 255, calculates a precipitation increase of 24 and 41 percent for the South and North Rims, respectively. Although consensus is lacking, the Pleistocene distribution of plants in Grand Canyon does not suggest a large increase in precipitation at river level.

5. Van Devender and Spaulding, "Development."

6. K. Cole, "Late Quaternary Zonation of Vegetation in the Eastern Grand Canyon," *Science* 217 (1982): 1142–1145.

7. J. I. Mead and A. M. Phillips, III, "The Late Pleistocene and Holocene Fauna and Flora of Vulture Cave, Grand Canyon, Arizona," *Southwestern Naturalist* 26 (1981): 257–288; Cole, "Vegetation Gradients," 242; idem, "Past Rates of Change, Species Richness, and a Model of Vegetational Inertia in the Grand Canyon, Arizona," *American Naturalist* 125 (1985): 289–303.

8. Van Devender and Spaulding, in "Development," 708, argue that Pleistocene winters were about as cold as those of today, a premise supported by the Pleistocene presence of frost-sensitive prickly pear (*Opuntia erinacea*) and barrel cactus (*Ferocactus cylindraceous*) in Grand Canyon.

9. Evidence for Pleistocene stands of desert shrubs without trees has been found at an elevation of 3,000 feet in southern Nevada. W. G. Spaulding, "Ice-Age Desert in the Southern Great Basin," *Current Research in the Pleistocene* 2 (1985): 83–85.

10. Researchers disagree about the precise timing of the climatic change at the end of the Pleistocene. Although the change is commonly held to have occurred about 11,000 years ago, many researchers find evidence for the change having occurred earlier, perhaps 12,000 years ago. P. J. Mehringer, Jr., "Pollen Analysis of the Tule Springs Site, Nevada," in H. M. Wormington and D. Ellis, editors, *Pleistocene Studies in Southern Nevada* (Carson City: Nevada State Museum Anthropological Paper 13, 1967), 129–200.

11. Cole, "Past Rates," 298–299.

12. Cole, "Vegetation Gradients"; idem, "Reconstruction."

13. K. L. Cole, "The Lower Colorado River Valley: A Pleistocene Desert," *Quaternary Research* 25 (1986): 392–400; idem, "Reconstruction."

14. W. G. Spaulding, "Vegetational and Climatic Development of the Mojave Desert, the Last Glacial Maximum to the Present," in Betancourt et al., *Packrat Middens*, 166–199; and idem, "A Middle Holocene Vegetation Record from the Mojave Desert of North America and Its Paleoclimatic Significance," *Quaternary Research* 35 (1991): 427–437. Phillips found scanty evidence of creosote bush in two middens but discounted it as contamination by younger material. A. M. Phillips, III, "Packrats, Plants, and the Pleistocene," University of Arizona, unpublished Ph.D. dissertation, 1977, 123.

15. Creosote bush probably became established along the river corridor of western Grand Canyon no later than 4,000 years ago. Spaulding, "Vegetational and Climatic Development," 182. Cole, in "Reconstruc-

tion," 363, speculates that creosote bush may still be advancing upstream along the river corridor because it is present in a 2,000-foot band above river level. Such a solid band suggests an invading species limited by its ability to invade upstream instead of a species limited by climate.

16. P. V. Wells and D. Woodcock, "Full-Glacial Vegetation of Death Valley, California: Juniper Woodland Opening to *Yucca* Semidesert," *Madroño* 32 (1985): 11–23. White bursage (*Ambrosia dumosa*) was present in the Skeleton Hills north of Las Vegas, Nevada, about 9,000 years ago. W. G. Spaulding, "Vegetation Dynamics during the Last Deglaciation, Southeastern Great Basin, USA," *Quaternary Research* 33 (1990): 188–203. This shrub probably invaded Grand Canyon before creosote bush. Perhaps as a consequence, white bursage occurs farther upstream (mile 133) than creosote bush (mile 174).

17. Phillips, "Packrats," 55. After reviewing the relevant midden records, Geoff Spaulding (written communication, 1993) has come to believe that catclaw (*Acacia greggii*) was probably present only after 10,000 years ago near the western Grand Canyon. *Acacia greggii* identified in sloth dung of Pleistocene age (R. M. Hansen, "Shasta Ground Sloth Food Habits, Rampart Cave, Arizona," *Paleobiology* 4 [1978]: 302–319) is likely to be false due to problems with species identification of plant parts in the sloth dung. See also note 55, Chapter 4.

18. Cole, "Past Rates"; Spaulding, "Vegetation Dynamics."

19. The description of desert plant assemblages of the river corridor is taken from P. L. Warren, K. L. Reichhardt, D. A. Mouat, B. T. Brown, and R. R. Johnson, *Vegetation of Grand Canyon National Park* (Tucson, Arizona: National Park Service, Cooperative Park Studies Unit, Technical Report Number 9, 1982), 104 (with maps, scale 1:62,500, 4 sheets).

20. Warren and his coauthors (ibid.) recognized the difference between plant assemblages on north- and south-facing slopes of the river corridor and mapped certain reaches with different types on opposing sides. Larry Stevens (written communication, 1993) has also measured fundamental dif-

ferences in desert plant assemblages on different orientations of slope.

21. S. W. Carothers and B. T. Brown, *The Colorado River through Grand Canyon* (Tucson: University of Arizona Press, 1991), 115.

22. B. G. Phillips, A. M. Phillips, III, and M.A.S. Bernzott, *Annotated Checklist of Vascular Plants of Grand Canyon National Park* (Grand Canyon Natural History Association Monograph Number 7, 1987), 79.

23. The best information on longevity of desert shrubs comes from repetitive readings of permanent vegetation plots. D. E. Goldberg and R. M. Turner, "Vegetation Change and Plant Demography in Permanent Plots in the Sonoran Desert," *Ecology* 67 (1986): 695–712. Using tree-ring dating techniques, one researcher found that many common shrubs were twenty to eighty years old, with variation among different species. C. W. Ferguson, "Growth Rings in Woody Shrubs as Potential Aids in Archaeological Interpretation," *The Kiva* 25 (1959): 24–30. An individual Great Basin sagebrush (*Artemisia tridentata*) collected at South Rim was over two hundred years old. C. W. Ferguson, "Annual Rings in Big Sagebrush, *Artemisia tridentata*," University of Arizona, unpublished Ph.D. dissertation, 1959.

24. L. Benson and R. A. Darrow, *Trees and Shrubs of the Southwestern Deserts* (Tucson: University of Arizona Press, 1981), 416.

25. Although Warren and coauthors report *Ephedra viridis* to be common, and even diagnostic, along the river corridor (Warren et al., *Vegetation*), we did not identify *E. viridis* at any camera station. Phillips and coauthors, in *Annotated Checklist*, 12, report *E. viridis* as rare along the river corridor. To avoid confusion, we report the assemblage types defined by *E. viridis* as "*Ephedra* assemblages."

26. By counting the stem rings in what probably was *Ephedra viridis*, one researcher estimated the age of one individual to be 81 years. Ferguson, "Growth Rings," 29. Alex McCord of the Laboratory of Tree-Ring Research, University of Arizona (interview, 1993), found slabs of the trunks of shrubs identified as *Ephedra trifurca* that Ferguson had cross-dated.

These plants were approximately 250 years old.

27. The vegetative propagation of Mormon tea presents a problem for plant measurements in the Mojave Desert. R. H. Webb, J. W. Steiger, and E. B. Newman, *The Response of Vegetation to Disturbance in Death Valley National Monument, California* (Washington, D.C.: U.S. Geological Survey Bulletin 1793, 1988), 15.

28. Establishment and mortality rates are calculated as the percentage of change per century. For example, mortality rate is equal to the number of individuals living in 1890 that are dead in the 1990s, divided by the total number of individuals visible in the 1890 view, multiplied by 100 percent, and divided by one century. I chose only those species whose individuals could live at least a century; short-lived plants are not suitable for this kind of analysis because their establishment and mortality rates would inevitably be 100 percent per century.

29. J. E. Bowns and N. E. West, *Blackbrush (Coleogyne ramosissima Torr.) on Southwestern Utah Rangelands* (Logan: Utah Agricultural Experiment Station Research Report 27, 1976), 27.

30. E. M. Christensen and R. C. Brown, "A Blackbrush over 400 Years Old," *Journal of Range Management* 16 (1963): 118.

31. A closely related species, *Lycium berlandieri,* can live in excess of seventy-two years. Goldberg and Turner, "Vegetation Change."

32. This creosote bush would be one of the oldest living organisms if the dating is correct. F. C. Vasek, "Creosote Bush, Long-Lived Clones in the Mojave Desert," *American Journal of Botany* 67 (1980): 246–255. Such longevity is unlikely, however, because creosote bush became established in the area only about 8,500 years ago. Spaulding, "Vegetational Development." In a study along the lower Colorado River, the average life span of creosote bushes was calculated to be 625 to 1,250 years. J. R. McAuliffe, "Markovian Dynamics of Simple and Complex Desert Plant Communities," *American Naturalist* 131 (1988): 459–490.

33. Using the method pioneered by Vasek in "Creosote Bush," one researcher has estimated that a clonal ring of creosote bush at Lava Falls Rapid is 2,200 years old. Theodore S. Melis, interview, 1991.

34. McAuliffe, "Markovian Dynamics," 471. Little data supports the characterization of white bursage (*Ambrosia dumosa*) as "extremely long-lived." C. H. Muller, "The Association of Desert Annuals with Shrubs," *American Journal of Botany* 40 (1953): 53–60.

35. Ocotillo is known to live for at least 72 years. Goldberg and Turner, "Vegetation Change," 706. Using extrapolated growth curves, one researcher has estimated a maximum age of 150 to 200 years for this species. R. A. Darrow, "Vegetative and Floral Growth of *Fouquieria splendens,*" *Ecology* 24 (1943): 310–322.

36. B. L. Kay, C. R. Brown, and W. L. Graves, *Fourwing Saltbush* (Davis: University of California, Department of Agronomy and Range Sciences, Mojave Revegetation Note 17, 1977), 12.

37. The cover of the only book on Arizona grasses shows cattle grazing in a grassland (R. R. Humphrey, *Arizona Range Grasses* [Tucson: University of Arizona Press, 1977], 159).

38. The results of the few studies of grass demography indicate that the typical life span of grasses is ten years or less. R. H. Canfield, "Reproduction and Life Span of Some Perennial Grasses of Southern Arizona," *Journal of Range Management* 10 (1957): 199–203; R. G. Wright and G. M. Van Dyne, "Environmental Factors Influencing Semidesert Grassland Perennial Grass Demography," *Southwestern Naturalist* 21 (1976): 259–274; N. E. West, K. H. Rea, and R. O. Harniss, "Plant Demographic Studies in Sagebrush-Grass Communities of Southeastern Idaho," *Ecology* 60 (1979): 376–388. However, the maximum longevity of individual clumps was twenty-nine to forty-three years, or the length of the study. West et al., "Demographic Studies," 380. Interestingly, West and coauthors report a maximum longevity of nineteen years for Indian rice grass (*Oryzopsis hymenoides*), which persists at least a century in one of the Stanton views. Clumps of big galleta grass (*Hilaria rigida*) could persist for "hundreds of years," according to

one study. P. S. Nobel, "Spacing and Transpiration of Various Sized Clumps of a Desert Grass, *Hilaria rigida*," *Journal of Ecology* 69 (1981): 735–742.

39. Shading by clumps of big galleta grass reduces soil temperatures substantially in summer and increases minimum winter temperatures. P. S. Nobel, *Environmental Biology of Agaves and Cacti* (New York: Cambridge University Press, 1988), 270. Clumps of big galleta grass are spaced farther apart as the clumps grow larger, indicating potential intraspecific competition for water. Nobel, "Spacing."

40. Little is known about the life spans of species in the genus *Opuntia*. However, in southern Arizona, several species of cholla can live for more than fifty years. Goldberg and Turner, "Vegetation Change," 706. Only one species also occurs in Grand Canyon; *Opuntia engelmannii* (listed as *Opuntia phaeacantha* in idem.) has been reported to live only thirty-two years. Goldberg and Turner may not have considered vegetative propagation of this species as persistence. F. Shreve, in "The Longevity of Cacti," *Cactus and Succulent Journal* 7 (1935): 66–68, speculated that chollas (e.g., *Opuntia fulgida*, not found in Grand Canyon) could live for sixty to eighty years and prickly pears (e.g., *Opuntia phaeacantha*) for thirty or more years. Shreve advocated the use of repeat photography to verify the longevity of cacti.

41. The maximum longevity reported for catclaw before this study was greater than 21 years. Goldberg and Turner, "Vegetation Change," 706. Recently, Alex McCord of the Laboratory of Tree-Ring Research, University of Arizona (personal communication, 1992), has cross-dated wood from catclaw trees in Grand Canyon with an established conifer record from the South Rim, which indicates that the rings are annual. By counting the rings and using the cross-dating technique to account for ones that are missing, McCord has found three trees in excess of 130 years in age.

42. Mesquites are commonly perceived as long-lived trees, but documentation of their supposed long life span is rare. Using tree-ring techniques, researchers found that eighteen trees from southern Arizona ranged in age from thirty-one to eighty-two years. C. W. Ferguson and R. A. Wright, "Botanical Studies," in B. L. Fontana and J. C. Greenleaf, "Johnny Ward's Ranch: A Study in Historical Archaeology," *The Kiva* 28 (1962): 108–114.

43. Hastings and Turner, *Changing Mile*, 3, 26.

44. Wright lippia has a maximum recorded age of seventy-two years. Goldberg and Turner, "Vegetation Change," 706. It could live much longer.

45. Conventional wisdom holds that brittlebush lives for about ten years. Muller, "Association," 56. Part of the problem with determining the longevity of brittlebush is its sensitivity to freezing. Despite considerable mortality during a severe freeze in January 1913, one brittlebush persisted at least twenty-two years (1906–1928) in southern Arizona. F. Shreve and A. L. Hinckley, "Thirty Years of Change in Desert Vegetation," *Ecology* 18 (1937): 463–478. Subsequent measurements have indicated that the maximum life span of brittlebush is thirty-two years. Goldberg and Turner, "Vegetation Change," 706.

46. Warren et al., *Vegetation*.

47. Benson and Darrow, *Trees and Shrubs*, 70. Utah agave (*Agave utahensis*) occurs farther north than any other agave in the southwestern United States.

48. Ibid., 64. The age until flowering for fifteen species of agave ranges from eleven to forty years with an average of about twenty years. H. S. Gentry, *Agaves of Continental North America* (Tucson: University of Arizona Press, 1982), 670. P. S. Nobel, in "Water Relations and Plant Size Aspects of Flowering for *Agave deserti*," *Botanical Gazette* 148 (1987): 79–84, estimates the age of flowering for *Agave deserti*, a species similar to *A. utahensis*, to be between fifty and fifty-five years in the wild. However, agaves reproducing by the offset of clones have remained in the same positions for at least sixty-eight years in Grand Canyon, and Gentry notes that clones for one species (*Agave toumeyana bella*) may persist for longer than a century.

49. The maximum recorded longevity for *Echinocereus fendleri* is nine years. Goldberg and Turner, "Vegetation Change," 706.

50. The oldest age reported for barrel cactus (*Ferocactus cylindraceus*) is about 30 years. P. W. Jordan and P. S. Nobel, "Height Distribution of Two Species of Cacti in Relation to Rainfall, Seedling Establishment, and Growth," *Botanical Gazette* 143 (1982): 511–517. A closely related species, *F. wislizenii*, has a maximum recorded age of 46 years. Goldberg and Turner, "Vegetation Change," 706. Exceptionally large individuals of *F. wislizenii* may be able to survive for 85 to 130 years. Shreve, "Longevity," 68.

51. Shreve, in "Longevity," speculated that upright chollas (e.g., *Opuntia versicolor*) are much longer lived (sixty to eighty years) than prostrate prickly pears (e.g., *Opuntia engelmannii*, about thirty years). Much of the problem arises from definition: prickly pears mostly reproduce clonally, making individuals difficult to define, whereas chollas have well-defined individuals. In addition, *O. engelmannii* in southern Arizona is more upright and more similar in form to *O. chlorotica* than the *O. engelmannii* in Grand Canyon. Clones of *O. engelmannii* can live at least a century in Grand Canyon.

52. As research has progressed on soil microbiology, nomenclature changes have been inevitable. Biological crusts have been called cryptogamic, microfloral, or microphytic crusts. I prefer the term cryptobiotic crusts (in accord with Jayne Belnap, interview, 1992) to avoid connotation of the types of life forms present. For a review of cryptobiotic crusts, see N. E. West, "Structure and Function of Microphytic Soil Crusts in Wildland Ecosystems of Arid and Semi-Arid Regions," *Advances in Ecological Research* 20 (1990): 179–223.

53. The life-form classification of *Microcoleus* appears to have shifted in the last thirty years. Once called a blue-green algae (L. W. Durrell and L. M. Shields, "Characteristics of Soil Algae Relating to Crust Formation," *Transactions of the American Microbiological Society* 80 [1961]: 73–79), *Microcoleus* is now considered a cyanobacterium (West, "Structure and Function," 181). *Microcoleus* is a primary component of soils on the Colorado Plateau, which includes Grand Canyon. J. Belnap and J. S. Gardner, "Soil Microstructure in Soils of the Colorado Plateau: The Role of the Cyanobacterium *Microcoleus vaginatus*," *Great Basin Naturalist* 53 (1993): 40–47.

54. Belnap and Gardner, "Soil Microstructure."

55. J. Belnap, "Potential Role of Cryptobiotic Soil Crusts in Semiarid Rangelands," paper presented at the Symposium on Ecology, Management, and Restoration of Intermountain Annual Rangelands, Boise, Idaho, 1990, 7.

56. Most work on trampling has concentrated on the effects of domestic livestock grazing and its exclusion. For an example, see D. C. Anderson, K. T. Harper, and S. R. Rushforth, "Recovery of Cryptogamic Soil Crusts from Grazing on Utah Winter Ranges," *Journal of Range Management* 35 (1982): 355–359. Most studies conclude that recovery can take decades to a century, but few studies combine restoration studies with changes in the species composition of the original crusts. In one study, researchers found that the re-establishment of lichens and mosses lagged behind that of fungi and, presumably, cyanobacteria. J. D. Brotherson, S. R. Rushforth, and J. R. Johansen, "Effects of Long-Term Grazing on Cryptogam Crust Cover in Navajo National Monument, Ariz.," *Journal of Range Management* 36 (1983): 579–581.

57. "Recovery" of cryptobiotic soils is difficult to define. Whereas restoration of a similar-looking crust may occur in as little as several years, restoration of productivity requires decades to centuries, even with inoculation of the soil with cyanobacteria and other components of the original crust. J. Belnap, "Recovery Rates of Cryptobiotic Crusts: Inoculant Use and Assessment Methods," *Great Basin Naturalist* 53 (1993): 89–95.

58. Radiocarbon sample GX-17721, Geochron Laboratories.

59. Radiocarbon sample GX-19327, Geochron Laboratories.

60. C. W. Ferguson, "Tree-Ring Dating of Colorado River Driftwood in the Grand Canyon," in *Hydrology and Water Resources in Arizona and the Southwest*, Tempe: Proceedings of the 1971 Meet-

ings of the Arizona Section—American Water Resources Association and the Hydrology Section—Arizona Academy of Sciences, 351–366.

61. S. C. Jones, "New Termite Records for the Grand Canyon," *Southwestern Entomologist* 10 (1985): 137–138; Susan C. Jones, written communication, 1993. The termites (*Incisitermes minor*) were found in dead tamarisk logs lying on the ground.

62. R. H. Beal, J. K. Mauldin, and S. C. Jones, *Subterranean Termites: Their Prevention and Control in Buildings* (Washington, D.C.: U.S. Department of Agriculture, Forest Service, Home and Garden Bulletin 64, 1989), 36.

63. Hoffmeister, *Mammals of Grand Canyon*, 88–92.

64. F. Shreve, "The Establishment of Desert Perennials," *Journal of Ecology* 5 (1917): 210–216; idem, "The Desert Vegetation of North America," *Botanical Review* 9 (1942): 195–246.

65. R. M. Turner, "Long-Term Vegetation Change at a Fully Protected Sonoran Desert Site," *Ecology* 71 (1990): 464–477.

Chapter 4

1. Dellenbaugh, *Canyon Voyage*, 224.

2. Edwards, "Diary," 35.

3. Ibid., 25. The Stanton expedition also saw many ducks downstream of Lava Falls Rapid and sign of cattle at the mouth of Diamond Creek.

4. Carmony and Brown, *Panthon*, 64, 67. Mostly because of the lack of game, Flavell ran Grand Canyon in only thirteen days.

5. J. F. Stone, *Canyon Country* (New York: G. P. Putnam's Sons, 1932), 96–97. One of the more interesting anecdotes related to "wildlife" in the river corridor is associated with Stone's expedition. Stone and his crew had paid the ferry operator to cache a food supply for them at Lees Ferry. When no cache could be found, Stone faced the dilemma of entering Grand Canyon with a meager food supply. A cowboy they met at Lees Ferry, Rowland Rider, apparently convinced Stone that he would find game in Grand Canyon. Sure enough, Stone and Gallo-

way saw five goats and killed one in the vicinity of 18 Mile Wash (ibid., 85). Rider claimed the "goats" were domestic sheep, the remnant of a herd of ten thousand thirsty sheep that jumped from the canyon rim to reach water in the river. R. W. Rider and D. M. Paulsen, *The Roll Away Saloon* (Logan: Utah State University Press, 1985), 66–68. Another tall tale from a notorious storyteller? During archaeological surveys several years ago, a large number of bleached bones were found below the cliffs near Soap Creek Rapid. Perhaps the number of sheep was exaggerated, but apparently domestic sheep had somehow gotten into the river corridor. Helen Fairley, National Park Service, interview, 1992.

6. C. Sheldon, *The Wilderness of Desert Bighorn and Seri Indians* (Phoenix: The Arizona Desert Bighorn Sheep Society, 1979), 144.

7. Most river runners in the summer observed bighorn sheep, always in small numbers. Bighorn sheep mostly use the river corridor in the summer. C. A. Stockwell, "The Behavior of Desert Bighorn at Grand Canyon National Park, Implications for Conservation," Northern Arizona University, unpublished M.S. thesis, 1989, 6. On a trip in 1938, river runners reported herds of 5–10 bighorn sheep below Deer Creek Falls and at the mouth of Havasu Creek (probably on the left bank). E. U. Clover and L. Jotter, "Floristic Studies in the Canyon of the Colorado and Tributaries," *American Midland Naturalist* 32 (1944): 618. Most bighorn sheep were sighted on the left bank, particularly between river miles 122 and 170. The scarceness of bighorn sheep along the river corridor may have reflected a regional decline in their populations; in 1941, bighorn sheep, which were hunted by the Havasupai, were characterized as exceedingly rare. S. A. Weber and P. D. Seaman, *Havasupai Habitat: A. F. Whiting's Ethnography of a Traditional Indian Culture* (Tucson: University of Arizona Press, 1985), 40.

8. The term *irruption* was coined to avoid confusion with volcanic "eruptions"; A. S. Leopold, *Deer Irruptions* (Madison: Wisconsin Conservation Department Publication 321, 1943), 3–11. For additional

history on the term *irruption* and another view of the history of deer populations on the Kaibab Plateau, see C. J. Burk, "The Kaibab Deer Incident, a Long-Persisting Myth," *Bioscience* 23 (1973): 113–114.

9. D. I. Rasmussen, "Biotic Communities of the Colorado Plateau," *Ecological Monographs* 3 (1941): 229–275, is the original source of information on the irruption of the Kaibab deer herd. Leopold in *Deer Irruptions* trivialized the complex issue by simplifying the conflicting estimates of the size of the deer herd and omitting reference to the cessation of overgrazing and its probable effect on initiating the irruption. The most thorough review of the problem is given in G. Caughley, "Eruption of Ungulate Populations, with Emphasis on Himalayan Thar in New Zealand," *Ecology* 51 (1970): 53–72. Although Caughley challenged Leopold's interpretation of the size of the deer herd and the circumstances leading to the irruption, he did not challenge the occurrence of the irruption; by contrast, while debunking the use of the Kaibab deer herd as the classic example of an irruption, Burk in "Kaibab Deer Incident" also implied that the irruption of the Kaibab deer herd did not even occur. D. Botkin, in *Discordant Harmonies: A New Ecology for the Twenty-First Century* (New York: Oxford University Press, 1990), 77–80, dismissed the occurrence of the irruption if the deer population rose to *only* 30,000 animals (seven and one half times the original population). This extreme revisionism appears unwarranted given the basic facts about the incident. For another perspective on Caughley's work, based on its application to the population boom of elk in Yellowstone National Park, see A. Chase, *Playing God in Yellowstone* (San Diego: Harcourt Brace Jovanovich, 1987), 464.

10. Billingsley, *Mining*.

11. Ibid.

12. Hughes, *House*, 49.

13. Ibid., 52.

14. Stanton and his crew found evidence of several attempts to gain access to the river corridor, probably for mining purposes. Just above Sockdolager Rapid (mile 78.6), they found a rope hanging over a twenty-foot cliff of schist and evidence of an unknown group camping next to the river. In the vicinity of Mohawk Canyon (mile 171.5), they found a placer-mining notice dated July 5, 1886. At Parashant Canyon (mile 198.5), they found part of a mill, a water wheel and sluice box, and large timbers of unknown age. Edwards, "Diary," 21, 34, 35.

15. The Lost Orphan Mine, a uranium producer between 1951 and 1966, was the last active mine in Grand Canyon National Park. Hughes, *House*, 111–112.

16. M. E. Musgrave, "Some Habits of Mountain Lions in Arizona," *Journal of Mammalogy* 7 (1926): 282–285.

17. T. L. McKnight, "The Feral Burro in the United States: Distribution and Problems," *Journal of Wildlife Management* 22 (1958): 163–179.

18. U.S. Department of the Interior, *Proposed Feral Burro Management and Ecosystem Restoration Plan and Final Environmental Statement, Grand Canyon National Park, Arizona* (U.S. Department of the Interior, National Park Service, Grand Canyon National Park, 1980).

19. For convenience, we lump the Bedrock Canyon herd into the Shinumo herd. For a discussion of the Bedrock Canyon herd, see G. A. Ruffner and S. W. Carothers, "Age Structure, Condition, and Reproduction of Two *Equus asinus* (Equidae) Populations from Grand Canyon National Park, Arizona," *Southwestern Naturalist* 27 (1982): 403–411.

20. G. A. Ruffner, "Distribution and Population Densities of Feral Burros, Grand Canyon, Arizona," in G. A. Ruffner, A. M. Phillips, III, and N. H. Goldberg, editors, *Biology and Ecology of Feral Burros (Equus asinus) at Grand Canyon National Park, Arizona* (Flagstaff: Museum of Northern Arizona, Final Research Report for Contract Numbers PX821060722, PX821071444, and CX821070015, 1977), 7–10.

21. McKnight, "Feral Burro," 172.

22. J. W. Jordan, "Diets of a Feral Burro Population during August and September from the Area between Parashant Canyon (River Mile 198) and Fall Canyon (River Mile 210.5), Grand Canyon, Arizona," in G. A. Ruffner et al., *Biology and Ecology*, 141–

143; G. A. Ruffner, S. W. Carothers, J. W. Jordan, and A. M. Phillips, III, *Diets of Feral Burros (Equus asinus) from the Bedrock Canyon Area, Grand Canyon National Park, Arizona* (Flagstaff: Museum of Northern Arizona, Final Research Report for Contract CS821050007, 1977), 14.

23. S. W. Carothers, M. E. Stitt, and R. R. Johnson, "Feral Asses on Public Lands: An Analysis of Biotic Impact, Legal Considerations, and Management Alternatives," in *Transactions of the Forty-First North American Wildlife and Natural Resources Conference* (Washington, D.C.: The Wildlife Management Institute, 1976), 396–406. No attempt has been made in this section to reconcile conflicting estimates of the number of animals present with those removed from various parts of Grand Canyon. Estimation of the population size of large ungulates is, at best, uncertain unless the animals are counted as they are killed, as was the case with the burros in Grand Canyon.

24. Ruffner, "Distribution," 8.

25. Ruffner et al., *Diets*.

26. U.S. Department of the Interior, *Feral Burro Management*, 4.

27. Ruffner, "Distribution," 9.

28. Stevens, *Guide*, 95.

29. Steven W. Carothers, interview, 1992.

30. Hughes, *House*, 53.

31. W. L. Rusho and C. G. Crampton, *Desert River Crossing* (Santa Barbara: Peregrine Smith, 1981), 126.

32. Larry Belli, National Park Service, interview, 1993; Carothers, interview.

33. J. P. Russo, *The Kaibab North Deer Herd: Its History, Problems, and Management* (Phoenix: Arizona Game and Fish Department Wildlife Bulletin Number 7, 1964), 195.

34. Considerable documentation exists for abnormal rainfall from about 1905 to 1928 on the Colorado Plateau. Using tree-ring reconstructions, researchers identified the period as one of the five wettest in the last thousand years on the Colorado Plateau. R. D. D'Arrigo and G. C. Jacoby, "A 1000-Year Record of Winter Precipitation from Northwestern New Mexico, U.S.A.: A Reconstruction from Tree-Rings and Its Relation to El Niño and the Southern Oscillation," *The Holocene* 1 (1991): 95–101. For a review of this information and documentation of the increase in warm-season rainfall between 1900 and about 1920, see R. Hereford and R. H. Webb, "Historic Variation in Warm-Season Rainfall on the Colorado Plateau, U.S.A.," *Climatic Change* 22 (1992): 239–256. The Colorado River, responding to the increased runoff, was abnormally high during this period. C. W. Stockton and G. C. Jacoby, Jr., *Long-Term Surface-Water Supply and Streamflow Trends in the Upper Colorado River Basin Based on Tree-Ring Analyses* (Los Angeles: University of California–Los Angeles, Lake Powell Research Project Bulletin Number 18, 1976), 70. Rasmussen in "Biotic Communities" summarizes the number of predators killed by hunters of the Predatory Animal and Rodent Control unit of the U.S. Biological Survey: from 1906 to 1931, 781 mountain lions, 30 wolves, 4,889 coyotes, and 554 bobcats were removed from the Kaibab Plateau. The last wolf in the region is thought to have been killed in 1928. D. E. Brown, *The Wolf in the Southwest* (Tucson: University of Arizona Press, 1988), 24. Despite severe reductions, the population of mountain lions eventually recovered somewhat. Populations of coyotes and bobcats appear not to have been seriously affected.

35. Caughley, "Eruption," 55.

36. G. Monson and L. Sumner, editors, *The Desert Bighorn: Its Life History, Ecology, and Management* (Tucson: University of Arizona Press, 1981), 202.

37. J. Walters, "Bighorn Sheep Population Estimate for the South Tonto Plateau, Grand Canyon," *Desert Bighorn Council, 1979 Transactions*, 96–106. Population estimates must be viewed skeptically, but few bighorn sheep have ever been in the river corridor. For example, only two hundred bighorn sheep were estimated to be in Grand Canyon in 1931. Stockwell, "Behavior of Desert Bighorn," 5.

38. Stockwell, "Behavior of Desert Bighorn," 14–16.

39. Currently, the Hualapai Tribe takes about six bighorn sheep per year; the tribe estimates that poachers kill an equal number.

40. Monson and Sumner, *Desert Bighorn*.

41. B. M. Browning and G. Monson, "Food," in Monson and Sumner, *Desert Bighorn*, 80–93.

42. An additional reason could be release from some disease or parasite. Sheldon (*Desert Bighorn*) noted several times in his diary that ticks infested the ears of rams he killed in 1912.

43. F. A. Branson, *Vegetation Changes on Western Rangelands* (Denver: Society for Range Management Monograph Number 2, 1985), 76.

44. Hastings and Turner, *Changing Mile;* Turner, *Long-Term Change.*

45. Turner, *Long-Term Change;* E. M. Schmutz, A. E. Dennis, A. Harlan, D. Hendricks, and J. Zauderer, "An Ecological Survey of Wide Rock Butte in Canyon de Chelly National Monument, Arizona," *Journal of the Arizona Academy of Sciences* 11 (1976): 114–125; E. M. Schmutz, C. C. Michaels, and B. I. Judd, "Boysag Point, a Relict Area on the North Rim of Grand Canyon in Arizona," *Journal of Range Management* 20 (1967): 363–369; R. M. Turner, L. H. Applegate, P. M. Bergthold, S. Gallizioli, and S. C. Martin, *Arizona Range Reference Areas* (U.S. Department of Agriculture, Forest Service General Technical Report RM-79, 1980), 34.

46. Utilization typically was 100 percent of each year's growth. W. W. Brady, S. Walker, and G. L. Whysong, "Evaluating Long-Term Utilization on White Bursage," in D. N. Hyder, editor, *Proceedings of the First International Rangeland Congress* (Denver: Society for Range Management, 1978), 524–525.

47. McKnight in "Feral Burro," 169, claims that creosote bush (*Larrea tridentata*) is utilized by burros during drought. Jordan and Nobel in "Distribution," 143, list undifferentiated *Opuntia* sp. as the seventh most important part of the August–September diets of burros in western Grand Canyon; however, these could have been fruits of *Opuntia engelmannii* and not the pads of *Opuntia basilaris*. Creosote bush was not found in the stomach contents of burros from western Grand Canyon. Jordan and Nobel, "Distribution."

48. Snakeweed is not reported for Pleistocene or Holocene packrat middens from the eastern Grand Canyon (Cole, "Vegetation Gradients"; idem, "Reconstruction"); however, fossil evidence of snakeweed may not have been identified or chosen for analysis because its presence or absence has no climatic significance. Moreover, packrats preferentially select materials for their nests, and snakeweed may be undesirable. Snakeweed (reported as *Gutierrezia lucida* instead of *G. sarothrae*) is reported as rare in packrat middens dated to 19,000 and 22,000 years ago from western Grand Canyon (Mead and Phillips, "Fauna and Flora"). Mead and Phillips recognized *G. sarothrae* in the modern flora; perhaps this species was not present in large numbers until this century.

49. Clover and Jotter, "Floristic Studies," 609, 639. Tanner Canyon is where the Tanner Trail, once known as the Horsethief Trail, ends. Horses perhaps could have brought the seeds of snakeweed into Grand Canyon, where it then could have spread to ungrazed areas.

50. We know of the presence of now-extinct herbivores in Grand Canyon because their bones are preserved in dry caves, particularly in the Redwall and Muav Limestones. Rampart Cave (mile 275) is the best known of these; its paleontological treasures were discovered in the early twentieth century. J. D. Laudermilk and P. A. Munz, *Plants in the Dung of Nothrotherium from Rampart and Muav Caves, Arizona* (Carnegie Institution of Washington, [D.C.,] Publication 487, 1938), 271–281; and R. W. Wilson, *Preliminary Study of the Fauna of Rampart Cave, Arizona* (Carnegie Institution of Washington, [D.C.,] Contributions to Paleontology, Publication 530, 1942), 169–185. Although archaeological materials were found in Stantons Cave (mile 31.7) in the 1930s, its bone and dung deposits were not systematically studied until 1969. R. C. Euler, editor, *The Archaeology, Geology, and Paleobiology of Stanton's Cave, Grand Canyon National Park, Arizona* (Grand Canyon Natural History Association Monograph Number 6, 1984), 141. Other dry caves scattered through Grand Canyon have also yielded significant paleontological materials. J. I. Mead, "Harrington's Extinct Mountain Goat (*Oreamnus*

harringtoni) and Its Environment in the Grand Canyon," University of Arizona, unpublished Ph.D. dissertation, 1983, 215; S. D. Emslie, "Age and Diet of Fossil California Condors in Grand Canyon, Arizona," *Science* 237 (1987): 768–770.

51. J. W. Olsen and S. J. Olsen, "Zooarchaeological Analysis of Small Vertebrates from Stanton's Cave, Arizona," in Euler, *Stanton's Cave,* 47–57.

52. A. Long, R. M. Hansen, and P. S. Martin, "Extinction of the Shasta Ground Sloth," *Geological Society of America Bulletin* 85 (1974): 1943–1948.

53. J. I. Mead, "The Last 30,000 Years of Faunal History within the Grand Canyon," *Quaternary Research* 15 (1981): 311–326.

54. A. M. Rea and L. L. Hargrave, "The Bird Bones from Stanton's Cave," in Euler, *Stanton's Cave,* 79–91.

55. Hansen, in "Shasta Ground Sloth," identifies mormon tea as *Ephedra nevadensis,* which was an unlikely component of the Pleistocene flora. Cole, "Vegetation Gradients." Although species of *Ephedra* are difficult to distinguish without cones and seeds, the more likely species is *Ephedra viridis,* which was common in the Pleistocene flora. *E. viridis* no longer is abundant along the river corridor. Other problems exist with Hansen's identifications. Globe mallow is identified as *Sphaeralcea ambigua,* yet the genus *Sphaeralcea* is one of the most difficult to distinguish without flowers and seeds. Globe mallows that now occur at higher elevations could have been the species preserved in the goat pellets. Finally, *Acacia greggii* probably was not present in Pleistocene packrat middens collected at Rampart Cave and adjacent caves, yet the species is listed as appearing in sloth dung dated at the glacial maximum. Although Hansen's argument concerning similarity between the diet of Harrington's mountain goat and modern floras of the river corridor is suggestive, the basic data appear to have substantial problems.

56. E. I. Robbins, P. S. Martin, and A. Long, "Paleoecology of Stanton's Cave, Grand Canyon, Arizona," in Euler, *Stanton's Cave,* 115–130.

57. Long et al., "Extinction." The density of large Pleistocene fauna is the critical missing piece of information on the amount of herbivory that occurred. Densities cannot be estimated given the sparse paleoecological materials that were preserved in only a few dry caves. One might assume, however, on the basis of similar diets and habitat preferences, that Harrington's mountain goat had a density similar to or slightly greater than that of bighorn sheep.

58. A. M. Phillips, III, "Shasta Ground Sloth Extinction, Fossil Packrat Midden Evidence from the Western Grand Canyon," in P. S. Martin and R. G. Klein, editors, *Quaternary Extinctions: A Prehistoric Revolution* (Tucson: University of Arizona Press, 1984), 148–158.

59. P. S. Martin, "Pleistocene Overkills," in P. S. Martin and H. E. Wright, Jr., editors, *Pleistocene Extinctions: The Search for a Cause* (New Haven: Yale University Press, 1967), 75–120.

60. Bighorn sheep were probably in the surrounding area, but no evidence of their presence in Grand Canyon appears before about 12,000 years ago. Mead, "Harrington's Extinct Mountain Goat."

61. Robbins et al., "Paleoecology," 124.

62. L. Spier, "Havasupai Ethnography," *Anthropological Papers of the American Museum of Natural History* 29 (1929): 83–392; Weber and Seaman, *Havasupai Habitat.*

63. Evidence for mule deer in Stantons Cave was found in the most recent sediments. Olsen and Olsen, "Zooarchaeological Analysis," 52. However, condors are known to transport parts of large animal carcasses to their nests. Emslie, "Age and Diet," 769. Two bones from mule deer were recovered from Pleistocene and Holocene provenances in Vulture Cave in western Grand Canyon. Mead and Phillips, "Fauna and Flora." The description of stratigraphic or dating controls on this evidence is vague, however, and I am unconvinced that mule deer were present at Vulture Cave in the Holocene. Mule deer are not present at this site today. Hoffmeister, *Mammals of Grand Canyon,* 87–92. Fossil remains of black-tailed jackrabbit and desert cottontail were found in the upper layers of Stantons Cave. Olsen and Olsen, "Zooarchaeological Analysis," 81. However, I do not accept from this evidence that rabbits

have been extirpated from the river corridor. Condors and other raptors also used Stantons Cave and could have scavenged dead rabbits from their current habitat above the rim and brought the bones into the cave.

64. I question whether the plants preserved in dung pellets are the same species that are now in the river corridor (see note 55). The environments and plant assemblages of the Pleistocene and Holocene are drastically different. For a negative view of whether Pleistocene herbivores would have survived in a Holocene climate, see S. W. Carothers, G. A. Ruffner, and A. M. Phillips, III, "Data Synthesis and Conclusions," in Ruffner et al., *Biology and Ecology,* 130–138.

65. Chase, *Playing God.*

Thinking Like a Canyon:
Wild Ideas and Wild Burros

1. Emslie, "Age and Diet." One condor nest revealed food scraps, bones of mammoth, camel, bison, and Harrington's extinct goat.

2. Hansen, "Shasta Ground Sloth"; Euler, *Stanton's Cave;* Phillips, "Shasta Ground Sloth"; Spaulding, "Vegetational Development"; Cole, "Vegetation Gradients." The evidence of mammoth comes from fossil dung in a dry cave near the Colorado River in Utah. O. K. Davis, L. Agenbroad, P. S. Martin, and J. I. Mead, "The Pleistocene Dung Blanket of Bechan Cave, Utah," in H. H. Genoways and M. R. Dawson, editors, *Contributions in Quaternary Vertebrate Paleontology* (Pittsburgh: Carnegie Museum of Natural History Special Publications Number 8, 1984), 267–282.

3. A. S. Leopold, S. A. Cain, C. M. Coltam, I. N. Gabrielson, and T. L. Kimball, "Wildlife Management in the National Parks," *Transactions of the North American Wildlife and Natural Resources Conference* 24 (1963): 29–44.

4. P. S. Martin, "The Equid Niche in the Grand Canyon," *Coevolution Quarterly* 19 (1978): 136–137.

5. A. S. Leopold, *A Sand County Almanac, with Other Essays from Round River* (New York: Oxford Uni-

versity Press, 1966), 129–132.

6. J. H. Brown and P. F. Nicoletto, in "Spatial Scaling of Species Composition, Body Masses of North American Land Mammals," *American Naturalist* 138 (1991): 1478–1512, state: "As human impacts inevitably increase and native species inevitably become extinct, the only way to restore lost diversity and ecological function will be through introduction of alien species."

Feral Burros: Old Arguments and New Twists

1. Carothers et al., "Feral Asses."

2. Davis et al., *Bechan Cave.*

3. Carothers et al., "Data Synthesis," 130–138; Carothers et al., "Feral Asses."

4. U.S. Department of the Interior, *Feral Burro Management.*

5. Although studies have not been rigorously undertaken to quantify rates and extent of recovery of areas previously occupied by burros in Grand Canyon, signs of burro trails still exist in many places where feral animals have been gone for decades. Other evidence of recovery (e.g., recovery of annual vegetation) can occur quickly. Within two years after burros had been removed from 209 Mile Canyon, the primary area from which the Carothers et al. ("Feral Asses") data were taken, annual vegetation was almost three feet high, and only detailed study indicated that burros had previously occupied the area.

Chapter 5

1. F. Shreve and I. L. Wiggins, *Vegetation and Flora of the Sonoran Desert* (Stanford: Stanford University Press, 1964), 26. Other variables considered to define deserts include strong winds, poor soils, and high rates of erosion.

2. For a review of the frost sensitivity of cacti and the effect of low temperatures on distribution of cacti, see Nobel, *Environmental Biology,* 103–109, 132–133. Other papers that discuss the effects of frost include Shreve, "Establishment"; idem, "Desert Vege-

tation"; W. V. Turnage and A. K. Hinckley, "Freezing Weather in Relation to Plant Distribution in the Sonoran Desert," *Ecological Monographs* 8 (1938): 530–550; J. R. Hastings, "Historical Change in the Vegetation of a Desert Region," University of Arizona, unpublished Ph.D. dissertation, 1963; and J. E. Bowers, "Catastrophic Freezes in the Sonoran Desert," *Desert Plants* 2 (1981): 232–236.

3. A preliminary version of the effect of frost on vegetation in Grand Canyon, based on results from replicate photography up to 1992, appears in R. H. Webb and J. E. Bowers, "Changes in Frost Frequency and Desert Vegetation Assemblages in Grand Canyon, Arizona," in K. T. Redmond and V. L. Tharp, editors, *Proceedings of the Ninth Annual Pacific Climate (PACLIM) Workshop* (Sacramento: Technical Report 34 of the Interagency Ecological Studies Program for the Sacramento–San Joaquin Estuary, 1993), 71–82.

4. Phillips et al., *Annotated Checklist,* 31.

5. Bowers, "Catastrophic Freezes"; James R. Ehleringer, University of Utah, interview, 1992.

6. R. M. Turner, J. E. Bowers, and T. L. Burgess, *Sonoran Desert Plants: An Ecological Atlas* (Tucson: University of Arizona Press, 1995); Turnage and Hinckley, "Freezing Weather."

7. Larry Stevens, National Park Service, interview, 1991. Low temperatures at Lees Ferry were 9°F on December 31, 1990, and January 1, 1991, but daytime temperatures were above freezing. At Phantom Ranch, the lowest low temperature was 21°F on December 23.

8. The first clearly visible brittlebush is in view number 362, taken on the right bank at mile 55.8 just above Kwagunt Rapid. Stanton had to wait for a lull to stabilize the tripod. Because of the wind and the long exposure time, the plant appears blurry, but the large, silvery leaves are unmistakably those of brittlebush. The individual in the view is next to a large, black boulder, which may be presumed to create a favorable, warm microhabitat, and the site faces southeast.

9. We used a contingency table analysis to test whether the differences in brittlebush between 1890 and 1990s views were significant. The table was a two-by-two matrix of the presence-absence of visible brittlebush in the 1890 and 1990s views. Of 137 camera stations with brittlebush present in the 1990s, 16 had brittlebush in both 1890 and 1990s views, 66 had brittlebush only in the 1990s, 1 had brittlebush only in 1890, and 54 showed no brittlebush in either view. The probability that such an arrangement could arise by chance alone is extremely low (chi-square distribution; $p < 0.001$).

10. Cole, "Past Rates." Brittlebush may have been in western Grand Canyon as early as 30,000 years ago. Phillips, "Packrats," 57. However, the type of plant assemblage in which brittlebush would occur did not become established in the region until after about 8,000 years ago. Van Devender and Spaulding, "Development." Brittlebush has been present in the Mojave Desert for 9,500 years. Spaulding, "Vegetational Development," 169–170.

11. Mass emergence of brittlebush seedlings is common after abundant winter rains in the Sonoran Desert. J. E. Bowers, "Natural Conditions for Seedling Emergence of Three Woody Species in the Northern Sonoran Desert," *Madroño* 41 (1994): 73–84. Few seedlings survive to develop into mature plants, however, but after rarely achieved ideal conditions, a pulse of establishment can create a population of individuals of the same age, called a cohort. One possibility for the rapid rate of brittlebush re-establishment is one or more pulse-establishment events between 1890 and 1923.

12. *Ferocactus cylindraceus* was formerly called *F. acanthodes.* N. P. Taylor, "Notes on *Ferocactus* B. & R.," *The Cactus and Succulent Journal of Great Britain* 41 (1979): 88–94.

13. J. Ehleringer and D. House, "Orientation and Slope Preference in Barrel Cactus (*Ferocactus acanthodes*) at Its Northern Distribution Limit," *Great Basin Naturalist* 44 (1984): 133–139.

14. E. U. Clover and L. Jotter, in "Cacti of the Canyon of the Colorado River and Tributaries," *Bulletin of the Torrey Botanical Club* 68 (1941): 413, incorrectly reported that *Ferocactus cylindraceus* was distributed from mile 26.5 to Lake Mead. They probably iden-

tified young *Echinocactus polycephalus* as young *Ferocactus*. The incorrect distribution was reported in Phillips et al., *Annotated Checklist*, 25.

15. Evidence for the prehistoric occurrence of barrel cactus in western Grand Canyon is from seven pack-rat middens dated between 8,500 and 19,000 years ago. Phillips, "Packrats," 57. Phillips notes that evidence of barrel cactus is lacking in most middens younger than about 9,000 years old (ibid., 74). Perhaps a change to more severe winters played a role in this anomaly; winters may have changed from relatively mild to much colder with the recession of the continental ice sheets about 11,500 years ago. Van Devender and Spaulding, "Development," 709.

16. M. Chamberlain, "Biosystematics of the *Echinocactus polycephalus* Complex (Cactaceae)," Arizona State University, unpublished M.S. thesis, 1991, 55. Although Chamberlain was discussing cottontop cactus, the possibility of seed dispersal by Native Americans also applies to the larger barrel cactus.

17. In a study in the northwestern Sonoran Desert 71 percent of barrel cactus seedlings were under nurse plants, particularly big galleta grass. Nurse plants provide benefits and drawbacks: although shading means less light for photosynthesis and more competition for water, it reduces the range of temperatures experienced by the plant and its roots. An added benefit is the higher soil nitrogen levels below big galleta grass, which provides a major nutrient for the growing plant. A. C. Franco and P. S. Nobel, "Effect of Nurse Plants on the Microhabitat and Growth of Cacti," *Journal of Ecology* 77 (1989): 870–886; and P. S. Nobel, "Temperature, Water Availability, and Nutrient Levels at Various Soil Depths, Consequences for Shallow-Rooted Desert Succulents Including Nurse Plant Effects," *American Journal of Botany* 76 (1989): 1486–1492.

18. P. S. Nobel, "Influences of Minimum Stem Temperatures on Ranges of Cacti in Southwestern United States and Central Chile," *Oecologia* 47 (1980): 10–15.

19. P. S. Nobel, "Low-Temperature Tolerance and Cold Hardening of Cacti," *Ecology* 63 (1982): 1650–1656.

20. The maximum difference between the temperatures juveniles and adults can withstand is 3.6°F. Nobel, "Influences." Field studies also indicate that seedlings can tolerate about 20°F. P. S. Nobel, "Extreme Temperatures and Thermal Tolerances for Seedlings of Desert Succulents," *Oecologia* 62 (1984): 310–317.

21. W. F. Steenbergh and C. H. Lowe, *Ecology of the Saguaro: II. Reproduction, Germination, Establishment, Growth, and Survival of the Young Plant* (Washington, D.C.: National Park Service Scientific Monograph Series Number 8, 1977), 106–107; Bowers, "Catastrophic Freezes."

22. Drought decreases the ability of seedling plants to become established. P. W. Jordan and P. S. Nobel, "Seedling Establishment of *Ferocactus acanthodes* in Relation to Drought," *Ecology* 62 (1981): 901–906.

23. The first view barrel cactus appears in is Stanton number 552, at mile 119.7. Barrel cactus appearing in this view do not appear to be in special microhabitats.

24. The difference between the number of visible barrel cactus in 1890 and the 1990s is statistically significant. Individuals were counted in each replicate view over an area in which individuals could be clearly identified in both views; this area varied among different views, but the variation in area size would not affect a comparison at any one site. In a paired-sample t-test, the mean difference between 1889–90 and 1990–93 views was 7.9 individuals ($p < 0.000$).

25. Field data on favorable conditions for germination are rare for these two species. Nonetheless, favorable conditions for brittlebush occurred seven times in seven years in southern Arizona (Bowers, "Natural Conditions"), whereas favorable conditions for germination of barrel cactus occurred in only eight of eighteen years in the Mojave Desert (P. W. Jordan and P. S. Nobel, "Infrequent Establishment of Seedlings of *Agave deserti* [Agavaceae] in the Northwestern Sonoran Desert," *American Journal of Botany* 66 [1979]: 1079–1084).

26. Jordan and Nobel, "Height Distribution."

27. One exception to the general increase in prickly pear in Grand Canyon is found in Hillers's view of Kanab Canyon. In views from 1872, 1968, and 1990, Engelmann's prickly pear has decreased considerably. R. H. Webb, S. S. Smith, and V.A.S. McCord, *Historic Channel Change of Kanab Creek, Southern Utah and Northern Arizona* (Grand Canyon Natural History Association Monograph Number 9, 1991), 70–72.

28. For an early review of the effects of cold on prickly pears, see J. C. Th. Uphof, *Cold Resistance in Spineless Cacti* (Tucson: University of Arizona Agricultural Experiment Station Bulletin 79, 1916), 119–124. *Opuntia erinacea* may decrease its uptake of water in the fall and winter, irrespective of rainfall, to maximize its frost tolerance. R. O. Littlejohn, Jr., and G. J. Williams, III, "Diurnal and Seasonal Variations in Activity of Crassulacean Acid Metabolism and Plant Water Status in a Northern Latitude Population of *Opuntia erinacea*," *Oecologia* 59 (1983): 83–87.

29. Several stations in Arizona and Utah have discontinuous weather records before 1890. Fort Mojave, approximately 150 miles southwest of Grand Canyon, was established in 1859 and abandoned in 1938 near the current site of Bullhead City, Arizona. B. H. Granger, *Arizona Place Names* (Tucson: University of Arizona Press, 1985), 216–217. The average winter temperatures currently recorded in Bullhead City are about 21°F warmer than Lees Ferry and 13°F warmer than Phantom Ranch. Temperatures were recorded for Fort Mojave from 1865 to 1892.

30. For a review of the Little Ice Age from the perspective of the last 10,000 years, see J. M. Grove, *The Little Ice Age* (London: Routledge Publishing, 1988); and N. Roberts, *The Holocene: An Environmental History* (Oxford: Basil Blackwell Ltd., 1989), 159–162.

31. D'Arrigo and Jacoby, "A 1000-Year Record."

32. R. H. Webb, "Late Holocene Flooding on the Escalante River, South-Central Utah," University of Arizona, unpublished Ph.D. dissertation, 1985, 204; Y. Enzel, D. R. Cayan, R. Y. Anderson, and S. G. Wells, "Atmospheric Circulation during Holocene Lake Stands in the Mojave Desert: Evidence of Regional Climate Change," *Nature* 341 (1989): 44–46.

33. K. L. Hunter, "Impacts of the Little Ice Age on the Vegetation of Southern Nevada," University of Nevada, Las Vegas, unpublished M.S. thesis, 1991, 66.

34. J. B. Benedict, "Recent Glacial History of an Alpine Area in the Colorado Front Range, U.S.A., II, Dating the Glacial Deposits," *Journal of Glaciology* 7 (1965): 77–87; idem, "Chronology of Cirque Glaciation, Colorado Front Range," *Quaternary Research* 3 (1973): 584–599; S. E. Porter, "Lichenometric Studies in the Cascade Range of Washington: Establishment of *Rhizocarpon geographicum* Growth Curves at Mount Rainier," *Arctic and Alpine Research* 13 (1981): 11–23.

35. V. C. LaMarche, Jr., and K. K. Hirschboeck, "Frost Rings in Trees as Records of Major Volcanic Eruptions," *Nature* 307 (1984): 121–126.

36. R. A. Kalnicky, "Climatic Change since 1950," *Annals of the Association of American Geographers* 64 (1974): 100–112.

37. Webb, "Late Holocene Flooding"; R. H. Webb and V. R. Baker, "Changes in Hydrologic Conditions Related to Large Floods on the Escalante River, South-Central Utah," in V. P. Singh, editor, *Regional Flood-Frequency Analysis* (Dordrect: D. Reidel Publishers, 1987), 306–320.

38. W. H. Quinn, V. T. Neal, and S. E. Antunez de Mayolo, "El Niño Occurrences over the Past Four and a Half Centuries," *Journal of Geophysical Research* 92 (1987): 14449–14461.

39. Accounts of extreme weather in nineteenth-century Arizona are given in Sellers et al., *Arizona Climate*. For example, a snowfall in the winter of 1848 was reported to have left three feet of snow on the level and drifts to the tops of houses on the Tohono O'odham (Papago) Reservation in southern Arizona. W. M. Tatom, editor, "A Chronology of Papago and Pima History Taken from Calendar Sticks," in *The Papago Indian Reservation and the Papago People* (Sells, Arizona: U.S. Public Health Service,

Bureau of Indian Affairs Papago Agency, 1975), 41–51. This story appears implausible, and newspapers were not published in southern Arizona in 1848 to allow independent verification of this snowfall. A second unusually deep snowfall occurred in the winter of 1870. In the twentieth century, snowfall of any depth has been unusual on this reservation.

40. D. D. Walker, "The Cattle Industry of Utah, 1850–1900: An Historical Profile," *Utah Historical Quarterly* 32 (1964): 182–197.

41. Wallace Stegner, *Beyond the Hundredth Meridian* (Boston: Houghton Mifflin Company, 1954), 294–296.

42. J. A. Young and B. A. Sparks, *Cattle in the Cold Desert* (Logan: Utah State University Press, 1985), 121–140.

43. Smith and Crampton, *Colorado River Survey*, 221.

44. T. R. Karl, L. K. Metcalf, M. L. Nicodemus, and R. G. Quayle, *Statewide Average Climatic History, Arizona, 1895–1982* (Asheville, North Carolina: National Climatic Data Center, Historical Climatology Series 6-1, 1983), 33.

45. D'Arrigo and Jacoby, "1000-Year Record," 95.

46. Hereford and Webb, "Historic Variation."

47. R. H. Webb and J. L. Betancourt, *Climatic Variability and Flood Frequency of the Santa Cruz River, Pima County, Arizona* (Washington, D.C.: U.S. Geological Survey Water-Supply Paper 2379, 1992), 40.

48. Idealized sea-level pressure and 500-millibar maps showing atmospheric conditions associated with extreme cold in Arizona are given in C. R. Green and W. D. Sellers, editors, *Arizona Climate* (Tucson: University of Arizona Press, 1964), 30–31. For a detailed discussion of the climatology of an extreme freeze at Phoenix, see A. J. Brazel and C. Blazek, *The Early December Freeze of 1978: A Climatological Perspective* (Tempe: Arizona State University, Laboratory of Climatology, Climatological Publications, Scientific Paper No. 16, 1981), 80. Extreme cold in Arizona originates in west-central Canada and is steered into the state by anomalous high pressure over the Gulf of Alaska.

49. B. L. Dzerdzeevskii, "Climatic Epochs in the Twentieth Century and Some Comments on the Analysis of Past Climates," in H. E. Wright, Jr., editor, *Quaternary Geology and Climate: Proceedings of the Seventh Congress, International Quaternary Association* (Washington, D.C.: National Academy of Sciences Publication 1701, 1969), 49–60; Kalnicky, "Climatic Change"; R. C. Balling and M. P. Lawson, "Twentieth Century Changes in Winter Climatic Regions," *Climatic Change* 4 (1982): 57–69.

50. Sellers et al., *Arizona Climate*, 104. The reading of −9°F at Phantom Ranch is either a typographic or a measurement error. For example, the probability of a minimum temperature of less than 0°F at Lees Ferry is extremely low (near zero probability). C. R. Green, *Probabilities of Temperature Occurrence in Arizona and New Mexico, Supplement No. 1 to Arizona Climate* (Tucson: University of Arizona, Institute of Atmospheric Physics Publication, 1962).

51. W. F. Steenbergh and C. H. Lowe, *Ecology of the Saguaro: III. Growth and Demography* (Washington, D.C.: National Park Service Scientific Monograph Series Number 17, 1983), 142–144; Sellers et al., *Arizona Climate*, 6–78.

52. W. P. Cottam, "Has Utah Lost Claim to the Lower Sonoran Zone?" *Science* 85 (1937): 563–564. Cottam's claim that all mesquites and creosote bushes were killed, based on his observations during the freeze, was disputed by observations in August 1937. F. R. Fosberg, "The Lower Sonoran in Utah," *Science* 87 (1938): 39–40. In the summer of 1938, only one year after the disastrous frost of 1937, Clover and Jotter in "Cacti," 409–419, observed what they interpreted as high-temperature damage to *Echinocereus*.

53. John D. Lee built and operated the first ferry near the mouth of the Paria River in 1872. Rusho and Crampton, *Desert River Crossing*, 32–33. Ferrymen after Lee, and operators of the gaging station, recorded freezes because of their effects on passage across the river or measurement of river flow.

54. J. H. McClintock, *Mormon Settlement in Arizona* (Tucson: University of Arizona Press, 1921), 95–96; E. C. LaRue, *Water Power and Flood Control of Colorado River below Green River, Utah* (Washington, D.C.: U.S. Geological Survey Water-Supply Paper 556, 1925), 13. Although it is hard to doubt the story

of wagons being driven across the river on the ice, the year in which this occurred is questionable. Temperatures recorded at Kanab, Utah, and Fort Mojave, Arizona, indicate that January 1878 was relatively warm in comparison to previous winters. This event more likely occurred in January 1879.

55. This story was contributed by A. Ralph Curtis of Tucson, Arizona (interview, 1992). Curtis's father, Ammon, was seven years old and part of the colonizing party. Several of Curtis's relatives, including his grandmother, Lucinda Curtis, and three great uncles, Charles Granderson, William, and Joseph Nahum Curtis, were members of the party. The group founded St. David, Arizona.

56. LaRue, *Water Power*, 13. In a history of ferry operations and stream gaging at Lees Ferry, only the 1866, 1878, and 1925 freezes are noted. J. H. Gardiner, "Lees Ferry," in F. B. Dodge, "The Saga of Frank B. Dodge: An Autobiography," U.S. Geological Survey unpublished manuscript, Tucson, 1944, 78–79.

57. The gaging station on the Colorado River at Lees Ferry was affected by ice until the closure of Glen Canyon Dam. For an example, see U.S. Geological Survey, *Surface Water Supply of the United States, 1960, Part 9, Colorado River Basin* (Washington, D.C.: U.S. Geological Survey Water-Supply Paper 1713, 1961), 335.

Chapter 6

1. Clover and Jotter, "Floristic Studies." Although Clover and Jotter were the first women to go through Grand Canyon, they were not the first to try. In 1928, Bessie Hyde made it to about 232 Mile Rapid before disappearing. Lavender, *River Runners*, 78–84.

2. Historic photographs of Grand Canyon, other than those taken by Stanton and Nims, show little perennial vegetation below the old high-water zone. Turner and Karpiscak, *Vegetation Changes*, 98, 102. Cottonwood trees were established below the old high-water zone at miles 194 and 222. A Goodding willow tree, which was still alive in 1993, was present at Granite Park (mile 209) in 1923. Other

than the scattered large trees, no other perennial vegetation was present below the old high-water zone.

3. Clover and Jotter, "Floristic Studies," 601, 608–610, 632. In plant lists, tamarisk was noted only at Lees Ferry, Vaseys Paradise (mile 31.8), Saddle Canyon (mile 47.0), Vulcans Anvil (mile 178.0), Separation Rapid (mile 239.6), and the delta of Lake Mead.

4. P. S. Martin, "Trees and Shrubs of the Grand Canyon, Lees Ferry to Diamond Creek," University of Arizona, Desert Laboratory, unpublished manuscript, 1971, 16. Although Martin was not the only botanist working along the river corridor during the late 1960s and early 1970s (see R. R. Johnson, "Historic Changes in Vegetation along the Colorado River in the Grand Canyon," in *Colorado River Ecology and Dam Management*, 178–206), his notes are complete enough to compare plant distributions with those of Clover and Jotter in "Floristic Studies."

5. Martin, "Trees and Shrubs," 11.

6. Turner and Karpiscak, *Vegetation Changes*, 14–15.

7. B. T. Brown, S. W. Carothers, and R. R. Johnson, *Grand Canyon Birds* (Tucson: University of Arizona Press, 1987), 302.

8. U.S. Department of the Interior, *Glen Canyon Environmental Studies, Final Report* (Salt Lake City: Bureau of Reclamation, Upper Colorado Region, 1989), 84; Carothers and Brown, *Colorado River*.

9. Johnson, "Historic Changes in Vegetation." The riparian vegetation of the southwestern United States is commonly reported to have been reduced by 95 percent. The source of this information is unclear but may reflect a reduction in native species compared with increases in tamarisk. It is difficult to assess the historical conversion of wetlands in terms of gains and losses. Riparian vegetation has been reduced along most rivers in the deserts of Arizona. J. C. Stromberg, "Hot Desert Riparian Ecosystems: Ecological Perspective of Hydrological Needs," in D. D. Young, editor, *Vegetation Management of Hot Desert Rangeland Ecosystems* (Tucson, Arizona: School of Renewable Natural Resources Publication), 294–302.

Groundwater pumping along the Santa Cruz River, for example, eliminated large mesquite bosques upstream of Tucson, Arizona. J. L. Betancourt, "Tucson's Santa Cruz River and the Arroyo Legacy," University of Arizona, unpublished Ph.D. dissertation, 1991, 273. Pumping and channelization projects eliminated stands of cottonwoods in town. However, releases of treated wastewater have created galleries of willows and tamarisks in reaches of the Santa Cruz River that probably did not have significant riparian vegetation. The extensive regulation and channelization of the lower Colorado River and other large southwestern rivers such as the Rio Grande has favored tamarisk at the expense of cottonwood and other native species. Wetlands have increased at the head of the numerous reservoirs in the region, but desert rivers robbed of perennial flow or shallow ground water by regulation or pumping have lost riparian vegetation.

10. D. B. Enfield, "El Niño: Past and Present," *Reviews of Geophysics* 27 (1989): 159–187; E. M. Rasmussen, "El Niño: The Ocean/Atmosphere Connection," *Oceanus* 27 (1984): 5–12.

11. During typical El Niño conditions, wetter-than-normal conditions occur in the Southwest whereas drought occurs in the Northwest. A. V. Douglas and P. J. Engelhart, "Factors Leading to the Heavy Precipitation Regimes of 1982–1983 in the United States," in *Proceedings of the Eighth Annual Climate Diagnostics Workshop* (Washington, D.C.: National Oceanic and Atmospheric Administration, 1984), 42–54. For a nearly complete listing of past years with El Niño conditions and their relative severity, see Quinn et al., "El Niño Occurrences."

12. D. R. Cayan and R. H. Webb, "El Niño/Southern Oscillation and Streamflow in the Western United States," in H. F. Diaz and V. Markgraf, editors, *El Niño: Historical and Paleoclimatic Aspects of the Southern Oscillation* (New York: Cambridge University Press, 1993), 29–68.

13. Frank Dodge worked at the Lees Ferry gaging station and discussed the incident of the cat in the apple tree with Jerry Johnson, son of the ferry operator in 1883. Johnson told Dodge that the stranded animal was a rabbit, not a cat. Dodge, "The Saga."

14. The discharge estimate for the 1884 flood is uncertain. Eugene C. LaRue, the hydrologist who made the estimate, states: "This determination, though subject to some uncertainties, was accurate enough for the purpose it was intended to serve as the probable error was no greater than is inherent in flood estimates" (LaRue, *Water Power*, 14).

15. U.S. Geological Survey, *Compilation of Records of Surface Waters of the United States through 1950, Part 9, Colorado River Basin* (Washington, D.C.: U.S. Geological Survey Water-Supply Paper 1313, 1954), 520.

16. J. M. Garrett and D. J. Gellenbeck, *Basin Characteristics and Streamflow Statistics in Arizona as of 1989* (Washington, D.C.: U.S. Geological Survey Water-Resources Investigations Report 91-4041, 1991), 133.

17. W. G. Hoyt and W. B. Langbein, *Floods* (Princeton: Princeton University Press, 1955), 469.

18. J. E. Stevens, *Hoover Dam* (Norman: University of Oklahoma Press, 1988), 326.

19. Ibid., 16–17.

20. Eugene C. LaRue devoted much of his career with the U.S. Geological Survey developing a plan for damming the Colorado River. On trips in 1914, 1921, 1922, and 1923, he explored most of the Green and Colorado Rivers. During the 1923 U.S. Geological Survey expedition, LaRue located twenty-one potential dam sites in Grand Canyon (LaRue, *Water Power*). After viewing all potential dam sites, LaRue favored a site about three miles upstream of Lees Ferry, although he acknowledged the feasibility of a high dam in either Boulder Canyon or Black Canyon. If LaRue's plan for water development of the Colorado River had prevailed, the entire length of the Colorado River in Grand Canyon would have become a lake. LaRue pushed hard for the first dam to be built upstream of Lees Ferry, and when he lost the battle he resigned from the U.S. Geological Survey. W. B. Langbein, "L'Affaire LaRue," U.S. Geological Survey, unpublished manuscript, n.d., 22. LaRue had a less-than-amicable departure from the U.S. Geological Survey. Lavender, *River*

Runners, 66. He died of a heart attack in 1948, a mere eight years before his dam, later named Glen Canyon Dam, was authorized by Congress.

21. For discussion of Boulder (Hoover) Dam and its effect on the United States, see Stevens, *Hoover Dam;* and H. Petroski, "Hoover Dam," *American Scientist* 81 (1993): 517–521.

22. The history of Glen Canyon Dam, including the political controversy surrounding its authorizing act—the Colorado River Storage Project—is given in R. Martin, *A Story That Stands Like a Dam* (New York: Henry Holt and Company, 1989), 354.

23. Numerous publications report the change in the hydrology of the Colorado River brought about by the closure of Glen Canyon Dam; for example, see D. R. Dawdy, "Hydrology of Glen Canyon and the Grand Canyon," in *Colorado River Ecology and Dam Management*, 40–53. Two particularly complete analyses were done before the high-water years of the 1980s (Turner and Karpiscak, *Vegetation Changes*, 3–8; and A. Howard and R. Dolan, "Geomorphology of the Colorado River in the Grand Canyon," *Journal of Geology* 89 [1981]: 269–298).

24. The streamflow statistics cited are for the gaging station "Colorado River near Grand Canyon, Arizona." Garrett and Gellenbeck, *Basin Characteristics*, 133–135.

25. Benson and Darrow, *Trees and Shrubs*, 270. An outlier stand of Apache plume is established across from Deer Creek Falls (mile 136). Johnson in "Historic Changes in Vegetation" reports that Apache plume along the river corridor is in poor condition, which he presumes is a result of dam operations.

26. In an analysis of aerial photography taken in 1965, 1973, 1980, and 1985, Mike Pucherelli of the Bureau of Reclamation found the amount of mesquite cover to be increasing in the old high-water line but at a rate five times slower than its increase in the new high-water zone. M. J. Pucherelli, "Evaluation of Riparian Vegetation Trends in the Grand Canyon Using Multitemporal Remote Sensing Techniques," in U.S. Department of the Interior, *Glen Canyon Environmental Studies: Executive Summaries of Technical Reports* (Salt Lake City: Bureau of Reclama-

tion, Upper Colorado River Region, 1988), 217–228. Mesquite increased until 1980 and then significantly decreased by 1985. The shifts documented by Pucherelli may not have been of the same magnitude as those shown in the Stanton repeat photography project.

27. J. T. Peacock and C. McMillan, "Ecotypic Differentiation in *Prosopis* (Mesquite)," *Ecology* 46 (1965): 35–51.

28. R. L. Glinski and D. E. Brown, "Mesquite (*Prosopis juliflora*) Response to Severe Freezing in Southwestern Arizona," *Journal of the Arizona-Nevada Academy of Sciences* 17 (1982): 15–18. Mesquites may have suffered damage during freezes in 1978 and 1984 in Grand Canyon. L. S. Anderson and G. A. Ruffner, "Effects of the Post–Glen Canyon Dam Flow Regime on the Old High-Water Zone Plant Community along the Colorado River in Grand Canyon," in Department of the Interior, *Glen Canyon Environmental Studies*, 271–286. Frost damage to mesquite can seem more severe than it really is; trees that appear to be dead immediately after a freeze can resprout from the trunk or base. Compare the reactions to the 1937 freeze of Cottam, "Lower Sonoran Zone," and Fosberg, "Lower Sonoran in Utah."

29. Stockton and Jacoby, *Long-Term Surface-Water Supply*.

30. Anderson and Ruffner, "Post–Glen Canyon Dam Flow Regime," 284. Larry Stevens (letter, 1993) observed no seedlings of mesquite in the old high-water zone in his decade of ecological work in Grand Canyon. This does not mean that mesquite cannot become established; instead, establishment may now be rare but not nonexistent.

31. Larry Stevens (letter, 1993) found high densities of catclaw seedlings and young plants in the old high-water zone, indicating that germination and establishment is occurring rapidly.

32. L. E. Stevens, "Mechanisms of Riparian Plant Community Organization and Succession in the Grand Canyon, Arizona," Northern Arizona University, unpublished Ph.D. dissertation, 1989, 115.

33. See Turner and Karpiscak, *Vegetation Changes*, for

a comprehensive (although dated) treatment of riparian vegetation in the new high-water zone. Johnson, in "Historic Changes in Vegetation," reviews what is known of vegetation changes and discusses consequent changes in wildlife populations. Carothers and Brown, in *Colorado River*, 111–128, provide an updated but more general review of the new high-water zone. For an in-depth analysis of the processes regulating the structure of riparian assemblages in the new high-water zone, see Stevens, "Mechanisms."

34. Turner and Karpiscak, *Vegetation Changes*, 15.

35. Martin, "Trees and Shrubs," 7.

36. Weber and Seaman, *Havasupai Habitat*, 209.

37. Clover and Jotter, "Floristic Studies," 623.

38. Turner and Karpiscak, *Vegetation Changes*, 14.

39. Discussion of tamarisk in the scientific literature is confusing, partly because of the problem of differentiation of tamarisk species and because the names of species have been changed. Initially, tamarisk species introduced into the United States were believed to be either *Tamarix pentandra*, *T. tetrandra*, or *T. aphylla*. T. W. Robinson, *Introduction, Spread, and Areal Extent of Saltcedar (Tamarix) in the Western States* (Washington, D.C.: U.S. Geological Survey Professional Paper 491-A, 1965). *T. aphylla*, known as athel tamarisk, and *T. tetrandra* are not invasive species; *T. aphylla* is a large ornamental tree. The literature is replete with suggested revisions to the genus. At one time, *T. gallica* was considered the invasive species, but Robinson (ibid., A3) confines its distribution to the Gulf Coast of Texas. Kearney and Peebles, in *Arizona Flora* (Berkeley: University of California Press, 1960), 557, consider *T. pentandra* (synonymous with *T. gallica*) to be the invasive species. Benson and Darrow, in *Trees and Shrubs*, 96–98, list four species of tamarisk in the southwestern United States but lump *T. pentandra* and *T. gallica* under *T. ramosissima* and consider *T. parviflora* as another invasive riparian species. For the most authoritative taxonomic treatment, see B. R. Baum, "Introduced and Naturalized Tamarisks in the United States and Canada (Tamaricaceae)," *Baileya* 15 (1967): 19–25. Stevens,

in "Mechanisms," uses *T. ramosissima* without commenting on taxonomic problems. I follow Turner and Karpiscak, *Vegetation Changes*, 14, and refer to the tamarisk in Grand Canyon as *T. chinensis* with considerable trepidation, despite the fact that tamarisk in Grand Canyon could be any one of three species (if these species really are distinct).

40. For several excellent reviews of the invasion of tamarisk in the western United States, see J. S. Horton, *Notes on the Introduction of Deciduous Tamarisk* (U.S. Department of Agriculture, Forest Service Research Note RM-16, 1964), 14; Robinson, *Introduction, Spread, and Areal Extent of Saltcedar*, 12; and D. R. Harris, "Recent Plant Invasions in the Arid and Semi-Arid Southwest of the United States," *Annals of the Association of American Geographers* 65 (1966): 408–422.

41. Robinson, *Introduction, Spread, and Areal Extent of Saltcedar*, 4–5.

42. I. Tidestrom, *Flora of Utah and Nevada* (Contributions from the United States National Herbarium 25, 1925), 665. The species is not listed in a previous flora of the region (C. H. Merriam, "Notes on the Distribution of Trees and Shrubs in the Deserts and Desert Ranges of Southern California, Southern Nevada, Northwestern Arizona, and Southwestern Utah," *North American Fauna* 7 [1893]: 285–343).

43. E. M. Christensen, "The Rate of Naturalization of Tamarisk in Utah," *American Midland Naturalist* 68 (1962): 51–57.

44. A. M. Woodbury and H. N. Russell, "Birds of the Navajo Country," *Bulletin of the University of Utah Biological Service* 9 (1945): 1–160; Turner and Karpiscak, *Vegetation Changes*, 14.

45. N. N. Dodge, *Trees of Grand Canyon National Park* (Grand Canyon Natural History Association, Bulletin Number 3, 1936), 67; P. M. Patraw, *Check-List of Plants of Grand Canyon National Park* (Grand Canyon Natural History Association, Bulletin Number 6, 1936), 44.

46. Tamarisk has been reported as having spread upstream along the Colorado River corridor from the Grand Wash Cliffs. W. L. Graf, "Fluvial Adjustments to the Spread of Tamarisk in the Colorado

Plateau Region," *Geological Society of America Bulletin* 89 (1978): 1491–1501. The spread of tamarisk up and through Grand Canyon is alleged to have occurred between 1900 and 1910, although no evidence supports this spread. Of about 120 views of Grand Canyon from the 1923 U.S. Geological Survey expedition that we have examined, none shows tamarisk. The first occurrence of tamarisk at Badger Creek Rapid is documented in a photograph taken during a 1938 trip. On the same trip, Clover and Jotter in "Floristic Studies," 632, reported the shrub to be common at Lees Ferry.

47. J. R. Irvine and N. E. West, "Riparian Tree Species Distribution and Succession along the Lower Escalante River, Utah," *Southwestern Naturalist* 24 (1979): 331–346.

48. R. H. Webb, unpublished observations in Cataract Canyon, 1992.

49. Martin, "Trees and Shrubs," 11; Turner and Karpiscak, *Vegetation Changes*, plate 2, figure 9.

50. Larry Stevens (letter, 1993) reports that most tamarisk stands are composed of individuals of the same age. The timing of germination is closely related to floods on the unregulated river, such as those in 1965, 1973, and 1983.

51. Pucherelli, "Riparian Vegetation Trends," 224.

52. L. E. Stevens and G. L. Waring, "Effects of Post-Dam Flooding on Riparian Substrate, Vegetation, and Invertebrate Populations in the Colorado River Corridor in Grand Canyon," in Department of the Interior, *Glen Canyon Environmental Studies*, 229–243.

53. Pucherelli, "Riparian Vegetation Trends," 224.

54. G. L. Waring and L. E. Stevens, "The Effects of Recent Flooding on Riparian Plant Establishment in Grand Canyon," in Department of the Interior, *Glen Canyon Environmental Studies*, 257–270. One study indicates that tamarisk produces a density of 100 viable seeds per square inch of ground. D. K. Warren and R. M. Turner, "Saltcedar (*Tamarix chinensis*) Seed Production, Seedling Establishment, and Response to Inundation," *Journal of the Arizona Academy of Sciences* 10 (1975): 135–144.

55. Warren and Turner, "Saltcedar," 142.

56. Stevens and Waring, "Effects of Post-Dam Flooding." For a brief summary of their findings, see Johnson, "Historic Changes in Vegetation," 192–193.

57. H. L. Gary, "Root Distribution of Five-Stamen Tamarisk, Seepwillow, and Arrowweed," *Forest Science* 9 (1963): 311–314.

58. Examination of root distribution diagrams in Gary, "Root Distribution," 313, suggests that tamarisk roots may be unable to penetrate even thin clay layers. Larry Stevens (written communication, 1993) has found tamarisk established in cracks in bedrock, which he views as a better anchor to prevent the scouring out of the plant during floods. Most tamarisk, however, is established in sandy substrate, whether in sand bars or in sand between rocks on debris fans.

59. Reaches of Grand Canyon that did not have tamarisk visible in replicates of the Stanton views included a reach of Marble Canyon with Redwall Limestone forming vertical cliffs adjacent to the river (miles 25–30); three reaches of the Inner Gorge (miles 77–87, 99–110, and 112–115); Middle Granite Gorge (miles 125–130); the Muav Gorge downstream of Kanab Creek (miles 143.5–164); and Lower Granite Gorge (mile 225 to 231 Mile Rapid.

60. Stevens, "Mechanisms," 100.

61. Ibid., 101.

62. Carothers and Brown, *Colorado River,* 10–105, 148–154. For example, the black-chinned hummingbird, which is common in the southwestern United States, now rears young in the river corridor. The nests of these hummingbirds are almost exclusively in tamarisk trees in the river corridor. B. T. Brown, "Nesting Chronology, Density, and Habitat Use of Black-Chinned Hummingbirds along the Colorado River, Arizona," *Journal of Field Ornithology* 63 (1992): 393–400.

63. This discharge was recorded at the gaging station "Colorado River near Grand Canyon, Arizona," on June 29, 1983. Garrett and Gellenbeck, *Basin Characteristics.*

64. Stevens and Waring, "Effects of Post-Dam Flooding," 235–236.

65. Waring and Stevens, "Effects of Recent Flooding." Unlike a flood on the unregulated river, the 1983 flood caused a loss of fine-grained substrate and nutrients that may retard plant growth in parts of the new high-water zone.

66. Marshes do not appear in any of the 389 Stanton views of the river or the approximately 500 other photographs we have replicated that show the Colorado River before the closure of Glen Canyon Dam. Several replicates, including the one shown of the mouth of Cardenas Creek and one at mile 55, show marshes today. Lois Jotter (interview, September 1994) reports no marsh vegetation along the river corridor except at major springs, such as Vaseys Paradise and the warm springs at Lava Falls Rapid. See also Carothers and Brown, *Colorado River,* 120, 123.

67. Gary, "Root Distribution."

68. Turner and Karpiscak, *Vegetation Changes,* plate 2, figure 15.

69. Clover and Jotter, "Floristic Studies," 608–611, 638. Long-leaf brickellbush (*Brickellia longifolia*) is common in Nims's photographs of Cataract Canyon, which typically showed the high-water zone.

70. Stevens, letter, 1993.

71. Anderson and Ruffner, "Post–Glen Canyon Dam Flow Regime," 280–281.

72. Benson and Darrow, *Trees and Shrubs,* 338.

73. Martin, "Trees and Shrubs," 14.

74. Johnson, "Historic Changes in Vegetation," 193.

75. Whereas tamarisk and Bermuda grass can be viewed in a favorable light, nothing good can be said for camelthorn.

76. Several issues concern the magnitude and timing of large dam releases from Glen Canyon Dam. Two proposals about releases have been made that would affect the new high-water zone. Large releases in late summer may benefit the germination of native species at the expense of tamarisk. Carothers and Brown, *Colorado River,* 127. Few seedlings of native species have been found in Grand Canyon, however, and a winter flood, which would not promote germination, may be a better alternative. Stevens, "Mechanisms," 66–67.

77. Stevens, "Mechanisms," 100.

78. The replacement of tamarisk by coyote willow, as described by Stevens in "Mechanisms," is a passive process. Coyote willow is not impeding tamarisk growth or killing adults; the conversion results from coyote willow being more shade tolerant than tamarisk and having the ability to vegetatively reproduce. Tamarisk must first die before coyote willow replaces it, and tamarisk can be relatively long lived. Also, it is unclear whether coyote willow will actually replace tamarisk or whether the two will share dominance of riparian stands.

Managing the New Riparian Zone for Its Naturalized Values

1. B. W. Anderson, A. Higgins, and R. D. Ohmart, "Avian Use of Saltcedar Communities in the Lower Colorado River Valley," in R. R. Johnson and D. A. Jones, technical coordinators, *Importance, Preservation, and Management of Riparian Habitat* (Fort Collins, Colorado: U.S. Department of Agriculture, Forest Service General Technical Report RM-43, 1977), 128–136.

2. B. T. Brown, *Breeding Ecology of Riparian Birds along the Colorado River in Grand Canyon, Arizona* (Tucson: National Park Service, Cooperative Park Studies Unit, Technical Report Number 25, 1989), 42.

3. S. W. Carothers, R. R. Johnson, and S. W. Aitchinson, "Population Structure and Social Organization of Southwestern Riparian Birds," *American Zoologist* 14 (1974): 97–108.

4. B. T. Brown and M. W. Trosset, "Nesting-Habitat Relationships of Riparian Birds along the Colorado River in Grand Canyon, Arizona," *Southwestern Naturalist* 34 (1989): 260–270.

5. Habitat fragmentation has the potential to reduce avian species diversity. L. D. Harris, *The Fragmented Forest: Island Biogeography Theory and the Preservation of Biotic Diversity* (Chicago: University of Illinois Press, 1984), 211.

6. Carothers and Brown, *Colorado River*.

7. B. T. Brown, "Breeding Ecology of a Willow Flycatcher Population along the Colorado River in Grand Canyon, Arizona," *Western Birds* 19 (1988): 25–33.

Chapter 7

1. Smith and Crampton, *Colorado River Survey*, 88.

2. This version of the debris flow at Diamond Creek relies heavily on a 1992 conversation with Dennis Silva, formerly of Outdoors Unlimited, and a 1986 telephone interview with Mike Walker of O.A.R.S, Incorporated. One excellent account of the debris flow at Diamond Creek, concerned mainly with what happened to the people involved in the incident and not the characteristics of the flow, has been previously published in M. P. Ghiglieri, *Canyon* (Tucson: University of Arizona Press, 1992), 270–276.

3. Ibid., 276.

4. Debris flow is a generic name for a flood with a sediment concentration higher than perhaps 60 to 80 percent. This phenomenon also has been called mudflow and debris torrent. Typical flows in Grand Canyon contain less clay than the typical mudflow, however, and warrant the generic name. For an overview of debris flows in the context of other types of floods and mass movements, see T. C. Pierson and J. E. Costa, "A Rheologic Classification of Subaerial Sediment-Water Flows," *Geological Society of America, Reviews in Engineering Geology* 7 (1987): 1–12. Debris flows in the southwestern United States were first described by Eliot Blackwelder in "Mudflow as a Geologic Agent in Semiarid Mountains," *Bulletin of the Geological Society of America* 39 (1928): 465–484. The first scientific descriptions of debris flows in Grand Canyon resulted from the flood of December 1966. M. E. Cooley, B. N. Aldridge, and R. C. Euler, *Effects of the Catastrophic Flood of December 1966, North Rim Area, Eastern Grand Canyon, Arizona* (Washington, D.C.: U.S. Geological Survey Professional Paper 980, 1977), 43). Additional information on these debris flows and the 1984 debris flow in Monument Creek is given in Webb et al., *Debris Flows*.

5. Interestingly, debris flows are most frequent in tectonically active terrains with fast uplift or in areas with frequent volcanic activity. Grand Canyon is relatively stable in comparison. Debris-flow activity in Grand Canyon owes its frequency to the rapid downcutting of a river through ideal types of bedrock. Those steep exposures result from the regional tectonism of the Colorado Plateau, which produced rapid uplift millions of years ago.

6. Melis et al., *Magnitude and Frequency Data*.

7. Cooley et al., *Catastrophic Flood*.

8. During surveys of bald eagles at Nankoweap Creek in February 1991, Bryan Brown witnessed a "car-sized boulder" fall into Nankoweap Rapid. The origin was a large rockfall, apparently in the Kaibab Limestone cliffs a thousand feet above the river.

9. Carothers and Brown, *Colorado River*, fn. 7, ch. 1, 212.

10. Observed rockfalls are listed in T. D. Ford, G. H. Billingsley, Jr., P. W. Huntoon, and W. J. Breed, "Rock Movement and Mass Wastage in the Grand Canyon," in Breed and Roat, *Geology of the Grand Canyon*, 116–128; and R. Hereford and P. W. Huntoon, "Rock Movement and Mass Wastage in the Grand Canyon," in S. S. Beus and M. Morales, *Grand Canyon Geology* (New York: Oxford University Press), 443–459.

11. K. L. Cole and L. Mayer, "Use of Packrat Middens to Determine Rates of Cliff Retreat in the Eastern Grand Canyon, Arizona," *Geology* 10 (1982): 597–599. This work was severely criticized by L. D. Hose and J. F. Haman in "Comments and Replies on 'Use of Packrat Middens to Determine Rates of Cliff Retreat in the Eastern Grand Canyon, Arizona,'" *Geology* 11 (1983): 314–316.

12. Downstream of about mile 15, the Chinle Formation is not close enough to the river corridor to produce debris flows that reach the Colorado River.

13. Cooley et al., *Catastrophic Flood*, plate 1.

14. Webb et al., *Debris Flows*, 24.

15. R. H. Webb, P. T. Pringle, S. L. Reneau, and G. R. Rink, "Monument Creek Debris Flow, 1984: Implications for the Formation of Rapids on the Colorado River in Grand Canyon National Park," *Geology* 16 (1988): 50–54.

16. Cooley et al., *Catastrophic Flood;* Webb et al., *Debris Flows.*

17. Two excellent review articles have been published on the basic mechanical properties of debris flows: A. M. Johnson and J. R. Rodine, "Debris Flow," in D. Brunsden and D. B. Prior, editors, *Slope Instability* (New York: John Wiley and Sons, 1984), 257–361; and J. E. Costa, "Physical Geomorphology of Debris Flows," in J. E. Costa and P. J. Fleisher, editors, *Developments and Applications of Geomorphology* (Berlin: Springer-Verlag Publishers, 1984), 268–317. Debris flows are much more complicated than even these reviews indicate, and a general model of debris-flow movement that explains all of the properties exhibited by flowing debris has not been developed.

18. Pierson and Costa, "Rheologic Classification."

19. Webb et al., *Debris Flows,* 31–35.

20. Melis et al., *Magnitude and Frequency Data.*

21. Webb et al., *Debris Flows,* 19–21; Melis et al., *Magnitude and Frequency Data.*

22. Melis et al., *Magnitude and Frequency Data.*

23. Webb et al., *Debris Flows,* 23.

24. R. M. Iverson and R. G. LaHusen, "Dynamic Pore-Pressure Fluctuations in Rapidly Shearing Granular Materials," *Science* 246 (1989): 796–799.

25. Despite its name, Redwall Limestone is gray. The red staining on its surface arises from chemical staining by runoff from the upper strata.

26. Concerns about the decreased competence of the regulated Colorado River were raised shortly after the dam was completed. T. L. Péwé, *Colorado River Guidebook: Lees Ferry to Phantom Ranch* (Phoenix: privately published by T. L. Péwé, 1968), 62. Of the debris fans in Grand Canyon, 25 percent were reported to have aggraded between 1965 and 1973. A. D. Howard and R. Dolan, "Changes in the Fluvial Deposits of the Colorado River in the Grand Canyon Caused by Glen Canyon Dam," in R. M. Lin,

editor, *Proceedings of the First Conference on Scientific Research in the National Parks* (Washington, D.C.: National Park Service, Transactions and Proceedings Number 5, 1979), 845–851. My observations suggest that this is too high a percentage for such a short period of time. Also see Howard and Dolan, "Geomorphology."

27. Recently, sufficient plant parts for radiocarbon dating have been extracted from debris-flow deposits plastered under overhangs in Grand Canyon tributaries. One radiocarbon date on a debris flow at mile 63.4 was 5,200 years B.P. Melis et al., *Magnitude and Frequency Data.*

28. Catclaw (*Acacia greggii*) is the best species for recording debris flows in tributary canyons. This species has diffuse rings, which are indistinct and difficult to ascertain as annual bands. However, careful analyses indicate that rings are added annually, which makes tree-ring analysis a viable option for dating the occurrence of debris flows or other floods. V.A.S. McCord, University of Arizona, unpublished data, 1992. Analyses are very labor intensive, however, and can be applied only to certain tributaries.

29. This number represents all tributaries greater than 0.06 square miles between Lees Ferry and Diamond Creek. Melis et al., *Magnitude and Frequency Data.*

30. Of the 529 tributaries of the Colorado River that periodically yield debris flows, 94 are greater than 4 square miles. The replicated views recorded 41 (43.6 percent) of these tributaries, of which 26 (63 percent) had at least one debris flow in the last century.

31. Of the 68 tributaries between miles 160 and 213, 15 were observed in Stanton views. Of these, 7 had debris flows during the last century.

32. Howard and Dolan, "Geomorphology"; J. C. Schmidt and J. B. Graf, *Aggradation and Degradation of Alluvial Sand Deposits, 1965 to 1986, Colorado River, Grand Canyon National Park, Arizona* (Washington, D.C.: U.S. Geological Survey Professional Paper 1493, 1990), 74.

33. Powell, *Exploration.*

34. W. K. Hamblin and J. K. Rigby, *Guidebook to the Colorado River, Part 1, Lee's Ferry to Phantom Ranch*

in Grand Canyon National Park (Provo, Utah: Brigham Young University, Geology Studies 15, part 5, 1968), 6–10; Howard and Dolan, "Geomorphology."

35. Hamblin and Rigby, *Guidebook*, 10.

36. Dolan and Howard, in "Geomorphology," refer to well-sorted, coarse-grained deposits as "cobble bars." Cobbles, which have diameters between 64 and 256 millimeters, are not the only constituents of these bars. I prefer to use the more generic term *debris bar*, which encompasses the range in particle size from gravel bars, which are common between mile 65 and 72, to rock gardens like the one just downstream of Crystal Rapid.

37. Lucchita, "History of the Grand Canyon," in Beus and Morales, *Grand Canyon Geology*, 311–332; W. K. Hamblin, "Late Cenozoic Lava Dams in the Western Grand Canyon," in Beus and Morales, *Grand Canyon Geology*, 385–433; idem, "Rates of Erosion by the Colorado River in the Grand Canyon, Arizona," in *Proceedings of the Twenty-Ninth International Geological Congress, Part B* (Washington, D.C.: International Geological Congress, 1989), 211–218.

38. L. B. Leopold, "The Rapids and the Pools: Grand Canyon," in *The Colorado River Region and John Wesley Powell* (Washington, D.C.: U.S. Geological Survey Professional Paper 669, 1969), 131–145.

Chapter 8

1. B. M. Goldwater, *A Journey down the Green and Colorado Rivers* (Phoenix: privately published by H. Walker Publishing, 1940), 80.

2. R. F. Nash, *The Big Drops: Ten Legendary Rapids of the American West* (Boulder, Colorado: Johnson Books, 1989), 216.

3. Stevens, *Guide*. Nash calls Lava Falls Rapid "the most difficult stretch of runnable whitewater in the West" (*Big Drops*, 173). Stanton thought that Lava Cliff Rapid, now drowned under Lake Mead, was the worst rapid he saw in Grand Canyon.

4. Nash, *Big Drops*, 151.

5. P. L. Fradkin, *A River No More* (Tucson: University of Arizona Press, 1984), 206.

6. Throughout this chapter, several special names are used to describe features in rapids. The *tongue* of a rapid, the glassy smooth water at the entrance, is shaped like a "V" pointed downstream; at most water levels, the tongue begins at about the upstream end of the debris fan. Within the main body of a rapid are different types of waves; for example, *lateral* waves appear at an angle to the flow, whereas *haystacks* are roughly conical and occasionally explode out in various directions. Laterals generally spawn from specific rocks near shore or from bedrock projections; they are surface turbulence caused by the constriction. If water barely covers a boulder and falls vertically on the downstream side, it is called a *pourover*. In a *hole*, water moving downstream appears to flow under a wave crashing upstream. Most holes form downstream of large boulders or piles of boulders; at high water, some waves may be related to the energy dissipation of the fast-moving water. In some holes, known as *keepers*, water appears to recycle endlessly, and objects that enter (such as boats and people) are not readily flushed out. Although laterals may be related to flow through the entire rapid, most waves and holes form downstream of rocks submerged just below the surface. For specific examples of these hydraulic features, see S. W. Kieffer, *The Waves and Rapids of the Colorado River, Grand Canyon, Arizona* (Washington, D.C.: U.S. Geological Survey Open-File Report 87-096, 1977), 69.

7. Harvey Butchart, pioneering hiker and mountaineer in Grand Canyon, and Don Davis tried to reconstruct the routes of McDonald and Stanton in May 1966. Butchart, *Treks III*, 30–31. Butchart reports that McDonald's route is unknown but must have been a severe climb. To survive freezing, McDonald was forced to break into a ranch building in House Rock Valley after he had crested the North Rim. The climb that Stanton's climbing group made was perilous and would now be attempted only by experienced climbers equipped with ropes and modern gear. As part of his efforts, Butchart attempted to replicate Stanton's view of Crystal Rapid from the top of the Tapeats Sandstone. He was a considerable distance from Stanton's camera position;

Ray Turner replicated Butchart's view in 1986. Webb et al., *Debris Flows*, figure 17.

8. Smith and Crampton, *Colorado River Survey*, 187–188.

9. This account was extracted from Lavender, *River Runners*, 51–54.

10. The seventeen-foot fall in Crystal Rapid was measured by the 1923 U.S. Geological Survey expedition. Stevens, *Guide*. The 1965 U.S. Geological Survey expedition reportedly measured a bed-elevation drop of twenty-one feet. S. W. Kieffer, "The 1983 Hydraulic Jump in Crystal Rapid: Implications for River-Running and Geomorphic Evolution in the Grand Canyon," *Journal of Geology* 93 (1985): 385–406.

11. W. Heald, "The Eighteenth Expedition," in R. Peattie, editor, *The Inverted Mountains* (New York: Vanguard Press, 1948), 184.

12. Leslie Jones, unpublished scroll map of the Colorado River, 1962. Boucher and Tuna Creek Rapids, upstream and downstream, were rated a 6 and a 4, respectively.

13. Meteorological data for this storm are given in E. Butler and J. C. Mundorff, *Floods of December 1966 in Southwestern Utah* (Washington, D.C.: U.S. Geological Survey Water-Supply Paper 1870-A, 1970), 40.

14. The flooding in southern California, southern Nevada, and central Arizona is documented in J. O. Rostvedt et al., *Summary of Floods in the United States during 1966* (Washington, D.C.: U.S. Geological Survey Water-Supply Paper 1870-D, 1971), D59–D91. Historic flooding on the Virgin River must be pieced together from several reports. The 1966 flood is the largest natural flood in the period of gaging record, which is 1930 to the present at Littlefield, Arizona (Butler and Mundorff, *Floods*). A second flood, which Butler and Mundorff equate in size to the 1966 flood, occurred during a much larger storm in January and February, 1862 (Webb, "Late Holocene Flooding," 4). However, the discharge of the 1862 flood may have been exceeded during flooding in December 1889. On December 7 and 15, floods on the Virgin River had a stage of

two feet higher in a wider and deeper channel than the flood of 1862. A. K. Larson, *"I Was Called to Dixie"* (Salt Lake City: Deseret News Press, 1961), 367–368. The fourth flood occurred September 1, 1909; billed "the greatest flood in the history of the county," this flood caused extensive damage along the Virgin River. R. R. Woolley, *Cloudburst Floods in Utah, 1850–1938* (Washington, D.C.: U.S. Geological Survey Water-Supply Paper 994, 1946), 100. Because the peak discharges for the 1862, 1889, and 1909 floods are unknown, the relative size of the 1966 flood is uncertain. I believe, in the absence of known discharges, that the 1889, 1909, and 1966 floods were of about equal size.

15. Nash, *Big Drops*, 153; Ghiglieri, *Canyon*, 4. One account states sixteen inches of rain fell. Christa Sadler, editor, *There's This River* (Flagstaff, Arizona: Red Lake Books, 1994), 54.

16. Annual rainfall typically increases with elevation, especially in the western United States. The difference in annual precipitation between the Colorado River and the North Rim is the largest in Arizona for such a short horizontal distance. W. D. Sellers and R. H. Hill, editors, *Arizona Climate, 1931–1972* (Tucson: University of Arizona Press, 1974), 7. The total recorded precipitation in the North Rim Entrance Station gage was seventeen inches for November 1 to December 7, 1966. Park rangers estimated that three inches fell during November storms; therefore, the exact amount of precipitation for December 3–7 at the North Rim Entrance Station is not known. The mean annual rainfall for the North Rim is twenty-five inches. Cooley et al., *Catastrophic Flood*, 4–6.

17. Cooley et al., *Catastrophic Flood*, 5.

18. Ibid.

19. The slope-area method is commonly used to estimate peak discharges for floods that cannot be measured directly. T. Dalrymple and M. A. Benson, *Measurement of Peak Discharge by the Slope-Area Method* (Washington, D.C.: U.S. Geological Survey, Techniques of Water-Resources Investigations, Book 3, Chapter A2, 1967), 12. This method uses the Manning equation to account for energy losses due

to friction against the channel bed. Unfortunately, substantial internal friction losses occur within debris flows that cannot be adequately accounted for using this equation.

20. Webb et al., *Debris Flows*.

21. Superelevation and runup methods are simplistic but are more appropriate for estimating the discharge of debris flows than the slope-area method. See Chapter 7.

22. Velocities for debris flows are typically less than twenty miles per hour, depending on channel slope and the viscosity of the flow. Pierson and Costa, "Rheologic Classification."

23. Nash, *Big Drops*, 153.

24. Unlike other diagnostic archaeological materials (for example, pot sherds), agave roasting pits cannot be dated accurately without radiocarbon analysis of charcoal used in the firing. Euler did not radiocarbon date any charcoal that may have been preserved in either of the pits affected by the debris flow, so the actual temporal significance is assumed, not known. Cooley et al., *Catastrophic Flood*, 16.

25. Cooley et al., *Catastrophic Flood*, 1.

26. Carothers and Brown, *Colorado River*, 41; Nash, *Big Drops*, 153.

27. Ghiglieri, *Canyon*, 5.

28. Nash, *Big Drops*, 151. Another account holds that the Crystal Creek basin had not experienced a comparable storm in recorded history. Carothers and Brown, *Colorado River*, 41. However, there is no recorded history of rainstorms in the Crystal Creek basin, including the 1966 storm. The one-day precipitation at Bright Angel Ranger Station and Phantom Ranch is not even the largest for days in December. Sellers et al., *Arizona Climate*, 122–123.

29. E. M. Hansen and F. K. Shwarz, *Meteorology of Important Rainstorms in the Colorado River and Great Basin Drainages* (Washington, D.C.: National Oceanic and Atmospheric Administration, Hydrometeorological Report 50, 1981), 167.

30. Statistically, estimates of the hundred-year rainfall of one-day duration are 3.8 and 5.5 inches at Phantom Ranch and the North Rim, respectively, which are greater than the one-day totals during December 1966. J. F. Miller, R. H. Frederick, and R. J. Tracey, *Precipitation-Frequency Atlas of the Western United States*, vol. 8, *Arizona* (Silver Spring, Maryland: National Oceanic and Atmospheric Administration, National Weather Service, NOAA Atlas 2, 1973), 41.

31. Garrett and Gellenbeck, *Basin Characteristics*, 136–139.

32. Ibid., 151–152.

33. Harvey Butchart, observations, in Webb et al., *Debris Flows*.

34. Webb et al., *Debris Flows*, 17.

35. Because of excessive inputs of carbon dioxide into the atmosphere during the Industrial Revolution in Europe, the radiocarbon calibration curve is flat between about A.D. 1650 and 1950. Any radiocarbon date with a mean age (in years B.P.) between 0 and 300 falls in this window of low resolution.

36. R. C. Euler and S. M. Chandler, "Aspects of Prehistoric Settlement Patterns in Grand Canyon," in R. C. Euler and G. J. Gumerman, editors, *Investigations of the Southwestern Anthropological Research Group, Proceedings of the 1976 Conference* (Flagstaff: Museum of Northern Arizona Publication, 1978), 73.

37. A. T. Jones, *A Cross Section of Grand Canyon Archaeology: Excavations at Five Sites along the Colorado River* (Tucson, Arizona: Western Archaeology and Conservation Center, Publications in Anthropology 28, 1986), 367.

38. Ibid., 105.

39. Cooley et al., *Catastrophic Flood*, 39.

40. Kieffer, "Hydraulic Jump"; idem, *Hydraulic Map of Crystal Rapid, Grand Canyon* (Washington, D.C.: U.S. Geological Survey Miscellaneous Investigations Map I-1897-H, 1988), 1 sheet; Webb et al., *Debris Flows*, 41; Nash, *Big Drops*, 155; Ghiglieri, *Canyon*, 9. The whole issue of damming at Crystal Rapid is somewhat contrived, either to formulate a descriptive model of debris fan evolution and reworking (e.g., Kieffer, "Hydraulic Jump") or to emphasize the severity of Crystal Rapid to navigation (e.g., Ghiglieri, *Canyon*). The first published account holds that the blockage was only partial.

G. C. Simmons and D. L. Gaskill, *River Runners' Guide to the Canyons of the Green and Colorado Rivers with Emphasis on Geologic Features, Volume III, Marble Gorge and Grand Canyon* (Flagstaff, Arizona: Northland Press, 1969), 79–80.

41. Ghiglieri, *Canyon,* 5.

42. The discharge was measured at the gaging station "Colorado River near Grand Canyon, Arizona." Garrett and Gellenbeck, *Basin Characteristics.*

43. The thirty-three-foot fall is based on a discharge of 5,000 cfs and accounts for the fall after 1983 between the head of Crystal Rapid and the base of the "Rock Garden," which is of comparable distance to that measured in 1923. The drop at the top of the rapid is twelve feet. Kieffer, *Hydraulic Map of Crystal Rapid.*

44. Simmons and Gaskill, *Guide,* 80; Kieffer, *Hydraulic Map of Crystal Rapid.*

45. Kieffer, in "Hydraulic Jump," 387–391, describes navigation before 1983 and many of the changes in Crystal Rapid caused by the 1983 flood.

46. In examining boulders transported by the 1966 debris flow in Crystal Creek, we found no large pieces of schist. Instead, most boulders were Supai Group sandstones or Redwall Limestone.

47. This story is condensed from L. Steiger, "My God, It's Waltenberg!" *Grand Canyon Professional River Guides News* 6 (1993): 22–26.

48. Nash, in *Big Drops,* 155, reports changes in Crystal Rapid caused by multiple floods in October 1972 on the Little Colorado River; however, low flow in the Colorado River diminished the size of these floods to less than the maximum discharge from the power plant at Glen Canyon Dam by the time the floodwaters reached the Grand Canyon gaging station. More likely, the changes Nash reports occurred during high releases from Glen Canyon Dam, which, in combination with high spring runoff on the Little Colorado River, peaked at 38,300 cfs on April 19, 1973.

49. For numerous stories about Lava Falls Rapid, some of which may be embellished, see Nash, *Big Drops,* 173–200.

50. Stevens, *Guide,* 90. Nash, in *Big Drops,* 179, gives a more accurate fall of twenty feet in a hundred yards. In actuality, the thirty-seven-foot drop, which was measured by the U.S. Geological Survey expedition of 1923, occurs over a distance of one and a half miles and accounts for the main rapid, Lower Lava Rapid, and several riffles further downstream. This certainly must have been the most inaccurate water-surface fall the expedition measured, because a flood of 112,000 cfs interrupted the surveying halfway through the rapid. The stage rise during this flood was twenty-one feet in twenty-four hours. Freeman, *Down the Grand Canyon,* 525–530. This sudden rise probably explains why the water-surface drop through Lava Falls Rapid is the only glaring inaccuracy in the 1923 survey, which adjusted elevations to a 10,000 cfs standard water-surface elevation. Richard Quartaroli (letter, 1994) reviewed all pertinent sources and found that the reported water-surface fall in Lava Falls Rapid (not including the thirty-seven-foot figure) varies from ten to twenty feet.

51. Water-surface fall is twelve feet at 5,000 cfs. S. W. Kieffer, *Hydraulic Map of Lava Falls Rapid, Grand Canyon, Arizona* (Washington, D.C.: U.S. Geological Survey Miscellaneous Investigations Series, Map I-1897-J, 1988), 1 sheet, scale 1:1,000. The amount of fall may change at different water levels.

52. Smith and Crampton, *Colorado River Survey,* 225.

53. Stevens and Shoemaker, *Footsteps,* 270–275.

54. There are several sites in Grand Canyon where numerous photographs have been taken; for example, numerous photographers beginning with Hillers have recorded the view from Toroweap Point high above Lava Falls. Beginning with the Stone expedition of 1909, numerous views have been made of crews portaging or lining boats down the left side of Lava Falls Rapid.

55. Hamblin, "Lava Dams." Lava flows occurred between 140,000 and 1.2 million years ago, both at Lava Falls Rapid and Whitmore Wash (mile 188). The fact that no large rapids occur at the mouth of Whitmore Wash, the site of massive lava dams, indicates another inconsistency in the idea that Lava Falls Rapid may be a residual of past lava dams.

56. B. H. Granger, *Grand Canyon Place Names* (Tucson: University of Arizona Press, 1960), 16; idem, *Arizona Place Names*, 149. Otis "Dock" Marston, the noted river historian, wanted to change the name of Lava Falls Rapid to Vulcan Rapid to avoid this confusion. John Weisheit, letter, 1993.

57. Powell, *Exploration.*

58. Fradkin, *River No More*, 206; Nash, *Big Drops*, 179.

59. Carothers and Brown, *Colorado River*, 39.

60. Richard Hereford, "Driftwood in Stanton's Cave: The Case for Temporary Damming of the Colorado River at Nankoweap Creek in Marble Canyon, Grand Canyon National Park, Arizona," in Euler, *Stanton's Cave*, 99–106.

61. Hamblin, "Lava Dams."

62. I found about 205 historic photographs of Lava Falls Rapid taken between 1872 and 1984. These views were taken on sixty different days over the 111-year period. Ted Melis and Tom Wise contributed extensively to the interpretations used here.

63. The quiescent water at the Black Rock is shown vividly in a movie made by a Dr. Inglesby in 1938 during a hike down from Toroweap Point. The movie pans across driftwood bobbing in front of the Black Rock. The original footage of Inglesby's movie is at the Utah State Historical Society in Salt Lake City. Moreover, in the 1939 movie of Don Harris and Bert Loper's trip, Loper's successful run at 7,600 cfs ends well above the Black Rock, and he is shown eddied out and waiting for Harris to complete his run.

64. Flavell must have had a good run; eight inches of water in a 15½-foot boat is a small amount compared to what it takes to fill up a modern 18-foot raft. Carmony and Brown, *Panthon*, 69.

65. Diary entry for Bert Loper, July 14, 1939. Manuscript is from the Marston Collection, Huntington Library, San Marino, California.

66. Diary of Don Harris, 1939 trip through Grand Canyon, entry for July 15.

67. Nancy Nelson, *Any Time, Any Place, Any River* (Flagstaff, Arizona: Red Lake Books, 1991), 19.

68. Two pieces of photographic evidence bracket the date of the largest debris flow in Prospect Canyon. A movie record of the runs of Don Harris and Bert Loper on July 15, 1939, clearly shows the Pyramid Rock and a completely different rapid than that of today. Photographs taken by Barry Goldwater on August 17, 1940, show a constricted rapid with no Pyramid Rock. As a result of a dissipating tropical cyclone, heavy rains fell in northern Arizona on September 4–6, 1939. W. Smith, *The Effects of Eastern North Pacific Tropical Cyclones on the Southwestern United States* (Salt Lake City: National Weather Service, National Oceanic and Atmospheric Administration, Technical Memorandum NWS WR-197, 1986), 229. This storm is the probable cause for the first historic debris flow in Prospect Canyon.

69. Melis et al., *Magnitude and Frequency Data.*

70. The "missing rock" is clearly visible in the low-altitude aerial photographs taken by P. T. Reilly in 1956 (L-26-15) and 1964 (L-71-33). Flow in the Colorado River was less than 3,000 cfs in both aerial photographs. At low water, guides running motorboats have reported hitting their propellers on a rock just upstream of the Big Wave. It is likely that the rock these boats are hitting is this "missing rock."

71. Goldwater, *Journey*, 93–94. Goldwater's photographs are the key ones that bracket the long period of stability (at least 1872 to 1939) of Lava Falls Rapid. The rapid shown in Goldwater's photographs was perhaps twenty feet narrower than the rapid was in 1993. The twelve-to-fifteen-foot fall does not appear in the photographs.

72. Heald, "Eighteenth Expedition," 195.

73. Photographs taken by Jorgen Visbak, on June 14 and August 29, 1954, bracket the date on which this debris flow occurred.

74. The photographs that bracket the period in which the debris flow must have occurred are among the best taken of Lava Falls Rapid. On March 19, P. T. Reilly made a series of low-altitude aerial views of the rapid, which also document the amount of constriction caused by the 1954 debris flow. Mary Beckwith, while on a river trip, inadvertently photographed the extent of change on July 20, 1955. On

an unknown day in October 1955, Parker Hamilton made views of the rapid from Toroweap Point that show a dramatically constricted channel.

75. H. E. Thomas, *The Meteorologic Phenomenon of Drought in the Southwest* (Washington, D.C.: U.S. Geological Survey Professional Paper 372-A, 1962), 42.

76. The largest discharge in the Colorado River between 1955 and the spring of 1957 was 67,200 cfs in June 1956.

77. A photograph taken by Harvey Butchart on August 29, 1957, shows the first clear evidence of the Ledge Hole in Lava Falls Rapid.

78. The photographs that bracket the date of the 1963 debris flow were taken by Bill Belknap on August 24 and an unknown person on September 22. The latter views, collected by Otis "Dock" Marston and preserved in his collection at the Huntington Library, San Marino, California, were attributed to Bud Rusho. However, Rusho was not at Lava Falls Rapid at that time (interview, 1991).

79. Webb et al., "Monument Creek." Hance Rapid is another notable example of a rapid controlled by debris flows from a tributary (Red Canyon) that has an unusual geological feature. A large dike of resistant rock appears to plunge beneath the water at the head of the rapid.

80. The 1939 movie showing the runs of Don Harris and Bert Loper suggest that, at least at 7,600 cfs, Lava Falls Rapid may have been easier to run before the September 1939 debris flow. The run consisted of several steep drops between the entry rock and where the V waves are now; the runs were completed before the boats reached the Black Rock. However, the rapid was littered with barely submerged rocks and probably was more similar to Hance Rapid (mile 76.6) than to any other on the modern Colorado River.

Chapter 9

1. Stanton was the first to challenge Powell's description of the rapids. Stanton, *Controversies*, 122–123.

2. Smith and Crampton, *Colorado River Survey*, 213.

3. This number was obtained from a count of all rapids rated 5 or higher at 10,000 cfs in Stevens, *Guide*.

4. Dellenbaugh, *Canyon Voyage*, 217.

5. Brown actually drowned a short distance downstream in Salt Water Riffle (see Chapter 1). But early river runners commonly believed that Brown died in the tailwaves of Soap Creek Rapid.

6. Smith and Crampton, *Colorado River Survey*, 70. Stanton's comparison to upstream rapids would place Soap Creek Rapid in competition with Dark Canyon Rapid and Big Drop 3 in Cataract Canyon, which are generally considered far more dangerous than Soap Creek Rapid is today.

7. Carmony and Brown, *Panthon*.

8. R. B. Stanton, "Through the Grand Cañon of the Colorado," *Scribner's Magazine* 8 (1890): 591–613.

9. Carmony and Brown, *Panthon*, 52–53.

10. Were it not for the group of spectators, Flavell also would have lined or portaged Hance Rapid. Ibid., 57.

11. G. W. James, *In and around the Grand Canyon* (Boston: Little, Brown, and Company, 1900), 233–238. James's view of Badger Creek Rapid, which he calls Soap Creek Rapid, appears opposite page 238.

12. E. L. Kolb, *Through the Grand Canyon from Wyoming to Mexico* (Tucson: University of Arizona Press, 1914, reprinted 1989), 344.

13. Ibid., 183–184.

14. Ibid., 188.

15. C. H. Birdseye, "Diary of the Grand Canyon Survey 1923," National Archives, Washington, D.C., unpublished manuscript, 1, 5.

16. C. Eddy, *Down the World's Most Dangerous River* (New York: Frederick A. Stokes Company, 1929), 293.

17. Ibid.

18. Webb, *Riverman*, 42. The boulder that caused the navigational difficulties is shown behind the boatman in a 1934 photograph. Ibid., 44.

19. Lavender, *River Runners*, 90; Amos Burg, postcard from Burg to A. W. Mendenhall dated October 16,

1938, National Archives, Washington, D.C.

20. Diary of Bert Loper, in the Marston Collection, Huntington Library, San Marino, California. The entry for July 6, 1939, concerns running Soap Creek Rapid.

21. Nelson, *Any Time*, 65–66.

22. Heald, "Eighteenth Expedition." A photograph of Soap Creek Rapid taken by Heald (number PO 341 3:2:9, Nevills Collection, University of Utah, Salt Lake City) shows no striking navigational difficulties.

23. Aerial photograph 6307, Navajo Project of the U.S. Soil Conservation Service, scale 1:31,600. The flight was at an unknown date in 1935. The negative for this photograph is stored in the National Archives, Arlington, Virginia.

24. Numerous historical photographs exist for Soap Creek Rapid, but the best were made before the 1923 U.S. Geological Survey expedition (number 309, U.S. Geological Survey Photographic Library, Lakewood, Colorado). Taken from the left rim, the photographs show substantial deposition of boulders and cobbles on the upstream side of the debris fan.

25. The replies to Dock Marston's questionnaire on the difficulty of rapids is in volume 190 of the Marston Collection, Huntington Library, San Marino, California.

26. Jones (map, 1962) erroneously reports a lining of House Rock Rapid by the Kolbs in 1911. The rapid the Kolbs lined was downstream of Boulder Narrows and probably was North Canyon Rapid. Inconsistencies occur in the early river guides to Grand Canyon. Whereas Jones lists House Rock as a 7, other guides list it as a 4–5 (Simmons and Gaskill, *Guide*, 37) or as a 7 (Hamblin and Rigby, *Guidebook*, 32).

27. Martin Litton, a long-time river guide, claims the debris flow occurred during the same storm that changed Crystal Rapid in 1966. Steiger, "My God, It's Waltenberg!" 22–26. John Cross II, who was the first boatman to run the river in 1967, did not observe changes in House Rock Rapid. Other professional guides state that the change occurred before their first river trips in the early 1970s.

28. Stephens and Shoemaker, *Footsteps*, 240–241; Webb et al., *Debris Flows*, 10–11.

29. Webb et al., "Monument Creek."

30. Carmony and Brown, *Panthon*, 57–59.

31. Nelson, *Any Time*, 18, 61. Nevills ran Hance Rapid in 1938 after thinking he might have to line it; in his eleven-year career, Nevills lined Hance only during high water in 1949.

32. Ghiglieri, *Canyon*, 139–140. Ghiglieri is not the only observer to blame the origin and severity of Hance Rapid on the dike. Péwé, *Guidebook*, 58.

33. P. W. Huntoon, G. H. Billingsley, Jr., W. J. Breed, J. W. Sears, T. D. Ford, M. D. Clark, R. S. Babcock, and E. H. Brown, *Geologic Map of the Eastern Part of the Grand Canyon National Park, Arizona* (Flagstaff: Museum of Northern Arizona Special Publication map, 1986), 1 sheet, scale 1:62,500. The second-largest area of landslides occurs in the Nankoweap Creek drainage, which feeds into the twenty-five-foot drop of Nankoweap Rapid. Nankoweap Creek also has the largest debris fan in Grand Canyon, built by a combination of rockfall and debris flows.

34. The rapid is rated a 10 between 3,000 and 9,000 cfs. Stevens, *Guide*, 76.

35. Nancy Brian, *River to Rim* (Flagstaff, Arizona: Earthquest Press, 1992), 72–73.

36. Smith and Crampton, *Colorado River Survey*, 177–178.

37. The origin of the phrase "lost in the Jewels" is claimed by Mimi Murov and Tom Brownold, but when the phrase is told to other river runners, they certainly can relate to the lack of identifiable geographical features in this reach.

38. Waltenberg Rapid is named for John Waltenberg, who worked for William Bass. Unfortunately, the Board of Geographic Names misspelled the rapid "Walthenberg" on official maps of Grand Canyon. Granger, *Grand Canyon Place Names*, 25; and Brian, *River to Rim*, 92. Despite the official name, I use the correct spelling of Waltenberg's name in this account.

39. Kolb, *Through the Grand Canyon*, 236–239.

40. Lavender, *River Runners*, 91; Amos Burg, postcards to A. W. Mendenhall dated October 28 and 29, 1938, National Archives, Washington, D.C. On Holmstrom's first trip, the discharge was about 7,200 cfs in Waltenberg Rapid; on the second, the discharge was about 10,000 cfs.

41. Unfortunately the Board of Geographic Names adopted a misspelling of Dubendorff's name. The official name for the rapid is Deubendorff. Granger, *Grand Canyon Place Names*, 9; Brian, *River to Rim*, 101. I use Julius Stone's spelling. Stone, *Canyon Country*.

42. Stone, *Canyon Country*, 95.

43. Bill Beer, *We Swam the Grand Canyon* (Seattle: The Mountaineers, 1988), 71.

44. Freeman, *Down the Grand Canyon*, 515–518. The mistaken notion that the rock in President Harding Rapid fell during the twentieth century has been perpetuated. See W. Cook, *The WEN, the Botany, and the Mexican Hat* (Orangevale, California: Callisto Books, 1987), 83.

45. Dellenbaugh, *Canyon Voyage*, 127.

46. In 1923, members of the U.S. Geological Survey expedition observed a log fitted into a piece of Muav Limestone. The log apparently had vibrated sufficiently to grind into the rock. Eugene C. LaRue, the expedition's hydrologist and photographer, took several close-up photographs of the log in the rock. Using one of these photographs, Tom Wise found the location (at mile 160.6) in 1992. The log was gone; apparently it had been washed from the rock during a flood.

47. I first observed suturing on a boulder deposited on the debris fan of 217 Mile Rapid. The newly deposited boulder, of unknown origin (no debris flow had occurred), was the only change in eighty-one years in a view photographed by Raymond Cogswell (Stone, *Canyon Country*, 404, Plate 135B). We also observed suturing in sandstone boulders deposited between 1937 and 1956 at the mouth of 205 Mile Canyon. The boulders were at an elevation overtopped only by discharges in excess of 30,000 to 40,000 cfs, which occurred only a few times since closure of Glen Canyon Dam. Suturing occurred quickly in the unregulated Colorado River.

Chapter 10

1. Dellenbaugh, *Canyon Voyage*, 185; G. C. Crampton, *Land of Living Rock* (Layton, Utah: Peregrine Smith Books, 1972), 142, 149.

2. C. G. Crampton and D. L. Smith, editors, *The Hoskaninni Papers: Mining in Glen Canyon, 1897–1902* (Salt Lake City: University of Utah Anthropological Papers 54, 1961), 182.

3. The annual suspended sediment load of 86 million tons per year is reported for the Colorado River at Grand Canyon gaging station (mile 87) for the period 1941–1957 by E. D. Andrews, "Sediment Transport in the Colorado River Basin," in *Colorado River Ecology and Dam Management*, 63. An amount of 65 million tons per year is reported for about the same period for the Colorado River at Lees Ferry in Department of the Interior, *Glen Canyon Environmental Studies*, A-30 to A-32. The difference may be attributed to sediment delivery to the Colorado River by the Paria and Little Colorado Rivers and small tributaries.

4. Howard and Dolan, "Geomorphology"; Andrews, "Sediment Transport," 61, 69.

5. Andrews, "Sediment Transport," 54–74.

6. The reasons for the initiation of arroyos is one of the most studied topics in the geomorphology of the southwestern United States. The amount of erosion was severe; for example, 250 million cubic feet of sediment was eroded from short reaches of Kanab Creek between 1883 and 1909. Webb et al., *Historic Channel Change of Kanab Creek*. Also see W. L. Graf, "Late Holocene Sediment Storage in Canyons of the Colorado Plateau," *Geological Society of America Bulletin* 99 (1987): 261–271.

7. J. B. Graf, R. H. Webb, and Richard Hereford, "Relation of Sediment Load and Flood-Plain Formation to Climatic Variability, Paria River Drainage Basin, Utah and Arizona," *Geological Society of America Bulletin* 103 (1991): 1405–1415.

8. Richard Hereford, "Climate and Ephemeral-

Stream Processes: Twentieth Century Geomorphology and Alluvial Stratigraphy of the Little Colorado River, Arizona," *Geological Society of America Bulletin* 95 (1984): 654–668; and idem, "Modern Alluvial History of the Paria River Drainage Basin, Southern Utah," *Quaternary Research* 25 (1986): 293–311.

9. A recent study relates the change in sediment transport of the Colorado River with floodplain storage in tributaries on the Colorado Plateau (A. Gellis, R. Hereford, S. A. Schumm, and B. R. Hayes, "Channel Evolution and Hydrologic Variations in the Colorado River Basin: Factors Influencing Sediment and Salt Loads," *Journal of Hydrology* 124 [1991]: 317–344).

10. The decline in bed elevation at Lees Ferry between 1940 and 1957 was about two feet. D. E. Burkham, *Trends in Selected Hydraulic Variables for the Colorado River at Lees Ferry and near Grand Canyon for the Period 1922–1984* (Springfield, Virginia: U.S. Department of Commerce, National Technical Information Service, Report PB88-216098, GCES/07/87, 1986), 58.

11. Interim flow regulations established in August 1991 have changed the maximum range to 6,000 to 20,000 cfs.

12. This amount was measured between 1983 and 1986. Department of the Interior, *Glen Canyon Environmental Studies*, A-30.

13. Ibid., A-32.

14. Melis et al., *Magnitude and Frequency Data.*

15. E. L. Pemberton, "Channel Changes in the Colorado River below Glen Canyon Dam," in *Proceedings of the Third Federal Interagency Sedimentation Conference* (Denver: Water Resources Council, Sedimentation Committee, 1976), 5-61 to 5-73. In the design of outlet works and spillways, engineers use mathematical models to predict downstream degradation. For an example of the modeling principles, see Z. L. Hales, A. Shindala, and K. H. Denson, "Riverbed Degradation Prediction," *Water Resources Research* 6 (1970): 549–556. Geomorphologists have also studied the downstream effects of dams and use empirical methods to describe the erosion. Typically, erosion is described using an exponential decay relation wherein erosion initially is rapid but declines with time. G. P. Williams and M. G. Wolman, *Downstream Effects of Dams* (Washington, D.C.: U.S. Geological Survey Professional Paper 1286, 1984), 83.

16. Burkham, *Trends*, 12.

17. Williams and Wolman, *Downstream Effects of Dams.*

18. E. M. Laursen, S. Ince, and J. Pollack, "On Sediment Transport through the Grand Canyon," in *Proceedings of the Third Federal Interagency Sedimentation Conference*, 4-76 to 4-87.

19. The analysis of Howard and Dolan in "Geomorphology" involves numerous assumptions about sediment inputs and storage on the bed. Few data exist to support or refute most of the assumptions, although current research on sediment mass balances may eventually yield more accurate values for inputs.

20. F. Y. Borden and W. A. Weeden, *Design and Methodology for Carrying Capacity Estimation for Camping Beaches along the Colorado River in the Grand Canyon Region* (Denver: National Park Service, Project Report for Contract No. CX0001-3-0061, 1973), 21. This inventory has served as one benchmark for observations on the status of camping beaches along the river corridor. The inventory begun by Borden and Weeden was redone in 1983 and 1991 (N. J. Brian and J. R. Thomas, *1983 Colorado River Beach Campsite Inventory* [Grand Canyon, National Park Service Report, 1984], 54; and L. Kearsley and K. Warren, *River Campsites in Grand Canyon National Park: Inventory and Effects of Discharge on Campsite Size and Availability, Final Report* [Grand Canyon National Park, Division of Resources Management Report, 1993], 65). Also see L. H. Kearsley, J. C. Schmidt, and K. D. Warren, "Effects of Glen Canyon Dam on Colorado River Sand Deposits Used as Campsites in Grand Canyon National Park, USA," *Regulated Rivers Research and Management* 9 (1994): 137–149.

21. Rasmussen, *El Niño.*

22. For a succinct detailing of lake levels and dam operations, see Figures 16.5 and 16.6 in L. D. Pot-

ter and C. L. Drake, *Lake Powell: Virgin Flow to Dynamo* (Albuquerque: University of New Mexico Press, 1989), 311. Details of the human effort to contain the flood at Glen Canyon Dam are given in Martin, *Story That Stands Like a Dam*, 315–318.

23. This discharge is the sum of discharges of 44,800 cfs in the Green River at Green River, Utah, and 61,900 cfs in the Colorado River near Cisco, Utah, for June 26, 1983.

24. Discharges are for the Colorado River at Lees Ferry and were collected by the U.S. Geological Survey.

25. The spillways were eroding because of cavitation induced by rapidly moving water in the tunnels. The three-foot-thick lining was removed in several sections, and the underlying bedrock of Navajo Sandstone was eroded. Martin, *Story That Stands Like a Dam*, 315–318.

26. Brian and Thomas, *Campsite Inventory*.

27. The differences between the inventories of Borden and Weeden (*Carrying Capacity*) and Brian and Thomas (*Campsite Inventory*) arose because of several fundamental differences in methodology. Whereas Borden and Weeden were inexperienced river runners, Brian and Thomas were familiar with which sand bars were used as camping beaches. Moreover, the definition of "camping beach" was different between the two inventories; Borden and Weeden based their definition on the size of sand, whereas Brian and Thomas considered those sand bars that were actually used.

28. Schmidt and Graf, *Aggradation and Degradation;* J. C. Schmidt, "Recirculating Flow and Sedimentation in the Colorado River in Grand Canyon, Arizona," *Journal of Geology* 98 (1990): 709–724.

29. Changes in flow patterns of eddies with increasing river stage is complicated and is mostly related to local channel geometry. Schmidt and Graf, *Aggradation and Degradation;* and Schmidt, "Recirculating Flow."

30. Schmidt and Graf in *Aggradation and Degradation* list four types of sand bars: separation, reattachment, upper-pool, and channel-margin deposits. Upper-pool deposits form immediately upstream of rapids where water is pooled behind the debris fan. These deposits may be classified as either separation or reattachment bars, depending on the flow pattern. In our interpretation of sand bars in Stanton photography, we chose to reclassify upper-pool deposits as one of the other three types of bars.

31. Kenton Grua, an experienced Grand Canyon guide who examined Stanton views from the vicinity of Havasu Creek, estimated that the flood experienced by the Stanton expedition probably peaked at about 30,000 cfs.

32. J. C. Schmidt, R. H. Webb, and P. Grams, unpublished data. These data, developed using numerous ground and aerial photographs of Badger Creek Rapid, show that the separation bar just downstream of Jackass Canyon fluctuated considerably in size before the closure of Glen Canyon Dam but was much larger than in 1992. After 1963, the separation bar was eroded severely and the reattachment bar, which is visible in only a few historical photographs, was completely removed.

33. S. Valentine and R. Dolan, "Footstep-Induced Sediment Displacement in the Grand Canyon," *Environmental Management* 3 (1979): 531–533.

34. I revised an existing classification based on bedrock geology at river level that distinguishes eleven reaches with an average length of 21.4 river miles; see Schmidt and Graf, *Aggradation and Degradation,* table 2; Department of the Interior, *Glen Canyon Environmental Studies,* A-8. These reaches have different geomorphic characteristics, such as channel width and depth and the width of the canyon, that influence the deposition of sand bars (A-26). The eight reaches we used are Glen Canyon Dam (mile +15.5) to Lees Ferry (mile 0); Lees Ferry to mile 35.9; miles 35.9 to 61.5; miles 61.5 to 77.4; miles 77.4 to 117.8; miles 117.8 to 125.5; miles 125.5 to 160.0; miles 160.0 to 213.9; and miles 213.9 to 238, the start of Lake Mead.

35. For maps showing camping beaches (large sand bars) in Grand Canyon by river mile, see Stevens, *Guide.* Kearsley and Warren in *River Campsites* provide a listing of camping beaches along the river corridor.

36. For a description of the effects of large releases in

1983 on the biological resources of the river corridor, see Carothers and Brown, *Colorado River.* The argument against large releases is predicated on the assumption that maximum biological productivity should be the goal of management of Glen Canyon Dam.

37. Ibid.

Chapter 11

1. Smith and Crampton, *Colorado River Survey,* 136. Incidentally, the photograph Stanton took did not turn out well (it was underexposed).

2. Ibid., 140.

3. Dellenbaugh, *Romance.*

4. Dellenbaugh's history unduly glorifies Powell's accomplishments and seriously criticizes Stanton's accomplishments. Stanton sought to learn the truth about certain events that occurred during Powell's first and second expeditions; he did not attempt to hide the shortcomings of his own trip.

5. Stanton, *Controversies;* idem, *Down the Colorado.*

6. J. Guilluly, A. C. Waters, and A. O. Woodford, *Principles of Geology* (San Francisco: W. H. Freeman and Company, 1975), 527.

7. J. H. Bretz, "The Channeled Scabland of the Columbia Plateau," *Journal of Geology* 31 (1923): 617–649. For a summary of the Spokane flood and descriptions of the Channeled Scablands, see V. R. Baker and D. Nummedal, *The Channeled Scabland* (Washington, D.C.: National Aeronautics and Space Administration, Planetary Geology Program, 1978), 186.

8. V. R. Baker, "The Spokane Flood Controversy," in Baker and Nummedal, *Channeled Scabland,* 3–16.

9. James, *In and around the Grand Canyon;* Hughes, *House,* 62.

10. Hughes, *House,* 87.

11. In the early 1970s, three Indian reservations, the U.S. Forest Service, the U.S. Bureau of Land Management, Grand Canyon National Park, Grand Canyon National Monument, and Lake Mead National Recreation Area were involved in management decisions that affected the river corridor. Ibid., 107. The existing national park was merged with the national monument lands, the part of Lake Mead National Recreation Area upstream of the Grand Wash Cliffs, and the river corridor and lands north of Marble Canyon. In addition, Glen Canyon National Recreation Area was expanded in 1972 to include the remaining fifteen miles of Glen Canyon between Lees Ferry and Glen Canyon Dam.

12. The National Park Service limits the use of the Colorado River not by the number of visitors but by user days, which was established in a permit system in 1972. In 1981, the number of user days was raised by about 60 percent. Drifter Smith, interview, 1993. In 1992, the maximum user days were 115,500 for commercial river companies and 54,450 for private individuals. In typical years, the quotas are met. The number of river runners is high because many river companies offer trips of short duration, thereby increasing the number of people who use the Colorado River.

13. Department of the Interior, *Glen Canyon Environmental Studies.*

14. U.S. Department of the Interior, *Operation of Glen Canyon Dam: Draft Environmental Impact Statement* (Salt Lake City: Bureau of Reclamation, 1993), attachment 2, att-3 to att-6.

15. If this theory is correct, and global warming results from the emission of carbon dioxide and other pollutants into the atmosphere, then the frequency of frost in the southwestern United States would decrease. I do not propose global warming as the cause for reduction in frost frequency over the last century, but that frequency may decrease still further if human-induced global warming becomes a reality.

Index

Page numbers in italics refer to figures.

Grand Canyon Protection Act of 1992, 208

Grand Canyon Supergroup, 132

Grand Junction, Colorado, 5

Grand River, 5. *See also* Colorado River

Grand Wash Cliffs, *6*, 103, 144

Granite Park (mile 209), 253n. 2

Granite Rapid (mile 93.5), 7, 153, 169, *170–71*

Grapevine Rapid (mile 81.5), 7, 20, *20–21*, 176, 183

grasses

    grazing of, 75, 80

    longevity of, 52–53, 219

Great Basin Desert vegetation, 45

Great Basin sagebrush *(Artemisia tridentata)*, 239n. 23

Green River, *8*

    Best expedition on, 26

    Brown-Stanton expedition at, 9, 10

    damming of, 103

    flooding of, 187

    proposed water-level railroad to, 5

    Stanton expedition at, 14

Green River (city), Utah, 5, 10, 31, 99

greythorn *(Ziziphus obtusifolia)*, 219

ground squirrels, 81

Grua, Kenton, 214, 270n. 31

Gunnison River, 103

Hakatai Shale, 173

Hamilton, Parker, 265–66n. 74

Hance, John, 71, 208

Hance Rapid (mile 76.8), 7

    debris flows upstream of, 141, 179, 266n. 79

    description of, 170–74

    Flavell trip through, 266n. 10

    mining downstream of, 71

    photographs of, *38–39*, 165, *172–73*

    scouting of, 163

    severity of, 169, 210

    Stanton expedition at, 18

Hansbrough, Peter

    burial of, 18, 19

    death of, 12, 17, 19, 30, 31

Haplopappus salicinus, 219

Harding, Warren, 177

Harper, S. S., 4, 71

Harrington's mountain goat, 80, 81, 82, 247n. 57

Harris, Don, 158, 168

Hatch, Bus, 168, 235n. 47

Havasu Canyon. *See* Havasu Creek

Havasu Creek (mile 156.9), 7

    Bermuda grass in, 112

    debris flows downstream of, 141, 180

    flooding of, 207

    non-native species along, 112

    prospecting in, 71

    sediment in, 185

    snakeweed in, 80

    Stanton expedition at, 24

    wildlife in, 70, 243n. 7

Havasupai Tribe, 74, 81, 112

hedgehog cactus *(Echinocereus fendleri)*, 58, 220

herbivores

    description of, 71–74

    impact on vegetation, 74–80, 81–86

    irruptions of, 70–71, 81

Hermit Rapid, 145, 147, 169

Hermit Shale, 127, 129, 131–32, 133, 134, 149

high-water zones

    description of, 99–100, *101*

    new, 100, *101*, 110–20, 122–23, 207

    old, 100, *101*, 103–10, 211–12

Hill, Betty, xviii

Hillers, Jack, 30, 38, 155–56, *157*, 169

Hislop, John

    evacuation of Nims by, 15

    fire set by, 24

    as railroad engineer in Alaska, 26

    on Stanton expedition, 14, 18, 21, 24

Hite, Utah, 3, 11

Hogue, James, 148

Holmstrom, Buzz, 158, 168, 176

Holocene era, 44–45

honey mesquite. *See* mesquite *(Prosopis glandulosa)*

Hoover Dam, 4, 26, 103, 209

Horn, Tom, 175

Horn Creek Rapid (mile 90.2), 7

    description of, 174–76

About the Author

Robert H. Webb is a hydrologist with the U.S. Geological Survey at the Desert Laboratory in Tucson, Arizona. His research—which spans the disciplines of climatology, plant ecology, and geomorphology—concerns historic changes in arid environments that can be attributed to climatic fluctuations or human effects. This book, his second, is based on seven months of fieldwork in Grand Canyon National Park. He has published in various scientific journals including *Science, Geological Society of America Bulletin, Water Resources Research, Quaternary Research, Ecology, Climatic Change, Journal of Arid Environments, Soil Science Society of America Journal,* and the USGS publication series.

Contributing Authors

Bryan T. Brown is an ornithologist and biologist with more than fifteen years' experience with boating and research in Grand Canyon. He is an environmental consultant in Salt Lake City.

Steven W. Carothers has more than twenty years' experience with boating and research in Grand Canyon. He is the president of SWCA, Inc., Environmental Consultants based in Flagstaff, Arizona.

Robert C. Euler is one of the premier anthropologists in the southwestern United States. He has been studying prehistoric peoples in the Grand Canyon area since the 1950s.

Paul S. Martin is a paleoecologist and Professor Emeritus of the University of Arizona. He has been involved in a variety of ecological issues in Grand Canyon since the late 1960s.

Constance McCabe is the photograph conservator at the National Gallery of Art in Washington, D.C. She was the photograph conservator at the National Archives when the Stanton negatives were restored.

P. T. Reilly ran the Colorado River between 1949 and 1964. His interest in the history of the Colorado River and northern Arizona has led to several publications on the region.